The Memoirs of
Jan Chryzostom
z Gosławic
Pasek

The Memoirs of Jan Chryzostom z Gosławic Pasek

Translated, with an Introduction
and Commentaries, by
MARIA A. J. SWIECICKA
Winner of
The Kosciuszko Foundation Dissertation Award
for 1973

The Kosciuszko Foundation
New York
Polish State Publishers
Warsaw
1978

Book cover and title-pages designed by
Andrzej Pilich

Volume VIII of The Library of Polish Studies
General Editor : Eugene Kusielewicz, Ph. D.

PREFACE

The present translation of the *Memoirs* is virtually based on the 1968 critical edition of Władysław Czapliński. The 1929 edition of Jan Czubek, that of Jadwiga Pietrusiewiczówna (1948), and the one of Roman Pollak (1955) were also consulted as well as the 1922 French translation of Paul Cazin and the 1967 German one of Günther Wytrzens. The introduction and all of the commentaries, unless otherwise indicated, were supplied by the author of this work.

ACKNOWLEDGEMENTS

I would like to express my deepest thanks to Professor Mieczyslaw Giergielewicz for his invaluable guidance and great concern in the preparation of this work as well as for his intellectual stimulation during my years of study with the Department of Slavic Languages and Literatures at the University of Pennsylvania.

I also gratefully acknowledge the invaluable advice received from Dr. Albert L. Lloyd of the University of Pennsylvania, Dr. Danuta S. Lloyd of Ursinus College, and Dr. Ludwik Krzyzanowski, editor-in-chief of *The Polish Review*.

My thanks are also due to Dr. Eugene Kusielewicz, President of The Kosciuszko Foundation in New York city, and general editor of the Foundation's series, Library of Polish Studies, and to Mary D. Van Starrex, Assistant to the President of The Kosciuszko Foundation, for her stallwart assistance in the preparation of this work for publication.

Maria A. J. Swiecicka, Ph.D.

Philadelphia, Pennsylvania
1977

TABLE OF CONTENTS

MEMOIRS
OF JAN CHRYZOSTOM Z GOSŁAWIC PASEK

INTRODUCTION

HISTORICAL BACKGROUND

Seventeenth-century European history presents a fascinating but at the same time a most complicated scene. Marked by religious conflicts, dynastic disputes, vast territorial changes and a shifting of power, it formed a nucleus of many problems with which the European states were to be faced in the centuries to come. Protestant and Catholic soldiery raised arms against each other in an endless war during this era ; the Bourbon, Hapsburg, Vasa, Romanoff, and other royal houses of Europe engaged in bitter struggles for the sake of their empires and crowns ; and all of Christendom was saved from the Ottoman might by ". . . a man sent from God, whose name was John."[1]

Amidst the swiftly changing fortunes of this turbulent century such controversial figures as Richelieu and Mazarin laid the foundations for absolutism in France and the illustrious reign of "Le Roi Soleil ;" Gustavus Adolphus and Oxenstierna made Sweden's name world-renowned ; Poland and Sweden shared a king and a Pole was to sit on the throne of Muscovy ; Jesuits and monarchs sought to control empires and monarchs.

The countries which were most strikingly affected in their territorial changes as a result of the dynastic disputes in the seventeenth century were Poland, Sweden, Russia, Turkey, and Brandenburg. The largest monarchy in the later Middle Ages

---

[1] *Fuit homo missus a Deo, cui nomen erat Joannes.* Words used by the preacher who celebrated the *Te Deum* in St. Stephen's Cathedral upon Sobieski's victory over the Turks at Vienna. See Nevin N. O. Winter, *Poland of Today and Yesterday* (Boston : L. C. Page and Company, 1913), 75.

and the foremost Slavic State in the sixteenth century,[2] the
Commonwealth of Poland still stretched over a territory of
some 350,000 square miles in the middle of the seventeenth
century, although already diminished in size, and after Muscovy
constituted the largest State of Europe.[3] But situated at the
crossroads of important trade routes between the northern and
the southern seas and between the western and eastern lands
of Europe, Poland has been an object of prey to her envious
and ambitious neighbors for almost all the centuries of her
existence. Tatar hordes attacked her beautiful city of Cracow
ninety-one times during the Middle Ages ; Russian, Cossack,
German, Turkish and Swedish armies involved her in eighty-
five years of various wars in the seventeenth century. It is no
wonder therefore that a statesman like Sully assigned to her
a very important place in his outline of an international organization of Europe,[4] and a military genius like Napoleon
called her "the true keystone to the arch," a country in which
"the security of Europe rested."[5]

In the dawn of her history, writes Halecki, Poland ex-
perienced an epoch of unquestioned splendor. Pomerania, Silesia, Lusatia, Moravia, Slovakia, and the territory on the upper
Wieprz and Bug on her eastern frontiers belonged to her vast
domains under Bolesław the Brave. Lithuania, White and Black
Russia, Ukraine, and Volhynia became incorporated into the
Polish Commonwealth under Ladislas, the first of the Yagiellons, and its sphere of influence was extended to the lower
Danube and the Dnieper and the shores of the Black Sea when
Moldavia, Walachia, and Bessarabia became her vassals of
their own free will. The Yagiellons gained access to the Baltic
Sea at Gdańsk, ruled over Marienburg, Chełmno and the
bishopric of Warmia, and held Brandenburg as a fief for nearly

[2] A. W. Ward, G. W. Prothero, and Stanley Leathes, eds., *The Cambridge Modern History, The Wars of Religion* (New York : The Macmillan Company, 1934), III, 73.
[3] F. L. Carsten, ed., *The New Cambridge Modern History* (Cambridge :
The University Press, 1964), V, 559.
[4] Oscar Halecki, *Borderlands of Western Civilization* (New York : The
Ronald Company, 1952), 193–229.
[5] Paul Cazin, *Poland* (Paris : Librairie Hachette, 1961), 48.

two hundred years. They defeated the powerful Teutonic Order, acquired Podolia and Kiev, sat on the thrones of Hungary and Bohemia, and took Livonia, Estonia, and Courland under their wings. During the reign of Casimir the Great, Poland assumed the leadership of east-central Europe in the sphere of culture and intellect and Sigismund II, the last Yagiellon, left her an immense, powerful, and most illustrious land. With his death the Yagiellonian dynasty officially terminated, even though, after a brief reign of Henry Valois and a ten-year-long reign of Stephen Batory, it indirectly continued through Sigismund III Vasa and his two sons Ladislas IV and Jan Kazimierz—the direct descendants of Katarzyna Yagiello, the sister of Sigismund II and Queen of Sweden—for eighty more years.

With the death of the last Yagiellon in 1572 the so-called Golden Age of Polish intellect and culture was drawing to an end, and it is generally believed that Poland began her gradual political and economic decline in the seventeenth century. Nevertheless Halecki writes that until 1648 Poland still "stood in the rank of a great power which the whole of Europe regarded seriously."[6] Her three subdivisions at the time, Great Poland with Pomerania, Chełmno and Marienburg; Little Poland included Galicia, Red Russia, Podolia, Bukowina, Volhynia and Western Ukraine; and Lithuanian Poland, which included Livonia, Courland, White and Black Russia,[7] were inhabited by some 10,000,000 people. Toward the end of the century, Poland's territories shrank considerably and her population decreased by a third.[8] In 1657 she lost Ducal Prussia to Friedrich Wilhelm of Brandenburg; in 1660 Livonia north of the Dvina to Sweden; in 1667 Smolensk, Siewiersk, Czernihów, and the Ukraine east of the Dnieper to Muscovy; and in 1686 Kiev.[9]

[6]Oscar Halecki, *The History of Poland* (New York : Roy Publishers, 1942), 123.

[7]David Ogg, *Europe in the Seventeenth Century* (New York : The Macmillan Company, 1968), 13.

[8]Carsten, *Camb. Mod. Hist.*, 559, 565.

[9]W. F. Reddaway, J. H. Penson, Oscar Halecki and Roman Dyboski, *The Cambridge History of Poland* (Cambridge : The University Press, 1950), see Treaty of Wielawa, 524 ; Peace of Oliwa, 525 ; Truce of Andrushow, 528.

The middle of the seventeenth century, which fell under
the reign of Jan Kazimierz, is considered one of the most disastrous periods in Polish history. Marked by great unrest throughout the whole of Europe, it was a time of interminable wars
on Polish soil and is commonly referred to as the "deluge",
Potop, in her history. The armed conflicts began when the
Dnieper Cossacks, the terror of the neighboring nations, rose in
rebellion in 1648 ; when Chmielnicki, their hetman, accepted the
suzerainty of the Tsar, the Cossack rebellion flared even more.
Since the Dnieper Cossacks owed allegiance to Poland, this led
her to a war with Muscovy, and Russian and Cossack armies
invaded her land.[10]

Encouraged by such a turbulent state of affairs in Poland,
Charles X Gustavus disregarded international law and the
Truce of Stumdorf and invaded Poland in the summer of 1655.
Flooded by enemy forces from all sides and already weakened
by the Cossack rebellion, Poland succumbed to the invaders.
By the end of the year all of Poland, with the exception of
Gdańsk and Lwów, was in Swedish, Muscovite, or Cossack
hands.[11]

The Swedish invasion of Poland was much more than
just a dispute between the two branches of the Vasa dynasty or
a territorial conflict over Livonia and Prussia :

What was at stake was the existence of Poland as an
independent nation, her union with Lithuania, and all that
remained of free development in East Central Europe.[12]

After the Polish victory over the Swedes at Częstochowa,
Polish peasants, noblemen, townsmen, and soldiers took up
arms against the invaders. In 1656 Brandenburg signed a treaty
with Sweden against Poland ; Jan Kazimierz reached an armistice with Russia, began to negotiate with the Tatars, and was
promised reinforcements by the Khan ; the Polish offensive
action began in full swing. At this point Jan Pasek's *Memoirs*
begin.

The reign of Jan Kazimierz was followed by that of Michał
Wiśniowiecki. The Polish provinces were ravaged by Cossacks,

[10]Ogg, 454–6.   [11]Reddaway, 520, 523.
[12]Halecki, *Bord. of West. Civil.*, 211.

Tatars, and Ottomans until, on November 11, 1673, the Polish Grand Hetman Jan Sobieski gained a splendid victory over the Turks at Chocim in Bessarabia. As subsequent Polish king, he restored peace to his land. "He is one of the few leaders of the seventeenth century." writes Ogg, "to whom the epithet 'great' is applicable."[13] By his famous victory over the Porte at the gates of Vienna in 1683 he made Poland's name shine with splendor in the world again. His rescue of Vienna

> ... was the last memorable historical success of independent Poland on the stage of European affairs... It remains in her everlasting credit that on this occasion she drew her sword chivalrously to help a neighbor who was not at all her friend. The victory of Vienna is the last noble reflex of the great crusading impulse of the Middle Ages, the last service generously rendered to a common European cause in an age of Machiavellian diplomacy and selfish national interest.[14]

THE GOLDEN FREEDOM

> Als die andern sich in Glaubenskriegen verzehrten übte Polen Toleranz, als die andern absoluten Herrschern dienten, trieb Polen die Freiheit bis zur Anarchie, als die andern sich dem nationalen Staat verschrieben, war Polen überhaupt kein Staat mehr.[15]

In the seventeenth century the Commonwealth of Poland, commonly referred to as *Korona i Litwa*,[16] represented a political

---

[13]Ogg, 460.

[14]Roman Dyboski, *Outlines of Polish History* (New York : Oxford University Press, 1924), 116–117.

[15]When the others were wearing themselves out in religious wars, Poland exercised tolerance, when the others served absolute rulers, Poland practiced freedom to the point of anarchy, when the others declared themselves for the national state, Poland was no longer a state. Günther Wytrzens, *Die Goldene Freiheit Der Polen, Aus den Denkwürdigkeiten Sr. Wohlgeboren des Herrn Jan Chryzostom Pasek (17. Jahrhundert)* (Graz : Verlag Styria, 1967), 7.

[16]Crown, i.e. Poland, and Lithuania.

entity, made up of two coordinate states, the Duchy of Lithuania and the Kingdom of Poland, as well as the feudal
Duchies of Courland and Prussia. The nearly autonomous
Livonia and the Duchy of Samogitia were part of the territories
of the Duchy of Lithuania. The Kingdom of Poland was divided into two provinces : Great Poland, which included Prussia,
and Little Poland, which included Ruthenia.[17]

The unity of the country was maintained by the Polish
king and the Polish Diet, *Sejm*. Since the death of the last
Yagiellon in 1572 the Polish monarchy was elective. By virtue
of the *Pacta Conventa* and the authority granted to the nobles
by the Diet, the power of the kings of Poland was limited. This
stood in sharp contrast to the situation in other countries of
Europe where the tendency was toward militarist states and
absolutism.[18] The commander-in-chief of the armed forces of
the Commonwealth was officially the king, but the actual command was in the hands of the grand hetmans, who were assisted
by field hetmans. The grand hetmans held the prerogative of
ministers of war and their office was for life. They made
decisions concerning the size, makeup, and financing of the
armed forces. Their authority was greater than that of any other
military commanders in Europe at the time. The Polish monarchs attempted to restrict the power of the grand hetmans
time and again.[19]

The autonomous provinces and all the voivodeships of the
Commonwealth enjoyed very abundant self-government. They
had their own governments and regional councils and sent their
dignitaries and deputies to the *Sejm*, which met every two years

---

[17]Great Poland numbered twelve voivodeships at the time : Poznań,
Kalisz, Sieradz, Łęczyca, Brześć Kujawski, Inowrocław, Płock, Rawa,
Mazowsze with the city of Warsaw, Chełm, Malbork, and Pomorze
(Pomerania). Little Poland numbered eleven : Kraków, Sandomierz,
Lublin, Ruthenia with the city of Lwów, Bełz, Podole, Wołyń (Vo-
lhynia), Podlasie, Bracław, Kijów (Kiev), and Czernihów (the Ukraine).
The Duchy of Lithuania numbered eleven : Wilno, Troki, Samogitia,
Nowogródek, Brześć Litewski, or Polesie, Połock, Mińsk, Witebsk, Mści-
sław, Smolensk, and Livonia with the city of Dyneburg.
[18]Ogg, 56–57.
[19]Carsten, 560.

for a period of six weeks. The *Sejm* was made up of the chambers of deputies and senators and was exclusively a parliament of nobles. Since there were no permanent taxes in the Commonwealth of Poland at the time, the finances of the army were taken care of by the resolutions of the Diet, which had the authority to pass levies and taxes. The weakness of the Diet as a legislative power resulted from the *liberum veto* which had been theoretically in existence since the middle of the sixteenth century. "No state can function unless minorities can at any time be ignored or crushed, but by the *liberum veto* the Polish Diet insisted on absolute unanimity."[20]

The *liberum veto* should not be taken literally, however, because up until the middle of the seventeenth century if a Diet was concordant it paid no heed to the protest of one single deputy, and only when a considerable minority voiced discontent could the *liberum veto* be exercised successfully. In 1652 a protest lodged by a deputy against the prolongation of the debates by one day resulted in the breaking up of the Diet for the first time. But the incident would have been of no consequence had it not been turned into a precedent. A split of the *Sejm*, occurred for the first time in 1669, right at the beginning of the proceedings, even before a marshal had been elected. During Jan Sobieski's reign, half of the Diets which were called into session were split. The *liberum veto* was detrimental in that it enabled foreign powers to exercise their influence upon the proceedings, and many protests were voiced at their instigation.[21]

Even though most scholars seem to agree that the baleful effect of the *liberum veto* was undoubtedly great, they also seem to stress that its principle was a true expression of the freedom-loving spirit of the Poles at the time. The Poles were the first in Europe to introduce a parliament based on the principle of liberty, equality and fraternity. In this country
    ... which was known as the asylum of heretics, where the
    churches stood next to synagogues and mosques and where

[20]Ogg, *Eur. in the Seventeenth Cent.*, 58.
[21]Carsten, 561–562.

there was a jealous spirit of liberty, a spirit partial to
novelty, subtlety, and discussion . . .
liberalism and tolerance had been practiced for centuries.[22]
Poland is the only example afforded by history of a nation
deliberately committing self-destruction for the sake of
absolute individual liberty.[23]

THE PRIVILEGED ESTATE

It is impossible to express the general
astonishment when we saw ambassadors in
long robes, wearing their scabbards, adorned
with jewels, the bridles, saddles, trappings
of their magnificent steeds and the air of
consequence and dignity by which they distinguished themselves in Latin, French, German and Italian. Those four languages were
as familiar to them as their own tongue.[24]

The Commonwealth of Poland was essentially a Commonwealth of nobles in the seventeenth century and only the Polish
nobility, together with the Polonized Ruthenian and Lithuanian
gentry, was identified with the Polish nation. The Polish nobles
were more privileged and influential than their counterparts
elsewhere in Europe and, in accordance with the saying "*szla-
chcic na zagrodzie równy wojewodzie,*"[25] every nobleman was

[22]Cazin, 18, 21.
[23]Winter, 8.
[24]Jacques Auguste De Thou (1553–1617), lawyer, magistrate, historian,
councilor of state and author of *Historia sui Temporis* (1604–08) on his
impressions of the Polish delegation which arrived on the nineteenth
of August, 1573 in Paris in order to offer the Polish Crown to Henry
Duke of Anjou, son of Charles IX. As quoted by Fletcher, 65–66. The
Polish embassy sent to receive Marie Louise of Gonzaga (Maria Ludwika) in 1645 is known to have been even more impressive. See
W. R. Morfill *Poland*, 133.
[25]"My home is my castle" or "the nobleman on his plot of ground is
equal to a voivode." (author's transl.) See Władysław Czapliński, *O Polsce siedemnastowiecznej* (Warszawa : Państwowy Instytut Wydawniczy,
1966), 14–22.

equal. There were no titles in the kingdom of Poland in the seventeenth century and all noblemen, regardless of office, addressed each other as *brat*, brother. Nevertheless, at least two strata among the nobility could be distinguished : the gentry and the magnates ;[26] and the economic and cultural differences between these strata were immense.

At the beginning of the seventeenth century, just as in any other feudal system, both Polish nobles and peasants lived from the soil.[27] Engaging in commerce was forbidden to the Polish nobility by law. After their education the gentry and the nobles usually spent some time at a magnate's or the royal court or might have travelled abroad ; they then settled on their land, participated in regional councils, and attended social and cultural functions.[28] The gentry quite often leased land, the noblemen either personally supervised the peasants' cultivation of their soil or had an administrator do it ; the average noble-man enjoyed thus a very comfortable and peaceful existence. The nobility kept many servants in their manors. The magnates lived in such affluence and splendor that some could afford to leave as many as forty villages to servants in a will ; some had to order 2000 gowns in order to attire their court for a funeral procession. They kept marshals, chaplains, singers, musicians, courtiers, and multitudes of various servants on their staff and an equipage of less than twenty-five horses was not considered respectable in Poland.

It was also universally accepted in the Commonwealth of Poland that every nobleman, and only a nobleman, possessed an innate feeling of what was good and noble, and that each cherished honor as his most priceless possession. A misde-meanor of an individual brought disgrace not only to his name but to his entire family as well. Foreign nobility was frowned

[26]Jan Stanisław Bystroń, *Dzieje obyczajów w dawnej Polsce wiek XVI–XVIII* (Kraków : Państwowy Instytut Wydawniczy, 1964), I, 158.

[27]Władysław Czapliński, ed., *Jan Pasek, Pamiętniki* (Wrocław : Biblio-teka Narodowa, Zakład Imienia Ossolińskich, 4th ed., 1968), XXXV–XXXVII.

[28]Aleksander Brückner, *Dzieje kultury polskiej* (Kraków : Nakładem Krakowskiej Spółki Wydawniczej, 1930), 377.

upon and only Polish noblemen could possess true old Polish virtues and traditions. This feeling of superiority of Polish nobility was connected with the so-called Sarmatian myth which asserted that the ancient Sarmatian tribe, once living along the banks of the Vistula, gave birth to the Polish ruling class. The glorification of the past represented an inseparable part of the Sarmatian ideology which excluded both plebeians and townsmen. The Polish noblemen found their fame and glory in the Sarmatians and their coats of arms in ancient Rome. They took pride in their individuality and independence with respect to the West. By the fourteenth and fifteenth centuries every Polish noble family had found links with the early Sarmatians and by the sixteenth and seventeenth centuries Sarmatian was often used interchangeably with Polish. Polish writers raised on Cicero and Seneca were primarily moralists who stressed the republican virtues of valor, simplicity in manners, discipline, and justice. Roman republican antiquity was set as an example of civic virtues to Polish knights and to the political system of the Polish Commonwealth of nobles. The ideology of Polish knighthood was generally much the same as that of its western counterpart and the ideal Polish or Sarmatian knight was a brave warrior of noble birth who served his fatherland, defended the Christian faith, and strove for fame.

In the fifteenth century, idealization of life on an estate became more pronounced, and in the sixteenth and seventeenth centuries Sarmatian ideology became more and more associated with landownership rather than knighthood. It established a style of life with its own moral code, religious upbringing, customs, family ties, and intellectual interests. The average nobleman was usually a faithful servant of the church and quite often the founder of chapels and churches. The hospitality and courtesy of the Polish nobility was renowned.[29] By the seventeenth century the Polish nobleman's fondness for country life

[29]An Italian by the name of Mosini writes : "A Polish nobleman is so hospitable that he never has refused his hospitality to anyone." As quoted by Zygmunt Wolff, in *Studia z dziejów kultury polskiej, podróżnicy włoscy o Polsce XVII wieku* (Warszawa : Nakład Gebethnera i Wolffa, 1949), 283.

and his pride in his exclusiveness had both reached excessive proportions.[30]

Women occupied a rather prominent place in the life of Poland. "The Polish women of the upper classes are undoubtedly charming and possessed of the graces of true womanliness," writes Winter and the opinion of many other writers is similar.[31]

In the fourteenth and fifteenth centuries, the Polish Academy of Cracow flourished as one of the most brilliant centers of European culture. Erasmus of Rotterdam corresponded with its many students and professors, and the German satirist Thomas Murner, the Swiss humanist Rudolph Agricola, the Spaniard Pedro Ruiz de Moros ("Roysius") either lectured or studied there. Polish creative contributions in the sphere of learning were considerable. In Poland's glorious age of the renaissance her noblemen received a most impressive education and Polish culture, intellectually linked with the West, penetrated deep into the Duchy of Lithuania, Muscovy, and the Ukraine, as well as into other European lands.[31] But when Poland lost her position of hegemony in eastern Europe as a result of her incessant wars in the seventeenth century, the gradual disintegration of social and economic life, the Reformation, Counter Reformation, and the Sarmatian myth resulted in a gradual drop of her cultural life as well. A high level of non-conformist education became accessible only to a small part of the dissenting gentry in the seventeenth century and the masses of the gentry attended Jesuit Colleges where they were taught mythology, classical literature and language, rhetoric, and Latin.[32] The uniform Jesuit system of education formed a uniform political outlook, attitude to other social classes, and mode of life, and discouraged independent thinking. Consequently the gentry began to view higher education as unnecessary. In no other country in the West did the education of the noble youth depend on the Jesuits to such an extent as it

[30]Tadeusz Mańkowski, *Genealogia sarmatyzmu* (Warszawa : Towarzystwo Wydawnicze Łuk, 1946), 36–87.
[31]Winter, 262, 264.
[32]Sobieski, 253–254.

did in seventeenth-century Poland.[33] The Jesuits, under the influence of such theoreticians of absolutism as Bellarmin and Bodin, also attempted to gain control of university education, and scholasticism even made its way to the Academy of Cracow. Polish noblemen, both Protestant and Catholic, went to pursue their studies in Italy,[34] the Netherlands, Germany, and France, and mostly commoners studied at home. Many of them distinguished themselves in mathematics, philology, philosophy, and science, and such worthwhile reforms as limitation of decentralization and strengthening of royal power were proposed by some of them,[35] while the gentry became more and more preoccupied with their Sarmatian myth. Their megalomania which developed in the course of the seventeenth century with a feeling of superiority over all social classes and nations, intolerance of other ideologies, civilizations, and cultural, political, and religious beliefs resulted in cultural isolation and xenophobia and did much to curtail the level of education. The gentry was convinced "that nothing could be learned from foreigners, for the system prevailing in Poland was perfection itself."[36] They feared that foreigners might plot against them, the universe of free souls ; and to safeguard their golden freedom they did all they could.

Nevertheless, in spite of the drawbacks of the seventeenth century the impact of the seventeenth-century Polish culture was great because it was no longer limited to the nobles but affected all classes alike and, in spite of the fact that Poland was gradually succumbing to her Muscovite invader in

[33]In Poland in the sixteenth and seventeenth centuries not only the nobility read, wrote, and spoke Latin, but also townsmen. In fact foreigners were stunned that they could make themselves understood in Latin even with servants and coachmen on occasion. See I. Wieniewski, *Podstawy kultury polskiej* (London :Wyd. Światowego Związku Polaków Zagranicy, 1946), 65–66.

[34]Chiefly in Padua and Bologna. Dyboski, *Out. of Pol. Hist.*, 95.

[35]Andrzej Frycz Modrzewski and Jan Zamoyski were interested in constitutional and social reforms in the age of the renaissance already. See Oscar Halecki, *Pol. as a Eur. Power* (Berkeley : University of California Press 1945), 44.

[36]Carsten, 90.

that century, she still continued to exert her cultural influence eastward, not only to her territories but to other countries as well, with great force. Polish fashion and speech persisted in Muscovy from the time of the False Demetrius until the reign of Peter the Great; the Ukrainian Hetman Chmielnicki, for example, continued to use Polish in his diplomatic correspondence with Tatar khans, Eastern Patriarchs, and Russian tsars, and the Ukrainian Academy was under a strong influence of Polish literature and learning.[87]

SARMATIAN BAROQUE

> Barok pozostanie w dziejach twórczości zjawiskiem odrębnym a splecionym z pierwiastków i prądów tak różnorodnych, że nie szukając porównań odległych, z określeń szerszych lub bardziej precyzyjnych, lepiej mu zostawić jako nazwę to słowo dziwne i tajemnicze, o którym nie wiadomo czy zrodziło się z nazwiska artysty, czy z perły niekształtnej poszło, czy z odległego przypłynęło średniowiecza.[88]

The term baroque, which was used by art critics in the late eighteenth century to describe works of architecture and art lacking in classic forms of true beauty, although of uncertain linguistic origin, can be linked to the scholastic term *baroco*. As one of the figures of formal logic, this term became associat-

[87]Dyboski, 110–111.

[88]The baroque will remain in the history of creativity a distinct phenomenon, interconnected with roots and currents so diverse that without looking for remote comparisons in broader and more precise descriptions, it is better to leave this strange and mysterious word as its name, about which we don't know whether it originated from the name of an artist, or was formed out of an imperfectly shaped pearl, or came floating from the distant past of the Middle Ages. Mieczysław Hartleb. "Początek Poezji Barokowej w Polsce." *Studia staropolskie*, 1928, 501. According to Barycz, the word baroque stems from Portuguese and originally designated pearls of irregular shape. See Henryk Barycz, *Historia nauki polskiej* (Wrocław : Zakład Narodowy Imienia Ossolińskich 1970), 9.

ed with the humanist dislike for scholasticism, and was taken
to mean intricate, eccentric, and perverse.[39] The idea of the
baroque as a distinct style, still rather unfamiliar several decades ago, has given rise to extended controversies and has
aroused great interest among the scholars of today.

The baroque style as a form of art, literature, and life
emerged clearly on the west European scene, according to most
scholars, in the decades after 1600 and reached its culminating
point about sixty years later, but it is very difficult to designate
the exact time of so "vast an array of grandiose creations," for
since the origin of baroque architecture is traced to various
Italian cities, including Rome, the baroque style must have
marked its beginning already sometime in the middle of the
sixteenth century. It is very difficult to ascertain the development from the "undoubted renaissance" to the "equally evident
baroque" through a gradual transitional period of change designated as *Manierismus* ;[40] when this mannerism began and
when it ended and whether this unique style is as important as
romanesque, gothic, renaissance, or baroque is still a controversial issue.

The origin of the baroque cannot be solely linked to the
spirit of the Counter Reformation, according to Friedrich, for
even though its violent clash of church and state produced
a new line of thought which was reflected in the baroque, and
even though it did revive religiosity—nudity was outlawed, rules
for the use of secular melodies in composition were established,
and the Index of forbidden books was decreed—the baroque
art was grossly sensuous, naturalistic, and worldly ; even though
many of the most beautiful baroque structures were Jesuit cloisters, abbeys, and churches, some of the most precious gems of
music and art were Protestant creations ; and even though the
origin of the Italian baroque did coincide with the Counter
Reformation after 1550, its spirit was nearly extinguished when
the baroque style reached its culminating point. Nor can the

[39]Carl J. Friedrich, *The Age of the Baroque* (New York : Harper and
Row, 1962), 38.
[40]*Ibid.*, 38–39.

baroque be merely considered the dominant impulse of abso-
lutist monarchy, even though it was concentrated in ducal
palaces and royal courts, for the beginning of baroque architecture was found in ecclesiastical Rome and beautiful baroque
town houses were built by the rich bourgeoisie, not only in the
absolute monarchies, but also in England, Holland, Venice, and
other countries ; even though kings and princes were usually
the patrons of the arts, art and music were supported by the
middle class as well, and the fact that the theatre and the church
were not exclusively the privilege of the few but the common
possession of all was the most significant characteristic of
the age.

Considered now one of the most significant forms of expression of occidental culture, this vivid, ornate, and dynamic
baroque style left its imprint in the operas and luxurious
palaces of the great capitals of Europe. Ornamental facades,
magnificent staircases, and decorative gardens were true signs
of its style in the West and its fabulous paintings of Rubens,
Rembrandt, Velasquez, and van Dyck reveled in the effects of
shadow and light ; fairy tale, knightly novel, extravagant com-
edy, and ornate lyrics were introduced as its literary genres ;
new forms of symphony, opera, and oratorio introduced the
combinations of human voices and instrumental music—its
epics and great chorals were filled with movement, tension, in-
tensity, and force. The costumes, with the exception of those
of the Puritans and the fellowship of Port Royal, were elaborate
and stately, and the wig[41] was perhaps the most revealing
symbol, the finest expression of its style in the West.

Preoccupied with expressing feelings, personality, and
Stimmung, the stormy age of the baroque was tormented by
doubts, perturbed by conflicts, contrasts, and tensions, torn by
mysticism and rationalism carried to extremes. Excesses in
eating and drinking marked that age ; gross sensuality alternated with moral fanaticism, debauchery with pangs of conscience ; skepticism and scientific discovery with dogmatism,

[41]Beards, which were in style in the early decades of the century, gave
way before shorter beards and moustaches in the latter part of the
century and eventually vanished. Friedrich, 38–42.

superstition, and intolerant persecution. There was endless quarreling and dueling, for nevertheless the baroque man held dignity and honor in highest esteem.

Living in an age when one could expect the unexpected and the irregular appeared regularly, not only architects, sculptors, painters, poets, and musicians, but also ordinary men were fascinated by the impossible, even though their quest for power and success often made them fall victims to an evil fate.

The meteoric rise and the cataclysmic fall of favorites, conquering heroes, royal concubines, were highly symbolic of the baroque... Gustavus Adolphus and Wallenstein, ... and ever so many others crowded the baroque period ... storming heaven, plunging into damnation, crying out : 'I shall yet force my fate.' It is almost as if baroque man had insisted that the final consummation of man's most striking exhibition of the never-ending quest for power was a violent death, or at least banishment, exile, oblivion.[42]

Even though the baroque style transcended all national boundaries and is considered to have been European in scope, national aspects of its style in the spheres of architecture, letters, art, and life did exist, and regional variations were most pronounced in cases of the most integrated national life. France displayed greater restraint in tensions and contrasts, Spain was most extreme, but "the Czechs, the Poles, and the Russians responded with truly baroque violence to the artistic possibilities of this style, especially in architecture ;"[43] the baroque seemed to be most expressive of the Slavic spirit in general.[44]

The Polish baroque, frequently referred to as Sarmatian, is believed to have marked its beginning in the early part of the seventeenth century, but belongs mainly to the decades after 1660, the year in which the Western baroque had reached its culminating point.[42] Originating as a blending of eastern and western cultures and marked by an artistic expression peculiar to local Polish tastes, the Sarmatian baroque, unlike the West-

[42]Friedrich, 47.
[43]Friedrich, 43.
[44]Andreas Angyal, *Die slavische Barockwelt* (Leipzig : E. A. Seemann, 1961), 202–210.

tern, centered mainly in residences of the magnates and manors of the gentry.[45]

The Western influence on Polish architecture, sculpture, and art was mainly Italian, but unlike Western baroque the facades of palaces and churches were often kept simple, and exuberant luxury, pageantry, and grandeur prevailed only inside; many Gothic palaces and churches were reconstructed and adorned with baroque gildings, sculpture, and original works of art. The costume of the Polish dignitaries[46] and nobles was the *kontusz*,[47] and in decorative arts, belts, ornamental weapons, harness, and hairstyles[48] the oriental influence was apparent. The manners of the Polish nobles were characterized by a mixture of authority, dignity, and casualness.

The seventeenth-century Polish literature, often called Sarmatian, qualitatively different from the preceding Golden Age of the Renaissance but according to the latest opinions and findings not really inferior, was to a large extent literature circulated in manuscript, for some of its most valuable and daring works were left unpublished. Poland's greatest Latin poet, Maciej Sarbiewski (1595–1640), made his name known and valued in all of Europe in that century; and among other published works there were Arian[49] poetical works of great

[45]Aleksander Gieysztor, ed., *History of Poland* (Warszawa: Polish Scientific Publishers, 1968), 262–264.

[46]Some dignitaries dressed in Spanish, German, or French costumes, however.

[47]Outer garment of the Polish noblemen; buttoned in the front with slit sleeves.

[48]Heads were either partly or completely shaved and long moustaches were in style.

[49]The name Arians was given to the so-called Polish Brethren, *Bracia Polscy*, the most radical religious sect in Poland during the Reformation who, like the original Arians (named after Arius, the Christian theologian of Alexandria who died in 336 A.D.), denied the divinity of Christ. After the resolutions of the Diets of 1658 and 1662 had singled them out for banishment from Poland, some of them settled in Transylvania; the Magyar Unitarians are to a large extent the descendants of these Polish Arians. See J. Czubek, *Pam.*, 2, note 6. "The enforced emigration of hundreds of the most enlightened families was a great loss to Poland, comparable with the loss later sustained by

value, middle class literature with elements of social criticism, and anonymous literature of plebeian origin. The impact of seventeenth-century Polish culture viewed thus was greater than that of the Renaissance, since its literature was so prolific and since all classes were affected by it. But how much of the seventeenth century Polish literature is baroque is a debatable question. The baroque is a dynamic, decorative, sensual, pompous, and aesthetically refined style, opposed to unconstraint, and only one or more of the above mentioned characteristics can decide about its stylistic expression. Yet Polish literary scholars, according to Dürr-Durski,[50] craved to see something mysterious and strange in the baroque, and it is not by chance that after many years of research such a prominent scholar as Roman Pollak perceived the baroque still as a great chaos :

> Bardzo kapryśny, sobie-pański jest ten polski barok literacki, dorywczo u tego i innego związany z włoską czy francuską manierą, tematyką, gatunkami ... Nie plewiony to zaiste ogród ... Pełno tam osobliwości, niespodzianek, nieoczekiwanych wyskoków, inwencji ...[51]

Polish literary scholars, he continues, failed to classify many of

France in her similar intolerance of the Huguenots. Among the Polish exiles were writers of first magnitude, such as Zbigniew Morsztyn, Erazm Otwinowski and Simon Budny, the last having distinguished himself by his masterful and critical studies of biblical texts which outdistanced modern biblical scholars by two centuries." E. H. Lewinski-Corwin, *Polit. Hist. of Pol.*, 256. It is to be remembered, however, that the anti-Arian movement was chiefly political in scope. In the sixteenth century, Poland was one of the most tolerant nations in Europe—if not the most tolerant—where all religious parties were allowed freedom of the press. Zygmunt August was the most tolerant king but even Batory's religious policy showed tolerance toward the Protestants and the Jews, even though he himself was a devout Catholic. A. W. Ward, *Wars of Rel.*, 102.

[50]Jan Dürr-Durski. "Od manieryzmu do baroku." *Przegląd Humanistyczny*, 1971, 15–17.

[51]Very capricious, quite lordly, is that Polish literary baroque, in some authors occasionally related to Italian or French mannerism in subject matter and kind, ... It is an unweeded garden indeed ... There is plenty of individuality in it, surprises, unexpected whims, inventions ... See Roman Pollak. "Zagadnienia periodyzacji historii literatury polskiej." *Pamiętnik Literacki*, 1950, 139–140.

the works of seventeenth-century Polish literature correctly, for not every literary work which is characterized by an abundance of words and richness of poetic figures, just as not every artistic creation abounding in decorative detail is baroque. As Würsten explains the principal identifying feature of the baroque ... "mit dem Unterordnen der Ornamente dem Gesamteindruck, beginnt eine neue Zeit."[52] The works of Marini are not baroque therefore because of their abundance of poetic figures but because they are so appropriately applied.

> Skoncentrowanie kompozycji, podporządkowanie zdobnictwa słownego jednemu mocnemu efektowi to są istotne cechy baroku.[53]

This also explains, according to Dürr-Durski, the later development of the baroque into a style of such great precision as the rococo. The baroque will continue to appear to all of us as a chaos, if we continue to confuse mannerism with baroque ; the feeling of chaos is bound to decrease automatically as soon as we weed out works in the manneristic style and treat works of the baroque separately.[54] The liberation of Polish literature of the seventeenth century from the reproach of chaos is important because such a reproach denies the literary works of this period their social function and merely brings everything down to formalistic problems. Dürr-Durski views the Arian literature, which appeared on the background of the conflicts between magnates and nobles in the second half of the seventeenth century just as the so-called *mieszczańska* had in the first half, as a current of opposition in the baroque utilizing the manneristic style. For the features of anarchy and unreliability are most characteristic of mannerism, and although mannerism proved such a good tool of social struggle in the hands of the oppressed, baroque could not prove a suitable weapon for the

---

[52]But therewith, with the subordination of the ornaments to the overall impression, a new era begins. Ernst Würsten, *Die Architektur des Manierismus in England* (Leipzig : E. A. Seemann, 1951), 210.

[53]The concentration of composition, the subordination of verbal adornment to one strong effect are the essential features of the baroque. J. Dürr-Durski, 15.

[54]*Ibid.*, 15–17.

same purpose. The chaos in the baroque is seen as manneristic and the baroque as a style of the era of absolutism which developed in Poland as a result of the futile attempts of the last Vasas to subordinate the oligarchy of the magnates in the early part of the seventeenth century. It is a style of the second half of the seventeenth century only, a style which was exploited by the oligarchy of the magnates and served to lend splendor to the luxurious and splendid ways of their lives. "Ecclesiastical and secular magnates were its representatives."[55] Baroque in its most characteristic form in Poland is for Dürr-Durski the style of the royal court and the courts of the magnates, a style which reflected the character of the social class of its leaders.[56] But limiting the baroque solely to the mighty and the few, if not quite wrong, is at the very least a debatable and controversial issue.

A CENTURY OF MEMOIRS

> 'The kings of Europe,' said the prince, white with agitation and anger, 'have not yet laid down the law to me in my palace; you shall not make me submit to yours, madame . . .'[57]

The word "biography" was coined by Dryden in 1683, "autobiography" was first used by Robert Southey in 1809; the literary genre was known as "journal", "diary", "memoirs", and "history by self" prior to that.[58] The instinctive desire to secure some kind of immortality for the story of his life had induced many a man beginning with the Assyro-Babylonian culture some 4500 years ago to record on clay, stone, parchment, and paper his innermost feelings and thoughts; this urge

[55]*Ibid.*, 15. *"Możnowładcy duchowni i świeccy są jego nosicielami."*
[56]*Ibid.*, 14–17.
[57]De Montespan, *Classic Memoirs* (New York: The John Day Company, 1901), I, 196–202.
[58]Richard D. Mallery, *Masterworks of Autobiography* (New York: Doubleday and Company, Inc., 1946), 4.

became more pronounced by the seventeenth century.[59] For in what age, except perhaps our own, could both men and women, both mighty and small, feel more of an urge and need to record their traumatic experiences and innermost thoughts than in this turbulent and most fascinating age of the baroque ?

There were the memoirs of Benvenuto Cellini and Girolamo Cardano in Renaissance Italy ; there were those of Santa Teresa de Jesus of Avila and Gracian in Renaissance Spain ; and there were those of Uriel Da Costa, De Montespan, Saint-Simon, De Maintenon, and Pepys, in Portugal, France, and England of the seventeenth century. But France produced the largest bulk of European memoirs in the seventeenth century.

The value of Polish memoirs as a most fascinating and useful historical and cultural source was recognized in the nineteenth century when many of them were re-edited or edited for the first time. Currently they have inspired a new wave of interest ; historians consult them, scholars delve into them, and ordinary readers find delight in them.

The various forms of Polish memoirs in the sixteenth century, such as autobiographies, diaries, chronicles, and journals, played a pioneer role in the formation of more mature forms of memoirs. They had no literary traditions or models. Qualitatively different from those of the seventeenth century, they nevertheless played a very important role in the development of this literary genre. The memoirs of the sixteenth century were innovative in nature. Even though the majority of the memoirists had no literary ambitions, each was known to develop a substantial art in this branch of writing by introducing an original metaphor, narrative dialogue, or character portrayal. In the seventeenth century this literary genre was in full blossom.[60]

The numerous Polish memoirs in the seventeenth century can be divided into those inspired by Poland's armed intervention against Russia during the revolts of the Impostors in the

[59]Saul K. Padover, *Confessions and Self Portraits* (New York : The John Day Company, 1957), XIII.
[60]Roman Pollak, *Antologia pamiętników XVI wieku* (Wrocław : Zakład Narodowy Im. Ossolińskich, 1966), LXXXIV–LXXXV.

early part of the century, the Cossack, Muscovite, and Swedish
wars in the middle of the century, and the military conflicts
toward its end ; also into those mainly concentrating on the
author, or on public events, or on both. Among the numerous
memoirists of the century were Stanisław Żółkiewski,[61] Bogusław Radziwiłł,[62] Samuel Maskiewicz,[63] Queen Maria Ludwika,[64] King Jan III Sobieski,[65] and Marysieńka, his charming
Queen.[66] The gallery of names is long and quite impressive but
the *Memoirs* of Jan Pasek,[67] according to Julian Krzyżanowski,
deserve special attention.

> Jedyne to dzieło polskie, które może zająć niepośled-
> nie miejsce w galerii ówczesnych pamiętników europej-
> skich, nic też dziwnego, że ogłoszenie go drukiem w r. 1836
> stało się prawdziwą rewelacją i dało silny impuls do po-
> wstania powieści gawędziarskiej.[68]

The original manuscript of Pasek's *Memoirs* is lost. Its
eighteenth-century copy, discovered among the holdings of the
Imperial Library of St. Petersburg, was transferred to the *Biblioteka Narodowa* (National Library) in Warsaw, where it is
located to this day (No. 4501). The preserved copy of the

[61]Stanisław Żółkiewski, *Progres wojny moskiewskiej* (Warszawa : Państwowy Instytut Wydawniczy, 1967), 5–197.
[62]Edward Raczyński, *Żywot księcia Bogusława Radziwiłła* (Poznań :
W Drukarni i Księgarni Nowej, 1841).
[63]Alojzy Sajkowski, ed., *Pamiętniki Samuela i Bogusława Kazimierza
Maskiewiczów* (Wrocław : Zakład Narodowy Im. Ossolińskich, 1961),
5–303.
[64]Edward Raczyński, ed., *Portfolio królowej Marii Ludwiki* (Poznań :
W Drukarnii i Księgarni Nowej, 1844).
[65]Leszek Kukulski, ed., *Sobieski, Jan III, King of Poland, Listy do
Marysieńki* (Warszawa : Czytelnik, 1966).
[66]Leszek Kukulski, ed., *Maria Kazimiera d'Arquien de la Grange*
(Warszawa : Czytelnik, 1966).
[67]Władysław Czapliński, ed., *Jan Pasek, Pamiętniki* (Warszawa : Biblio-
teka Narodowa, 1968).
[68]Only this Polish literary work can take an important place in the
gallery of contemporary European memoirs. No wonder therefore that
when it was published in 1836 it became a true revelation and gave
a strong impulse to the rise of the chatty style novel. Julian Krzyżanowski, *Historia literatury polskiej* (Warszawa : Państwowy Instytut
Wydawniczy, 1963), 367.

Memoirs covers the years 1656–1688, thus stretching over a period of thirty-two years of the seventeenth century. Its first fifty pages, some middle ones, and the end are missing. The bulk of the *Memoirs* appears to have been copied by one hand, but two other handwritings can be detected.[69]

When excerpts of the *Memoirs* came to light in 1821, they instantly became a literary sensation. Edward Raczyński edited the text in 1836 but made various changes and translated all the Latinisms into Polish. A much more careful edition was prepared by Lachowicz (1843). A complete list of these early editions appears on page 89 of the *Nowy Korbut* (1964).[70] The 1929 edition of Jan Czubek is considered the best among them. All later editions are based on it.

Proofs of the popularity of the *Memoirs* till this day are their many editions, the interest of literary historians in them, and the influence which they have exerted and exert on poets or historical writers such as Słowacki, Kaczkowski, Sienkiewicz, and others. "In Sienkiewicz's opinion, the personality of Pasek perpetuated in his memoirs was more accessible and understandable than that of many contemporaries."[71] Without Pasek's *Memoirs*, Sienkiewicz's "novelistic attempt would have been one more repetition of the literary formula ; Pasek's colloquial Polish breathed life into Sienkiewicz's dialogue."[72]

Shortly after the first editions of the *Memoirs*, numerous doubts were raised as to their authenticity. They were silenced by the discovery of numerous facts pertaining to the author's life. Aleksander Kraushar and Jan Czubek made the greatest contributions in this field ; their discoveries established the authenticity of the *Memoirs* beyond any doubt.[73]

---

[69]Jan Czubek, ed., *Jan Chryzostom z Gosławic Pasek, Pamiętniki* (Kraków : Polska Akademia Umiejętności, 1929).

[70]The latest source of Polish bibliography.

[71]Mieczysław Giergielewicz, *Henryk Sienkiewicz* (New York : Twayne Publishers, 1968), 79.

[72]Jerzy Pietrkiewicz. "A Polish 17th-Century Diarist." *Slavonic and East European Review*, 1953–1954, 448.

[73]Czapliński, *Pam.*, LVIII.

JAN PASEK : A POLISH NOBLEMAN AND SOLDIER

> Pasek is more than a symbol of the
> past, he is its personality, and personality
> outlives the symbols we fashionably attach
> to the past.[74]

Jan Chryzostom z Gosławic Pasek was born in the Polish Mazovian voivodeship of Rawa around 1636, but neither the exact date nor place of his birth is known to us.[75] Marian Władysław Pasek and Jadwiga Pasek, née Piekarska, the memoirist's parents,[76] came from Polish gentry, the so-called *szlachta zaściankowa* or *zagrodowa* (yeomanry). His mother was the only daughter of the judge of that district ; Jan was their only child and apparently a very much beloved son.

His surname, unlike those of most of the gentry, was derived from the Christian name Paweł (Paul.) [77] Paweł eventually developed into its diminutive from *Paszek* which on the lips of the Mazovians, who pronounce the sibilant *sz* as *s*, became "Pasek" ; Pach, the augmentative form of *Paweł*, exists as a plebeian surname to this day.[78]

The original home of the Paseks is believed to have been the village Paski in the Mazovian district of Sochaczew, but by the sixteenth century, several members of the family settled in other parts of the Commonwealth ; Wawrzyniec Pasek moved to Podolia, and Jan,[79] a judge and frequent escort of Muscovite envoys to Poland, moved to the then Polish city of Smolensk. When in 1654 Poland lost the territories of Smolensk to Muscovy, Daniel and Piotr, the two sons of Jan Pasek, judge of the city of Smolensk, divided their father's fortune and became

[74]Pietrkiewicz, 439.
[75]Czubek, *Pam.*, XV–XVI.
[76]Franciszek Kamocki, "Kilka uwag o nazwisku i rodzie z Gosławic Paska." *Myśl Narodowa*, 1929, 220–223.
[77]Jan Stanisław Bystroń, *Dzieje obyczajów w dawnej Polsce wiek XVI–XVIII* (Warszawa : Państwowy Instytut Wydawniczy, 1960), I, 173.
[78]Czubek, *Pam.*, III.
[79]This Jan Pasek was the memoirist's uncle.

subjects of the Tsar, but Jan, his third son and the Chancellor of the Lithuanian Confederacy,[80] went over to the Polish side. The descendants of Daniel and Piotr are still living in the region of Smolensk to this day ; the traces of those of Jan Pasek, the Chancellor of the Lithuanian Confederacy, seem to have been lost forever. The memoirist's branch of the family remained in Mazovia and at the outset of the seventeenth century, N. Pasek, the father of Stanisław and Marcin, still lived there. Stanisław seems to have had only one son, also named Stanisław, whose branch of the family was extinct in the beginning of the eighteenth century. Marcin was the memoirist's father and since the latter died childless, even Niesiecki makes no mention of the Polish Paseks' Mazovian branch since then.

The memoirist was the first member of his family to sign his name z Gosławic (i.e. from the village Gosławice)—and later Stanisław also signed his name this way—but Czubek found no record of such a village ever having belonged to the Pasek family and thus found no justification for their doing so. Czapliński assumes that Pasek might have been born on one of the many estates named Gosławice but neither Czapliński nor Czubek make any mention of Kamocki's discovery that an Andrzej Pasek was already listed under the year 1528, in the Słownik geograficzny ziem polskich, under Gosławice,[81] which justifies Pasek's use of the name.

Little is known of the memoirist's childhood and youth before he entered the army, except that he was educated at the Jesuit College of Rawa, and that he must have joined the army in December, 1655, and Domaszewski's armored company in 1657. In Domaszewski's official register, Zaręba and Olszewski, Pasek's companions at arms mentioned in the Memoirs, are also listed.[82] From then on Pasek himself records the story of his life quite accurately.

From the Memoirs we learn that in 1656 Pasek participated in the battles with the Swedes under his beloved commander Stefan Czarniecki, "experiencing sometimes misery and some-

---

[80]The army's protest against Jan Kazimierz because of back pay.
[81]Kamocki, 222.
[82]Czapliński, Pam., XVI, XLI.

times good fortune,"[83] and that at Trzemeszno Czarniecki's division, together with 2000 Crimean Tatars, put six thousand Swedes to the sword. His military service under Czarniecki, "a leader in the style of all great and lucky warriors,"[84] Pasek found very enjoyable indeed.

Together with his relative Filip Piekarski, Pasek fought Rakoczy during his invasion of Poland the following year. Pasek's descriptions of the Swedish and Hungarian wars, although quite brief and to the point, give us a linking, from the very start, of his political credo, his robust sense of humor, and his narrative skill. From his speeches to the senators in Grodno we learn that during all these trying years of the "Deluge" in Polish history, he stood steadfastly on the side of his fatherland and his king.

Pasek loved warfare and his military career was both diversified and exciting. He spent 1658 and 1659 with Czarniecki's division fighting the Swedes in Denmark, on land and sea ; he fought the Muscovites at Mohylew, Basia, and Połonka in 1660 and shared in the glory of the Polish victory in these battles ; he participated in the civil war and fought at the battle at Mątwy in 1666. Military events and turmoils of war seemed such an inseparable part of his life that even when he no longer took part in them he continued to write about them in his *Memoirs.* He wrote down, for example, that in 1671 the Crimean Tatars were attacked at Kalnik and in 1672 the Tatars captured Kamieniec ; that in 1673 the Poles gained a splendid victory over the Turks at Chocim and again at the gates of Vienna ten years later, and even though Pasek learned of the course of the Vienna campaign only from his relative Stanisław, his accounts of it are interesting, quite accurate, and detailed.

As an outspoken man, Pasek willingly and quite readily expressed his various opinions at all times. He commented on the Great Elector's secret ambitions, the latter's attitude toward the Polish army, and on the behavior of the imperial troops in Denmark in 1658. He complained about extravagance in

[83]*Memoirs*, 1656, 80.
[84]*Ibid.*, 80.

Polish fashions and commented on the life at the Polish court ; he confessed his ambivalent feelings toward the confederacy of 1661 and his reluctance to be bound to it by an oath of allegiance. After his arrest on false suspicion of spying for the confederacy he revealed his courageous determination to speak his mind, his equality as a nobleman even before his superiors, and his true loyalty to his country and the king. He spoke freely of his hatred for Archbishop Prażmowski, the French-born Queen Maria Ludwika, and their schemes to bring a Frenchman to the Polish throne ; he could find no logical explanation for Lubomirski's being tried for aspiring to the Polish throne, and during the civil war his sentiments were with Lubomirski, even though his regiment stood on the side of the king.

So far as his personal life and loves are concerned, he fell in love with a Danish noblewoman, and wedding bells seemed inevitable for him when sudden orders for the Polish army to retreat cut his romantic episode short ; his drinks became seasoned with tears, so strong were his passions and his love. He courted two young ladies in Węgrzynowice eight years later and frankly admitted his preference for the one who had fertile soil rather than cash as dowry, but married neither. Being introduced to a forty-six-year old widow that same year—he was barely thirty at the time—he proposed to her shortly after their encounter and married her three days later. He acquired a good wife and a nice dowry, but also six stepchildren[85] and many problems to boot, and complained about the lot of marrying a widow years later. "I withered and lost my health for the interests of others. What I could have earned for myself, I spent on lawsuits and I still incurred ingratitude instead of thanks,"[86] yet added that he would have been happy with that marriage if he had had a child of his own with his wife.

With Pasek everything happened according to the Will of God, and his piety was typical for his day. In the *Memoirs* we learn of Father Piekarski's admonishing words before the battle

[85]They were : Jadwiga, Marianna, Aleksandra, Barbara, the second Marianna, and Krzysztof.
[86]*Memoirs*, 734.

at Kolding, of Pasek's ordering his men to shout "Jesus,
Mary !" in hopes of bringing them good luck, of the Polish
army singing the *Te Deum laudamus*, and the thanksgiving
Mass being celebrated in the field. Pasek prayed to God when
lost during a storm at sea ; he concluded that apparently his
marital plans to the Danish girl were not in the Will of God ;
he wrote that "one should never despair even though fortune
grows somewhat dim, for God disposes of man and his fortune ;
He saddens a man whenever He desires to ; He comforts him
when such is His Holy Will." It is God who willed the election
of Wiśniowiecki and Sobieski as Polish kings, and in 1683 it
was God who favored Christendom so with His blessings that
year.

A man of truly baroque contrasts, Pasek was a witty,
clever, curious, and eccentric man. Sent to Ebeltoft because of
his knowledge of Latin in order to obtain provisions for Czarniecki's army, he clownishly pretended not to understand the
language until receiving what he wanted, and thus managed to
fulfill his mission with great success. Quite anxious to see and
hear everything that he could not find in Poland, he observed
Danish customs, enjoyed their delicious food and drinks, and
marvelled at their landscapes, sea animals and fish. Especially
interesting are his descriptions of his famous otter, his aviary,
greyhounds and wild animals, under the year 1680, as good
examples of his habits and tastes. "If some stranger met me on
my way to a hunt," he writes,

> he would see several greyhounds, several scenting dogs and
> a fox, a martin, a badger, and an otter running among
> them ; a hare with bells hopped behind a horse, a hawk
> sat on the hunter's arm, a raven flew right over the dogs,
> from time to time it would sit down on the back of one in
> order to ride for awhile. The stranger would just cross
> himself then and say : 'For Heaven's sake ! This is a sor-
> cerer ; animals of all kind run among his dogs. What is he
> looking for ? Why does he not bait these animals which
> run behind him ?'[87]

[87]*Ibid.*, 655–656.

Pasek also took an active part in the regional councils and Diets of the Polish Commonwealth and admonished all young men to do the same, for "all the public meetings in the world are mere shadows as compared to the meetings of the Diet! There one learned etiquette, law, and many things which one never heard of in school. I wish every one such a chance."[88] He attended the Diet in 1662 in Warsaw and the regional council meetings in Węgrzynowice in 1667 ; he gave precise instructions pertaining to the agenda of the Diet to the deputies of Rawa, while serving in the capacity of a deputy chamberlain there. He attended the funeral of Queen Ludwika in 1667 and the Diet in 1668 in Warsaw during which King Jan Kazimierz voluntarily proposed his abdication. He attended many more Diets in Warsaw and even several in Grodno. In 1669 he was present at the election of the king, and rejoiced over the choice of Michał Wiśniowiecki, a native Pole. He also attended the coronation ceremonies, the Coronation Diet immediately following, and the royal wedding in Częstochowa the next year. He participated in the election of King Jan Sobieski in 1674 and witnessed the burial of two Polish kings, Jan Kazimierz and Michał Wiśniowiecki, and the coronation ceremonies of a third, all at the same time, in Cracow, two years later.

The range and scope of Pasek's experiences and interests are immense. He enjoyed the best military encampment of his life on the estate of the Castellan's wife at Strzała in 1660, gave an eloquent eulogy in honor of Jan Rubieszowski and Jan Wojnowski, two companions at arms, fought duels with the Nuczyński brothers and Jasiński in Kozierady, and went on a mission to rescue the Polish envoys in Mińsk during the battles with the Muscovites. He escorted the Muscovite envoys to Warsaw in 1662, saw Mazepa[89] at the royal court once again, and went on an adventurous trip to Wilno. He witnessed Lubomirski's apology to the King and his taking of the oath of allegiance. He sent his three stepdaughters to the Bernardine convent, for such was their vocation and will, gave away

[88]*Ibid.*, 503.
[89]A Cossack ennobled by the Polish King Jan Kazimierz (John Casimir) ; later Hetman of the Ukraine.

another, Jadwiga, in marriage to his nephew, and settled his stepson comfortably on land in Smogorzów. He also proved to be a concerned son and a good friend to those he liked, but could be nasty if provoked.

Following his marriage in 1667, Pasek spent most of his time in the voivodeship of Kraków (Cracow), cultivating land and sailing with his shipments of grain to Gdańsk. He gave us accounts of his losses and incomes, of prices and harvests. His fondness for nature and its blessings are easily detectable in Pasek. "Right in the beginning of the year we lived to see something different," he writes in 1680,

> for there were no frosts, the weather was nice and warm, flowers sprouted, the earth yielded grass and people began to sow.[90]

"The winter this year was truly Italian, entirely without snow and frost," he continues in 1682,

> one did not ride in sleighs, the rivers did not freeze, the grass was green, there were leaves on the trees and flowers all winter long. People plowed and sowed at a time when otherwise severe cold persisted. Even March was so warm, dry and cheerful, that it was truly contrary to its own nature. Only in April was there snow and frost. Snow fell again during the Easter holidays, whereby the already sprouting vegetables, especially peas, froze in certain areas.[91]

Like many of the poorer gentry of the time, Pasek never owned land, but merely leased it. In 1667 he settled with his wife in Olszówka but since its lease was drawing to a close he signed another.[92] He lived in Smogorzów for a time and moved to Skrzypiów in the middle of Lent of 1671, where he stayed until 1677. In 1680 he complained of his stockyards burning down in Smogorzów, and in 1681 and the following four years, of the cost of living being high in Great Poland and crops being bad in Olszówka.

[90]*Ibid.*, 640.
[91]*Ibid.*, 662.
[92]On the estates of Miławczyce and Biegłów.

In 1688 we find Pasek involved in a lawsuit with Margrave Myszkowski in Lublin, and his wife living in Madziarów, pretending to be held there by the Margrave by force, since the latter refused to acknowledge Pasek's loan to his deceased brother and to extend further the leasehold of Brzeście and Olszówka. Pasek took the case to the Diet in Grodno and entreated the King, who was Jan Sobieski at the time, to intervene on his behalf. The King who remembered Pasek well, partly for his merits as a soldier and partly for his gift of the marvellous otter, treated him with exceptional kindness, promised to help, and entrusted the Voivode of Sieradz with the case. At this point the *Memoirs* break off.

Thanks to the research of Aleksander Kraushar,[93] we know today that on November 18, 1690, Pasek won the case, and that the court decreed that the Margrave should pay Pasek 6000 zlotys, but at the same time sentenced Pasek to the tower for one week for abusing the Margrave's honor and denied him the continuation of his leasehold of the two estates.[94] Pasek was forced to look for another leasehold, but the King came to his help once again. After the death of Teodor Denhof, the Starost of Wiślica, he gave Pasek a lifetime lease on the royal estate Ucieszków, and things would have gone ideally for the memoirist there, had it not been for a certain Mikołaj Wolski, the Master of the Royal Hunt of Owrucz, a vindictive neighbor. Frequent clashes occurred between the neighbors, such as Wolski's men confiscating a couple of Pasek's horses and Pasek forcing one of Wolski's hunting companions to eat half a rabbit raw in revenge ; court summonses and lawsuits started again. Consequently on February 15, 1696, one month before his wife's death, Pasek sold his lifetime lease of Ucieszków to Aleksander and Anna Tudorowski-Lisowski and leased a near-

---

[93]In the *Księgi wyroków trybunalskich lubelskich* Kraushar discovered Pasek's case with Myszkowski and with Wolski and his sentence to eternal banishment in 1700 for disturbing public safety and peace. Aleksander Kraushar, *Nowe epizody z ostatnich lat życia IMci Jana Chryzostoma z Gosławic Paska* (Petersburg : Księgarnia B. R. Rymowicz, 1893), 28–30.
[94]Brzeście and Olszówka.

by village, Górna Wola, from Denhof's widow Katarzyna, née Potocka, at a very low rent. Things seemed to go well for the memoirist there until the expiration of the lease three years later, when the widow refused to renew the contract and Pasek refused to leave.

Pasek was sentenced to eternal banishment on June 23, 1700 by the court of Lublin for disturbing law and peace ; he had already lawsuits with Marcjan Chełmski, Warszycki, Ajchinger, the Cistercians, Chotecki, Myszkowski, and Mikołaj Wolski on his record by that time. Many literary critics accuse Pasek of being silent about many of the turbulant episodes in his life, even though he was not at fault at all times.

Pasek learned of the sentence from the law authorities of Lublin on August 2, 1700, in Niedzieliska, which is the last known reference to Pasek during his lifetime. Thanks to the weakness of law enforcement at the time, the sentence was never executed, and Pasek evidently died peacefully at home some time in the summer of the following year. On August 5, 1701 Pasek's heirs, his nephews Jan Remiszowski and Stanisław Pasek, appeared in the municipal court of Cracow claiming their rights to Pasek's granary in Nowokorczyn. That same year Krzysztof Łącki made an endowment for his stepfather's and mother's souls in the Pilczyn church.[95]

THE MEMOIRS

According to the findings of both Czubek and Czapliński, Pasek began recording his *Memoirs* around 1690, that is late in life, and must have finished them approximately five years later. He seems to have recorded them for his own pleasure as well as for his close circle of family and friends to whom he must have narrated them scores of times.

Czapliński attributes the varying length of the chapters to the interest which Pasek's listeners displayed in his respective stories, which quite justifiably accounts for the fact that certain

[95]See Jan Czubek, *Pam.*, XII–XV, and Władysław Czapliński, *Pam.*, XLIII.

portions of the *Memoirs* are treated in greater detail than others. The Swedish and Hungarian wars are described very briefly, for example ; Czarniecki's expedition to Denmark, Pasek's debates with the senators in Grodno, the battles at Basia and Połonka, and the victory at Vienna, on the other hand, with greater detail and length ; the years 1670, 1671, 1675, 1679, 1681, and 1682 are covered in several sentences, while still other incidents are omitted in their entirety.[96] The omissions of various facts can be attributed to the fact that the *Memoirs* were not written as the events occurred ; quite naturally, the details of the less interesting stories fell into oblivion, while thanks to the many repetitions, the more popular ones were retained in his memory and faithfully recorded. The legal papers, royal letters, speeches, and other documents in the *Memoirs* can safely be considered authentic, for Pasek, like other Polish noblemen of the time, must have safeguarded and treasured them.[97]

The historical significance of the *Memoirs* and their element of truth have been investigated by many Polish historians and other scholars, yet their judgments are not uniform. Brückner did not attach to them much historical value and Pollak maintained that Pasek was silent about some facts of his life and generally was not sincere about his life at all. Czermak disbelieved Pasek's narratives about the size of the enemy forces and smiled at his political credo, yet admitted that he willingly read the descriptions of battles, beaming with life and full of enthusiasm, vivacity, and humor.[98] Mickiewicz referred to the *Memoirs* as a historical romance, and Czubek went so far as to say that they are full of historical mistakes, that the dates are inaccurate, and that we cannot rely on them safely and should use them with great care.[99] But the historical facts in the *Memoirs* serve merely as a background to the story of

[96]For example, his relations with the Śladkowski family after his marriage, about which we know from other sources.
[97]Czubek, *Pam.*, XV–XXI.
[98]Wiktor Czermak, "Szczęśliwy rok", *Przegląd Polski*, 1887, 509.
[99]For example, Pasek cites as the fourth battle with the Swedes in 1656, the battle at Warka of April 7, after the battle at Warszawa of July

the author's life, a fact of which the author reminds us several times. "Not a history but a *cursum vitae meae* do I write, *non statum Reipublicae*, in order to remind myself of my deeds in case my memory were to fail me."[100]

> Pasek did not record his life day by day and in cipher, like Pepys ; he viewed the years from the comfortable perspective of old age. He had no political or religious cause to protect from the commentators of history, like the great masters of self-justification, e.g. the Duc de Saint-Simon. He wrote no spiritual autobiography like the prominent Jesuits or Saint Theresa. He possessed no intellectual subtlety, like John Evelyn, to deprive his record of that redeeming triviality after which novelists yearn in their quest.[101]

Since the *Memoirs* were recorded toward the end of his life, historians should not expect any special accuracy in details such as numbers and dates. Historical precision is by no means to be expected in memoirs.[102] It is amazing indeed that he remembered so much accurately.

Czapliński went further than most other Polish historians and literary scholars and quite correctly concluded that the *Memoirs* are an important historical source despite their want of precision ; even though Pasek on occasion tends to magnify some events or change their course for the sake of witticism,[103]

28–30 ; the capture of Kolding under 1658 rather than the following year ; Marcjan Chełmski as camp commander in 1677, a post which he did not receive until February 20, 1680 ; Dymitr Wiśniowiecki's death in 1681 instead of 1688 ; Marek Matczyński as Master of the Horse of the Crown in 1686, whereas he was already at the Voivode of Bełz at the time ; he claims to have leased Smogorzów for seventeen years in the year 1687 and in another chapter he claims to have leased it for twenty ; he gives the date of his father's death as 1677, yet he is known to have been alive two years later. See J. Czubek, *Pam.*, XVII.
[100]*Memoirs*, 158–159.
[101]Pietrkiewicz, 448.
[102]Margaret Botrall, *Every Man a Phoenix, Studies in Seventeenth Century Autobiography* (London : John Murray, 1958), 9.
[103]He merely jokes sometimes, as in the case of Rakoczy invading Poland in order to taste some Polish garlic, or Xerxes waging war against Greece for the sake of Attic figs. *Memoirs*, 1657 A.D., 74, 75.

he never completely invents them ; though no expert in politics, he is nevertheless not quite ignorant of it. Numerous facts can be cited as examples of this theorem, such as Denmark's attitude toward Poland during the Swedish wars, the Great Elector's aspirations to the Polish throne, and the capture of Kolding ; France's schemes in Poland, Condé's attitude toward Louis XIV, and the battle at Mątwy ; the election of Michał Korybut Wiśniowiecki to the Polish throne, the confederacy of Gołąb,[104] as well as many other facts, are shown in complete accordance with historical truth. The accusations of many scholars that Pasek augmented the successes of his army by depicting the greatness, righteousness, unconquerability, valor, and courage of Polish soldiers and presented them in the most favorable colors are not justifiable in view of the findings of Czapliński[105] and others, which prove Pasek to be correct. Furthermore the historical skeptics should keep in mind that Pasek was above all a military man, and a brave soldier at that, and that his idolization of his army and his commander Stefan Czarniecki is quite genuine and sincere ; also that the opinions of Polish historians on the seventeenth century are rather divided.

The *Memoirs* are filled with numerous authentic details. Pasek remembered correctly, for example, that his father died in a Christian way on the eve of St. Barbara, whom he worshipped, fully conscious, and as if falling asleep. He also recalled many years later that on August 8, 1667, when he was courting the widow, he was heartened when he saw her youngest daughter, Marysia, who was two years old at the time, and hoped that God might still give him a son.[106] He remembered specific accounts of individuals, such as of Łukasz Wolski or the dragoon who killed the famous otter, and recalled well the reactions of various individuals to the events of the time. We can also rest assured that Czarniecki's words quoted in the *Memoirs* are authentic, for apparently nothing sticks more in

[104]Memoirs, 1658, 1664, 1665, 1666, 1668, 1669, and 1672.
[105]Władysław Czapliński, "Polacy z Czarnieckim w Danii (1658–1659)." *Rocznik Gdański* IX and X, 1937.
[106]Czubek, *Pam.*, XVII–XIX.

the memory of old soldiers than the image of their leaders and their warm and encouraging words. Pasek remembered such visual details as that when the Voivode twisted his beard it was a sign of anger or worry, and recorded these for us many years later; and even such fantastic stories as those of the bear at the court of Jan Kazimierz, Sułkowska's encounter with the King during the civil war, and the mysterious coral reef in the vicinity of the island Anholt in the middle of the Kattegat were not invented by him. It is quite true, therefore, that "if we, at times, suspect a liar in Pasek, his literary genius is to blame, not a pedantic regard for his private annals," for

> Pasek was ridiculous enough, cruel enough, and humble enough to preserve that strange balance between sincerity and style ; his personal record asks for no excuse, it claims as little from life as does true literature, because it reveals before it justifies.[107]

The *Memoirs* are furthermore an excellent reflection of the living speech of an ordinary Polish nobleman in the second half of the seventeenth century, a fine example of chatty style, and an excellent source of Polish customs of the time ; a vivid picture of a nobleman-knight, citizen, and farmer. So far as the depiction of customs is concerned, the views of most literary scholars are in general agreement that no other work of the seventeenth-century Polish prose can compare with the *Memoirs*. Far too much emphasis seems to be placed, however, on the memoirist being a typical representative of the Polish gentry of his time.

> Pasek was to the seventeenth century something of what Rey was to the sixteenth, with the difference, however, that while Rey represented the cultured and partly educated gentry, Pasek was a thoroughgoing representative of the undistinguished and mediocre masses of the gentry.[108]

By closer analysis of the situation we are bound to discover that words such as "typical" or "thoroughgoing", as used

[107]Pietrkiewicz, 441, 448.
[108]Manfred Kridl, *A Survey of Polish Literature and Culture* (New York : Columbia University Press, 1956), 117, trans. from the Polish by Olga Scherer-Virski.

above, are both misleading and vague. Although the intellectual level of the Polish nobles was very high in the sixteenth century and even though, as a result of the endless wars and invasions with which the Polish Commonwealth was faced in the seventeenth century, the deepening feudalism, and growing megalomania, the country had already lost its leading role among other east European nations and the high cultural and economic position of priority, its gentry was by no means "mediocre". Furthermore, Pasek, who was in many ways a typical representative of the masses of the gentry from his native voivodeship of Mazovian Rawa, who were unique in their own way, and rather different from those of the other voivodeships of the Commonwealth, and whose sense of humor and quick temper were typically Mazovian, did not consider himself a Mazovian in the true sense of the word, and even said so to Kordowski who was pinpricking the Mazovians :

> You should not refer to the Mazovians as night approaches, because you might see them in your dream and because there are none here. But since I am a neighbor of the Mazovians I must answer your Lordship in their behalf.[109]

Pasek did not consider himself a Mazovian because his native voivodeship of Rawa was already annexed to the Polish Crown, i.e. Poland proper, in 1462, while the rest of the Duchy of Mazovia was not annexed until 1529. Even though Pasek's training in rhetoric, his knowledge of Latin, mythology, and ancient history, and his political outlook are true signs of the schooling which the young gentry received in the uniform Jesuit system of college education throughout the Commonwealth, and his feeling of Polish superiority over other nations and his distrust of foreigners are traits planted by the Sarmatian ideology of the time, viewing the memoirist in the perspective of his own native Polish environment is not enough in order to do justice to a full analysis of his personality.

Negative descriptions of Pasek such as : a liar and an undistinguished man, a nationalist who disdained foreigners,

[109]*Memoirs*, 565.

a patriot who fought for both duty's and booty's sake, a super-
ficially educated man without a broader political outlook, a
fanatic without a deeper spiritual life, have appeared much too
frequently in Polish criticism.

In reply to the argument that Pasek lies concerning his
own personal affairs, we can quite safely maintain that truth-
telling memoirists are virtually nonexistent. Every memoirist,
whether intentionally or not, tries to represent himself and his
deeds as favorably as possible, that is in a better light than his
contemporaries would, and there is no reason why Pasek should
be an exception to the rule. Though the aim of most of them
is to give the truth about themselves, we can see that even in
the case of St. Augustine the toil to recollect the truth proved
futile at times. While our "inner censor" prevents us from
hiding unpleasant memories from our consciousness, "we are
often still incapable of speaking of our secret shame, however
well we may know it is nothing abnormal or shocking to
others."[110]

It can furthermore be maintained that even though Pasek
was not a man of extremely high position, it seems quite unfair
to call him undistinguished. Clever and greedy to the point that
he called money the interpreter of his wishes he was nevertheless
capable of moderation, which he proved with the Danes and on
numerous other occasions ; as a soldier he showed bravery, valor,
vitality, and courage, and did not side with the Swedish invader
in 1657 or join the confederacy of rebelling soldiers in 1661, but
remained faithfully on the side of his country and his king
throughout, even though he stood to gain less by doing so.
Pasek's misdemeanors need not be emphasized too much, for
he was quite often in the right ; nor should his weaknesses be
stressed too much, for they can easily be explained in the light
of the baroque. Viewed in the perspective of all men living in
that age of endless quarreling and dueling, boasting, and the
restless search for power and personal success, indeed his faults
seem relatively insignificant in the perspective of the entire

[110]Roy Pascal, *Design and Truth in Autobiography* (Cambridge : Harvard University Press, 1960), 61.

European scene. To cite the strange careers of Wallenstein or the adventures of Alonso de Contreras, a soldier of Spain,[111] would be sufficient to illustrate this point. Pasek's acts of charity, piety, and occasional modesty by far surpassed his faults of boastfulness and pride, but the fact that he possessed so many contradictory traits, that he was so unpredictable at times, benevolent and good, yet sometimes heartless to extremes, makes him merely so much more human, so much more representative of that stormy and dynamic age; for amidst all the baroque struggle for power and success, mere survival presented a challenge and a quest.

So far as Pasek's education is concerned, it is true that he was a product of a system of education which had already stepped down from the high position which it had held in the previous century, but he was not ignorant by any means. He boasted of his knowledge of mythology, ancient history, and Latin; although he made mistakes in quoting his mythological sources, these are rather rare. His common sense and judgment are both amazing and sound.

A very pious man, Pasek wholeheartedly trusted his God and the Saints and accepted all that befell him as coming from the Will of God, which did not make him blind to the evil doings of the Archbishop, however, nor stop him from making a parody of the prayer for indulgence.

> When the poor Lithuanian souls began to pray for indulgence and to offer themselves to God there,

he writes about the clash during the civil war in Częstochowa between Lubomirski's men and the royal Lithuanian army,

> they prayed so ardently that they broke out in a bloody sweat. They left such offerings behind that they were completely stripped of everything. They arrived elegantly dressed, on horseback, with beautiful saddles, but returned on foot and practically naked with the exception of those who had extremely poor robes or boots which were not accepted as offerings.[112]

[111]Sorrano y Sanz, ed., *Vida del capitan Alonso de Contreras*, as quoted by D. Ogg, 24–27.
[112]*Memoirs*, 498.

Anyone who is surprised at Pasek comparing a ray, a Scandinavian delicacy of the seventeenth century, to a devil, might be interested to learn that today the Scandinavians find it just as abominable as he did then ; anyone who shakes his head over Pasek's naiveté in describing the Danish house spirits as real might be surprised to learn that an Italian writer of the seventeenth century, by the name of Torquato Rechi, informed his readers that winds, wrapped in handkerchiefs, were sold to sailors in Denmark.[113]

A born story-teller, Pasek must have disarmed his listeners with the vividness and color of his stories, with the sincerity and humanity of his self-portrayal. His *Memoirs* are considered by many the most interesting, entertaining, and instructive Polish memoirs in existence.

Much has been written to indicate an analogy between Pasek and Pepys ; many similarities have been repeatedly stressed. But according to Pietrkiewicz,[114] it is in Boswell rather than Evelyn or Pepys that the English reader should search for an analogy with Pasek in the literature of his native land. Educated at Cambridge, Pepys rose high in government service under his patron the Duke of York, and chose to share in the latter's fall as well. He retired from public life, devoted much of his time to the Royal Society and became author of the Memoirs of the Royal Navy.[115] Pasek never received the royal post he was promised for his loyalty to the king, yet as a free citizen of the most freedom-loving republic in Europe at the time, he participated in the social, military, and political life of the Polish Commonwealth of nobles in many different spheres. The exciting careers of both, even though different in nature, carried them through the most acute vicissitudes of life. Yet Pepys's meticulous diary, designed primarily to discipline and analyze himself, was a transcript of his innermost feelings and thoughts stretching over a period of ten years ; the preserved pages of Pasek's *Memoirs* stretch over a period of thirty-two

[113]Czapliński, *O Pol. Sied.*, 209.
[114]Pietrkiewicz, 447.
[115]O. F. Morshead, ed., *The Diary of Samuel Pepys* (New York : Harper and Row, 1960), IX–XVIII.

years and his narrative was spontaneous and broader in scope. The Diary is a document filled with jealousies and quarrels, moral failures and self-condemnation; the *Memoirs* neither justify nor condemn. But if one takes the initiative to assume that neither Pasek nor Pepys ever dreamed that their *cursus vitae* would be read by students of literature some day, one can safely conclude that at least that they did have in common.

COMMENTS ON THE TRANSLATION

"The mentality of a people is recorded in the words of its language, Felician Mars told me when I confided in him my difficulties as a translator," writes Cazin,

> The Polish vocabulary is less rich than the French on the subject of poverty. Even their slang, with which I flatter myself I am quite familiar, for all its color, abundance, and savor when it describes drinking, eating, or rudeness, does not provide terms angry enough, crushingly contemptuous enough, to growl out the necessary curses against destitution, poverty, starvation, exhaustion and pain.[116]

It is generally assumed that Polish, the most inflected of the Slavic languages, does not lend itself easily to translation, and Old Polish is obviously far more difficult to translate than modern; furthermore in general Polish renders itself better into German or French than into English.

The difficulties encountered in the actual translation of the text were both numerous and complex; to discuss them in great detail would be a tedious and lengthy task. The memoirist's language, which reflects the everyday language of the middle strata of the Polish gentry of the time, is under some influence of German, French, and Italian, and richly intertwined with Latin words, expressions, and phrases.[117] Pasek's style varies,

---

[116]Paul Cazin, 26.

[117]According to Lednicki, the Polish nobleman cultivated not only the land but also all his national, and particularly domestic, habits and virtues, in the end of the seventeenth century, but his education became scant, cursory, and badly organized. The one thing he still knew well was Latin. "Take Pasek's *Memoirs* and you will see that in his Polish

as if recorded by several pens : conversations, descriptive passages, adventures, and other points of interest are described briefly, vividly, and to the point ; speeches and poems are couched in a heavy and burdensome style. The enthusiastic statements of the critics concerning the narrative parts of Pasek's style are in general agreement. Pasek wrote just as he spoke ; he varied his style with short and verbless sentences, with *praesens historicum,* proverbs and sayings. He used his pen pointedly and vividly. "One cannot resist the charm of his narrative, the liveliness of his style, the vividness of his pictures and scenes."[118] His lively and colorful style, full of baroque contrasts and rhetorical effects and overlaid with a thin varnish of classical learning "overflows linguistic boundaries and even a modest translation cannot fail to preserve its lasting quality."[119]

Wytrzens disagrees with the judgment of most Polish literary critics in their classification of Pasek's verses, letters, and speeches as "*Schwulst, Barock im schlechten Sinne* :"

> Wir können uns dieser völligen Verwerfung nicht ganz anschliessen : Prunken mit tatsächlicher oder vorgeblicher Bildung, das Exzellieren und Paradieren mit rhetorischen Kniffen und Finten gehört ebenso zu Pasek und damit zur ambitionirten polnischen Szlachta wie der geschickte Gebrauch von Säbel und Feuerwaffen.[120]

Pasek's poems are nevertheless utterly clumsy, his letters and speeches very difficult to translate. In their translations of the

---

there are more Latin words than capital letters—every sentence contains a great number of them. He knows Aristotle and Plato, and the Latin poets, whom he cites with the greatest ease. There is also eloquence. When it is necesary, he becomes a truly inspired orator." Wacław Lednicki, *Life and Culture of Poland* (New York : Roy Publishers, 1944), 123.

[118]Kridl, 117.

[119]Pietrkiewicz, 438, 445.

[120]Pomposity, baroque in bad taste. We cannot quite agree with this entire censure : ostentation with actual or pretended education, the excelling in and demonstrating one's skill in rhetorical devices and artifices belongs just as much to Pasek and therewith to the ambitious nobility as the skilful use of sabres and firearms. Wytrzens, 14–15.

Memoirs into German and French, Wytrzens and Cazin respectively simplified their task by not only leaving out the poetry, letters, and speeches, but many difficult passages and phrases as well. In this translation, however, all the prose, including letters and speeches, is faithfully rendered into English in its entirety and without exception, regardless of its complexity in the original text. Only the verse is omitted.

Edward Raczyński's edition of the *Memoirs* in 1836 received harsh criticism for distorting the text by Polonizing the Latinisms. A decision concerning the Latin had also to be reached in this translation. Wytrzens retained very few of the Latin expressions or words ; Cazin retained some of the Latinisms with their French translation following in the text. In preparing this translation at first all the Latinisms were rendered into English, then all of them were reinstated in Latin, until finally a decision was reached to retain only a certain portion of them. All the Latinisms which are retained are translated into English in the footnotes unless :

1) their meaning is obvious as for example *Gratulor* ! *Gratulor* !, obviously meaning congratulations.

or

2) they occur often in the text, as for example *sufficit*, suffice it to say ; *ex ratione*, because ; *interim*, in the meantime. In such instances they are translated only once in the text.

It is perhaps safe to say that a native speaker of Polish is not able to understand or read freely seventeenth century Polish texts without consulting a dictionary. Seventeenth-century Polish syntax is very involved and complex. Pasek's sentences are very long and their structure extremely intricate. An effort was made to retain his long sentences in English if possible, but it became necessary to break them up into shorter sentences on numerous occasions. Pasek's vocabulary is very rich. Old Polish dictionaries were consulted for the exact meaning of his words, either to make sure what the word actually stood for, if the meaning was unclear, or to check whether the meaning of the word has not undergone a change in the course of the centuries. The words have been carefully weighed and considered. The word *fantazyja*, for example, which Pasek uses on numerous occasions, has some of the following meanings : animation, spirit, verve, vigor, zest, readiness, willingness, whole-heartedness, fervor, zeal, enthusiasm, eagerness, keenness, courage, daring, boldness, nerve, pride, self-respect, stateliness, lordliness, ambition, honor, disposition, temper, nature, character, intention, design, view, purpose, whim. Before a word was rendered into English it was examined in the perspective of the entire setting, paragraph, or sentence. An attempt was made to give as precise a translation of the text as possible, and to keep the translation as concise as possible. If Pasek used three words to express some thought for example, the same number of words was used in the English with the exception of such phrases as : *wybuchnął śmiechem*, which has no English equivalent as such and has to be translated as "burst out into a loud laughter" in order to acquire its full meaning. For a small number of words no English equivalents could be found as, for example, *hulajgorods*, and their meaning had to be supplied in the footnotes. The selection of words proved a very complicated and tedious task.

All the localities, both Polish and foreign, were checked in geographical dictionaries and atlases, for spellings and locations. All last names were checked in biographical dictionaries or historical sources. All historical data in the text were checked in both Polish and foreign historical sources. Mythological quotes and those of Latin poets were also checked. Books on Polish and foreign customs were also consulted.

The question which arose over and over again in the translation of the text is : what is a real translator's task ? The viewpoints of writers vary concerning the methodology. Nabokov for example maintains that :

> In the first place, we must dismiss once and for all the conventional notion that a translation should read smoothly ... should not sound like a translation ... In point of fact, any translation is bound to be inexact upon inspection ; while, on the other hand, the only virtue of a good translation is faithfulness and completeness. Whether it

reads smoothly or not depends on the model, not on the mimic.[121]

In Poland most of the translations of literary works were attempted by some of the best writers who devoted as much enthusiasm and creative skill to the translation as they would have to their own piece of work.[122] Among the gallery of names were such prominent writers as Mickiewicz, Słowacki, Norwid, and Boy-Żeleński, but not all of them were equally successful, for indeed it is not a very easy or rewarding task.

If the genius and character of all languages were the same, according to Woolhouselee,[123] only fidelity and attention would be required of a writer and it would be easy to translate from one language to another. But since the genius and character of languages are different, two opinions have arisen as to the proper translator's task.

1) that it is the duty of a translator to attend only to the sense and spirit of his original, to make himself perfectly master of his author's ideas, and to communicate them in those expressions which he judges to be best suited to convey them.

2) that, in order to constitute a perfect translation, it is not only requisite that the ideas and sentiments of the original author should be conveyed, but likewise his style and manner of writing, which, it is supposed, cannot be done without a strict attention to the arrangement of his sentences, and even to their order and construction.

In this translation the attempt has been made to remain as faithful as possible to the original text and at the same time to render it in a readable and unobjectionable English.

---

[121]Vladimir Nabokov, *Introduction to Mikhail Lermontov's A Hero of Our Times* (New York : A Doubleday Anchor Original, 1958), XIII.
[122]Michał Rusinek, ed., *O sztuce tłumaczenia* (Wrocław : Zakład Narodowy Imienia Ossolińskich, 1955), 8–11.
[123]Alexander Fraser Woolhouselee, *Essay on the Principles of Translation* (Edinburgh : Neil and Co., 1813), 13–14.

BIBLIOGRAPHY

Alpatov, Mikhail. *Russian Impact on Art*. New York : Philosophical Library, 1950.

Andersson, Ingvar. *A History of Sweden*. Translated from Swedish by Carolyn Hannay. New York : Praeger, 1956.

Angyal, Andreas. *Die Slavische Barockwelt*. Leipzig : E. A. Seemann, Buch- und Kunstverlag, 1961.

Arnold, Stanisław. *Geografia historyczna Polski*. Warszawa : Państwowe Wydawnictwo Naukowe, 1951.

— ed. *Odrodzenie w Polsce*. Warszawa : Państwowy Instytut Wydawniczy, 1955–56.

Bain, R. Nisbet. *Slavonic Europe*. Cambridge : At the University Press, 1908.

Banaszkiewicz, L. "Sprawa polskiego baroku". *Czasopismo dla Nauczycieli*, IV (Sept./Oct., 1949), 31–32.

Barbirecki, Jan. *Trzy mapy Polskie, wiek XVI, wiek XVII*. Warszawa: Gebethner i Wolff, 1815.

Bardach, Artur, and Herbst, Stanisław. *Kultura polska*. Warszawa : Ludowa Spółdzielnia Wydawnicza, 1961.

Bartoszewicz, Julian. „Nowe dowody autentyczności kroniki Jana Chryzostoma Paska". *Dziennik Warszawski*, 1852.

Barycz, Henryk, and Hulewicz, Jerzy. *Studia z dziejów kultury*. Warszawa : Gebethner i Wolff, 1949.

Biegeleisen, Henryk. "Rozbiór krytyczny 'Pamiętników' Paska". *Dziennik Warszawski*, 1852.

Bobrzyński, Michał. *Dzieje Polski w zarysie*. Vol. 3. Kraków : Nakładem Krakowskiej Spółki Wydawniczej, 1931, 4th ed.

Botrall, Margaret. *Every Man a Phoenix, Studies in Seventeenth-Century Autobiography*. London : John Murray, 1958.

Brückner, Aleksander. *Dzieje kultury polskiej*. Vol. 2. Kraków : Nakładem Krakowskiej Spółki Wydawniczej, 1931.

Bugiel, Władysław. "Materiały ludoznawcze w pamiętnikach Paska". *Studia i Szkice Literackie*, 1910.

Bujnicki, J. "Struktura artystyczna 'Trylogii' a pamiętniki polskie XVII wieku". *Pamiętnik Literacki*, LVII, 1966, 105–137.

Bukdahl, J., et al. *Scandinavian Past and Present*. Odense, Denmark : Arnkrone, 1959.

Bulfinch, Thomas. *The Age of the Fable*. New York : The New American Library, 1962.

Butlin, F. M. *Among the Danes*. New York : James Pott and Co., 1909.

Bystroń, Jan Stanisław. *Dzieje obyczajów w dawnej Polsce, Wiek XVI–XVII*. Vol. I, Warszawa : Państwowy Instytut Wydawniczy, 1960, 2nd ed.

Carsten, F. L. ed. *The New Cambridge Modern History*. Vol. V, Cambridge : The University Press, 1964.

Cazin, Paul. *Poland*. Paris : Librairie Hachette, 1961.

Charges, R. D. *A Short History of Russia*. New York : E. P. Dutton and Co., 1956.

Chlebowski, Bronisław. "Jan Chryzostom Pasek i jego pamiętniki". *Pisma*, III, 1952.

— *Rozwój kultury polskiej* Warszawa : Gebethner i Wolff, 1917.

Chrzanowski, Ignacy. *Historia literatury niepodległej Polski (965–1795)*. London : Interim Treasury Committee for Polish Question, 1947.

Clark, George N. *The Seventeenth Century*. New York : Oxford University Press, 1961, 2nd ed.

Corsi, Edward C. *Poland, Land of the White Eagle*. New York : Wyndham Press, 1933.

Cronholm, Neander N. *A History of Sweden, From the Earliest Times to the Present Day*. Chicago : Published by the Author, Vol. II, 1902.

Cross, Samuel Hazzard. *Slavic Civilization Through the Ages*. Cambridge : Harvard University Press, 1948.

Czapliński, Władysław. *O Polsce siedemnastowiecznej, problemy i sprawy*. Warszawa : Państwowy Instytut Wydawniczy, 1966.

— and Długosz, Józef. *Podróż młodego magnata do szkół, Studium z dziejów kultury XVI i XVII w*. Warszawa : Państwowy Instytut Wydawniczy, 1969.

— "Polacy z Czarnieckim w Danii (1658–1659)". *Rocznik Gdański*, IX and X, 1937, 293–339.

Czermak, Wiktor. "Przeprawa Czarnieckiego na wyspę Alsen." *Przewodnik Naukowy i Literacki*, XII, 1884, 1024–1039.

— "Szczęśliwy Rok." *Przegląd Polski*, LXXXIII, 1887.

Czernik, Stanisław. *Z życia pańszczyźnianego w. XVII*. Ludowa Spółdzielnia Wydawnicza, 1955.

Czubek, Jan. "Jan Chryzostom z Gosławic Pasek w oświetleniu archiwalnym (1667–1701)". *Rozprawy Akademii Umiejętności*, XXVIII, 1900.

De Battaglia, Otto Forst. *Jan Sobieski, König von Polen*. Zürich : Verlagsanstalt Benziger and Co., 1946.

Dürr-Durski, Jan. "Od manieryzmu do baroku". *Przegląd Humanistyczny*, XV, 1971, 1–17.

Dyboski, Roman. *Outlines of Polish History*. New York : Oxford University Press, 1924.

— *Poland*. London : Ernest Benn Limited, 1933.

— *Poland in World Civilization*. New York : 1950.

Dzięcioł, Witold. *The Origins of Poland*. London : Veritas Foundation Publication Centre, 1967.

Fay, Sidney Bradshaw. *The Rise of Brandenburg Prussia to 1786*. New York : Henry Holt and Company, 1937.

Fletcher, James, Esq. *History of Poland*. London : Cochrane and Pickersgill, 1931.

Freytag, Gustav. *Bilder aus der deutschen Vergangenheit*. Leipzig : Verlag von G. Hirzel, 1896, Vols. 1–4.

Friedrich, Carl. J. *The Age of the Baroque, 1610–1660*. New York : Harper and Row, 1952.

Giergielewicz, Mieczysław. "Fredro's Comedies in English". Review of *The Polish Review*, No. 4, Vol. XIV, 92–103, 1969.

— *Henryk Sienkiewicz*. New York : Twayne Publishers, Inc., 1968.

Gieysztor, Aleksander; Kieniewicz, Stefan; Rostworowski, Emanuel; Tazbir, Janusz; and Wereszycki, Henryk. *History of Poland*. Warszawa : Polish Scientific Publishers, 1968.

Grabiec, Jan. *Dzieje Polski niepodległej*. Warszawa : Towarzystwo Wydawnicze w Warszawie, 1916.

Grabski, A. F., et al. ed. *Zarys dziejów wojskowości polskiej do roku 1864*. Warszawa : Wydawnictwo Ministerstwa Obrony Narodowej, Vol. 2.

Gubrynowicz, Bronisław. "Cenzura 'Pamiętników' Paska". *Ruch Literacki*, 1932, 204–205.

Halecki, Oscar. *A History of Poland*. New York : Roy Publishers, 1943.

— *Borderlands of Western Civilization, A History of East Central Europe*. New York : The Ronald Press Company, 1952.

— *Dzieje Unii Jagiellońskiej*. Warszawa : Gebethner i Wolff, 1920, Vols. 1 and 2.

— *Europa Grenzen und Gliederung seiner Geschichte*. Darmstadt : Wissenschaftliche Buchgesellschaft, 1957.

— *Poland*. New York : Frederick A. Praeger, 1957.

— *Przyłączenie Podlasia, Wołynia i Kijowszczyzny do Korony w roku 1569*. Warszawa : Gebethner i Wolff, 1915.

— *The Crusade of Varna*. New York : Polish Institute of Arts and Sciences in America, 1943.

— *The Limits and Divisions of European History*. New York : Sheed and Ward, 1950.

Hartleb, Kazimierz ; Bardach, Artur ; and Bielak, Franciszek. *Kultura Polski*. Kraków : Wiedza, Zawód, Kultura, 1948.

Harvey, William James; and Reppien, Christian. *Denmark and the Danes, A Survey of Danish Life, Institutions and Culture*. London : T. Fisher, Unwin, Ltd. Adelphi Terrau, 1916, 2nd ed.

Hayes, Carlton ; Huntley, Joseph ; Baldwin, Marshal Whithed ; and Cole, Charles Woolsey. *History of Western Civilization*. New York : The Macmillan Company, 1962.

— *History of Europe*. New York : The Macmillan Company, 1949.

Hensel, Witold. *Polska przed tysiącem lat*. Wrocław : Zakład Narodowy im. Ossolińskich, 1960.

Jump, J. D. *The Diary of Samuel Pepys*. New York : Washington Square Press, 1964.

Kaczmarek, M. *Antologia pamiętników polskich XVI wieku*. Wrocław : Zakład Narodowy im. Ossolińskich, 1966.

Kamińska-Linderska, A. *Między Polską a Brandenburgią*. Wrocław : Zakład Narodowy im. Ossolińskich, 1966.

Kamocki, Franciszek. "Kilka uwag o nazwisku i rodzie z Gosławic Paska". *Myśl Narodowa*, Vol. XIV, 222–223, 1929.

Kersten, Adam. *Sienkiewicza 'Potop'*. Warszawa : Państwowy Instytut Wydawniczy, 1966.

— *Stefan Czarniecki*. Warszawa : MON, 1963.

Kijas, J. *'Potop' Henryka Sienkiewicza*. Warszawa : Państwowe Zakłady Wydawnictw Szkolnych, 1965.

Kinser, S. *The Works of Jacques-Auguste DeThou*. The Hague : Martinu Nijhoff, 1966.

Kleiner, Juliusz. *Zarys dziejów literatury polskiej*. Wrocław : Zakład Narodowy im. Ossolińskich, 1959.

Kliuchevsky, V. O. *A History of Russia*. Translated by C. J. Hogarth, New York : E. P. Dutton, 1911.

Konovalov, S. *Russo-Polish Relations, An Historical Survey*. Princeton : The University Press, 1945.

Kosman, Marcel. *Na tropach bohaterów 'Trylogii'*. Warszawa : Książka i Wiedza, 1966.

Kraszewski, Józef Ignacy. "Historia czy Pamiętniki ?" *Studia Literackie*, 1842, 142.

Kraushar, Aleksander. *Nowe epizody z ostatnich lat życia Imci Jana Chryzostoma z Gosławic Paska*. Petersburg : Księgarnia B. R. Rymowicz, 1893.

— "Stryj Imci Pana Paska". *Obrazy i Wizerunki Historii*, 1906.

Kridl, Manfred. *A Survey of Polish Literature and Culture*. Translated from Polish by Olga Scherer-Virski. New York : Columbia University Press, 1956.

— and Malinowski, W ; Witlin, J., eds. *For Your Freedom and Ours*. New York : Frederick Ungar Publishing Company, 1943.

Krzyżanowski, Julian. *Historia literatury polskiej.* Warszawa : Państwowy Instytut Wydawniczy, 1963.

— "J. C. Pasek 'Memoirs' by Czubek and Brückner". *Pamiętnik Literacki,* 1925.

— "Pasek i Sienkiewicz". *Pamiętnik Literacki,* Vol. 47, 4, 1956, 301–322.

Kubała, Ludwik. *Wojny duńskie i pokój oliwski.* Lwów : Księgarnia Wydawnicza H. Altenberga, 1922.

Kuchowicz, Z. "Echa konfliktów szlachecko-magnackich w literaturze drugiej połowy XVII w." *Prace Polonistyczne,* 1955, 45–59.

— "Literatura szlachecka wobec elekcji Michała Wiśniowieckiego". *Prace Polonistyczne,* XII, 1955, 171–186.

Kukulski, Leszek, ed. *Maria Kazimiera d'Arquien de la Grange.* Warszawa : Czytelnik, 1966.

— "Pośmiertna nobilitacja wydry pana Paskowej". *Ruch Literacki,* Vol. V, 1965, 75–76.

— ed. Sobieski, Jan (King of Poland). *Listy do Marysieńki.* Warszawa : Czytelnik, 1962.

Laing, Samuel. *Observations on the Social and Political State of Denmark, and the Duchies of Sleswick and Holstein in 1851.* London : Longman, Brown, Green and Longmans, 1852.

Lauring, Palle. *A History of the Kingdom of Denmark.* Translated by David Hohnen. Copenhagen : Høstand Søn, 1960.

Lednicki, Wacław. *Life and Culture of Poland as Reflected in Polish Literature.* New York : Roy Publishers, 1964.

Lehr-Spławiński, Tadeusz. *Od piętnastu wieków, szkic z pradziejów i dziejów kultury polskiej.* Warszawa : Instytut Wydawniczy Pax, 1961.

Lengyel, Emil. *1,000 Years of Hungary.* New York : The John Day Company, 1958.

Lewicki, Anatol. *Zarys historii Polski.* London : Orbis Ltd., 1947.

Lewiński-Corwin, Edward Henry. *The Political History of Poland.* New York : The Polish Book Importing Company, 1917.

Łempicki, Stanisław. *Renesans i humanizm w Polsce.* Kraków : Czytelnik, 1952.

Łepkowski, Tadeusz, ed. *Mały słownik historii Polski.* Warszawa : Wiedza Powszechna, 1964.

Łopalewski, Tadeusz. *Między Niemnem a Dźwiną.* London : Wydawnictwo Polskie, 1955.

Łowmiański, Henryk, ed. *Historia Polski.* Vol. 1. Warszawa : Państwowe Wydawnictwo Naukowe, 1957.

— *Początki Polski.* Vols. 1 and 2. Warszawa : Państwowe Wydawnictwo Naukowe, 1964.

Łoziński, Władysław. *Prawem i lewem.* Kraków : Wydawnictwo Literackie, 1960, 6th ed.

— *Życie polskie w dawnych wiekach.* Jerozolima : Nakładem Wydziału

Kultury i Prasy DTWA Jednostek Wojska na Śr. Wschodzie, 1946.

Madej, A. "Pamiętniki Paska". *Tygodnik Warszawski*, IV, 1948, 10.

Mahan, A. T. *The Influence of Sea Power upon History, 1660–1783*. Boston : Little, Brown and Company, 1918.

Mallery, Richard D. *Masterworks of Autobiography*. New York : Doubleday and Company, 1946.

Mańkowski, Tadeusz. *Genealogia sarmatyzmu*. Warszawa : Towarzystwo Wydawnicze "Łuk", 1946.

Marriott, J. A. R. *The Eastern Question, An Historical Study in European Diplomacy*. Oxford : The Clarendon Press, 1956. 4th ed.

Mieleszko, T. "Wyspa Paska". *Nowy Świat—Dodatek Tygodniowy*, (July, 1970, 25), 3, 5.

Morfill, W. R. *Poland*. New York : G. P. Putnam's Sons, 1903.

Morshead, O. F., ed. *Introduction to the Diary of Samuel Pepys*. New York : Harper and Row, 1960.

Morton, J. B. *Jan Sobieski, King of Poland*. London : Eyre and Spottiswoode, 1932.

Mousset, A. *The World of the Slavs*. New York : F. A. Praeger, 1951.

Murryat, H. *A Residence in Jutland, the Danish Isles and Copenhagen*. London : John Murray, 1860.

Nabokov, Vladimir. *Introduction to Mikhail Lermontov's 'A Hero of Our Times'*. New York : A Doubleday Anchor Original, 1958.

Nałkowski, Wacław. *Materiały do geografii ziem dawnej Polski*. Vol. 1. Warszawa : Nakładem Komitetu Wydawnictw Krajoznawczych, 1913.

Ogg, David. *Europe in the Seventeenth Century*. New York : The Macmillan Company, 1968.

Padover, S. K. *Confessions and Self-Portraits, 4600 Years of Autobiography*. New York : The John Day Company, 1957.

Pascal, Roy. *Design and Truth in Autobiography*. Cambridge : Harvard University Press, 1960.

Pasek, Jan. *Pamiętniki*. Edited by Aleksander Brückner. Kraków : Biblioteka Narodowa, 1928.

— *Pamiętniki*. Edited by Władysław Czapliński. Wrocław : Zakład Narodowy im. Ossolińskich, 1952.

— *Pamiętniki*. Edited by Władysław Czapliński. Wrocław : Zakład Narodowy im. Ossolińskich, 1968, 4th ed.

— *Reszty rękopisu Jana Chryzostoma na Gosławicach Paska, deputata z powiatu lelowskiego*. Edited by S. A. Lachowicz. Wilno : Nakładem Księgarni J. Hussarowskiego, Drukiem A. Syrkina, 1843.

— *Pamiętniki*. Edited by Jadwiga Pietrusiewiczówna. Warszawa : Spółdzielnia Wydawnicza "Książka", 1948.

— *Pamiętniki*. Edited by Roman Pollak. Wrocław : Zakład Narodowy im. Ossolińskich, 1955.

— *Pamiętniki Jana Chryzostoma Paska z czasów panowania Jana Ka-*

zimierza, Michała Korybuta i Jana III. Edited by Edward Raczyński. Poznań : 1836.

— *Les Mémoires de Jean-Chrysostome Pasek, Gentilhomme Polonais (1656–1688).* Translated by Paul Cazin. Paris : Les Belles-Lettres, 1922.

— *Die Goldene Freiheit Der Polen, Aus den Denkwürdigkeiten Sr. Wohlgeboren des Herrn Jan Chryzostom Pasek (17. Jahrhundert).* Translated by Günther Wytrzens. Graz : Verlag Styria, 1967.

Pełczyński, M. "Zdrowaś Maryja Polaków. Nieznany paszkwil z czasów rokoszu Lubomirskiego". *Pamiętnik Literacki*, Vol. 45, 1954, 195–196.

Pepys, Samuel. *The Diary of Samuel Pepys.* New York : Harper and Row, 1960.

Pertek, Jerzy. *Polacy na szlakach morskich świata.* Wrocław : Zakład Narodowy im. Ossolińskich, 1957.

Phillips, W. Alison. *Poland.* New York : Henry Holt and Co., 1956.

Pietrkiewicz, Jerzy. "A Polish 17th Century Diarist". *Slavonic and East European Review*, Vol. 32, (1953–1954), 438–448.

Pigoń, Stanisław. "Relacja Imci Pana Paska z poselstwa do Moskwy 1671–1672". *Pamiętnik Literacki*, Vol. 45, 199–204.

Platonov, S. F. *History of Russia.* New York : The Macmillan Company, 1925.

Pollak, Roman, ed. *Antologia pamiętników polskich XVI wieku.* Wrocław : Zakład Narodowy im. Ossolińskich, 1966.   •

— *Miscellanea staropolskie.* Wrocław : Zakład Narodowy im. Ossolińskich, 1966.

— *Od renesansu do baroku.* Warszawa : Państwowe Wydawnictwo Naukowe, 1969.

— "Zagadnienia periodyzacji historii literatury polskiej". *Pamiętnik Literacki*, Vol. XXXIX, 1950, 139–140.

— ed. *Nowy Korbut : Bibliografia literatury polskiej.* Warszawa : Państwowy Instytut Wydawniczy, 1964, Vol. 1.

Pollard, A. F. *The Jesuits in Poland.* London : Methuen and Co., 1892.

Przyboś, Adam ; and Żelewski, Roman, eds. *Diariusz poselstwa polskiego do Francji po Henryka Walezego w 1573 roku.* Wrocław : Zakład Narodowy im. Ossolińskich, 1963.

Ptaśnik, Jan. *Miasta i mieszczaństwo w dawnej Polsce.* Warszawa : Państwowy Instytut Wydawniczy, 1949, 2nd ed.

Raczyński, Edward, ed. *Portofolio królowej Marii Ludwiki.* Poznań : Drukarnia Nowa, 1844.

— *Żywot księcia Bogusława Radziwiłła.* Poznań : Drukarnia Nowa, 1841.

Reddaway, W F. ; Penson, J. H. ; Halecki, Oscar ; and Dyboski, Roman. *The Cambridge History of Poland*, Cambridge : The University Press, 1950.

Riegl, Alois. *Die Entstehung der Barockkunst in Rom*, Wien : Verlag von Anton Schroll and Co., 1908.

Roberts, Michael. *Gustavus Adolphus, A History of Sweden, 1611–1632*. London : Longmans, Green and Co., 1953.

— *Sweden as a Great Power, 1611–1697* : *Government, Society, Foreign Policy*. New York : St. Martin's Press, 1968.

Rose, William John. *Poland, Old and New*. London : G. Bell and Sons, 1948.

Rusinek, Michał. *O sztuce tłumaczenia*. Wrocław : Zakład Narodowy im. Ossolińskich, 1955.

Rytel, Jadwiga, ed. *Pamiętniki Paska na tle pamiętnikarstwa staropolskiego*. Wrocław : Zakład Narodowy im. Ossolińskich, 1962.

Sajkowski, Alojzy. "Jan Pasek, 'Pamiętniki' by Władysław Czapliński (1952)". Review of *Pamiętnik Literacki*, Vol. XLIV, 1953, 329–334.

— *Od Sierotki do Rybeńki, W kręgu radziwiłłowskiego mecenatu*. Poznań : Wydawnictwo Poznańskie, 1965.

— *Pamiętniki Samuela i Bogusława Kazimierza Maskiewiczów*. Wrocław : Zakład Narodowy im. Ossolińskich, 1961.

Savory, Theodore. *The Art of Translation*. London : Jonathan Cape, 1957.

Schevill, F. *The Great Elector*. Chicago : University of Chicago Press, 1947.

Schmitt, Bernadotte, E., ed. *Poland*. Berkeley : University of California Press, 1945.

Schulze, J. *Forschungen zur brandenburgischen und preussischen Geschichte*. Berlin : Walter de Gruyter and Co., 1964.

Segel, Harold B. *The Major Comedies of Alexander Fredro*. Princeton University Press, 1969.

Shaw, Desmond. *The Soul of Denmark*. New York : Charles Scribner's Sons, 1918.

Smoleński, Władysław. *Dzieje narodu polskiego*. Kraków, 1921, 6th ed.

Stolpe, Sven. *Christina of Sweden*. New York : The Macmillan Company, 1966.

Strakhovsky, Leonid I., ed. *A Handbook of Slavic Studies, Slavic Civilization Through the Ages*. Cambridge : Harvard University Press, 1949.

Svanström, Ragnar, and Palmstierna, Fredrik, C. *A Short History of Sweden*. Oxford : The Clarendon Press, 1934.

Szenic, Stanisław. *Larum na traktach Warszawy*. Warszawa : Wydawnictwo Ministerstwa Obrony Narodowej, 1960.

Szpruch, Jan. "Jan Pasek, 'Pamiętniki', by Roman Pollak, 1955". Review of *Pamiętnik Literacki*, Vol. XLVII, 1956, 560–569.

Święcicka, Maria A. J. "Die Goldene Freiheit der Polen, Aus den Denkwurdigkeiten Sr. Wohlgeboren des Herrn Jan Chryzostom Pasek". (review), *The Polish Review*, Vol. XIV, 1969, 117–118.

Święcicki, Józef Marian. "Historia czy romans". *Tygodnik Powszechny*, IV, 1953, 4–5.

Tarnowski, Stanisław. *Historia literatury polskiej*. Kraków : Drukarnia *Czasu*, 1900.

Tazbir, Janusz. *Reformacja a problem chłopski w Polsce XVI wieku*. Wrocław : Zakład Narodowy im. Ossolińskich, 1953.

Tennant, A. E. *Studies in Polish Life and History*. London : George Allen and Unwin, 1924.

Trzynadłowski, Jan. "Sztuka pamiętnikarska Jana Chryzostoma Paska". *Prace Polonistyczne*, Vol. 20, 266–277.

Vernadsky, George. *History of Russia*. New Haven : Yale University Press, 1959.

— *The Origins of Russia*. Oxford : The Clarendon Press, 1959.

Waliszewski, K. *Poland the Unknown*. London : William Heinemann, 1919.

Ward, A. W.; Prothero, G. W.; and Stanley, Leathes, eds. *The Thirty Years' War*. New York : The Macmillan Company, 1934, Vol. IV.

— *The Wars of Religion*. New York : The Macmillan Company, 1934, Vol. IV.

Wedgwood, C. V. *The Thirty Years' War*. New York : Penguin Books, 1957.

Whitton, F E. *A History of Poland—From the Earliest Times to the Present Day*. New York : Charles Scribner's Sons, 1918.

Wieniewski, Ignacy. *Podstawy kultury polskiej*. London : Wydawnictwo Światowego Związku Polaków z Zagranicy, 1946.

Winter, Nevin O. *Poland of To-Day and Yesterday*. Boston : L. C. Page and Company, 1913.

Wojciechowski, Zygmunt. *Poland's Place in Europe*. Poznań : Instytut Zachodni, 1947.

Wojtasiewicz, Olgierd. *Wstęp do teorii tłumaczenia*. Wrocław : Zakład Narodowy im. Ossolińskich, 1957.

Wolff, Zygmunt. "Podróżnicy włoscy o Polsce XVII wieku". *Studia z Dziejów Kultury*, 1949.

Woolhouselee, Alexander Fraser. *Essay on the Principles of Translation*. Edinburgh : Neill and Co., 1813.

Wójcik, Zbigniew. *Traktat andruszowski, 1667 r. i jego geneza*. Warszawa : Państwowe Wydawnictwo Naukowe, 1959.

W. P. and Zelda K. Coates. *Six Centuries of Russo-Polish Relations*. London : Lawrence and Wishart, 1948.

Zajchowska, S., ed. *Warmia i Mazury*. Poznań : Instytut Zachodni, 1953.

Żółkiewski, Stanisław. *Początek i progres wojny moskiewskiej*. Warszawa : Państwowy Instytut Wydawniczy, 1966.

Żółkiewski, Stefan. *Stare i nowe literaturoznawstwo, Szkice krytyczno-naukowe*. Wrocław : Zakład Narodowy im. Ossolińskich, 1950.

— *Zagadnienia stylu, Szkice o kulturze współczesnej.* Warszawa : Państwowy Instytut Wydawniczy, 1965.

Żółtowski. *Border of Europe.* London : Hollis and Carter, 1952.

Aarhus, Meeting-Place of Tradition and Progress, Denmark in Print and Pictures. An account written by a group of its citizens. Copenhagen, 1956.

Voprosy khudozhestvennovo perevoda. Moskow : Sovetskij Pisatel', 1955.

J. C. PASEK

Memoirs

ANNO DOMINI 1656[1]

The second battle with the Swedes this year was fought at Gniezno[2] at a great loss to the Swedish army. There were still many Poles in the service of the Swedish King;[3] the Arians[4]

[1] The first fifty pages of the manuscript are missing. They contained the memoirist's childhood and adolescence, the beginning of his military service as well as the first stanzas of a poem mourning the death of his beloved roan which was most likely killed during an encounter with the Swedes on February 8, 1656 at Gołąb. See Jan Czubek, *Pam.*, p. 1, note 1. The last six stanzas of this poem, with which the preserved portions of the *Memoirs* begin, are left out in this edition and translation.

[2] The battle at Gniezno which took place on May 7, 1656 was also referred to by historians as the battle at Kłecko. J. Czubek, *Pam.*, p. 2, note 4. The battle at Jarosław on the San may be considered the first battle of the year.

[3] Charles X Gustavus (1543–1590), King of Sweden (1654–1660). Son of John Casimir (1543–1590), Count of Palatine of Zweibrücken and Catherine, sister of Gustavus Adolphus and daughter of Charles IX Vasa. He was made Commander-in-Chief of the Swedish army (1642–1648) during the Thirty Years' War by his cousin Christina (Queen of Sweden 1632–1654) whose hand he unsuccessfully had sought in marriage. Upon her abdication the Riksdad elected him as her successor to the Swedish throne. See N. N. Cronholm, *A History of Sweden* (Chicago: Published by the Author, 1902), p. 2.

[4] See Introduction, p. 28, note 47. During the Swedish invasion they indeed often stood on the side of Charles X Gustavus hoping that he would assure them religious tolerance. Charles Gustavus made promises of religious tolerance to the Polish Catholics as well. He had no intention of keeping them however since he assured Cromwell at the same time that "there would soon be not a single papist left in Poland." W. F. Reddaway *et al.*, p. 521. The ideology of the Arians expressed a protest against the social conditions which existed in Poland at the time.

and the Lutherans had their own companies in which many Catholics served, some *per nexum sanguinis*,[5] others for booty and out of wantonness.

Because of bad leadership, the third battle[6] took an unfortunate turn after our successful retaking[7] of Warsaw and the

[5] On account of blood relationship.

[6] A three day battle at Warsaw, July 28–30. Czubek, *Pam.*, p. 2, note 8.

[7] Warsaw was recovered for a short time in June 1656 but then again fell into the hands of the enemies after the three-day battle which was fought on the outskirts of the city with the combined enemy forces, i.e., the Swedish and Brandenburg ones. A. Gieysztor, p. 249.

capture of Wittenberg,[8] the Swedish Field Marshal, for we could have defeated the Swedish King before the Great Elector of Brandenburg[9] arrived with 16,000[10] of his army ; but after they had joined forces, the auxiliary Tatar troops[11] were the first to desert us and later our army was driven off the battlefield and many of our good soldiers perished, but also many Swedes.

The fourth and very successful victory took place at Warka[12] where under the command of Czarniecki[13] we killed several thousand elite Swedish troops, filling the Pilica river with Swedish blood and corpses. From that time on, the Swedish might began to waver and to weaken considerably.

The fifth battle and also really the last one with the Swedes *inter viscera*[14] took place at Trzemeszno,[15] during, which, with only Czarniecki's division and two thousand Crimean Tatars, we put to the sword six thousand Swedes who had assembled from various fortresses with much booty acquired in Poland

[8]Count Arfwid von Wittenberg, Swedish general who entered Great Poland via Pomerania in the summer of 1655. Charles X Gustavus, at the head of another Swedish division, joined him there. N. N. Cronholm, pp. 4–5. Wittenberg died the following year as Polish prisoner in Zamość. J. Czubek, *Pam.*, p. 3, note 1.

[9]Frederick William, Ger. Friedrich Wilhelm (1620–1688), the Great Elector of Brandenburg (1640–1680), became Sweden's ally on January 17, 1656. W. F. Reddaway, p. 521.

[10]According to N. N. Cronholm, p. 7, and other sources he had 18,000 men with him.

[11]2000 armed Tatars under the leadership of Ghazie, sent by Mohamed Giraj. Juliusz Kijas, *Potop Henryka Sienkiewicza* (Warszawa : Państwowe Zakłady Wydawnictw Szkolnych, 1965, 40–41.

[12]The battle at Warka (a town on the Pilica river) took place on April 17, 1656, i.e., earlier than the battles of Gniezno and Warsaw. The Swedish forces were completely crushed there. Grabowski, p. 18.

[13]Stefan Czarniecki (1599–1685), one of Poland's greatest warriors. Was appointed Deputy Hetman of the Crown on January 3, 1656 and given the leading command in the war with the invader. Was appointed Field Hetman of the Crown in 1665 ; Voivode of Ruthenia in 1657, and Voivode of Kiev in 1664.

[14]Within boundaries, i.e., on Polish soil.

[15]The battle at Trzemeszno (now Strzemeszna) took place on August 25, 1656. Trzemeszno lies about 12 km from Rawa, Pasek's hometown. J. Czubek, p. 3, note 8.

and were trying to cross over to Prussia to join their King.[16]
We killed them to the very last man so that as the saying goes
nec nuntius cladis,[17] not one be left to report to the King the
news of the destruction of this army ; those who fled from the
battlefield to the forest or to the marshes met with an even
more cruel death at the hand of the peasants.[18] Those who were
not tracked down by the peasants were forced to go to a village
or city but they also had to die, for there were no longer any
Swedish forces in the area. (This battle took place about a
league from Rawa.)

I don't know if among all the slaughtered Swedes even one
could be found who was not disemboweled, and this was for the
following reason : while collecting spoils on the battlefield, the
peasants came across one fat corpse of a soldier whose stomach

[16]Charles X Gustavus.
[17]Not a single survivor ; not even the messenger of the defeat.
[18]The Swedes robbed Polish manors, desecrated the churches, outraged
the population. The Poles eventually rebelled and peasants armed with
scythes, sickles and flails began a guerilla warfare. The provincial
armies of Great Poland, Little Poland, and Lithuania became united
in a confederation and in December 1655 began to attack the Swedish
occupying forces. W. F. Reddaway, p. 521.

was so sharply cut open with a sword that the intestines were showing. Since the intestine was cut open, one of the peasants saw a ducat[19] inside ; looking further he found more. Then the peasants began ripping open others, finding in some gold and in others dirt. Even those Swedes whom they found alive in the forests they searched for money belts, then they cut their stomachs open with a knife and searched the intestines. Only when nothing was found would they say : "Go home, you thief and villain ; since you have no booty I grant you life."[20]

The Swedes were also defeated badly at other places this year. But it would be difficult to write about those where I was not present. During all the military turmoils I stayed with Czarniecki and with him I experienced sometimes misery and sometimes good fortune, since he was after all a leader in the style of all great and lucky warriors ; *sufficit*[21] that during the entire time of my service in his division I ran away only once but the times I chased the enemy I could count by the thousands. In short, all of my military service was *sub regimine eius*[22] and it was very pleasant indeed.

[19]Red *złoty* ; a gold coin.
[20]This behavior can be explained as revenge on the crimes committed by the Swedes against the Polish population.
[21]Suffice it to say.
[22]Under the command.

ANNO DOMINI 1657

We were at war with Hungary, for which purpose new recruitment was called. Filip Piekarski, a relative of mine, enlisted
among others; for this reason I also joined the forces. The
Hungarian thief, the mad Rakoczy[1] wanted a good beating. He
was fed up with peace and acquired a fancy for some Polish
garlic, which somebody praised to him in jest, saying that it
was better tasting than the Hungarian.

Like Xerxes[2] who waged war against Greece *ob caricas
Atticas*,[3] so with similar luck Pan[4] Rakoczy set out with 40,000
Hungarians and Moldavians[5] and just as many Cossacks in
order to taste some Polish garlic. In Poland he was not only
given garlic but a hard time as well. For as soon as he crossed
the border, Jerzy Lubomirski[6] invaded his land, burning and

[1]George II Rakoczy, György Rákóczi II, Prince of Transylvania (1648–
1660); also ruler of the large adjoining counties of Szatmar and
Szaboles. The principality was then a federation of three nations: the
Magyars, the Magyar-speaking Szklers of its eastern part and the
Saxons. Charles X Gustavus promised him southern and southwestern
Poland in terms of the alliance. Rakoczy entered Poland in January
1657 and joined forces with Charles X on April 11. After his unsuccessful invasion of Poland he was deposed that same year. F. L. Carsten,
pp. 478, 486.

[2]Xerxes I, called "The Great", King of Persia (486–465 B.C.).

[3]For the sake of Attic figs.

[4]Polish for Mr., used ironically here.

[5]I.e., Walachians since Moldavia was a part of Walachia at the time.

[6]Jerzy Sebastian Lubomirski (1616–1667), Polish Grand Hetman. He
distinguished himself in the battles with the Swedish and the Transylvanian invaders (1655–1660) and later in the battles with the Muscovites (1661).

killing all around and leaving only land and water. Then taking
a big ransom from Rakoczy's mother,[7] he went to persuade her
son not to eat up all the Polish garlic, but to leave at least some
for seeding. Also those of us with Czarniecki did the best we
could : and Rakoczy so happily satisfied his appetite for garlic
that he lost his whole army and fell into our hands himself.
Then bargaining for his skin,[8] he agreed to pay millions, and
having saved his life, he went to the border like an escorted
Jew, accompanied only by a small retinue. *In oppigneratione*[9]
for the agreed ransom he left behind the illustrious Counts
Katanas,[10] who at first drank wine and ate off silver china in

[7]She was Zsófia Báthory.
[8]He was surrounded by the Polish army and deserted by the Cossacks
at Czarny Ostrów on July 22, 1657. He capitulated and pledged himself
to break the alliance with Sweden, to return his Polish towns, and to
pay an enormous war contribution. The Tatars decimated his army
during his retreat and the Sultan deprived him of the Transylvanian
throne. W. F. Reddaway, p. 523. Some of his forces Rakoczy left
behind under the command of János Kemény ; at the battle of Trembowla, July 31, Kemény suffered a defeat and was taken with some of
his men as prisoner to Crimea. F. L. Carsten, *The Camb. Hist.*, p. 487.
[9]As security.
[10]Pasek seems to confuse here the Hungarian word *Katona*, soldier,
with a last name. The hostages were then the two Magyar magnates
István Apaffy (who was married to Rakoczy's aunt, i.e., his mother's
sister) and György Gyeröffy. J. Czubek, *Pam.*, p. 7, note 5.

Łańcut;[11] but when no ransom was to be seen, they drank water. Later they chopped and carried wood for the kitchen and ended their lives in such destitution.

The ransom was lost and so was Rakoczy, for he found nowhere a cheerful face ; wherever he turned he heard crying and cursing on account of the sons, husbands, and brothers whose death he had brought about in the war with Poland. He then fell into despair and died. Well, that's garlic for you !

As he was setting out for this war and was taking leave of his mother, he mounted his horse ; right in front of her the horse fell under him to the ground. When his mother tried to persuade him to give up that war, saying that this was a bad omen, he answered her that the horses' legs were bad and not the omen. He then changed to another horse ; a plank in the bridge broke under him and he again fell off the horse. To this he said the plank was bad. Isn't it amazing how these *praesagia*[12] usually do come true ?

[11]A town 15 km east of Rzeszów, at that time the residence of the Lubomirskis.
[12]Auguries.

ANNO DOMINI 1658

The King[1] was with one army near Toruń;[2] another army stayed in the Ukraine; whereas our division under Pan Czarniecki was stationed for three months near Drahim.[3] *In decursu Augusti*[4] we went to Denmark to help the Danish King,[5] who had launched a diversionary attack during the Swedish invasion of Poland.[6] He surely did not do so *ex commiseratione*[7] for us, although his nation had been *ab antiquo*[8] favorably inclined

[1]John II Casimir, sometimes known as Casimir V (1609–1672), Jan Kazimierz in Polish; son of Sigismund III Vasa and brother of Władysław (Ladislas) IV; king of Poland (1648–1668). A Jesuit and Cardinal (1640) he was absolved by the Pope on becoming king (1648) and married his brother's (Władysław's) widow, the French-born Marie Louise (Maria Ludwika) Gonzaga.

[2]A city in the northwestern part of Poland in the province of Poznań. Birthplace of the Polish astronomer Copernicus.

[3]A small town 65 km south of Koszalin, now Drawsko. Pasek is mistaken here. According to other sources, Czarniecki's division did not rest that long in Drahim. When Czarniecki received orders to march to Denmark he was already at Peplin in Pomerania. W. Czapliński, *Pam.*, p. 9, note 1.

[4]Toward the end of August... This date is wrong. Czarniecki was in Peplin on August 9 and in Wałcz on the 16th. W. Czapliński, *Pam.*, p. 9, note 2.

[5]Frederick III (1609–1670), king of Denmark (1648–1670), second son of Christian IV, born in Haderslev. He was Bishop of Bremen prior to that.

[6]Denmark declared war on Sweden on May 2, 1657 while Charles X Gustavus was still in Poland. N. N. Neander, *A Hist. of Sweden*, p. 9.

[7]Out of compassion.

[8]For a long time.

toward the Polish nation, as old documents show, but because of an *innatum odium*[9] which he cherished toward the Swedes. On account of the bitter hostility between neighbors and in order to avenge the injustice inflicted upon him, he took advantage of the occasion when the Swedish King was busy in Poland and invaded the latter's country with his own army, attacking, destroying and killing.[10] Gustav, who was a great and lucky warrior, returned from Poland, leaving his garrisons at some Prussian fortresses and *oppressit*[11] the Danes so violently that he not only took back his own but conquered almost their whole country as well. The Danish King, in an attempt to make his behavior look more justified, then declared that he broke the *pacta*[12] and made war against Sweden just *per amorem gentis nostrae*.[13] He, therefore, asked the Poles as well as the Emperor[14] for help. Giving as an excuse his pacts[15] with Sweden, the Emperor refused to send troops. The second excuse he gave was that he had no army at the time, since he had allowed the Polish King to hire it. The Polish King sent Czarniecki with six thousand of our army. He also sent in his

[9]An innate hatred.
[10]Actually the Danish King had assaulted the Swedish territories and started war with Sweden in 1657. Overcome by the Swedes he was forced to conclude the treaty of Röskilde in February 1658. By the humiliating peace of Röskilde, February 27, 1658, Denmark yielded Scania, Halland, Blekinge, Bohuslän, and the Trondheim to Sweden. Ragnar Svanström, Carl Fredrik Palmstierna, *A History of Sweden* (Oxford : The Clarendon Press, 1934), p. 158. Charles Gustavus promised to withdraw his forces of 5000 men from Denmark but failed to keep his promise and in the fall attacked the Danes once again. Hølstand Søn, Copenhagen, 1960.
[11]Oppressed.
[12]Agreements.
[13]Out of love for our nation.
[14]According to Czapliński the Emperor was not causing any difficulty at the time. *Pam.*, p. 10, note 17. He was Leopold I (1640–1705), second son of Ferdinand III ; king of Hungary (1655–1705), Holy Roman Emperor (1658–1705) ; Emperor of the hereditary Hapsburg dominions of Austria and Hungary (1657). His father, Ferdinand III, had concluded the alliance with Poland against Sweden in 1657.
[15]Peace of Westphalia, 1648, which concluded the Thirty Years' War. Czubek, *Pam.*, p. 9, note 7.

name General Montecucculi[16] with the imperial army. We were ordered to ride there unencumbered by supply wagons ; Wilhelm, the Great Elector of Brandenburg,[17] was *in persona*[18] of the Polish King and was so to speak the commander-in-chief of these troops. We left our transport and supply columns in Czaplinek,[19] hoping to return to them within half a year at the latest.

In Czaplinek, as we were leaving, the military men had various reflections. Many were alarmed at the prospect of going beyond the sea where no Polish foot had ever stood ; at going with six thousand troops into the land of that enemy[20] whose might we could not withstand with all our strength in our own fatherland. Moreover, no final decision had yet been made as to whether the imperial army was to go with us. Fathers wrote to their sons, wives to their husbands that they should not go to Denmark even if they were to lose pay and retinue, because all considered us as good as perished. My father, however, although I am his only son, wrote to me commanding me to call upon the Name of God for assistance and not to let myself be disturbed by all this but to boldly follow the will of the leader with father's and mother's blessing. He promised to beseech the Divine Majesty ardently and assured me that not even one hair would fall from my head without the Will of God.

As we were going toward Cielętnice[21] and Międzyrzecz[22]

---

[16]Raimondo Montecucculi or Montecuccoli, Conte di (1609–1680) ; Italian general in imperial service. He defeated the Turks in the battle of St. Gotthard in 1664. He commanded the imperial army in the war of the Empire and Holland against France (1672–1675).

[17]See the treaties of Wehlau and Bromberg. W. F. Reddaway, pp. 524–525.

[18]I.e., represented.

[19]Germ. Tempelburg, a town in the starosty of Drahim in western Pomerania, southwest of Drawsko.

[20]Sweden.

[21]Now Sulęcin, called Zielenzig at the time, a town in the voivodeship of Gorzów. W. Czapliński, *Pam.*, p. 11, note 31.

[22]A city about 34 km east of Sulęcin. Obviously the Poles must have reached Międzyrzecz before Sulęcin. W. Czapliński, *Pam.*, p. 11, note 32.

already near the border, many companions[23] and retainers[24]
turned back to Poland, especially those from Great Poland,[25]
from the newly recruited district banners,[26] such as the regiment
of the starost of Osiek[27] and that of Opaliński,[28] the voivode
of Podlasie. The entire banner of Kozubski[29]dispersed, only he
with the standard-bearer and another officer went with us. The
banner of hussars[30] of Zamoyski,[31] the voivode of Sandomierz,
did remain, but *verius dicam*,[32] the rest of the regiment had
fled ; only six officers with the second in command[33] remained
with the banner. They went with us and stayed on with the
army ; we used to call them Gypsies, because their retainers
wore red overcoats. From other banners two or three men
remained. Thus these cowards discouraged even good lads so
that many hesitated. After we had already crossed the border,
each made his vows to God in his own way. The entire army
began to sing in the Polish manner : *O gloriosa Domina* ![34] The
horses in turn began to snort so noisily in all the regiments
that all plucked up courage. Everyone took this *pro bono
omine*,[35] which turned out to be the case.

[23]Pol., *towarzysze*, i.e., officers of noble origin.
[24]Every nobleman was accompanied by two or three such retainers.
W. Czapliński, *Pam.*, p. 12, note 34.
[25]Western region of Poland.
[26]Hist., any number of men marching behind a banner, Pol. *chorągiew*.
Here meaning such banners which were sustained by the districts of
the various voivodeships. J. Czubek, *Pam.*, p. 11, note 5.
[27]At that time he was Adam Uriel Czarnkowski. W. Czapliński, *Pam.*,
p. 12, note 36.
[28]Piotr Opaliński (1600–1665) ; later the voivode of Kalisz. J. Czubek,
Pam., p. 11, note 7.
[29]Mikołaj Kozubski. J. Czubek, *Pam.*, p. 11, note 8.
[30]*Husaria* (a word of Hungarian origin, *huszár*), a choice, heavy armored cavalry, armed in sabres, swords, and spears. J. Czubek, *Pam.*, pp.
11–12, note 10.
[31]Zamoyski, Jan, grandson of the Chancellor Zamoyski and married to
Maria d'Arquien, who after his death married Jan Sobieski. Czapliński,
Pam., p. 12, note 4.
[32]To tell the truth.
[33]*Namiestnik*, a temporary substitute of a lieutenant-colonel. J. Czubek,
Pam., p. 12, note 2.
[34]Oh, Glorious Queen !
[35]As a good omen.

From Międzyrzecz we continued along the same road. The army passed a hill from which one could still see the Polish border and some towns. Many a man turned around and thought : "Dear Fatherland, will I ever behold you again !" As long as we were close to home, some strange longing overcame us, but as soon as we had crossed the Odra[36] the nostalgia was swept away and after we had gone further, Poland was soon forgotten.

The Prussians received us rather *honorifice* ;[37] they sent us their delegates even beyond the Odra. We were given the first provisions near Kiestrzyń[38] and kept receiving them everywhere until we had crossed the land of the Great Elector. One had to admit that all went smoothly, because a regulation had been issued concerning quarters for the night across his whole country[39] and provisions were brought to these places in advance. In our army the German custom was adopted : when we were crossing through cities, or marching on parade, the regular officers rode in front of the banners with their swords drawn, the officers of noble birth held their pistols high and the retainers their guns. Offenses were no longer punished by beheading or shooting but by tying the offender in full uniform, just as he was caught in the act, to a horse by his legs and dragging him two or three times, depending on the sentence, around a public square. At first this appeared a trivial punishment but it is a frightful torture because not only the victim's clothes but also his flesh fall off, so that only the bones remain.[40]

[36]Germ. Oder.

[37]Courteously.

[38]Now Kostrzyn (Germ. Küstrin), a city on the Oder at its confluence with the Warta in western Poland. It belonged to Brandenburg at the time.

[39]I.e., Brandenburg.

[40]All Brandenburg commentaries seem to agree that the Polish army behaved in exemplary fashion during that march. W. Czapliński, *Pam.*, p. 14, note 54.

Then the army moved to Nyböl;[41] thence to Apenrade[42] and from Apenrade again to Haderslev[43] to spend the winter. In Hadersleben the Voivode set up quarters with only his regiment of dragoons[44] and our royal regiment, whereas other Polish regiments got stationed in Kolding,[45] Horsens[46] and in other Danish towns and villages. Although the army was to penetrate even deeper into the Danish kingdom, the commander[47] decided that we should take up winter quarters as close as possible to the enemy's border in order to eat more Swedish than Danish bread—and this was the way it happened. Throughout the entire winter our raiding parties would penetrate the Swedish villages and avenge the wrongs inflicted upon our own nation. One could write much about what the raiding parties did to these people, whenever they visualized the injustices committed recently by the Swedes in Poland.

A great abundance of provisions was brought back from all the patrols : cattle and sheep in sufficient number ; one could buy a good ox worth a whole thaler for two Danish marks. Honeycombs were brought to us in great quantities, because everywhere in the fields there were spacious apiaries where bees were kept in straw boxes, not in beehives.[48] Many varieties of

[41]Nübel, a town in southwestern Denmark. The route of Czarniecki's division to Denmark is not sufficiently well known but the army marched via Wriezen, Eberswalde, Templin, Ferbelin, and Hamburg. W. Czapliński, *Pam.*, p. 14, note 55.

[42]Aabenraa, a town at the head of the fiord opening on Little Belt, in southwestern Denmark, 15 km south of Haderslev. The Poles reached it in November. W. Czapliński, *Pam.*, p. 14, note 56.

[43]Germ. Hadersleben, a seaport in southeastern Jutland, south of Apenrade. The Poles arrived there in November. W. Czapliński, *Pam.*, p. 15, note 57.

[44]Mounted infantry in the seventeenth century, armed in spades or maces and fire-arms. J. Czubek, *Pam.*, p. 14, note 1.

[45]A seaport in southeastern Jutland, Denmark, on inlet of Little Belt.

[46]A seaport in eastern Jutland, Denmark, south of Kolding at head of Horsens Fjord.

[47]Hist., Deputy Hetman, here Czarniecki.

[48]Bees in Denmark were indeed cultivated in huge flagons woven of straw. Since Pasek probably never got close to them, they appeared to him as straw boxes. See Czapliński, *O Pol. Sied.*, p. 206.

fish were in abundance and plenty of bread. The domestic wine was bad, but the Spanish wines[49] and the mead were good. Since wood was scarce, one heated with cut and dried peat, which yielded such excellent coal that even oak wood could not have produced any better.

There were stags, hares, and deer[50] beyond all expectations and not very timid because not everyone was allowed to hunt them. There were no wolves and also for that reason the game was not timid ; it let itself be approached and shot at from close up. We used to hunt it in the following manner : after we spotted a herd of stags in the field—since these wretched creatures used to come up to the village like cattle—we rode down the herd from the side of the open field, then picking up speed and uttering a cry we drove the stags into the peat-pits, which were very wide and deep. The animals fell into these in heaps, and one only had to pull them out and slaughter them. As I had already mentioned, there were no wolves there, because the law was such that whenever a wolf was spotted, all village and city dwellers to the very last man had to leave their homes and to pursue the wolf until they managed to starve it to death, drown or capture it. Then without flaying it they would hang it by a heavy iron chain from high gallows or from a tree, and thus it hung until only the bones remained.[51] They not only did not let a wolf propagate, but did not even let it spend the night in their country, whenever it managed to make its way there through the only possible narrow entrance be-

[49]Malaga wine. Its actual name was *Pedro Ximenes* which later became called *Petersimenis*, and in Polish *petercyment*. J. Czubek, *Pam.*, p. 14, note 6.

[50]Red deer were so numerous in 1610 that Christian IV shot thirty-six deer one morning at Kirsholm, about eight miles from Copenhagen. Now the deer are very rare and live mostly in the forests between Halborg, Viborg and Aarhus. The falow deer were important to Denmark in the 17th century. See William J. Harvey and Christian Reppien, *Denmark and the Danes, A Survey of Danish Life, Institutions and Culture* (London : T. Fisher Ltd., 1916), p. 25.

[51]According to the ordinance of 1650, mass hunts for wolves were to take place in December. Wolves were hung next to criminals... W. Czapliński, *Pam.*, p. 16, note 69.

tween the seas in search of some cervine meat. There is no access from the other sides, because on one side the kingdom is washed by the Baltic Sea, on the other side, as well as *a septemtrione*,[52] by the Ocean.[53] From all these sides the wolf had no access, unless he were to hire a small smack in Gdańsk[54] from his Honor the Mayor and pay for it well.

For this reason there is a great abundance of game in Denmark. There are no partridges however, because they are so stupid that they are frightened by mere trifles, fall down into the sea and drown.

The Danish people are good-looking; the women are pretty but somewhat too fair. They dress nicely but in cities as well as in villages they wear wooden clogs. Whenever they walk on the city's sidewalks they make such a clatter that one cannot hear one's own words. The upper class women, however, wear shoes as our Polish women do.

In showing affection, the Danish women are not as restrained as the Polish women are, for even though they show some unusual shyness at first, they fall madly and passionately in love at the first meeting after exchanging merely a few words and they do not know how to conceal this amorousness. They are all too eager then to give up father and mother and a rich dowry, and are ready to follow their beloved even to the ends of the earth.

They have their beds hidden in the walls like closets and they use lots of bedding. They sleep in the nude, just the way their mothers bore them, and they do not consider it shameful to dress and undress in front of one another. They do not even heed a stranger, but take off all their attire by candlelight and

[52]In the North.
[53]This long peninsula extends about 300 miles from Altona on the Elbe to the Scaw Point at the entrance of the Cattegat. Samuel Lang, Esq., *Observations on the Social and Political State of Denmark, and the Duchies of Sleswick and Holstein in 1851* (London : Longman, Brown, Green, and Longmans, 1852), p. 200.
[54]A city in northern Poland on Gulf of Gdańsk and a major Baltic seaport.

in the end they take off their chemises too. Then they hang everything on pegs and in the nude they bolt their doors, put out the candle and crawl into the closet to sleep.[55]

When we told them that this was shameful and that in our country even a wife did not do this in front of her husband, they used to tell us that in their land no shame was attached to

[55]Czapliński finds the information about the beds hidden in the walls as well as about the Danes going nude to bed true. W. Czapliński, *O Pol. Sied.*, pp. 206–207.

this because one should not be ashamed of one's limbs, which were created by God.

As for their sleeping in the nude, they said : "The chemise and other articles of clothing which are of service to us and cover us during the day, deserved a rest and should be allowed to have one at least at night. Besides, of what use are they to us and why should we take fleas and bugs to bed with us and allow them to bite us, thus interfering with our sweet dreams ?" Our lads used to pull all sorts of practical jokes on them, but nevertheless, the custom was not broken.

Their eating habits are very peculiar, because they seldom eat anything warm, but cook various dishes all at once for the entire week ; then they eat them cold, bit by bit and frequently.[56] They even eat while threshing, since women thresh there with flails just as men ; after almost every sheaf which they have threshed, they sit down on straw, take bread and butter, which always lies in a wooden dish, butter the bread and eat it, then get up once again and work. They do this repeatedly.

When they slaughter an ox, a pig or a ram, they don't waste even the smallest drop of blood but drain it all into a container, mix into it barley or buckwheat groats, stuff the tripe of the animal with it and cook everything together in a boiler. Then they put this stuffed tripe on a big dish in the shape of a wreath around the head of the slaughtered animal and set this on the table at every dinner and eat it as a great delicacy. They do this even in the homes of the gentry, and they kept treating me to this *ad nauseam* until I finally told them that we Poles should not be eating this because dogs would become our enemies, since this is their dish.

---

[56]Shaw Desmond describes this frequent eating as follows : "Talk-talk-talk. Snak-snak-snak. Not only at dinner table, but wherever men do congregate ... Snak-snak-snak. Talk-talk-talk. It's Denmark's curse— that and the hospitality which prompts it. But it is a delightful curse and a delightful hospitality." Shaw Desmond, *The Soul of Denmark* (New York : Charles Scribner's Sons, 1918), pp. 597–599.

They have no ovens in their homes, with the exception of the great gentlemen, because ovens are heavily taxed by the king. It was said that the tax was one hundred silver thalers for every oven per year.[57] They have spacious fireplaces, however, in front of which they put as many stools as there are people in the house. They sit down on them to warm themselves. Also for better heating of the room they have a little trench like a trough in the middle of the room. They fill it with coal, fan it from one end so it glows and heats.[58]

The churches are very beautiful. They were formerly Catholic churches. The services are also more beautiful than those of our Polish Calvinists, because the churches still have altars and paintings. We used to be present at the sermons, since they prepared them in Latin especially for us and invited us to them. They preached so *circumspecte*[59] in order not to utter one single word *contra fidem*[60] that one could have said that a Roman Catholic priest was preaching and they *gloriabantur*[61] about this and said : "We believe in what you believe, and you call us dissenters in vain." Still Father Piekarski[62] scolded us for going there. To be sure many went there just to see the beautiful Danish girls and to observe their customs. They have a service similar to that of the Germans, during which the men cover their eyes with their hats, the women with their veils and then bend over and put their heads under the

[57]According to Rosznecki, this is not quite correct. See Czapliński, *Pam.*, p. 19, note 77.
[58]The statement about the little trenches according to Czapliński is true. He saw them in the National Museum in Copenhagen. Czapliński, *O Pol. Sied.*, p. 207.
[59]Cautiously.
[60]Against the Faith.
[61]Boasted.
[62]Adrian Piekarski, or rather Pikarski, a Jesuit army chaplain and later royal preacher. He was Pasek's uncle ; died in 1679. J. Czubek, *Pam.*, p. 18, note 5. Adrian Pikarski, Filip, a lieutenant and standard-bearer under Czarniecki, and Anzelm were brothers and sons of Jan Pikarski a provincial judge, and brothers, or half brothers, of Jadwiga Pikarski, the memoistist's mother. Pasek never refers to them as uncles however. F. Kamocki, p. 223.

pews.[63] On such occasions our lads used to snatch their prayer books, scarves, etc. Once the minister noticed this and burst out laughing so that he could not finish his sermon because of it. Also we who were watching this had to laugh. The Lutherans *stupebant*[64] that we laughed and that their preacher was laughing with us. He later cited a parable about a soldier who begged a hermit to pray for him. The hermit knelt down to pray ; in the meantime the soldier snatched away from him the little ram which carried his little knapsack, and ran away. At the end of this parable, the preacher *exclamavit* : *O devotionem supra devotiones* ! *Alter orat, alter furatur* ![65] From that time on, whenever the women had to cover their heads again, they first put away their prayer books and scarves, but they still continued to exchange glances and laugh.

When I questioned them as to why they concealed their heads and covered their eyes, since neither Christ nor the Apostles did that, no one could answer me. One of them did say that this was done in memory of the days when the Jews covered Christ's eyes and ordered him to prophesy. To that I retorted : "If by this you want to express properly *recordatio passionis Domini*,[66] then while you are covering your eyes one should beat you on the neck with a fist, because this was the way it was done then." But they would not agree.

The Great Elector of Brandenburg learned soon about these services and when the Starost of Kaniów[67] was visting

[63]Some even dozed with their heads under the pulpits in Aarhus, Jutland, since in 1646 Christian the IV decreed that, "as a great disorder is caused in churches through sleep, it is our gracious will that in every parish in your diocese some persons shall be appointed to walk round the churches with long cudgels, with which to rap on the heads of those who are asleep, and in this way keep people awake to hear the sermon." F. M. Butlin, *Among the Danes* (New York : James Pott and Co., 1909), p. 124.

[64]Were astounded or amazed.

[65]Cried out. Oh, piety of all pieties ! One prays, another steals !

[66]A remembrance of the Passion.

[67]Stefan Stanisław Czarniecki, the Voivode's nephew ; a colonel and a brave soldier. He took part in all the battles under the reign of Jan Kazimierz and during the rebellion of Lubomirski he sided with the King. He fought at Vienna and Parkany (1683). He was awarded the

with him he said : "For God's sake, your Honor, please warn
his Excellency the Voivode on my behalf to forbid the Polish
gentlemen to go to church, for surely many of them will be
converted to the Lutheran faith, since I hear that they have
been praying so ardently that this fervor engorges the scarves
of the Danish girls." The Voivode had a good laugh on account
of this warning.

That same Prince Wilhelm behaved very courteously toward us, accommodated us on all occasions, entertained us and
dressed in a Polish manner. Whenever troops were passing by,
as a rule some men would deliberately ignore others; he,
however, came out and stood in front of his tent—or quarters,
if he happened to be staying in a town—and held his cap in his
hands until all banners had passed. Perhaps he also cherished
the hope of being offered the Polish crown *post* Jan Kazimierz'
fata.[68] As a matter of fact it might even have come to that if
an envoy[69] of his had not blundered during the election, for
when one senator said to him : "Let his Highness the Elector
renounce Luther, and he will become our King," the envoy
angrily declared that the Elector would not do such a thing
even for an empire. Prince Wilhelm was displeased when he
learned of this and reproached the envoy for having said this
so *absolute*[70] without first having asked him about it.

During our stay in Denmark, the Voivode dealt with him
often, because he was *in persona*[71] of the Polish King and had
command over our army as well as over the Imperial army
whose fourteen thousand troops were under General Montecucculi ; the Elector had under him twelve thousand Prussians,

starostys of Kaniów, Lipniszki, Brańsk. He was elected the marshal
of the Confederacy of Gołąb in 1672. He fought at Chocim in 1673.
[68]After ... death.
[69]The envoy was Jan Hoverbeck. Lubomirski had suggested this to
Hoverbeck in 1661. Hoverbeck excluded the possibility of the Elector
changing his religion. Even though the Elector did approve of what
the envoy said he was not content that the emphatic answer of the
envoy excluded the possibility of further discussion on the subject.
W. Czapliński, *Pam.*, p. 21, note 96.
[70]Categorically.
[71]He represented the Polish King.

better men than the imperial troops, and we always preferred
to go into combat with them. It was also not good to make
camp close to the imperial forces, because they immediately
would send seamstresses to our camp. It was strange that in
such an affluent country where we had plenty of everything in
our winter quarters, scarcely had the imperial troops stayed in
one place for a week and they sent their wives begging to us.
A young woman, fair but emaciated, as if after the heaviest
siege, would come to the tent with this oration : "Sir Pole, do
give me some bread and I shall sew shirts for you."

When one saw such a miserable creature one had to give
alms and for a week or two she made shirts for whoever needed
them. These women came in handy, for it was not difficult to
get linen, since enough of it was brought back from patrols,
and we had no one to sew for us because we had only one
woman in our army, a trumpeter. When their husbands grew
weary awaiting them, they would come looking for them from
one tent to another. Whoever found his wife took her home
and thanked us for having fed her well. If we still needed her,
that is, if she had not finished sewing shirts, we had only to
give the husband some biscuits and he would go away, leaving
her for a longer time. He visited her only now and then. And
so many a wench looked so much better in the course of two
weeks that her husband could not recognize her ...[72]

. . . .

They debated how to entrench themselves and how to fell
the palisade walls ; however, they failed to consider with what
they were to fell them. Where was one to get axes ? Finally the
light cavalry sergeant[73] ordered the men to search all the villages in a radius of two or three leagues for axes and even

[72]The manuscript breaks off here. The section describing the events
preceding the capture of Kolding is left out. Czubek, *Pam.*, p. 22,
note 1. It should also be noted that the capture of the island Als which
Pasek places under A. D. 1659 took place before the capture of Kolding.

[73]He was Piotr Mężyński. Hist., a military officer or official who looked after the camp watch and was responsible for its order and
discipline. Czubek, *Pam.*, p. 22, notes 2 and 3.

before dawn some five hundred of them were already stacked
in a heap. As soon as the clocks struck four o'clock in the
morning, orders were given to sound the reveille. The Voivode,[74] who had hardly slept that night, got up and gave orders
to distribute the axes among the cavalry banners and the infantry. One hour after reveille he ordered the trumpets to sound
once again, this time to summon everyone to be ready in an
hour for assault. Everyone was to carry a sheaf of straw on
his chest as protection from musket shots. All were to leap
forward together under the battlements and press toward the
walls as close as possible to avoid being struck down from
above and in order to be able to shoot back.

As soon as it began to grow light, the army sneaked closer
to the city and I went to see the army chaplain. Later the
Voivode said to me : "Lieutenant Charlewski volunteers to be
in command of the soldiers. Let him do so then and you, Sir,
will stay here." I answered him : "Everyone heard that your
Honor had asked me to go. Someone might think that I am
afraid, so I shall go."[75]

When we dismounted, Paweł Kossowski and Łęcki did the
same. With the retainers there were five officers from our
banner, but I was in command, since it had already been
delegated to me before these senior officers made up their
minds to volunteer. We commended ourselves to the protection
of God and His Holy Mother and everyone made a vow to
Almighty God. We took leave of our companions as if parting
for eternity and then stepped back to a place apart from the
mounted men. Father Piekarski, the Jesuit, gave us an encouraging sermon of more or less the following content :

> Even though every sacrifice made sincerely from the heart
> is well pleasing to God, the most pleasant *victima*[76] of all
> is, nevertheless, when one offers one's blood on the battle-
> field for the Honor of Almighty God. Why did He bless

[74]Czarniecki.
[75]Most likely Czarniecki appointed Pasek to be in command of the
retainers during the assault. This was probably mentioned in the omitted section.
[76]Sacrifice.

Abraham so that his race should inherit the entire world ?[77]
Only because, at one single command of God, he had been
ready to sacrifice the blood of his beloved Isaac. We are
summoned by the injustice which the Almighty has suffered from the Swedish nation ; we are summoned by the
temples of God desecrated all over Poland by the Swedes ;
we are summoned by the blood of our brothers and by our
fatherland devastated by their hand ; we are summoned
by the Holy Virgin, Our Lady, whose immaculate name
was blasphemed by their nation ; they all summon us to
intercede sincerely for these inflicted offenses, so that the
world should still see in us the unfading glory and courage
of our ancestors. You brave knights bring here, as Isaac
did, your blood as a sacrifice to God. I assure you,
however, in the name of God, that each one of you whom
God leads out of this danger safely as He did Isaac, being
content with the mere intention, will be rewarded with
glory and with all His blessings. He who will be injured
in any way, however, will have the power to wash away
even the most mortal sins for every drop of blood shed in
the name of Almighty God and His Mother and will
assuredly secure for himself an eternal crown in heaven.
Sacrifice yourselves then for Him, who today lies poor in
the manger and who willingly offers his own blood for
your salvation to God His Father. Offer then your *actiones*[78] of today instead of an early mass, which we usually
celebrate at this time to welcome the new guest—the God
sent in human shape to the world. I, however, have faith
in Jesus, whose Most Holy Name I utter, and in the intervention of His Most Holy Mother to whom I call : *'Vin-
dica honorem Filii Tui.'*[79] Through Your intercession, oh
Holy Mother, bring about that He may bless this undertaking, that He may lead our excellent knightly company
successfully out of this tribulation and preserve it for
further glory of Almighty God. Such are the commanders,

[77]Gen. 11–25.
[78]Deeds.
[79]Defend the honor of Your Son.

the protectors, the custodians whom I give to you for this undertaking and I have faith that I shall greet all of you on your return in good health.

He then recited with us the act of penitence and all the additional prayers which are customary for those whom death awaits. I approached him more closely and said : "I ask your Reverence for a special blessing." Leaning down from his horse he placed his hands on my head and blessed me, then he took off his relic and put it on me and said : "Go boldly, have no fear !" Father Dąbrowski,[80] another Jesuit, also rode up to other regiments, but he cried more than he preached. He had such a *vitium*[81] that even though he was not a bad preacher, he burst into tears as soon as he began to preach, so he could not finish his sermons and provoked laughter.

In the meantime the trumpeter who had been sent to the Swedes to propose to them an honorable surrender, if they wanted one, had returned. The Swedes replied : "Do with us whatever your knightly fancy bids you ; as for us, we were not afraid of you in Poland, so much the less are we afraid of you here." Immediately afterwards they also began to shoot. They esteemed us lightly since they saw that we did not even have one small cannon, but only one infantry regiment, four squadrons under Piaseczyński[82] and three hundred choice Cossacks.[83] The cavalrymen, they believed, were people not accustomed to assaults, and would disperse under the first fire ; so their prisoners had told them. Each one of our retainers held his sheaf of straw in front of him. The officers were only in coats of mail but some also had round shields.

Suddenly the Voivode came and said : "May God and His Holy Name grant you His protection. Rush forward, and when

[80]Felicjan Dąbrowski, the chaplain of Czarniecki's division until the death of the Voivode in 1665.
[81]Weakness.
[82]Kazimierz Piaseczyński, starost of Ostrołęka and Mława, married to a Czartoryska. J. Czubek, *Pam.*, p. 26, note 1.
[83]There were only 100 of them in Czarniecki's division. W. Czapliński, *Pam.*, p. 26, note 116. In Polish Semenowie (from Turkish), choice troops ; the Cossacks were under the command of Captain Kobyłecki. Czubek, *Pam.*, p. 26, note 2.

you have crossed the rampart ditch leap under the battlements as fast as you can, because under the walls the Swedes can no longer harm you so much." Since the clergymen had told us to offer our deeds of today *in memoriam*[84] of an early mass—for this took place on the very dawn of Christmas Day—I began to sing a carol with those who were under my command: "Let us praise the King"![85] Also Paweł Wolski, who later became the Starost of Lityń, but at that time was an officer of the royal armored cavalry squadron[86] and like myself a commander of his squadron's retainers, ordered his people to sing the same. God ordained it so that in our squadrons not one man perished, while those who did not sing were decimated.

As soon as we reached the rampart ditch, the sheaves of straw began to prick terribly. Some men got tired and began to throw the sheaves into the ditch; others, who saw those ahead of them do it, did the same and the ditch became levelled with sheaves, so that it was far easier to get across for those who were marching at the end than for us in the royal regiment, who marched ahead. It was hard to climb the slope in the snow carrying those sheaves; whoever managed to drag his along,

[84]In remembrance or instead.
[85]*Już pochwalmy Króla tego* ... etc., a Polish carol from the sixteenth century.
[86]Hist., cuirassiers; dressed in coat of mail, casques on their heads, iron nets, which fell on the shoulders and were fastened under the chin, they used bows during reviews but short spears and oblique sabres, pennons, rifles and pistols during battle. Pasek served in the royal armored squadron. Czubek, *Pam.*, p. 26, note 5.

however, learned that it helped, for bullets were found in some which had even penetrated to the middle.

When we scrambled up out of the ditch I ordered my men to shout : "Jesus, Mary !", even though others called : "Hu, hu, hu !" as I hoped that Jesus Christ would help me more than this Lord Hu. We rushed in with all speed under the battlements. The bullets showered like hail ; some men groaned and some fell to the ground. It so happened that by a huge pillar, or rather corner, where I was with my unit, there was a window with a very thick iron grating. I immediately ordered my men to take turns hacking at the wall under it ; when some got exhausted, others took over. On the second floor, directly above us, there was another such window with the same grating. From that window the Swedes shot at us, but only with pistols. They could not shoot at us with other weapons, because the grating prevented them from leaning out and they could, therefore, shoot only at those further away. I then ordered about fifteen rifles to be pointed at that window and to fire whenever anyone stuck out his hand. This was done and presently a pistol fell to the ground. Now they no longer dared to show their hands and only threw stones at us through the grating ; but after all it was easier to take shelter from these than from bullets. Meantime our men kept hacking at the wall all around the grating, circling around it as one did around that little stove in Pińczów,[87] and we were still unable to get at the Swedes. We were glad indeed when we saw the ends of the grating because bullets were showered on us like hail. We eagerly wished to get under a roof as soon as possible, but since we had nothing with which we could break open the grating we still had to continue hacking. As soon as the opening was big enough for one man, I told the retainers to crawl in one by one.

[87]In Pińczów, a city in the district of Kielce, on the Nida river. The bath house of Pińczów was famous in the XVII century. It was built by one of the Myszkowskis according to Italian models. According to an unknown author it was a splendid structure built in the shape of a little tower. Pasek, who had lived in the vicinity of Pińczów since 1657, must have seen and admired this stove. Czubek, *Pam.*, p. 28, note 1.

Wolski, a man who always wanted to be the first said : "I shall crawl in." He barely got in when the Swedes grabbed him by the head. He screamed. I grabbed him by the legs. Those within invited him to join them and we struggled to get him back. We almost tore the man apart. He called to us : "For Heaven's sake, let me go, you will tear me apart !" I shouted at my men : "Fire into the window !" They put several rifles into the window and fired : the Swedes let go of Wolski instantly. We then crawled in one by one.

Already about one hundred and fifty of us had crawled in through that window. *Interim*[88] several companies of musketeers[89] came toward us. They had learned of us apparently from those Swedes who escaped. They were just entering the cellar when our men fired into the crowd. Six of them fell ; others escaped into the courtyard. We got out of the cellar all right and fell into line in the courtyard. More and more of our men kept coming through that opening. When the Swedes saw us in the courtyard they began to sound the trumpet and to wave a white flag as a *signum*[90] of surrender. In a short period of time they thus altered a custom of their swinish nation, since they had previously said : "We do not ask for clemency !" I did not allow my men to disperse before a general confusion of the enemy could be seen. Wolski gave his men the same order.

There was nobody in the courtyard as all men were arrayed and each guarded his own post. Suddenly the musketeers came down the steps from the rooms where the commander himself had stayed. I said to my companions : "Look, we are having company." We ordered our retainers to stand in a semicircular line, not in a crowd, for a line is less vulnerable than a crowd. We also gave orders to attack with swords right after the first firing. Behind the troops the music resounded, the kettledrums banged, there was an uproar and shouting. The musketeers entered the courtyard and immediately took position in a fighting line. We also advanced toward them ; firing

[88]In the meantime.
[89]Infantrymen armed with muskets.
[90]Sign.

could commence at any moment. Meanwhile the Swedes began to run away from the rooms close to the gate, as lieutenant-colonel Tetwin[91] had already broken in there with his dragoons. We leaped toward those who were facing us. They fired; several men fell on both sides and a fight with swords began. Several of the Swedes reached the stairs from which they came. The remaining ones were immediately cut off from the stairs from the left side and the fighting with swords resumed. Those who ran away from Tetwin came to us as if to a slaughter-house. We killed all of them.

Now our soldiers scattered hastily, plundered in the rooms, seized and killed everyone that they came across in all corners of the castle, and dragged away the booty. Tetwin also came with his dragoons, assuming that he was the first one to enter the castle. A mass of corpses lay around and only about fifteen of our companions stood by, since the others had already dispersed. Tetwin crossed himself and said : "Who slaughtered these people when only so few of you are here?" Wolski retorted : "We did but there will also be enough for you; they are looking down from the tower."

A youth came leading a fat officer. I said : "Let me kill him." He begged : "Let me undress him first, because he wears beautiful clothes and they would get splashed with blood." He began to undress him when Adamowski, an officer of the Royal Sewer[92] and friend of Leszczyński[93] came and said : "Pan brother, his neck is too thick for your hand, let me kill him."

We kept haggling over who was to kill him while in the meantime some men rushed into the cellar, where gunpowder lay in barrels. Along with other things, our men also took the gunpowder in their caps and handkerchiefs, each in whatever

[91]Jan Tedtwin, the Chamberlain of Derby, a Catholic convert, and officer of the Polish army. Czapliński, *Pam.*, p. 29, note 132.

[92]Hist., a household officer of rank who was in charge of serving dishes at the table.

[93]Wacław Leszczyński, Polish captain of horse of a Cossack banner. Czapliński, *Pam.*, p. 30, note 134.

way he could. One dragoon, the scoundrel, came with a lighted
fuse and also took gunpowder ; somehow a spark ignited it.
Oh Almighty God, what a detonation it was when the walls
began to crumble, when the marble and alabaster figures began
to fly !

At the very corner of the castle,[94] overlooking the sea,
there was a tower. It was roofless and covered with a flat roof
of tin, like the floor in a room ; its brazen rain-water gutters
were gilded ; all around stood balustrades with gilded brass
statues in the corners, in places also figures of white marble, as
if alive. Even though I had not seen them from close up *in
integro*,[95] we nevertheless examined them carefully after the
explosion. One of them was thrown by the explosion safe and
sound to the side where our army was. It looked just like
a living woman. To marvel at her, people rode there and told
others that the commander's wife lay there, hurled by the explosion. So lay this dummy with her arms spread out, like
a beautifully shaped human body which was difficult to
distinguish from a living one ; only when one touched its stony
hardness did one know for sure.

In that tower, or rather in that hall, kings used to indulge
in their pleasures, to eat their suppers, to dance and entertain
themselves in various ways. From there the view was very
beautiful : the king could see almost all the provinces of his
kingdom and a part of Sweden as well. The commander and
his entire suite had fled to that tower. From there they asked
for clemency, although not right away. We might have granted
it to them, but the gunpowder which ignited *directe*[96] under
that tower elevated them very high. It blew up all the floors
and when the impetus seized them they flew so high upward
that they waltzed in the clouds of smoke : one could hardly
see them up there with the naked eye. Only after their speed

[94]The Kolding castle was one of the most ancient in Jutland. It was
built by King Abel and was formerly called Ørnsborg or Eagle Castle.
It was burnt down during the occupation of Bernadotte and is now
a ruin. Horace Murryat, *A Residence in Jutland, the Danish Isles, and
Copenhagen* (London : John Murray, 1960), p. 59.
[95]In their entirety.
[96]Directly.

was diminished could one see them better, when they came back and fell into the sea like frogs.[97]

The wretches wanted to flee from the Poles to Heaven, but they were not admitted there. St. Peter closed the gate immediately and said : "Ah, scoundrels ! You maintain that the grace of the Saints is useless, that their intercession with God is meaningless and unnecessary. In the churches of Kraków you wanted to house horses, to the horror of the Jesuits, so that the poor souls collected ransom for you as for pagans. Now Czarniecki has offered you peace and wanted to spare your lives, but you have contemptuously refused. Do you remember when you treacherously blew up the Poles in the castle of Sandomierz ?[98] Even there God saved those who should have been saved. The explosion threw Pan Bobola, a local nobleman, with his horse to the other bank of the Wisła,[99] and yet he was safe and sound. Also now you have directed heavy fire at the Poles and yet you did not kill many of them—why ? Because they are guarded by the angels and you by the black devils—now you see what their service is like !"

Dear God, how just Your judgments are ! The Swedes did such wrong to our Poles in Sandomierz when they treacherously planted mines in the castle, but here they set a trap for themselves. Our men did not do this to them intentionally, because this explosion killed about twelve of our own men. Nobody knew which of our people perished there ; we only surmised this, if anyone was not found either dead or alive.

Both the Danish and the Swedish kings[100] saw this *spectaculum*[101] and the entire imperial and Brandenburg armies saw it. They assumed, however, that the Poles were celebrating *in laudem Dominicae Nativitatis.*[102] Then Radziejowski and Ko-

[97]According to the Danish historian Rosznecki, the explosion was not severe. Pasek evidently exaggerates here. W. Czapliński, *Pam.*, p. 32, note 144.
[98]In the summer of 1656. W. Czapliński, *Pam.*, p. 33, note 145.
[99]Vistula.
[100]According to Czapliński, the kings could not have seen such a small explosion from Zealand. *Pam.*, p. 34, note 147.
[101]Spectacle.
[102]The glory of Christmas.

rycki[103] told the Swedish King, at whose side they still were, that this was something else, because there is no such custom among the Poles but at Easter.

After this lucky victory, which we attained in three hours, the Voivode garrisoned the fortress with Captain Wąsowicz and his men. We went to our quarters, because one had to attend a Holy Mass on such a solemn occasion. We had a priest, but there was no liturgical equipment. Only when we reached the forest did father Piekarski receive the equipment for which he had sent during the night. The army came to a halt; the altar was prepared on the trunk of a felled oak and there the Mass was celebrated. Fire was lit to warm the chalice, because it was freezing cold. We sang the *Te Deum laudamus*[104] so loudly that it resounded all over the forest. I knelt down to serve Father Piekarski at Mass. Bloodstained, I began to dress the priest when the Voivode remarked : "Pan brother, you should at least have washed your hands." The priest retorted : "This does not matter. God does not loathe blood shed in His Name." Soon after, we came upon many of our retainers, who brought us all sorts of provisions. Whoever found his servant sat down and ate, compensating for yesterday's hunger.

The Voivode rode along happily, for it was an unusual instance to take such a fortress without cannon and regular infantry. He could have had both from the Great Elector, who was stationed in the vicinity, but he had pride and did not want to bow down to anyone, wishing to draw fame to himself. Trusting in God, he plunged in and he won.

[103]Hieronim Radziejowski (1622–1666), vice-chancellor of the Crown, 1651 ; he was exiled to Sweden in 1652 as a result of his plottings in Poland. He was later suspected of plotting with the Poles and was arrested in Sweden in Jutland, 1658. In 1662 he returned to Poland, served as envoy to Turkey, died in 1666 in Adrianopol. Czubek, *Pam.*, pp. 33–34, note 4.
Krzysztof Korycki. He remained in Swedish service for a long time. In 1659 he came over to the Polish side ; he died in 1676 as chamberlain of Chełm. Czubek, *Pam.*, p. 34, note 1.
[104]"You God We Praise," a Latin hymn sung during solemn services, especially as thanks for a war victory. Czapliński, *Pam.*, p. 35, note 153.

ANNO DOMINI 1659

By the grace of God we began the year happily in Haderslev; we also celebrated the carnival season there, but not with the same gaiety as in Poland. The island Als,[1] which lay behind, still constituted a big hindrance to us : our retainers were captured on patrols and our booty was taken away, since its *praesidium*[2] was large. The Brandenburg troops passed near it with cannon and with infantry, but they neither wanted to attack nor dared to, for as the saying goes : "Crows will not pick out crow's eyes."

Once, the Voivode went on patrol with three hundred horsemen, *quidem*[3] for a ride. He did not say anything but gave orders for a full alert on the following day and for the entire company to ride out.[4] We did not forget to make a careful preparation : we told the retainers to fill the bags *ad victum*[5] and we set out.

We cut the ice with axes in one spot, because it had not yet melted along the sea-shore, even though it was not very cold and very nice weather had prevailed ; on the other side the dragoons

[1]Germ. Alsen, Danish Als. Pasek consistently calls it Alsen, which is its German equivalent. It is an island off the eastern coast of South Jutland, Denmark, separated from the mainland by the Sound of Alsen. The island is about 33 km long and 5–15 km wide. It was conquered in December 1658, before Kolding. Czapliński, *Pam.*, p. 37, note 1.

[2]Garrison.

[3]Supposedly.

[4]This is not quite accurate. Czarniecki was informed about the expedition and was asked to participate. W. Czapliński, *Pam.*, p. 37, note 6.

[5]With provisions.

did the same. We managed everything so suddenly that the *prae-sidiarii*[6] did not know about us until we were already on the other shore, for they were stationed quietly in the towns and villages. We had to swim approximately the same distance[7] as that from Praga[8] to Warsaw across the Vistula, but in the middle of this inlet there was a spot over 100 meters wide where the horses could reach the bottom and rest. The Voivode made the sign of

[6]Here, the Swedish occupying forces.
[7]The width of the straits was about 500 meters there.
[8]Suburb of Warsaw, Poland, situated on the right bank of the Vistula.

the cross and rode ahead into the sea; the regiments followed him—there were only three of them, not the entire army. Each soldier put his pistol in his waistcoat and tied his ammunition pouch around his neck. As soon as the Voivode swam to the middle he stopped and ordered each banner to rest for awhile, and then to move on. The horses had already been tested for their swimming ability; if one swam poorly, it was put between two good ones which did not let it drown.

The day was fortunately quiet, warm, and without frost. It had thawed a little, but later there was again severe winter. Not one banner had reached land yet, when the Swedes appeared.[9] They began to shoot. The first banner out of the water dashed at the enemy instantly. When the Swedes saw that even though we had just come out of the water our firearms were not wet but could shoot and kill, they began to run away. The others who came to their rescue were cut off by our cavalry and then we attacked the enemy with great force. Our prisoners later said: "We thought that you were devils, not people."

The Danish King sent for the Swedish commander, begging to turn him over alive, since he had some great grudge against him. I don't know how he was received there.[10] After that encounter, when the soldiers reached a warm peasant hut, each grabbed whomever he could—either a man or a woman— and stripped off his or her shirt in order to change into it himself. After the Voivode had thoroughly searched this island, which was not large, only seven leagues in all, with several towns and several dozen villages, he set up a brave captain, a Danish nobleman, as commander with newly enlisted men under him. For there was a regulation that as soon as our army

[9]Pasek here seems to contradict his previous statement that the Swedes were unaware of the Polish forces until they reached land. According to Kersten all of Czarniecki's cavalry was transported by boats, pulling the horses behind them. Kersten, *Stefan Czarniecki*, p. 39. According to some, the cavalry was transported by boats. Before the cavalry all of the infantry was transported to the other shore. Czapliński, *Pam.*, p. 38, note 11.

[10]The Danes asked for someone else. W. Czapliński, *Pam.*, p. 39, note 12.

marched in, officers of the Danish King were to enlist soldiers and man the conquered fortresses with them. The Voivode took 100 good Swedish soldiers for himself and he put them among his dragoons, in order to replace those who were lost here and there, for usually : "where wood is chopped chips fall."

Later the army returned to its quarters, but this time the inlet was crossed by ship. Just as the previous year had ended well with our famous capture of Kolding, so the new one began successfully with the *gloriosus*[11] capture of the island Als. Then we rested quietly for several weeks. Later we went to Friederichs-Odde.[12] It is a very powerful fortress ; there is no city there, only the entrenchments ; the fortification is excellent, both facing the land and the sea. This entrenchment stretches in the shape of a wedge into the sea in such a way that a ship can come right up to the rampart by sea from which the fortress can prohibit the passage of ships and paralyze almost the entire Danish fleet.

Even though we saw that it was beyond our power, we still tried our luck, for one is free to dare even the impossible, and so we attacked often. The Swedes came out to put up a fight in front of the fortress, and went back into their hole when it became too hot for them. They attacked us vigorously with their heavy cannon. Every day horses and people were shot down, because a ball from a long cannon carrried almost anywhere. God was merciful to us, however, for later in spring this fortress miraculously fell into Polish hands, without much bloodshed. We had thus spent the winter fighting constantly and attacking the Swedes on raids.

Later we went to a Danish province called Jutland. After we crossed it, the royal regiment went to Aarhus[13] and set up quarters in this beautiful city. Our banner was allotted a street where no horses could be accomodated. There was also no building material for stables nor even room for building them, since the city lies on a narrow strip of land on water like Venice. We, therefore, asked the Voivode to be allowed to be stationed

[11]Glorious.
[12]Now the city of Fridericia. A city on the eastern shore of Jutland.
[13]A city on the eastern shore of Jutland.

in a village. We set up billets in Hoerning[14] thus while other regiments and banners were stationed in different towns and villages. A regulation was passed to take ten silver thalers per horse for every *plug* (what we call *lan* they call *plug*).[15] During the first month we took ten thalers according to the regulation, in the second twenty, in the third as much as one could get, that is, as much as it was possible to bargain for, according to the peasant's wealth. The town of Ebeltoft[16] and its surroundings and villages was assigned to our banner as provisions supply area. This region lies on the spot of land between the Baltic Sea and the Ocean ; from there one cannot go further by land.[17] Here the province is called Jutland, around Hadersleben, however, Suder-Jutland.[18]

The banner would gladly have stayed in Ebeltoft. It was not permitted to do so, however, *ex ratione*[19] it could be trapped, since this town lay too far from the army. It was only ten leagues from Copenhagen by sea, a distance which was as easy to cover for the enemy as a league by land.

I was sent there as a delegate, mainly because of my knowledge of Latin, since almost every peasant there speaks Latin,[20]

[14]Hurnum-Hoerning, a village not far from Aarhus.

[15]*Lan* was a Polish unit of cultivated land equal to from seven and a half to thirty acres, the English equivalent of which was a hide. Pasek, who was at first in the regions of Denmark which are nowadays designated as Sönderjylland, but which formerly constituted the Duchy of Schleswig, confused here the *ploug*, the Schleswig measure of land, with the *tönder*, the unit of measure of cultivated land in northern and central Denmark. Czapliński, *O Pol. Sied.*, pp. 207–208.

[16]A city in northern Jutland northeast of Aarhus. It is the capital of the beautiful Mols countryside.

[17]Ebeltoft, i.e., this provision area did not actually lie between the Baltic Sea and the Ocean, but between the Baltic Sea and the Kattegat.

[18]Actually Soenderjylland.

[19]Because.

[20]Pasek exaggerates here no doubt. It is true however that all the educated people wrote, spoke, and thought in Latin as it was the language of the church, universities, the schools and civil functionaries, and military commanders communicated with each other in Latin still during the reign of Christian IV. Danish was simply neglected by the learned man. Samuel Laing, *The Social and Political State* (Brown, Green, and Longmans, 1852), p. 351.

few speak German, and none Polish, and the difference between the language of the Jutlanders and the Germans is like that between Latvian or *Samogitian* and Polish.[21]

I felt a little uneasy about going there amidst the two big seas—for on this strip of land one sees the sea on both sides : *ad meridiem*[22] the Baltic Sea, *ad septemtrionem*[23] it is as if one saw clouds ; although both are of water, it is apparent that the nature of the two seas is different. I also could notice that sometimes simultaneously one appears azure, the other black ; one of the same color as the sky, the other always different from it. When one moves and tremendous waves roll, the other remains quiet, and even when both are calm and one looks at them where they meet, especially in the evening, one can *visibiliter*[24] distinguish some kind of a border. It was a little unpleasant for me to go there, as I had already said, but since I always had the urge to see the world, I did not try to make excuses.

I was given over a dozen retainers, and I left. When I arrived in Aarhus, the Piekarski brothers said to me : "Have a good trip ! Greet King Gustav from us, since you will sooner find yourself in Copenhagen than back with us." I did not care and rode on. The Voivode also said to me : "Pan brother, I should also get a share there for my kitchen. I am sending my Lanckoroński[25] too. Be careful, so that you will not have to pay Copenhagen[26] a visit." The Voivode had picked this place because he was told that there the people were the wealthiest. I went in spite of everything, and Lanckoroński, the Voivode's chamberlain, followed me a week and a half later.

When I arrived there I pretended not to know any Latin and showed the commissioner's order. They asked me : *"Kann*

---

[21]The difference between Latvian and Polish is greater than that between Danish and German. Samogitian is Low Lithuanian, closely related to Latvian.

[22]To the south.

[23]To the north.

[24]Clearly.

[25]The Voivode's chamberlain.

[26]Copenhagen was then besieged by the Swedes.

der Deutsch ?"[27] I answered : *"Nix."*[28] They brought someone who could speak Italian. He asked me : *"Italiano pierla, franciezo ?"*[29] I said : *"Nix."* So these rascals almost went mad from frustration that they could not communicate with me. Whatever they said to me I only answered : *"Geld."*[30] They asked me : "What would you like to eat ?" *"Geld."* They asked me : "What would you drink ?" *"Geld."* They begged me not to insist on money right away. I kept saying : *"Geld."* Most of all they tried to speak Latin to me, because it is a familiar language to the Poles. They brought a nobleman to me who lived not far from them and whose possessions and castle could be seen from Friederichs-Odde. He had served in the army and was well travelled. The Danes believed that he would communicate with me somehow. He addressed me thus : *"Ego saluto Dominationem Vestram"*[31] I answered : *"Geld."* He said : *"Pierla franciezo ?"* "Geld." He said : *"Pierla italiano ?"* *"Geld."* He said to them : "He does not understand any language," and left after a while. The Danes deliberated seriously and this lasted a whole day. They were on the point of sending someone to the Brandenburg army to get an interpreter. One of them was already getting ready to go. Meantime, early next day, they brought me as a present a huge live salmon in a tub, a fattened ox, and a tame live stag on a rope, and also a hundred silver thalers in a mug. Since they already knew that they could not make me understand them in any language, they said in their *lingua nativa* :[32] "We brought you a present." I pointed to that mug with thalers and finally addressed them thus : *"Iste est interpres meorum et vestrorum desideriorum."*[33] Oh, how these Germans[34] jumped for joy, how they began to shriek

[27]Do you know German ?
[28]No.
[29]Do you know Italian, French.
[30]Money.
[31]I greet your Honor.
[32]Native tongue.
[33]This is the interpreter of my wishes and yours.
[34]Pasek calls them Germans (Pol. *Niemcy*) because they don't understand him. The etymological origin of the word *Niemiec* (German) comes from the word *niemy* meaning mute. Here Danes.

with laughter and to embrace me, how they rushed to the city saying: "Our guest has spoken." They sent after the one who had already left for the interpreter. Then the conversation and the discussion began—the Danes got drunk out of joy.

We began to bargain next day. I showed them the commissioner's register, how many *plugs* he assigned to every village, and then there was no arguing. They could not disagree when they saw that it was not my invention but the commissioner's specific order. In two days they collected the money for the first month. Now whenever there was any talk about thalers they did not call them thalers but *interpretes*.[35] I ordered them to deliver this money to the banner at once and sent three of my own men along with them. I also wanted to go but they begged me very much not to do so, since they were afraid that the Brandenburg patrols which were only six leagues away could pester them. Indeed these did come later but caused no damage, because even if one of them snatched some cattle, he released it at once and fled when he saw the garrison troops.

When the Danes delivered the money to the banner they told about this "interpreter" incident, which was also reported to the Voivode. When I was back in Aarhus the Voivode said to Polanowski,[36] a colonel of the starost of Bratyan ! "My dear Colonel ! I have an officer in my army who speaks various languages, but *conditionaliter* :[37] one must first place a big silver mug full of silver thalers before him and then he is ready to converse in any desired language." Polanowski did not understand this anecdote so the Voivode explained it to him, and from that time on in the army thalers were called *interpretes*. Even the Voivode himself did so when he wrote Lanckoroński, his chamberlain, in somewhat the following manner : "The treasurer had counted the money delivered by you only after your departure, and over a dozen bad thalers were found in it. Be sure that you yourself will receive them as pay, for it is a disgrace when a nobleman is not competent with money. You have Pan Pasek near you and you can learn from him what a *bonus interpres*[38] stands for.

In the following month the colonel wrote to me that "all banners collect twenty thalers per *plug* and you should do the same." The poor souls grumbled that this was *contra constitu-*

---

[35] Interpreters.
[36] Aleksander Polanowski, a colonel of the armored banner of the Starost Adam Działyński, the castellan of Lublin, the starost of Bratyan. J. Czubek, *Pam.*, p. 43, note 2. He accompanied Jan Sobieski in his military campaign ; he also took part in the battles of Podhajce (1667), and Chocim.
[37] Conditionally.
[38] Good interpreter.

tum ;[39] they paid up and delivered the money to the banner, however.

For the third month it was decided to collect even more, but seeing the devastation of these people by war I no longer wanted to have anything to do with this even though it could be noticed that they had been affluent before. I did not want to anger them, for they were good people who had been ruined by the enemy. I wrote to the banner : "Either be content with what you had the previous month, that is with twenty thalers per *plug* or remove me from here for I shall not undertake to be a murderer of people who are our *foederati*,[40] not our enemies." *Conclusum*[41] to divide the *plugs* among the banners and each was to get from his peasants as much as he could. So it was done. The retainers were sent there and squeezed out what they could. I was told to stay on to watch over the retainers to prevent excesses ; the sooner one scared his peasant out of the money the faster both would leave to settle the dues. As for myself, I took the responsibility for collecting taxes from those Danes whom I knew or who paid for this favor.

My mind was freer then and I had a marvellous life *in victualibus*.[42] Everything I desired was there : good drinks, especially mead, which the people there do not drink themselves but brew and send to other provinces by ship ; a multitude of all kinds of fish : for two Leipzig shillings, which equalled four Polish pennies, one could send a peasant out fishing, and he would bring back a sack of fish of such size that he would bend under it. They bake bread from peas, of which there is a great abundance there ; however, I was also provided with wheat and rye bread, especially by the gentry. During Lent even the preachers ate meat there and rebuked those who failed to do so. I would have had pangs of conscience to eat meat when such an abundance of fish was available. I did not even want to eat the eels which were cured together with flitches of bacon in a trough. Plenty of various kinds of fish was available

[39]Against the arrangement.
[40]Allies.
[41]It was decided.
[42]So far as food was concerned.

there, of the talking and the groaning kind[48] except for carp, which was scarce.

I had much fun and recreation there, for I saw things which it would be difficult to see in Poland. It was also a joy to be present during deep sea fishing for there were unusual *genera*[44] and *species*[45] of fish. When a huge quantity of them was pulled to the shore, those which appeared to me to be the nicest and the best turned out to be bad and not edible and were thrown on the sand for dogs and birds ; the others, though good for eating, were so ugly that it was even unpleasant to look at them. They have a horrible fish there, resembling the demon painted on church walls, with flames coming out of its mouth,[46] and I said : "No matter how hungry I might be, I would not eat this fish." When I was a guest once in the house of a nobleman, among other dishes (for they serve meat and fish there at the same time) I began to eat a fish which was very tasty. I ate it with such an appetite that I almost finished the entire plate of it. The nobleman said : *"Hic est piscis, quem sua Dominatio diabolum nominavit."*[47] I became very confused but noticing that the others ate this fish with pleasure I did not believe it to be the same one, because it seemed improbable to me that in such an ugly body such good taste could be found ; nevertheless, I never ate it again. The host remarked that it cost a ducat per pound when smoked. I can no longer remember its name, since it was as strange as the fish itself : it had a head and eyes as horrible as those of a dragon and jaws wide and flat like those of a monkey ; on the head two bent horns like those of a wild goat, and so sharp

[48]Some fish in Denmark make certain sounds but there are no talking ones. W. Czapliński, *Pam.*, p. 47, note 65.

[44]Kinds.

[45]Varieties.

[46]Czapliński writes that it is quite probable that such a picture could be found on the walls of some church since in the Denmark of the Middle Ages frescoes wall-paintings, appeared on the white walls of Gothic village churches, the famous *Kalkmaleri* which are an iconographic source filled with various phantastic representations of evil spirits and monsters. Czapliński, *O Pol. Sied.*, p. 208.

[47]This is the fish which your Lordship called a devil.

that they prick like a needle, on the neck a hook, not much smaller than the horns, bent upwards toward the head, and then others across the entire back, one after another, gradually becoming smaller up to the very tail ; the trunk was round like a stump ; the skin was like that of a shagreen, the kind which is used for scabbards, and on that skin, small hooks again such as on the back, but smaller, like claws of a hawk, and very sharp ; the mere touching of these can draw blood.[48] There are also other very marvellous ones which have wings like birds, beaks and heads like storks ; when their heads stick out of a hole in a sack, many would swear that a stork was inside.[49] Much more could be told about all this.

We enjoyed ourselves in various ways on the sea whenever we boarded a barge. When the sea was calm, all we had to do was keep still and not to row ; one would see many creatures of all varieties then, all sorts of reptiles, sea animals, and peculiar fish. They were especially visible when one stopped where the seaweeds grow, out of which salt is made, because in those spots the sea is so transparent that one can see the smallest fish and everything else that swims against the seaweed a hundered fathoms deep. Since this grass is as white as snow, every little thing is clearly reflected against it *in profundo*.[50] This grass is weeded out with iron hooks which are dropped to the bottom of the sea on a long cord. It is pulled out, brought to the shore, scattered over shrubs, dried, and burned immediately after. Very good salt is obtained from it then. But salt is made not only out of sea-weeds ; there is also a kind of earth from which salt can be derived. Whenever it was necessary to salt a dish, they would put a handful of this earth into a bowl, rinse it, then pour the water into a pot and in half an hour very good salt would settle.

One could observe all sorts of unusual things at the

---

[48]Pasek describes here rather accurately a ray. In the 17th century in the Scandinavian countries it was considered a delicacy. Today it seems as horrible and abominable to the Scandinavians as to Pasek at the time. Czapliński, *Pam.*, p. 48, note 68.
[49]A fish common in the western part of the Baltic Sea.
[50]In the depths.

bottom of the sea. In some spots there was only pure sand, in other spots weeds grew and something resembling small trees ; elsewhere rocks towered like poles or buildings and on these rocks sat some strange creatures. Whenever we wanted to take a good look at these beasts—there was an empty castle on the shore, four leagues from Ebeltoft on a big rock, which was called Ryf van Anholt[51]—we would go to this castle before noon, leave our barge on the shore, conceal ourselves *inter rudera*[52] and not make a sound ; then those frightful porpoises, huge sea lions, and various other animals would crawl to the cliffs. They would stretch in the sun and spread out their awful fat stomachs. After we had seen enough of these marvels, we only had to throw a small stone in that direction and all of them would instantly disappear in the sea. The natives said that even if one were to shoot at them with a rifle, one would only waste ammunition, because they would jump into the sea with the bullet ; and even if one of them were to fall there, someone else would get it, because the sea would wash it who knows where.

I enjoyed the excursions on the sea, but once I became very frightened and it was for the following reason : I wanted to sail to an Easter Mass in Aarhus, where the Voivode was stationed, and since it was closer by sea than by land, I did not want to wear out the horses. We left on Saturday. The sea was rough, but after it had calmed down at midnight, we set out, trusting the skippers that they would not lose their way. The night was pitch-dark ; we headed toward Zealand.[53] From the very start I did not like the fact that it took so long to cover a distance of only six leagues. I asked whether we were heading in the right direction. They said : "It's nothing new for us to

[51]A coral reef in the vicinity of the island Anholt which lies in the middle of the Kattegat. Pasek confused here the reef near the island Anholt with the island Hjelm lying in the vicinity of Ebeltoft according to Czapliński. *Pam.*, p. 50, note 78. Recent findings indicate that Pasek was right.

[52]Among the ruins.

[53]Largest of the Danish islands, situated east of Jutland. Copenhagen is located on it. It is true that going to Aarhus one had to first go in the direction of Zealand. Czapliński, *Pam.*, p. 51, note 81.

sail at night. We surely will not lose our way." Only after we had sailed for some time, did they finally become disturbed, for they recognized their mistake. They consulted with each other in order to correct the course. They made it even worse. We sailed, it seemed, for an eternity and saw nothing except sky and sea. As I had very good eyesight, I perceived some buildings before they did. "*Ecce in sinistris apparet forte civitas.*"[54] They could not see it and said : "*Deus avertat, ne nobis a sinistris appareat civitas* ; *a dextris debet esse nostra civitas.*"[55] When we came closer we saw the ships in the port of Nikoping,[56] and now we were really frightened. We grew quiet until a clock began to strike. Then we moved quietly to the side. A sentry had already noticed us and shouted : "*Wer do ?*"[57] We did not answer. He called a second time : "*Wer do ?*" I then said to our steersman : *Dicas, quia sumus piscatores.*[58] He did so. The sentry asked again : "From where ?" He answered : "From this shore." Then the sentry began to scold and to wish us ill luck : "You rascals ! It is a holiday. It is Easter Sunday !" Oh how we began to row with all our strength ! We steered toward the shore and not toward the open sea so that they would not suspect anything. It had begun to dawn a little. Suddenly we heard gunfire in back of us ; then I realized that it was already time for matins and I said : "*Ecce ibi videtis, quia ibi est Aarhusen, ubi iaculantur.*"[59] "*O, per Deum* ! *non Aarhusen, sed Koppenhagen est, circa obsidionem iaculantur.*"[60] I told them that it is a custom with us to shoot during matins on *Resurrectionis Domini.*[61] Then they realized that Aarhus was really there and they recognized its shores and

[54]There is a city here on the left side.
[55]God help us if we were to see a city on our left. Our city should be on the right.
[56]A city on the western side of Zealand. It was at that time in Swedish hands. It is about 100 km from Aarhus.
[57]Who is there ?
[58]Tell him that we are fishermen.
[59]Look, over there, where the shooting is coming from is Aarhus !
[60]Oh, for God's sake, it is not in Aarhus where they shoot during a siege but in Copenhagen.
[61]Resurrection of Christ, i.e., Easter.

port; they already made out where we were. We then commended ourselves to God and began to row straight in the direction from where the shooting was coming so vigorously, so that our ribs cracked. We had not yet sailed a league away from the ships in port when it dawned and they noticed us (for one can see for a league at sea as well as for a few furlongs on land). They set out after us in six barges—and we also began to row more briskly! They pursued us for about two leagues. But after they noticed that we, who wanted to escape, were rowing as eagerly as they, who wanted to catch up with us— they also probably had noticed something about the sea—they halted and then turned back. We continued to row until the older skipper remarked: *"Evasimus de manibus unius hostis, alter imminet ferocior, nempe tempestas. Orandum et laborandum est."* [62] Oh, how we again began to bend and to pull! We could already see Aarhus well, when the sea began to heave in places. Terrible fear and sincere piety penetrated us as well as the Lutherans. The Almighty granted that the storm did not break right away, however, and the sea did not become restless for a good hour. The closer we came to the city, the higher the waves began to rise. We were glad that the wind was not away

[62]We have escaped from the hands of one enemy but now another more dangerous one is threatening us, namely a storm. We have to pray and keep working.

from it but a little to the side, which helped us to row toward the shore, and the steersman also utilized it very skilfully. They saw us from the city and watched to see what was coming from the side of the enemy. Now the storm really broke loose and we began to be tossed around. Some of us rowed while others kept bailing. The Germans did so with their hats and the others with whatever they had, for we only had one container for this purpose. When a wave came up, it covered us and the barge. When it passed and we regained control of ourselves, another one like it would catch up with us and again it felt as if a new foe and the ultimate peril had reached us : hardly had one passed when another followed immediately. The barge would crack when the waves broke over it. The Lutherans called out : *"Oh, Herr Jesu Christ !"*[63] They only besought the Son, while the Catholics besought both the Son and the Holy Mother— indeed the proverb was verified : *"Qui nescit orare, discedat in mare."*[64] This came to my mind and I had to exclaim : "God ! don't let us perish. For you see that we set out here with the intention of serving You and extolling Your Glory."

From the city people came running. They had ropes which were customarily thrown to the sinking ones. They called to us and waved their hands, but we heard nothing. Neither could those on the shore hear us, for whenever the sea heaved, there was a noise like cannon fire. Meanwhile we had already approached the quay. Whenever a wave brought us up to the quay, the impetus of the water would throw us back into the sea. Whenever another wave pushed us toward land, it also tossed us back again. Finally we managed to seize the rope and when we were thrown up to the quay by a wave, we hit it so hard that the steersman fell onto it ; the rest of us fell sideways in the barge. The barge was now almost full of water, even though we kept bailing. We crawled out onto the quay like mice. We had hoped to be in time for matins. We could not even hear the High Mass, however, as we arrived just before vespers.

[63]Oh, Jesus Christ.
[64]Whoever does not know how to pray should sail on the sea.

I went to an inn and the innkeeper gave me a dry shirt. The room was heated—fire was lit in the middle of the room in a trough-like trench filled with coal, since such was the custom—my garments and those of my retainers were hung up to dry. Food was offered but I refused it. I did order a large pot of mead to be brought, however, since their wines are bad. I poured cloves and ginger into this mead and I drank it so. After I recuperated a little, I began to feel hungry. I sent someone to Father Piekarski and asked him to send me a blessed Easter egg. I also instructed the messenger to tell him what hardships I had experienced. He sent me a little lamb, an Easter cake and eggs. I enjoyed some blessed food then and it was already evening. Several good friends came to see me after they found out what had happened to me. I sat by the fire in just a shirt and kept warming myself with mead. They began to ask : "What did you do ? How did it happen ?" I told them about the fright which I had experienced. They congratulated me on my lucky escape and dispersed. I lay down to sleep then, for after such a bath I needed rest. When I got up next day my garments were dry. I went to the commander and told him at his request of the hardships of the previous day and my twofold fear : of the Swedes and of the water. The Voivode said : "You surely experienced some hardships but you, Pan brother, are superior to the rest of the army since the army fights only on land while you fight also on sea. You wanted to demolish the *regnum Sueticum*[65] all by yourself and to take the palm of victory before we would do so." I replied to this : "Since Jesus Christ destroyed the *regnum*[66] of the spiritual enemies on this day, we should try to destroy the kingdoms of the material ones. But since your Honor claims that I fight in a dual manner, I ask for a dual pay : as a sailor and as a soldier."

We joked in this manner for a while and then we went to hear Mass. I attended church services also on Monday and Tuesday. Some companions said to me : "Now you will surely

[65]The Swedish kingdom.
[66]Kingdom.

prefer to go ten leagues by land rather than by water." But I answered them : "I don't believe that I will again have to fear the misfortune from which I was spared yesterday, for whoever saved me then will also preserve me tomorrow." I did this. Indeed after attending Mass on Wednesday, I boarded a boat and set out. This time I kept close to land. For it is not danger- ous to sail on the sea, even in a small vessel, as long as one keeps close to the shore. By doing so one can escape as soon as some change in weather is perceived. It was not the weather but the sailing error in the night which caused our misfortune, however.

After Low Sunday[67] the Voivode became ill *periculose.*[68] We were very frightened. Various doctors were summoned, and the Great Elector sent his. The Dutch Admiral[69] sent by ship his doctor, a very famous one, but I don't remember from which city. They tried to save the Voivode by all possible means. *Ex consilio generali*[70] the doctors decided that music should play for him *continue,*[71] so musicians kept playing softly in the next room on lutes, zithers, theorbos and other instru- ments. He came back to health then to the great joy of our army, and we gave thanks to God. The army remained in its billets until he became very well ; I was also present and I was never idle but always tried to see whatever I could not see in Poland. We always had to be on guard, however, since as soon as it became warmer, the Swedes came more often than before to the mainland from Zealand and from Fionia.[72]

Once seven Dutch ships arrived in Ebeltoft and anchored in the harbor.[73] They were to hinder the Swedes from passing through that body of water and were also to transport our army to Fionia. They stayed there for a week or more. They were our

[67]First Sunday after Easter. It fell on April 20 at the time. Czapliński, *Pam.,* p. 55, note 105.
[68]Dangerously.
[69]Jakub van Wassenaer Obdan. W. Czapliński, *Pam.,* p. 55, note 106.
[70]At a general consultation.
[71]Continuously.
[72]An island between Jutland and Zealand.
[73]Pasek is mistaken here, there were five ships altogether, two Danish and three Dutch. Czapliński, *Pam.,* p. 56, note 112.

allies and also their *princeps* Wilhelm *Auriacus*[74] was the brother-in-law of the Prussian Prince, for his sister[75] was married to Wilhelmus. His wife accompanied him in this war. They were friendly with us and when this Admiral[76] came from the ships to Ebeltoft to attend Mass, he also made our acquaintance and was not at all conceited, even though he was actually of a rank equivalent to that of our hetman. He used to come to our billets after church and he also used to invite us.

Once he invited Lanckoroński and me to his ship on a Sunday.[77] Even though the port was still and quiet it was inaccessible. Big war ships could not approach the quay ; only small merchant vessels and boats could do so. One therefore had to take a boat to the ship and we got in a barge and sailed there. We had just been served some food when a sailor, who kept watch on the crow's nest, called out that two ships were approaching from Zealand. A mate told the Admiral about this in German. The latter immediately translated it for us into Latin and added : "*Isti duo nobis prandium non impedient.*"[78] He ordered the flags to be identified and to find out whether they were Swedish or some other ones, for it was difficult to distinguish them from a distance. The mate announced again that two more ships were coming, and soon after, that still more were coming, but that they were still far away. They looked through their telescopes. "What do you see ?" They said : "We still cannot identify them." The Admiral ordered his telescope to be brought. It was apparent that either his eyesight was better or he had a better telescope, as is usually the case. He recognized instantly from the flags of the first two ships that they were Swedish. Later more and more ships appeared. When fifteen[79] of them could be seen, he ordered his

[74]Prince of Orange. Wilhelm (William) III. Czapliński, *Pam.*, p. 56, note 114.
[75]Louise Henrietta, wife of the Elector of Brandenburg, was sister of Wilhelm II, father of Wilhelm III. Czapliński, *Pam.*, p. 56, note 115.
[76]Peter Bredal.
[77]The battle at Ebeltoft took place on Sunday, August 2. Czapliński, *Pam.*, p. 58, note 119.
[78]These two ships will not interrupt our dinner.
[79]Actually only seven. Czapliński, *Pam.*, p. 58, note 124.

ships to stand at a greater distance from each other. He wanted to take up the entire port, and stay close to shore, so that he could not be surrounded. He would have attacked the Swedes boldly, even though there were more of them, but had no men on board. He had only a few guns, cannon and the crew of the ships, for he was, as I have already mentioned, to transport our army to Fionia. For that reason the ships were sent without soldiers, since it was known that we had infantry. After the Swedes had found out that these ships had little garrison, they came to seize them. We learned that the Swedes had been informed by someone from the Brandenburg army. It is not difficult to find a traitor anywhere.

When the first two ships were already not far away, the Admiral said to us : *"Forsam abeundum est in civitatem ?"*[80] I replied : *"Manebimus adhuc."*[81] But Lanckoroński said : "I shall go for I have fifteen thousand thalers with me which I had collected and during a commotion someone might grab it." He got into a barge and was taken to the pier. I stayed behind.

When the Swedish ships approached from the left side, two of our ships sailed forward toward them. They rushed in at full sail. Both sides fired at each other so vigorously that cannon balls flew as thickly as bullets. Then they quickly withdrew to a distance of at least ten furlongs away from each other and began to tack about and load the cannon in the meantime. Also both of our ships retreated back to the port and then kept tacking and waited for the approach of the enemy. Two more Swedish ships came then and lined up with the others after they had set their sails. Later a third pair of ships made the same maneuver. When still others came, the city bells and drums resounded loudly. People rushed to the quays. Whoever had any knowledge of navigation boarded barges and rowed to the ships. The Swedes were arming themselves in the meantime. When they got ready, they began to approach us close-ranked. They came closer than a furlong to us. The ships began to fire briskly at each other, and the sky became dark

[80]Perhaps you would like to return to the city ?
[81]We shall remain here.

with smoke. One Swedish ship sped too far. It fell among the Dutch ones like the moon among the stars. Suffice it to say that when we fired at it from the sides and from the Admiral's ship its planks went flying. It immediately moved aside, limping like a dog whose leg was hurt. They sailed forward for the second time and fired their cannon. They moved away a little and then drew close again. The Swedes were desperately eager to get behind the Dutch. They could not do so, however, since the Dutch remained close to the port. They kept shooting at each other until evening. Later they dispersed and grew quiet.

I boarded a barge and sailed to the quay. During that night the Swedes stole a merchant vessel from the pier. As soon as it dawned they let it sail with the wind, set the sails and set it on fire. Then they pushed it among the Dutch ships, one of which immediately caught fire, for these ships are as inflammable as sulphur. The Swedes then advanced right behind those ships and began a terrible cannonade. A tragic *spectaculum*[82] resulted then when one did not know whether to fight the fire or the enemy ! People had to avoid the burning ship and at the same time to take care that the enemy would not blow them to pieces. In trying to escape from that burning ship, they grabbed planks, beams, or whatever they could, and jumped with it into the sea.

From the city some bold ones came with barges. They rescued those who were sinking by throwing ropes for them to grab. Meanwhile cannon thundered from both sides. Considering that every ship was armed with anywhere from eighty to a hundred cannon,[83] one could imagine how dense the firing must have been ! Surely, land warfare is dreadful but far more dreadful is war on the sea, when masts fly, when sails fall into the sea, when man is an enemy to man and when in addition to all this there is the water.

The shots which missed the ships hit on the mainland those people who came from the city. If the Dutch had been conquered, the Swedes would have surely plundered the city. At that time people still kept everything at home because they felt secure, since they had an army to defend them. Only when they saw how the ships caught fire did they begin to hide their *pignora*[84] in the water.[85] The most certain hiding place for

[82]Spectacle.
[83]The ships in those days usually had a smaller number of cannon. Czapliński, *Pam.*, p. 61, note 140.
[84]Valuables.
[85]The custom of concealing valuables in the sea was quite common in Denmark at the time. Czapliński, *Pam.*, p. 61, note 142.

these people is the sea, and not only for *comestibilia*[86] but also for *vestimenta*,[87] silver, and money. *Sufficit* for them to submerge these valuables in whatever they want to and to haul them up whenever they want to. They have such methods and adapted containers so that nothing will spoil or get wet in them. They submerge these containers in places where the sea does not wash out, as in bays, inlets, etc. Also on a Swedish ship the sails caught fire : the masts were cut instantly, however, and were thrown into the sea. Another Swedish ship was pierced through by a cannon so that it immediately went to the bottom with everything in it ; only a few men from its crew were saved. A third one lost two masts, a fourth its mainmast ; these Swedish ships thus had suffered *mutilationem*.[88] The ship which in yesterday's battle was damaged could not be of any help and stood at a distance. Sufficit that the Dutch would have taken the ships if they had had more troops. When the Swedes saw their mutilation and that their damage was greater than that which they inflicted on the enemy, they immediately turned back. The wind, which was blowing from the side, was not so calm as before. It no longer favored those who were turning back. The poor Dutchmen patched the holes in their ships, carried their dead on land, buried them and later they recovered the Swedish cannon as well as their own. They told us about all this when they came to see us in Friederichs-Odde.[89]

The Dutch have great *scientiam*[90] in the art of concealing things in the sea. They also have divers who dive into the sea, walk around on its very bottom and apply *instrumenta* there by which they can hoist everything *ex profundo*.[91] The members

[86]Food supplies.
[87]Articles of clothing.
[88]Damage.
[89]This battle, fought on July 23, 1659, ended with a severe defeat of the Danes and the Dutch. The Swedes destroyed four of their ships and burned down transport vessels in the port.
[90]Knowledge.
[91]From its depth.

of their crew are trained to swim very well so that they can swim far *in necessitate.*[92] One woman, who was on the Dutch ship which burned down, swam a distance of more than three fourths of a league and reached the quay.

Three thousand of the Brandenburg infantry arrived after the Swedish retreat. The ships were manned with it according to need, the remainder returned to the army.

The Swedes often apply this stratagem *in pugna,*[93] especially when they find in the harbor *aemulos debiliores*[94] than themselves. Later it was said that they used this trick against the Dutch yet a second time. A traitor from the Prussian army had notified the Swedes. At that time these Swedes were under the command of Wrangel.[95]

After the Swedish retreat we went to the Admiral with condolences, but found him cheerful. He did not complain about the loss at all, because for them to lose a ship is like firing a cartridge. He considered it a victory, since he did not give in and inflicted damage on the enemy. He thanked me because I did not abandon him on the first day, even though I did not help him there in any way. He also told the Voivode [Czarniecki] that even though I was a field soldier I did not shrink from a sea battle. About the sunken cannon he said: "They will all be yours." Yet this seemed improbable to me when I considered what drudgery it is when a cannon gets stuck in mud: What must it be like when it gets stuck in the sea? I very much wanted to watch this and to be present at the salvage. They had to wait for the water to become warmer, however. Meanwhile I was recalled from there, since the army was already marching to camp.

As soon as I had some time, I would indulge in such pleasant conversations that even among my relatives in Poland they could not have been more enjoyable. I already had various temptations not to go back to camp. But I nevertheless decided

[92]If necessary.
[93]In battle.
[94]An enemy weaker.
[95]Karl Gustav Wrangel, Swedish count and general.

to do so. I took leave of my dear friends[96] with many assurances of friendship as well as with pledges for the future. I was to go there with the army again next winter.

I went back to the banner after receiving a certificate of good behavior addressed to the overseer in which the *incolae*[97] of that area asked him to send me and no one else to them again next winter. Yet one of my retainers, a gentleman from the vicinity of Brzeziny,[98] named Wolski, married a daughter of a rich farmer, subject of this nobleman, and remained there. This fact strengthened their hope that I would probably return to them. But he did not keep his promise. He deserted his wife and went back to Poland with the regiment of Piaseczyński. He later related that, awake and asleep, he felt as if someone were calling behind his ear : "You have forsaken God."

After I had met my banner, we set out immediately on the fourth day for camp, which was established between Friederichs-Odde and Ribe.[99] This Friederichs-Odde is not a city but a very powerful fortress on a neck of land. Ribe, on the other hand, is a very beautiful city, once famous for its archbishopric[100] during the times of Catholicism. This mentioned fortress Friederichs-Odde lies on the sea (on Elsinore's outermost low stony tongue of land) on the side of Fionia. It has two more outlets, *Helsonariam et Cronaburgum*[101] which lie *directe*[102] opposite each other. No one in the world, even with the mightiest fleet, can reach the ocean *ex mari Baltico*[103] without the permission of the Danish King and without the payment of

[96]This already ties in with Pasek's love which is discussed later in this chapter. The friends he is talking about are the members of the Dyvarne family.
[97]Inhabitants.
[98]The city of Brzeźnica.
[99]A city on the eastern shore of Jutland. Ribe is one of the most ancient cities of Jutland.
[100]Actually it was only a bishopric. Czapliński, *Pam.*, p. 64, note 168.
[101]Helsingborg and Kronborg. Elsinore (Helsingør).
[102]Directly.
[103]From the Baltic Sea.

a toll.[104] This Kronborg[105] was founded *mirabiliter*[106] by a *Fridericus Daniae rex*[107]—I do not know which one[108] of the several Fredericks. He had a great multitude of stones be thrown into the depth of the sea. They became the subfoundations *in profundo*[109] of the sea for the foundation-walls which rose higher than all the waters and stormy waves and which until this day resist the most violent sea storms. Whoever navigates between these fortresses must bow, beg and pay the *vectigal constitutum*,[110] or rather the *portorium*.[111] The Danish people boast about the fact that once when Alessandro Farnese,[112] *dux Parmensis*, was waging war *contra Belgas foederatos*,[113] five hundred Dutch ships were locked, at the command of the Danish King, *in mari Baltico*.[114] All the people on the ships would have smothered there and no one would have escaped had not their *confederati*[115] collected large sums of money and ransomed them. The profit derived from these Sunds[116] *in mari Baltico*[117] is considerable. The Danish King receives a large income from them. In his kingdom there are no gold or silver mines,

[104]The tolls were first collected in 1425. In 1855 the countries who used the Sound agreed to pay Denmark 26,000,000 dollars to cease demanding tolls. Hudson Strode, *Denmark is a Lovely Land* (New York : Harcourt, Brace and Company, 1951), p. 43.

[105]Hamlet's castle. The castle is solidly built, creamy beige in color with a green copper roof. Hudson Strode, p. 93.

[106]In a very amazing way.

[107]Frederick, a Danish King.

[108]Frederick II (1534–1588), king of Denmark (1559–1588), son of Christian III. This fortress of Kronborg at Helsingör was built between the years 1577–1585.

[109]At the bottom.

[110]Established toll.

[111]Port fee, i.e., Sound Dues.

[112]1542–1592. He was in service of Philip II in Netherlands (1577–1586) ; duke of Parma (1586–1592) ; head of the Spanish armies in Netherland (1586–1592).

[113]The duke of Parma... against a confederate of Belgium, i.e., the Dutch.

[114]In the Baltic Sea.

[115]Allies.

[116]Two Straits (Large and Small Sund) between Sweden and Zealand.

[117]In the Baltic Sea.

but there are provinces fertile in game and abundant in fish and mead. The provinces supply each other with whatever is needed. Greenland[118] has so much fish that if people did not keep fishing there would be no *fretum navigabile*.[119] There is an especial abundance of herring and codfish which are caught *in Januario*[120] and dried in the frost and wind, so that they become as stiff as a board. In one province they have one thing, in another, other things, and therefore nothing is lacking.

I shall leave aside the descriptions of those provinces and their natural resources however, as I have not undertaken here to write a history, rather, I *proposui*[121] to write *cursum*[122] *vitae meae*.[123] I return, therefore, to the subject matter which I left off.

With the orders to move, a regulation was passed that all the regiments were to move into camp on the same day. These orders were carried out by the Polish troops *cum aedificatione*[124] of the foreigners because the Polish regiments arrived on one day as if shaken out of a sleeve. The German imperial troops, however, assembled for a week and a half. The armies set up billets only a league away from each other. General Montecuccoli had a grudge against the Voivode since all the officers of the Danish King along with their newly enlisted men did not go to him, but went to the Voivode from whom they took orders because such was their King's order. At their first meeting the two generals had an argument about this. The Voivode said to him: "We should not quarrel and be angry. This preference can be settled between us with the sword. You are a soldier and I am a soldier. You are a general and I am a general: tomorrow I shall give you satisfaction." He sent to

[118]A large island in the northern Atlantic, a Danish possession. Apparently Pasek is thinking about Zealand since he mentions the straits. Czapliński, *Pam.*, p. 66, note 183.
[119]Navigable straits.
[120]In January.
[121]Have undertaken.
[122]The course.
[123]Of my life, rendered in Polish in the original text.
[124]To the amazement.

him Skoraszewski,[125] the Royal Sewer Leszczyński's lieutenant,
challenging him to a duel face to face,[126] in order not to disturb the army. But Montecuccoli was clever. He did not want
to go himself and only sent some officers with some kind of
proposal. When Czarniecki saw them, he jumped like lightning toward them. *Supponendo*[127] that the general was trying
to leave the camp. But when he saw that it was not so, he
stopped and agreed to see the delegation.

The Great Elector was with his army about three leagues
away from us at that time. When he saw Montecuccoli again
he supposedly said this : "You did well not to go. If you had
gotten into some conflict with Czarniecki, surely you would
have also had to deal with me, since here I am representing the
Polish King." On the third day, however, God punished Montecuccoli as he was wounded by a cannon ball. Allegedly he was
not hit by the shot itself but by a splinter ripped off a ship by
that shot. Both of his calves were wounded. He had really
wanted to show off and achieve something without us, since for
two winters he had accomplished nothing and was idle. He
manned those Dutch ships and other merchant vessels, which
he had brought together with his people and sailed to the Sund
between Fionia and Friederichs-Odde. The Sweedes attacked
him so from various sides that he turned back in confusion and
injured his calves.

It was obviously the Will of God that such a splendid
fortress and the province as well were to be conquered not by
a German sword, but by a Polish sabre. Surely God wanted to
repay our nation for the defeat, which at His permission we
suffered from the Swedes when they invaded our country.

From that time on the Voivode gave orders not to let the
Swedes rest. We were to attack them, to shoot at them and to
lure them out of the entrenchments. At first they were so stupid
that they fell into the trap. Later they stopped doing so and

[125]Michał Władysław Skoraszewski. Czubek, *Pam.*, p. 64, note 5.
[126]Other sources also indicate that there were disagreements between
Czarniecki and Montecuccoli but do not mention the duel. Czapliński,
Pam., p. 67, note 193.
[127]He assumed.

stayed in the fortress. We entrenched ourselves then. We pushed our trenches forward very close to the fortress during the night. We could now shoot at the enemy both from cannon and muskets. The fortification of these entrenchments was not perfect however. Thus the army stood guard there on all sides the whole day, so that the Swedes would not make a sally against these entrenchments and would not drive our men away. Only when night came again could we reinforce them better : sand baskets were brought and filled up. cannon pulled in, and everything was done very quietly. It had been difficult to do this during the day, since the Swedes had been firing vigorously at us. On Friday the Swedes saw these fortified entrenchments. At dawn of the same day our dragoons under Colonel Tetwin attacked them from very close range. The two sides shot at each other with muskets. Our men drove them off one rampart. The Swedes lost heart. In the afternoon of that day they made a sally, but our men withstood them mightily and rushed headlong at them from the camp. The Swedes ran back and left several dozen corpses behind.

During that night, that is, from Friday to Saturday, they boarded their ships. Meantime they shouted, made noise and shot from the ramparts facing our camp. They escaped to Fionia, since on Saturday morning they expected a general assault.[128]

We kept wondering the next day why our neighbors were so quiet. When we realized what had happened, we waved flags on the ramparts and shouted : *"Vivat rex Daniae !"*[129] The retainers rushed eagerly from camp to take booty, but the Voivode sent Sergeant Mężyński after them immediately. All were to leave the entrenchments at once under penalty of death. Tetwin was to put a watch all around so that no one would enter the place, but by the time the sergeant had arrived the men had robbed whatever they could find. There was not

[128]It took place on the night of 26/27 of May, that is Monday to Tuesday. The Austrians also took part in the siege. Since the main fortifications were destroyed the Swedes defended themselves in their fortification Björsodde. Czapliński, *Pam.*, p. 69, note 200.
[129]Long live the Danish King !

much to take except for some food supplies which were stored almost in the very place where the mines were set. Only after everyone had left the entrenchments did the mines ignite, but no one was hurt. Even the rampart and buildings were in no way damaged. Only two oblong shed-like buildings burned down. They were presumably storage houses. Other buildings remained unharmed.

The duty of a wise leader is thus to foresee correctly and to act accordingly in order not to destroy the army. For most likely serious damage could not have been avoided there. Also our soldiers had quickly noticed that the enemy had escaped. They immediately rushed there and plundered whatever there was. The Swedes *supponebant*[130] that we would not notice this so soon. They set such slow fuses therefore. So that fortress whose capture had cost twenty thousand dead when the Swede had taken it away from the Danish King—since as the delegates themselves said, nine thousand Swedes and eleven thousand Danes had perished there[131]—was regained without any harm to our army. The delegates related that the earth had been soaked with human blood as with water after a downpour. The Swedes thus fled from Friederichs-Odde to Fionia to escape death. They hoped that it would not find them there between the seas. They were mistaken in that, however, for in a short time it followed them even across the sea. More will be said about this later.

The Great Elector congratulated the Voivode upon this good fortune, but jealousy showed in his eyes and in those of the Germans, since God had handed over to us a famous fortress. The Swedes also were very much ashamed for failing to accomplish anything with their mines.[132] Only on the third day the Voivode set up a Danish *praesidium*[133] there under a commander of that same nation. He was afraid that there could

---

[130]Assumed.

[131]According to Czapliński, in November 1657, the Polish forces numbered only five thousand, the Danish garrison numbered five thousand men. *Pam.*, p. 70, note 204.

[132]When they had planted the gunpowder.

[133]Garrison.

be still more mines. Dutch ships landed by that fortress in a very fine port. *Et interim*[184] we debated how to deal with Fionia, as Friederichs-Odde, such a strong fortress, fell into our hands. It was an ally of Fionia and now turned to a rival. We stayed in camp but, after all, our old man[185] was never idle, for we had about two hundred barges. He constantly kept filling these with dragoons and elite Cossacks, who attacked the Swedes in Fionia and disturbed them considerably. Especially the Cossacks, of whom there were only three hundred, accomplished amazing things. These were men sorted out according to age and height as if one mother had borne them. The Swedes had enough to do in Fionia. That province had a dimension of fourteen leagues and they had to guard all the shores well. They did not know where the enemy would land, especially at night. In general God has been obviously gracious to us in all the combats there, during surprise attacks as well as during assaults. Wherever we came across the Swedes, we defeated them. The Swedes esteemed the Imperial army lightly, however.

Once on patrol the Swedes had captured an officer named Myśliszowski. They sent him to their King at Copenhagen. Among other things the King asked : "What kind of an army is there under Czarniecki ?" He replied : "The one which customarily belongs to his division." The King asked : "Where were you at the time when I was in Poland ?" He answered : "We were also there and we fought against the army of your Majesty." "Why didn't you fight as well then as you do now ?" He answered : "Such was apparently God's Will." The King said : "This is surely a reason but I shall tell you of another : not everyone would find a way home if you were to lose now. Try therefore to win all the time." The officer fell silent. The King asked : "Why are you silent ?" "Because I do not know what to say against the truth." Also the Swedish prisoners admitted that they saw a complete change of fortune.

As soon as the Swedish King found out about the capture of Friederichs-Odde, he began to negotiate with the Danish

[184]Meanwhile.
[185]Czarniecki.

9*

King about peace. In his army he ordered to sound the trumpets so that whoever wanted to go back to Poland, could do so
in gratiam[186] to Radziejowski, after receiving a discharge and
being paid. Not many were found however. There were thousands of Poles in the Swedish army. Along with Radziejowski
only one hundred and fifty men left, all noblemen, among
whom were Kompanowski, Przeorowski,[187] Kaznowski and Rafał Jarzyna,[188] son of Marcin, the castellan of Sochaczew. Korycki[189] still remained and so did many Poles, who already had
become accustomed to life there and who did not expect to be
so well off in Poland if they returned to their possessions.

We who had been stationed in camp close to the imperial
troops for eight weeks or longer, got really tired of each other.
They complained about us : "The patrolmen steal from us."
We, on the other hand, complained that their wives kept eating
bread in our camp. We moved away from them by three
leagues. The women still kept finding their way there, but not
so often as before. *Interim* manifestos came from our King.
They reported of the dangers threatening our fatherland from
Moscow. We were told to be in full alert *ad regressum*[140] march
toward the border upon receiving a second order.[141]

The kindling of my affection caused me a lot of anxiety.
Letters circulated frequently between us. At one moment the
thought would occur to me to stay, at another, not to do this.
Sometimes I considered the stay indispensable, for I regretted
less abandoning such wealth than the love whose equal it would
be difficult to find. I struggled with these thoughts as with
a bear. Whenever I leaned toward staying, some joy came over
me, when swayed not to do so, some worry would overcome

[136]Thanks to the grace granted to Radziejowski.
[187]Both names might have been twisted by Pasek. Czapliński, *Pam.*,
p. 72, note 213.
[138]As seen from Czarniecki's letters he returned in April to the Polish
camp. Czapliński, *Pam.*, p. 72, note 214.
[139]Korycki went over to the Polish side already in January of 1659.
Czapliński, *Pam.*, p. 72, note 215.
[140]For a retreat.
[141]This is not quite correct. The Polish forces were to be moved to
Pomerania around Szczecin. Czapliński, *Pam.*, pp. 72–73, note 231.

me again. I regretted the love that these people had for me and I visualized how they would suspect me of insincerity and ingratitude. Some of my companions noticed my mood and asked: "How come that sometimes you are so engrossed?" I replied that no one could always be the same. I would not give away my secret to anyone in the world. They would not have known anything, if Lanckoroński had not blabbed a little of my affection before our standard-bearer. But also he did not know for sure, even though he visited them with me quite often. He saw only the attention I paid her. From this he made an assumption and arrived at a conclusion. Only then my companions *investigarunt*[142] some of my feelings and began to tease me about them. Besides, a letter came by special messenger, as they had learned that the Polish army was approaching the frontier. Many other letters were lost but the contents of this one were the following:

Your Honor N.N. ![143]

What is dear to the heart, we cherish readily in spirit, we desire to assure with words, we demand to look at with our eyes. The respect which my noble father had conceived for a splendid hero of a famous nation and companion of such a commander, the love with which he honors him, is proven by a frequent mention of the name of your Honor for he has a strong resolution which he preserves, to love you not like an adopted son but like one born from his own blood. If my father loves you, however, his daughter does not love you less, for this tender inclination has so firmly taken root in her heart that if it were possible to send in this letter her careworn heart, everyone would read with ease, the open and clear proof of her sincerity. I confess now what I concealed for long, that in all my past life I did not feel for any man, among so many competing for my hand, an attachment in my heart except for you, your Honor; and I readily believe that this comes from the Will of God and as a result of His decision. If you, your

[142]Here meaning guessed.
[143]The letter is written in Latin in the original text. N.N., *Nomen nescio*, I do not know the name.

Honor nourish the same in your heart, which you have
expressed in words I call that happiness. But if your lips
had only declared for my reassurance what you did not
feel, it would be a great sin against the love of fellow man.
Imagine my love which will forsake you neither because of
the distance between us nor because of the bashfulness of
my sex. This love runs swiftly between the shots, through
fire and so many dangers. It hurries, to see the temple of
Bellona, fearless of all her followers. She only thinks of
how she could enter the camp, and the sound of the
trumpets of Mars does not scare her. She is determined to
go where fate leads her and the secrets of her heart call
her. May it be spared violent reproaches and rejoice in the
fulfillment of the vows. I offer you my faithful heart in
sacrifice. Accept it and remember your word, which kindled hope in me. By the grace of God the home of my
parents is distinguished enough and can be compared with
the most ancient families of the Polish Kingdom. Their
wealth is not a secret. Although of little value, you used to
praise my upbringing nevertheless. If you found it appeal-
ing do not let it be discouraging. Religion is not a hindrance, for I also believe in the Holy Trinity, by Whose
grace human hearts are inspired. The words of my father
that the property cannot be taken out of our kingdom,
should not be a hindrance. The creator of this rule is my
father. You can be its interpreter. You, your Honor, can
be its plenipotentiary executor. It will be yours to command and mine to obey. The Honorable Richaldus, the
general delegate and secretary of our kingdom, conveyed
to me proof of your favorable feeling. For their confirmation I beg God and my dearest sister, who certainly will
convey clearly my feeling. As many words as many sighs.
As many recollections as many sobs. If someone had
asked : "Why do you do this ?"—it is sufficient for me to
say : "Answer for me, my heart." My heart no longer
belongs to me but to you. It has forsaken me. It accom-
panies you, it lives in you. Find out whether I am saying
the truth ! Advise me what to do with a rebelling heart !

You will find a cure for everything with ease, as soon as you desire. If you forsake me remember that God's anger always punishes ingratitude. This, however, I do not wish for myself and I do not question your promises. I only warn against the repetition of infamies which we condemn in people of former ages. Now there is nothing else left for me to desire but the presence of your Honor in the house of my father. With your presence, so I believe, everything will turn to the best. Come for at least one hour. I ask imploringly for this. I summon you eagerly. I await you with impatience as one affectionately attached to your Honor to the end of her life.

Eleonora of Croes Dyvarne

Under the signature she also added an intercession for a retainer of mine who got married there *me inscio.*[144] It reads as follows : *"Dominus Wolski sperat hac occasione procumbere ad pedes Dominationi suae una cum supplici nostrum omnium libello et deprecari gratiam Magnificentiae."*[145]

This letter did not conform to a woman's mentality in its style. I myself would not have believed that it was of her writing if I had not known about her education and had not listened often enough to *extemporanei discursus.*[146] I felt as if shackles had been put on my heart and I decided to go there without fail. I answered the letter promising to come. I composed it so that it would conform to her style. I left on the third day and no one knew where to and what for. On my way there, going past Piaseczyński's regiment I stopped at the regimental banner whose flag-bearer was Rylski,[147] a relative of mine. I confided my secret to him *in toto* :[148] I showed him the letters and took *consilium*[149] as from a relative. He persuaded me in

[144]Without my knowledge.
[145]Pan Wolski expects on this occasion to fall on his knees before his master with fervent entreaties of all of us in order to acquire forgiveness of your Honor.
[146]Extemporaneous conversations.
[147]Beniamin Rylski. According to Niesiecki he fought with Czarniecki in Denmark. Czubek, *Pam.*, p. 76, note 3.
[148]Completely.
[149]Advice.

omnibus modis[150] not to cast aside such an opportunity. He offered to go there with me himself. We drank to this occasion for one day and yet another. On the third day we left ; when the news came that a few thousand Swedes had landed near Skanderborg,[151] a city which we had to cross on our way there. In spite of that we went on riding ; but near Vejle[152] we found things in a state of alarm. The Prussians were arming. They asked us where we were going and, when we told them, they argued that : "It is impossible for you to get through since the Swedes have already landed there. They are fixing up the old field works. They want to settle there in order to have some *dominium*[153] in Jutland as a compensation for Friederichs-Odde. His Highness the Great Elector is now arming himself against the Swedes, for he wants to drive them out of there." We listened to their advice and turned back.

When we came to our camp, we found our men arming for a raid. The Voivode also wanted to go, and was in all readiness to do so when a lieutenant came galloping from the Great Elector and reported that the latter wanted to save the Polish army the trouble, being closer to the enemy, and wanted *sufficere*[154] this combat himself. The Voivode said : "When a woman gets off the carriage, it is easier on the wheels. Let them at least make good with this one battle, for until now they have not accomplished anything worthwhile, and have been consuming a lot of bread." We made ourselves at home. But I still intended to leave as soon as the Swedes had been expelled from there. The Prussians had not finished readying themselves against the Swedes when we received orders from our King to turn back to Poland.

[150]In every way possible.
[151]A city about 22 km southwest of Aarhus. It is located on a lake. Since Skanderborg lies about 20 km from the sea it is impossible for the Swedes to have left their ships here. Since it lies on a lake Pasek might have just remembered the water. Czapliński, *Pam.*, p. 78, note 239.
[152]Vejle, a seaport, SE Jutland, Denmark, at the head of Vejle Fjord. A city about 45 km southeast of Skanderborg.
[153]Territory.
[154]To manage.

I reflected over all these *impedimenta*,[155] and thought : "Dear God ! Apparently this intention is not in accordance with Your Holy Will." Then Rylski came in and asked : "What about our plans ?" I answered : "Probably nothing will come of them." And he said : "I too think that we should let it be." So we talked about it and drank at the same time, in the Polish fashion. After a few drinks, whenever I recalled my love, the drink became seasoned with tears ; later we parted.

The night did not bring sleep to my eyes, even though I drank a lot. I drank even more in order to fall asleep, but it could not come about by natural means. So powerful are passions in young people ! What moved me so was neither the noble origin nor the beauty of the maiden, which together with such intelligence and education were unusual, considering her sex, but the love which she felt for me, an insignificant man, or actually they felt for me. For not only she herself but also both her parents loved me. Their servants and subjects regarded me as their master's own son.

I submitted everything to God's will and embraced the feet of Jesus Christ, whose picture I had with the Holy Virgin. I felt greatly relieved upon that and I was ready to go to Poland. I no longer wanted to stay behind.

Trumpets announced departure in three days. It was postponed for a week, however, as the Great Elector sent a messenger asking to leave some of our cavalry behind for him as a token that not all Poles had left the Danish kingdom.

The Voivode concluded to designate Piaseczyński with fifteen hundred men. As soon as this order was given, the *consilium*[150] of my relative Rylski also changed. He had persuaded me not to remain before. Now he advised me *in contrarium*,[157] *ex ratione*[158] he had to stay behind. He gave me many reasons for doing so. He said that many opportunities would present themselves to stay and to decide about further actions, that later we would be able to do whatever we liked.

155Obstacles.
156Opinion.
157To the contrary.
158Because.

Now my mind began again to lean toward this argumenta-
tion, but when Father Piekarski found out about this plan, he
began to reproach me : "Don't do this ! What will you gain by
this ? Don't you know what end things will come to ? Since
you were lured by the *dulcedo*[159] of the imposing property and
the charm of married life, you would never leave for Poland.
They will constantly keep persuading you and will bring things
so far that you will settle in Denmark ; whoever you associate
with, such you become, so you will become a Lutheran. What
a great gain it would be to win a wife and to lose your soul !
Besides, what consolation would this good match bring to your
parents and to your relatives when they would only hear about
you by mail and would not see you ? It would be just as if you
had died and had entered Heaven, where the most beautiful
kingdom is, filled with greater treasures than the estates of Lord
Dyvarne. It is not a pleasure to hear that a relative is well off
when he is some two or three hundred leagues away ; but only
when he is close by. Don't do this, please !"

Things turned out that way, and probably for the good,
for Rylski perished in Fionia soon after. *Qui scit*[160] if I would
not have perished there too ? Had I remained there, I would
have surely had to participate in that battle.

We took leave of those staying behind and went toward
the border without mishap. With tears in my eyes I looked in
the direction where they expected me for the winter. When they
found out that our army was moving back to Poland, they sent
Wolski with a letter. They ordered him, if he no longer found
the army in camp, to pursue it even as far as Hamburg and to
ask me to wait in Hamburg for a further message. They dressed
the man in German garments, but his language was Mazovian.
The only words he could say in German were : "*Gib Brot, gib
Speck, gib Haber !*"[161]

In this they made a mistake, for if he had been dressed
in Polish garments, he would have surely overtaken our army
some fifteen leagues from the camp (as far as I could judge the

[159]Sweetness.
[160]Who knows.
[161]Give bread, give bacon, give oats.

time from his story). But when he passed the places which had previously been occupied by the Swedes—that is, before they had fled back to where they had come from, since they did not want to try their luck with the Great Elector—he came across the imperial men. They addressed him in German—no response; in Latin—no response; so they said: "You are a spy. You are wearing German garments, but you don't speak according to your outfit." They took away his horse, robbed him, read the letters and sent him back on foot. So I did not get the chance to read those last letters of which Wolski related later, upon his return from there. According to him I would have surely yielded to these letters from the parents.

These letters the emperor's men read in his presence. Later some who knew Polish asked him *de statu rerum*,[162] how and what. When he told them about it, some considerate ones took it ill of those who had stopped him and had robbed him because he was sent on such a mission. They released him on the fourth day. When he returned to his master the house was filled with lamentations. They still had hoped that, because of these letters, after he had caught up with me, I would have remained in Hamburg, from where some means of crossing over could be found.

It is strange: I compared the time with that according to Wolski's report—exactly when things went wrong there, when he was stopped with the letters, and when the lamentations began in the house after his return—my heart also felt so heavy that I did not know whether I was alive.

Jędrzej Zaręba did not yield an inch from me, when he saw my *alterationes*.[100] What premonition does a heart have! All this surely was not in the Will of God, and therefore it turned out so.

After we left Jutland, Kazimierz Piaseczyński, an ambitious man, almost Czarniecki's *par*[164] in military craft, tried diligently to fight *pro gloria gentis*.[165] He also wanted those who

[162]About the state of affairs.
[163]Sorrow.
[164]Equal.
[165]For the glory of the nation.

had stayed with him to see that he earned his bread well. Having chosen the right time, he wanted to earn a good name for Poland and for himself. He saw that the Swedes were not guarding the shore of Fionia as *diligenter*[166] as they had before our army had passed through there, but that they were arming still more against the men of the Emperor and those of Brandenburg. He took from the Great Elector three regiments of infantry and put the cavalry and infantry across by ship.

Even though the Swedes vigorously opposed our landing, they, as has been mentioned before, had already dispersed their forces among different field works along the coast. Before the first Swedish troops had gathered, the others could no longer withstand us and had to let our troops land. Our cavalry rushed at them, crushed them down, and killed them. Then they stopped and waited for more guests. There were twelve thousand Swedes there, and among the *incolae*[167] each man was a rifleman, a soldier, and also a sorcerer. An overwhelming crowd of them thus came against a small handful of our men.

They rushed at our men from both sides, and Colonel Piaseczyński was killed by a bullet in the chest during the first assault. Rylski, my cousin, perished simultaneously with him, likewise several officers and retainers. But since our men withstood the fire and began to fight with swords, the Swedes had no time to reload their guns. *Et interim*,[168] more Prussians landed in another place, which had been already abandoned by the Swedes. The Swedes were killed both by bullets and swords. They were massacred. The cities and villages were plundered. All were severely punished, since the Poles took revenge for the blood of their colonel. Also all the *incolae*[169] had their share. Half of them perished, since they were found *in armis*[170] and defended themselves like the Swedes. They already considered the Swedish King their lord and did not even suspect that he would allow them to be snatched from

[166]Carefully.
[167]Inhabitants.
[168]And meanwhile.
[169]Inhabitants.
[170]Armed.

him.[171] But as they abandoned their Lord, so did their infernal protector, in whom they *totaliter*[172] believed, abandon them. For even the Devil himself will resign when God wants to punish someone.

In the entire Swedish kingdom and in some Danish provinces, the devils are handled like the slaves in Turkey. They do whatever they are ordered to and they are called *spiritus familiares*.[173] When Rej[174] went as an envoy to Sweden, his beloved coachman fell ill. He was compelled to leave him in the house of a certain nobleman and intended to take him along on his way back to Poland. The sick man lay in an empty room, and when the fever left him, he heard some beautiful music. He thought that someone was playing in another room and remained lying down. Then a small boy dressed in a German costume jumped out of a mousehole, after him a second and a third one, and later also ladies. The music could be heard better and better, and they began to dance in the room. The coachman was petrified. Then they grouped themselves in pairs in order to leave the room through the door. The musicians left with them. A maiden in a wedding dress also came through. All of them left the room through the door. They did not harm him but the coachman almost died of

---

[171]The allied forces under the command of the Danish Field Marshal Ernest Albrecht Eberstein crossed over to Fionia on Nov. 14th. The Polish divisions got over on the 15th. Piaseczyński perished in the battle at Nÿborg on November 24th. Czapliński, *Pam.*, p. 84, note 288.

[172]Totally. The Fionians were commonly known as outstanding sorcerers at the time. Czapliński, *Pam.*, p. 84, note 289.

[173]House spirits. In Scandinavia the peasants believed in benevolent and serviceable dwarfs, called *nisser*. Rosznecki claims that Pasek's description of Denmark excels in precision over other descriptions, among others of the descriptions of the Italian Torquato Rechi who was in Denmark at the end of the 16th century. Those authors who ridicule Pasek's descriptions of the little dwarfs in Fionia may compare this narration with Rechi's, who seriously informs his readers that one sells winds, enclosed in handkerchiefs, to sailors in Denmark. Czapliński, *O Pol. Sied.*, p. 209.

[174]Perhaps Pasek confused him with Andrzej Morsztyn, who was an envoy to Sweden in 1655. It is not known which Rej he is talking about here. Czapliński, *Pam.*, p. 84, note 291.

fear, however. Later they sent back a little fellow who said: "Don't worry about what you see, because not even a hair will fall off your head, for we are the house spirits. We are celebrating a wedding, for one of us is getting married. We are going to the wedding feast and shall return the same way. We shall also have you participate in the feast." He did not wish to look at this *spectaculum*.[175] He got up and bolted the door, so that they could not return that way. On their way back from the wedding they found the door locked. This music could be heard once again. *Interim*[176] they tried the door. It was locked. A little fellow crawled in through a crack under the door. He grew before the coachman's eyes into a big man, threatened him with his finger, loosened the bolt and opened the door. They then took the same way as before and then crawled into that mousehole. An hour or so later one of them came out of the hole again and brought him a cake on a plate filled richly with jams and raisins. He said: "The bridegroom sends this so that you can also taste the wedding desert." The coachman took it with great anxiety, thanked him for it and put it next to him. Later, those who nursed him during his illness and also the physicians who took care of his health, came to him. They asked: "Who gave this to you?" He told him of the whole incident. They asked: "Why don't you eat it?" He said: "I am afraid to eat this." They said to him: "Don't be foolish, have no fear: these are good things. They are members of our household, our friends. Do have some of it!" He did not want to do so. They took the cake, ate it before his eyes and said to him: "We get something to eat from them often. It does not harm us."

They also used these spirits for work and for various services. The Fionians trusted very much in their protection, but I did not hear of any Pole whose sabre got notched from cutting their neck. True, before a battle the Poles put a spell on the bullets, and rubbed the sabres with various consecrated objects.

[175]Spectacle.
[176]In the meantime.

We marched back toward Poland as far as Hamburg along the same route as we had taken before. We saw an Augustinian monastery there, from which Martin Luther ran away to his apostasy.[177] The Voivode had set up billets there. I was *curiosus*[178] enough to view all the places, the beauty and the ornamentation of the monastery as well as the cells. I even went to the cell where he had lived. Some of us said that we were Lutherans and the Germans took us around with confidence and showed us all the *antiquitates*[179] of this place, with accompanying explanations as to what had happened and how. We also kept sighing. This monastery, if I remember correctly, is called Uraniburgum.[180] It was an extremely beautiful structure, situated in a spot which was very suitable for defense, since on three sides it was washed by a huge lake as if by a sea. It was accessible only on the fourth from a great plain. Each of the monastery's cells was so beautiful that it could have been called a royal chamber ; and there were about five hundred of them. The windows in all of them were huge, bright, and painted. In some cells there were various paintings of the Saints. But in most of them there were pictures of the Most Holy Virgin and all of these paintings *cum inscriptionibus*.[181] Other windows were made out of glass as white as crystal. The church itself was so splendid and beautiful that I had not seen

[177]Czubek assumes that Pasek is talking about a Franciscan monastery in the vicinity of Hamburg which was demolished in the 19th century. Now a stock exchange and a town hall stand in its place. Czubek, *Pam.*, p. 85, note 1. Czapliński says that he talks about a large monastery, also located on a lake, called Brodesholm in Schleswig, north of Neumünster. The armies of Czarniecki stopped there while going to Denmark in 1658. It is possible that Pasek visited it on his way back. This convent had earlier belonged to the Augustinians and Luther was a member of that order for a while. The monastery of Bordesholm was indeed a very splendid one. Czapliński, *Pam.*, p. 86, note 298.
[178]Curious.
[179]Antiquities.
[180]Uranieborg, renowned observatory and scientific institute built by Tycho de Brahe, the noted Danish astronomer and nobleman, on the island Hven in the middle of the Sound. Czubek, *Pam.*, p. 85, note 4.
[181]Had (with) inscriptions. Citations from the Holy Scriptures and others.

its equal in Poland. The altars and paintings were of ancient workmanship. The paint, varnish and gilding on them were very beautiful and kept in such fine condition that one could not even see a speck of dust anywhere : one could have said that the monks were driven out of there only two days ago. The income of the monastery was considerable—they said—but they also said that there had been allegedly four hundred monks there.

All these cells, wherever one looked, were swarming with women and children, who had fled from the army. They had feared very much that we might rob them ; they were more afraid of us on our retreat than they had been previously on our march thither. But when they saw that we did not do them any unpleasantness, even though in the monastery a few hundred men had stayed overnight with the Voivode and the entire army had camped in front of the monastery, they were already more cheerful on the next day. When the army was leaving, they came out before the monastery, blessed us, and thanked the Voivode.

From there we marched to Reinbeck,[182] Berstede,[183] toward Wismar,[184] into the Duchy of Mecklenburg toward Güstrow,[185] Tomaszów,[186] Żuraw,[187] Tobel,[188] Wistock,[189] into the land of Brandenburg to Szczecin,[190] toward the border. We reached our camp in Czaplinek, in Tempelburg[191] that is. The camp de-

[182]A city east of Hamburg.
[183]Or Bersztede, a name apparently twisted by either the copyist or the author. Bergstedt.
[184]A city and Baltic seaport.
[185]A city in Mecklenburg.
[186]Perhaps Teterów, a city east of Güstrow. Czubek, *Pam.*, p. 87, note 6.
[187]Or Żurów, a city east of Wismar.
[188]Perhaps Dabel.
[189]Wittstock, a city in Mecklenburg.
[190]From Czarniecki's correspondence we know that he was in Wittenburg, in Mecklenburg, on August 20 and on 29 in Schwedt on the Oder. Czapliński, *Pam.*, p. 88, note 213.
[191]The names of the localities Pasek most likely cited from a map and he twisted them around. Some of them might have been changed by the copyist.

teriorated. Some retainers died, others went back home, and still others got married. The wagons had rotted and nobody knew where things had disappeared to.

We crossed the border and thanked God, that He let us see the fatherland in good health. We sang merrily to the honor and glory of the Name of the Almighty. Right beyond the border the banners dispersed. Great Poland and Warmia[192] were assigned to our army for winter quarters. From Marienburg an army also returned with Field Hetman Lubomirski. When the banners had mingled during the march, it was not necessary to ask which division a banner had belonged to, for when one looked at it, it was obvious. When the men were emaciated, poor, shabby, barefooted and on foot, they came from Marienburg; if, however, they were on horseback, armed, well dressed, they were those from Denmark, or *Czarnieczykowie*[193] as we were called.

God punished, moreover, those who had escaped from us at the border, being afraid to go with us, for they either perished or suffered losses fighting here, in Poland.

Our banner was assigned to Oborniki[194] and Mosiny,[195] near Poznań. On my way there I caught typhus in the following manner: There was a sick officer being carried on a stretcher; he turned out to be a good friend of mine whom I had known since youth. I knew him when I was still in school at Rawa, for he worked in the chancellery[196] there and I was also friends with his brother. I felt sorry for him. I did not know what he was ill with, but I realized that he had to follow his banner for a league or even more to stop for the night. I invited him to spend the night in my quarters. Several days later I fell gravely ill. My companions had already doubted my recovery, but they nursed me with great care. Shortly after, I began *convalescere*.[197]

[192]Ermland.
[193]Czarniecki's men.
[194]A city about 30 km north of Poznań.
[195]A town 18 km south of Poznań.
[196]In the chancellery of Grodno. The starosty of Grodno was in the Mazovian Rawa.
[197]To come back to health.

When we arrived in Poznań, I thanked God that He had returned me to my former health and also for preserving my health in foreign lands, as not even a finger of mine had been hurt there, thanks to His Most Holy Grace and that of His Virgin Mother.

Half of my banner had stopped in Mosiny and the other half in Oborniki. I was stationed in a house in the market place, but both landlords were great rascals. I moved to Poznań Street, therefore, to an indentured weaver, a decent man, at whose house I enjoyed full comfort after that illness. Since I wanted to eat only poultry, that man sent everyone in his house all around and did his best to see that I would have it all the time. He also performed all the services with great kindness. Thus I soon returned *ad perfectionem.*[198] Only my crop of hair fell out. But I say this : Oh God, protect me from such an illness a second time in my life !

We thus ended the old year—may the Name of God be praised—in 1659 in Mosiny.

[198]To full health.

ANNO DOMINI 1660

By the grace of God we began this year in Mosiny, where, after such trying battles and the long expedition beyond the Baltic Sea, we were to stay encamped for the entire winter ; but dangers threatening us from the Muscovites and the Cossacks resulted in our not being allowed to celebrate peacefully the Bacchus holiday[1] in our winter quarters.[2] Manifestoes[3] which no longer contained ardent orders, but rather ardent entreaties, were sent acknowledging that the army deserved compensation and rest for its privations and courage. At the same time they begged that out of love for God and the fatherland no one consider it unjust that the army had to be put to marching during such a severe winter, a necessary measure since the Muscovites had already conquered all of Lithuania, had overrun the fortresses in Podlasie, and intended to take Warsaw. Our division was promised that it would be compensated on another occasion.

We set out from our winter camp. Ever since Czarniecki had been given his own division and had become practically a third hetman, we could no longer spend the entire winter in camp. We had to fight the enemies constantly. Still our army

[1]Here Shrovetide. In classical mythology Bacchus or Dionysus was the god of wine and son of Zeus (Jupiter) and Semele. He personified both its good and bad qualities. The carnival season ended on February 10 at the time. Czapliński, *Pam.*, p. 91, note 1.

[2]A great Russian army under Dolgoruky and Khovansky was marching towards Warsaw. Reddaway, p. 527.

[3]The royal proclamation summoned men to assemble in the vicinity of Łuków in Podlasie. Czubek, Pam., p. 90, note 3.

10*

was the best and the most orderly, for God so rewards sincere devotion toward the fatherland.

We began to march then, not just simply the way soldiers are believed to march, but in a straight line, *magnis itineribus*[4] through Łowicz[5] towards Warsaw. This quick response was to the astonishment of all, for such eager obedience[6] was not expected of us.

The military men came *in veste peregrina*[7] to see the King. They were well dressed: a linen *żupan*[8] and a *kontusz*[9] of the same material, a jerkin made out of a cavalryman's tunic; high boots with German bootlegs that went almost up to the waist. (The *kontusz* came only up to the knees.) From this garb originated the short costume that had buckled boots and which was incorrectly called Circassian, for we originated it *ex necessitate*[10] when we were in those foreign lands where on account of the long and wide bootlegs we had to keep our

[4]In forced marches, an expression from Caesar's "Commentaries."
[5]A city on the Bzura river in the district of Sochaczew, the voivodeship of Warsaw.
[6]Czarniecki's soldiers were in Warsaw already at the end of January. Czapliński, *Pam.*, p. 92, note 6.
[7]In novel costume, i.e., foreign garments.
[8]Pol., undergarment of the Polish national dress.
[9]Pol., a nobleman's overcoat with split sleeves.
[10]Out of necessity.

frocks short. We would have looked like scarecrows if we had allowed the long frocks to bounce in back and front against those heavy bootlegs. We had no Polish bootlegs there in the foreign lands for our army had come only on horseback and without transport and supply columns. Everyone came only with those boots which he had on his feet at the time and which could not have been so durable as to last us during our entire stay abroad.

This costume became the fashion. Even the most beautiful frocks were cut short. Even Polish boots were made with long bootlegs and with silver or gold buckles which were set with diamonds or rubies, depending on what one could afford. To make these buckles ostentatious the frocks were made short. Everyone went along with this fashion, even the shoemakers and the tailors. Such is the custom here in Poland that even if one were to wear a frock inside out, people would call it a fashion. Later such fashion would enjoy great popularity until the common folk would begin to wear it.

How many continuously changing styles I remember in frocks, caps, boots, swords, harness, and in every other kind of military garment and household utensils, as well as in hairstyles, gestures, walking and greeting habits! Oh Almighty God, one could not manage to list them on ten ox skins! Surely this is the *summa levitas*[11] of our nation and the cause of great *depauperatio*.[12] The outfits which I bought abroad would have lasted me a whole lifetime—even my children would have profited by them—had they not gone out of fashion and become unstylish in a year or less. These outfits had to be taken apart and restyled, or else had to be sold in a second-hand market. Then others would have to be purchased, since old ones could be worn only *inter domesticos parietes*.[13] Otherwise people would rush at you like sparrows at an owl: "Look, look!" They would point their fingers at you. They would say that the outfit reminded them of the days of

[11]Greatest frivolity.
[12]Impoverishment.
[13]Within domestic walls, i.e., within one's four walls.

the Deluge. About the ladies and their fancies I shall not say anything because I could fill an entire book with this subject.

This fashion then, which we had introduced out of pure necessity in Denmark, came into general use. When the soldiers arrived in Warsaw so dressed, Queen Ludwika[14] and her ladies in waiting could not take their eyes off them. They made the soldiers turn around and they looked at them with wonderment. Even if someone had a nice old frock, he nevertheless would dress in the colorful new costume whenever he needed a favor from the King.

We were paid from the treasury, but only for two quarters of the year. I collected the money and went straight from Łowicz to Bieliny,[15] some three leagues beyond Rawa, to see my parents. When they saw me return in good health and good fortune, they greeted me with such abundant tears of joy that they could not calm themselves for almost an hour. I also brought many unusual gifts to them, such as special *nummismata*[16] which could not be found anywhere in Poland. I also brought a pair of lindenwood sandals as a present for Miss Teresa Krosnowska, the daughter of the cupbearer of Rawa and the lady of my heart, for we were in love.

Especially for these sandals I had bought an incrusted box in Poznań. It was set with ebony and with mother-of-pearl and lined with crimson damask. Pan Franciszek Ołtarzowski,[17] a companion and a neighbor of mine, presented this gift to Miss Teresa as a great rarity on my behalf. He performed his task *cum facunda oratione*.[18] He fulfilled his task cleverly. He did not reveal the contents of the box right away. He only called it a present which had never before been seen in Poland. Those present, looking at the beautiful box, assumed that something marvellous and costly was inside.

---

[14]Maria Ludwika Gonzaga (1611–1667) a princess of Mantua, she was the second wife of King Władysław IV. After his death in 1648 she married on March 31, 1649, Jan Kazimierz, his brother.

[15]A village in the district of Rawa.

[16]Coins.

[17]Later Lord High Steward of Rawa. Czubek, *Pam.*, p. 94, note 4.

[18]An eloquent speech.

I cannot remember Pan Ołtarzowski's entire speech but he spoke in somewhat the following manner :

My Ladyship !

Love is a volunteer in human flesh. It does not take orders from the other senses. It lets itself be guided only by its own whim, and can be turned in any desired direction by the inclination of the heart. Whether it climbs over high Alps, whether it swims across rapidly flowing rivers, whether it lingers in the abysmal depths of an impenetrable ocean, it has a goal towards which it strives with the inclination of its heart. To this goal it turns its friendly thought even from a distance.

His Lordship Pan Pasek, my friend and companion, did not want to miss an opportunity to be of service to you. He reflected for a long time with what kind of present he could please your Ladyship upon his return from long wanderings away from his native borders. To bring something from abroad which is esteemed among the people solely for its price and value but which is commonplace here in Poland would not be anything remarkable. It would have been even inappropriate to bring something from abroad of which we already have enough here in Poland. To bring such a rarity as Poland has not seen up until now would be thrilling however. Let the bold Jason show off his Golden Fleece for which he dared go to Colchis seeking his own gain. Let Hippomenes win the favor of fair Atalanta by throwing the golden apple. Such presents cannot compete with the one in this box. And why ? Because the only rare thing about those valuables was that they were made out of pure gold. But I am proud to hand over my friend's most unusual present. For it could be found neither in royal nor in imperial treasuries, in possession of which or joy of which even such a cunning world famous lady of fashion as Cleopatra could pride herself with. Upon seeing this most unusual gift Your Ladyship will surely be ready to admit this herself. I beg your Ladyship on my friend's behalf now to accept it gratefully and to enjoy it.

After this eulogy everyone assumed that a gem of inestimable value was concealed inside the box. But when they saw the wooden sandals, they received the gift with the same courtesy as they had displayed before. Almost all the relatives and neighbors from the surrounding area came to see the sandals.

I celebrated the Carnival in the good company of my neighbors, especially with the same Mikołaj Krosnowski, the cupbearer of Rawa—he at my father's house and the two of us at his. Later I followed my squadron, even though I had little desire to do so. But hard discipline existed in our division at the time. God help the officer who was absent from his banner for a long time. If he happened to be absent during its arrival at camp, during its march off, or if he missed a battle, he would be tried and sentenced immediately and those articles of law, which any true officer knew by heart, would be cited.

When I caught up with my banner, troops were mingled and one banner was encamped close to another. By the time we reached Podlasie, the Muscovites had retreated toward Mścibów.[19] Prior to that they had instigated combats in the vicinity of Siemiatycze[20] and Brześć[21] under the command of Trubetzkoy[22] and Słoński.[23] The Voivode received orders from the King to spread out the army for the Easter holidays all over Podlasie, to set up quarters in the estates of the nobles, and to seek sustenance by soliciting whatever the nobles would give willingly.[24] The royal and the ecclesiastical estates would no longer *sufficere*[25] for feeding the army. They had been devastated by the Lithuanian army and by the enemy. The various units of the hetman's divisions remained encamped far from each other

[19]A town 15 km east of Wołkowysk.
[20]A city 55 km northwest of Brest Litovsk.
[21]Brest Litovsk. The Russians had occupied it since January. Czapliński, *Pam.*, p. 97, note 51.
[22]Alexey Nikitich Trubetzkoy, prince and voivode of Moscow. Died in 1680. Czapliński, *Pam.*, p. 97, note 51.
[23]A White Russian nobleman who fought on the Muscovite side. Czapliński, *Pam.*, p. 97, note 52.
[24]The estates of the nobility were not obliged to supply the army with either provisions or billets. Czapliński, *Pam.*, p. 97, note 53.
[25]Suffice.

in order to keep guard on Warsaw from that side, and to be ready to move on after Easter. The Town of Sielce,[26] together with three parishes, which were made up of only poor gentry, were assigned to us for repose. Pan Wawrzyniec Rudzieński— who later became our flagbearer—and I were delegated to assign billets and to allot these poor provision areas to our army.

Once we arrived there we were received cordially and *nemine reclamante*,[27] for the Lithuanians had already so disciplined the local nobility that they had almost converted them into peasants.[28] We arrived there on the fourth Sunday of Lent.[29] First of all we paid a visit to her Ladyship, the Castellan's wife. She lived near by, right outside of town, on an estate called Strzała,[30] but her husband[31] lived somewhere far away. They had always lived separately since he was suffering from insanity at that time. This estate belonged to her as the *haeredissa*[32] of the Wodyński family.

When we rode to see her we said to ourselves : "They will oppose the billeting orders *ratione iuris bonorum terrestrium*.[33] When we announced the reason for our visit and showed our authorization, however, there was no contradiction, but every kindness and hospitality. We obtained permission to set up billets. After our return to town, we examined the billets on the very next day. Since the townsmen had read the authorization, they knew which parishes were assigned to supply us with provisions. Two gentry delegates from every village, usually consisting of 50 or 60 farmsteads, came on behalf of their people to greet us. They brought along with them oats, grains

[26]Siedlce.
[27]Without opposition.
[28]I.e., had impoverished them so.
[29]The fourth Sunday of Lent. It fell on March 7 at the time. Czapliński, *Pam.*, p. 98, note 64.
[30]A village some three kilometers north of Siedlce. Czapliński, *Pam.*, p. 98, note 66.
[31]Tomasz Olędzki na Chłędowie. Czubek, *Pam.*, p. 97, note 9.
[32]Heiress.
[33]On the grounds of the rights of landed estates (i.e., estates of the nobles.)

for bread, oil, and other things, even though they were not
asked to do so. They besought us to show them consideration
and to treat them in a friendly manner. Some also asked that
only good men be assigned as chief collectors in their villages,
for they expected us to treat them the way the Lithuanians had.
We fixed provision areas on Tuesday. On Wednesday we went
to the various villages. We rode around until Friday and we
still did not manage to finish our tour, because the villages were
densely populated and located close to each other. There were
even as many as thirty of them in one parish.

We returned to town and gave orders that only two men
were to come from every village. These men were to bring the
tax vouchers[34] which were to serve as the source of information
about the size of the villages and their lands. The men arrived
promptly on the next day. But since we had to ride out to
welcome the remainder of our banner, which was due to arrive,
they had to wait. On Passion Sunday,[35] right after early Mass,
we sat down to study the vouchers. We kept calculating until
evening.

The representatives of the gentry asked for good collectors
for their villages. They promised as a reward a goose for the
holidays, a capon, or a little lamb. We told each one of them
in secret: "We have assigned for you the best man and one
who will be companionable." One of the men thanked us while
another made a declaration of his intended gift. They did not
leave until we had finished writing all the assignations and had
distributed them. They kept their word to such an extent that
whatever they had promised *nomine*[36] of their village they
delivered during Holy Week. They brought all sorts of things
for us so that even if we had not had any allotment we would
have been well off could feed other people.

When the collected provisions were delivered, some thirty
or forty members of the gentry came along. Our companions
invited them to join us at the meal table and treated them *per*

[34]Such vouchers were handed out by the tax-collectors. Czapliński,
Pam., p. 99, note 76.
[35]Fifth Sunday of Lent.
[36]In the name.

respectum[37] for their being of the gentry—and therefore our brothers—and also because they brought provisions without being obliged to do so. Sometimes they drank more liquor than they had brought along. But *in recompensam*[38] for our hospitality they would again deliver something without being asked to do so. They praised us to the heavens and said that the soldiers of Pan Czarniecki were angels and that the Lithuanians were devils. Not one of those who had especially asked for a good one complained that he had been given a bad man.

This encampment, or rather, as we used to call it, a place of repose, was a rather nice place. To myself I assigned the Strzała village, the estate and place of residence of the Castellan's wife, who had personally asked me to do so. I was very satisfied with my post. The Castellan's wife was such a nice lady that not only did she give orders that I be rendered various services and that provisions be put at my disposal but she also allowed me to live there for the duration of the banner's encampment. The village was situated quite close to town. The retainers as well as my horses received an abundance of everything. I myself ate and drank in the manor and indulged in the most boisterous speech, just as if I were in Paradise.

The Castellan's wife was a dignified and respectable lady, but cheerful. She had only one daughter, her sole heiress, who later married Oleśnicki, son of the Chamberlain of Sandomierz.[39] She asked me to invite my companions for the holidays. She also wanted me to be present. She said that I could invite them to her house to dance and to play cards, for she had her own musicians and over a dozen ladies-in-waiting from fine homes with nice dowries. She herself had only one daughter, the heiress of several hundred thousand. Later Stefan Czarniecki,[40] the starost of Kaniów at the time, began to court this daughter. He joined the competition for the daughter's hand. He followed the wishes of the Voivode, his uncle, who had

[37]With consideration.
[38]In order to repay.
[39]Her first name was Joanna. She married Stanisław Oleśnicki, who later became the starost of Radziejów. Czubek, *Pam.*, p. 101, note 2.
[40]The nephew of Hetman Stefan Czarniecki.

provided him well for this courtship and sent him out from the camp with a group of brave soldiers. Stefan had no luck however. Apparently God had not willed it so. I was told later that he was turned down because he was too moody and too eager. Within the same year the daughter married the son of Oleśnicki, the Chamberlain of Sandomierz.

The post seemed blissful to me since things went so well. During my entire military service I never had another post like it. My wagons were loaded with all sorts of special goodies which usually were to be had only at home during the holidays, not at camp. These things were sent to my camp at Kozierady,[41] which was only six leagues away, until my departure. Suffice it to say that not all mothers would have been so generous.

The Castellan of Zakroczym, the husband of this noble lady, was a kind and capable man and also a very good soldier. But he became somewhat insane. He and his wife were separated after the birth of their only daughter. He managed his estates and she managed hers. Each of them kept a household staff. He was such a valiant man, when still in good health, that everyone feared him. Once, in a company of nine other men, he killed off the banner[42] of Karol Potocki[43] in the first attack. He had said to his opponents : "I shall not wait for you in my village but in the open field so that you cannot say that I believe in a numerical superiority." He did just that. When they met, he first challenged the lieutenant and then both rode away from the banner. Now they said to each other : "To swords !" The Castellan rode toward Potocki and thrust at him twice so mightily that the latter fell off his horse. The Potocki banner then rushed in a mob. The Castellan withstood their assault with his group of men. They soon overcame and massacred their foes : they killed them all and took possession of their flag and kettledrums, which they sent to the hetman.

The Castellan did no evil—as the insane usually do—he

---

[41]A town east of Siedlce, in the voivodeship of Lublin. Now Konstantynów. Czubek, *Pam.*, p. 101, note 5.
[42]About one hundred men.
[43]The cup-beared of Podolia. He was the standard-bearer of an armored banner at the time. Czapliński, *Pam.*, p. 102, note 93.

only became somehow terribly devout. He sewed a small cross with the image of Christ onto his cap and when he went through a church or a room he would not look at any one, would not greet anyone, and only held in both hands that cap with the picture of the Crucified before his eyes and kept staring at it. A page boy carrying a sword accompanied him. He never laughed. The servants who had served him a dozen or so years related that they never saw him laugh. He used to visit his wife but would never stay overnight in her house. He ate his dinner in the evening when one would normally eat supper and then for the whole night through he would ride to his home which was four leagues away. Sometimes he spoke wisely and sometimes deliriously. Once at his usual dinner time he visited his wife. Four of our officers were also present at her table. When it was announced that his Lordship had arrived, I said : "Your Ladyship, should we go out to greet him ?" She said : "It is not necessary to do so because he considers himself unworthy of such a gesture."

He entered the room looking grave and devout and held that cap with the little cross before his eyes. He went directly to his wife and knelt down. She, in a manner of a bishop, put her hands on his head, because such was their habit. Had she not done so he would have remained kneeling until she did. Next to her Ladyship sat Kościuszkiewicz, an old and a very brave officer from Volhynia. He was a respectable man, vigorous and tall, with a beard down to his waistline. The Castellan, rising, said to this Kościuszkiewicz : "Greetings, Sir hetman !" Kościuszkiewicz answered : "Greetings, Your Majesty !", whereupon they shook hands. Then the Castellan asked : "Is his Lordship Sir Pasek also here ?" I spoke up : "At your Lordship's service." We, too, shook hands with each other and he then said : "I surmised immediately that it was you because they spoke of a young officer." And he continued : "I came here to thank your Lordship for being the guardian of my wife." All the while the page boy held that sword right under his elbow. I answered : "In no way do I claim the honor of being the guardian of her Ladyship but only of your subjects who for the time being find themselves in my provisions supply area." To that he said : "It must be so ; God in Heaven has so commanded." Kościuszkiewicz said : "Dear Sir Castellan, please sit down and, as the master of the house, also invite us to do so because the dishes will get cold." "Agreed, Sir Voivode, I also have not eaten as yet !" He shook hands with those companions whom he had not yet greeted and who were sitting next to Kościuszkiewicz and then he went to the far end of the table, almost up to the door. We began to move and begged him to take the place of honor. His wife said : "It is wasted effort ! He will not do that for anything in the world and if you insist on it, he will leave. Such is his habit." He then sat down behind all his wife's domestic servants and our retainers. He ate and drank well, but with every glass of liquor he drank, he went up to his wife to ask for permission, knelt down, and she had to put her hands on his head. He talked sensibly at times and then deliriously. At all times the page boy stood there holding the sword. I kept a keen eye on that sword because one never knows what to expect from the insane.

After dinner he said : "My Dear Ladyship, don't you have any musicians in the house, for there is no gaiety ?" She answered : "Surely, your Lordship, but they have no money to buy themselves strings." He said : "Call them to me, Brzeski !" He put his hand in the pocket of the page boy who held the sword. He took therefrom three golden zlotys for the musicians, who then came and played. We began to dance. We bowed before him and he blessed us with that cross and kept drinking. After drinking he no longer spoke a word to anyone. Before he departed he knelt in front of his wife again and then left. She began to cry out of her sorrow that, though having a husband she really did not have a companion, for he behaved so strangely.

Still prior to his departure one of our companions, a Pan Łącki from Lithuania, said to him : "Why don't you, your Lordship, contribute to the gaiety in this your house ? He struck his sword with his two fingers and pointing to it he said : "I am only accustomed to dance with this Lady. If I began to dance with her, however, things could prove unpleasant for someone in an encounter." Łącki left him alone at that and he no longer encouraged him to dance. We were told that at his own house as well he would order music when he was tipsy and then he would perform various fencing tricks. He would attack and retreat until he exhausted himself. He was an excellent fencer, they said.

When we were stationed in Siedlce two old fellow officer soldiers died. They were Pan Jan Rubieszowski[44] and Pan Jan Wojnowski. It was *mirabile*[45] that these two men were so close to each other that if one was well off so was the other, and if things did not go well for one neither did they go well for the other. Both were from Mazowsze[46] and both old. Both were soldiers and both had Jan as their first name. Both were married, and in their banner register they were listed next to each other. Both were equally brave. At Chojnice,[47] when the Swedes attacked us during the night,[48] both were seriously cut and stabbed all over with rapiers. They were both believed dead and both left on the battlefield. Both recovered from their grave injuries at the same time. Later both thanked the King for the money which he had contributed for their funeral and burial, for when the King saw their severe injuries after the battle, he ordered six hundred zlotys to be paid to each, saying that it was meant for a funeral rather than for a recovery. When they were thanking the King for his money, he gave to each man one thousand zlotys more. They continued to fight in the war. They also were with us in Denmark, just as if they had made *a pactum*[49] with each other concerning their mutual fortunes and misfortunes. They both fell ill in Siedlce and died

[44]In the accounts of the *Sejm* for the time of the Swedish war there is a mention : "P. Rubieszowski who was seriously wounded by the Swedes, was given 120 zlotys for recompense." Czapliński, *Pam.*, p. 104, note 102.

[45]Strange.

[46]Mazovia, an historic region in the central part of Poland which in 1526 became part of the Polish Crown.

[47]A city near Gdańsk, Pomerania. The battle took place on January 1, 1657. Czapliński, *Pam.*, p. 105, note 106 and 107.

[48]It was on New Year's Day, January 1, 1657. Czapliński, *Pam.*, p. 105, note 107.

[49]Pact.

on the same day. When it was a question of rendering them the last service, Jan Domaszewski, our lieutenant, arranged for them such a splendid funeral ceremony in the church of Siedlce that even a senator could not have had a better one. The funeral was attended by the local nobility, by military men, and by many clergymen as well. *Ex mente*[50] of Lieutenant Domaszewski and other officers, both Pan Jan and I were asked to invite for the funeral dinner. I began my speech, though I did not have the time for an adequate preparation, for my billets were a hindrance to me as I was *provocatus*[51] to play cards, chess, or checkers constantly. But I took pains not to say any nonsense, for I knew that very many people would be present there. I also knew that Pan Gumowski, the cupbearer, who was an excellent *orator*,[52] would speak on behalf of the guests. Pan Wolborski, the lieutenant of Rokotnicki, the starost of Dobrzyń, was to express condolences in the name of the army. I began to speak then in the following manner :

I do not know which books of this Constitution to contradict, before which Parliaments to complain, among which of the world's mightiest monarchs to seek protection from the inevitable injustice of mortality of the human race and I do not find the way to do so. But I do see even the law cannot help when I read the motto of the Commonwealth of Genoa : *Parcam*[53] *falcitenentem minaci manu superbam*,[54] which bears the following inscription : '*Leges lego, reges rego, iudices iudico.*'[55] Who can oppose such power ? For ceremony's sake only an equal can complain about his grief to an equal, a man to a man, a mortal to another mortal. One has to stop and grow silent after complaining however, because *diutius accusare fata possumus, mutare non possumus.*[56] It is a painful separation, to

[50]According to the wishes.
[51]Summoned.
[52]Orator.
[53]Parka, one of the fates, fatal sisters.
[54]A proud Parka holding a scythe in her fierce hand.
[55]"I establish the laws, I rule rulers, I judge judges."
[56]Although we can complain about our fate for a long time we nevertheless cannot change it.

be sure, when innate kinships are broken as a result of death, when bonds of love fixed by marriage are broken; when father has to abandon son or when son has to abandon father; when a friend has to abandon a most intimate friend. What is to be done about it when even Aristotle has attributed such fate[57] to human nature: *Homo est imbecilitatis exemplum temporis spolium, fortunae lusus, inconstantiae imago, invidiae et calamitatis trutina.*[58] To be sure, it is a great misfortune to our company, to our mother,[59] to lose simultaneously two such prominent sons; a heavy and unbearable loss to the fatherland to lose through ruthless *fata simul et semel*[60] two such warriors who generously shed their own blood in all the battles in order to extinguish the *periculosissima incendia*;[61] a great *iactura*[62] to the entire company to lose such good, intimate, unbothersome knights, so desirable at one's side during every clash with the enemy and so capable of withstanding all sorts of attacks. But since the Holy Scripture itself gives such a proverb as this to the entire world: *'Metenda est seges, sic iubet necessitas.*[63] *Necessitatem ferre [portius], quam flere decet,*[64] keeping in mind the terms of the *pactum*[65] made *ante saecula*[66] between Heaven and Earth that we were promised *morte renasci*[67] up there and to be returned *ad communem societatem.*[68] *Veniet iterum, qui nos reponat in lucem, dies.*[69]

---

[57]The meaning of this sentence is not clear. Perhaps it means that since Aristotle attributed such fate to mankind. Czapliński, *Pam.*, p. 107.

[58]"A man is a model of helplessness, a prey of time, a frolic of fate, a picture of fickleness, a composite of equal parts of envy and adversity."

[59]Figuratively of the banner.

[60]Fate together and at the same time.

[61]Most dangerous fires.

[62]Bereavement.

[63]Grain should be reaped, so bids necessity.

[64]It is more fit to endure necessity than to mourn over it.

[65]Agreement.

[66]Years ago.

[67]To be revived.

[68]To the universal community.

[69]A day will come again which will lead us back to light.

In the ancient state of Athens the law was that a dead soldier could not be buried until he was properly praised before the largest possible assemblage of his people. *Laudabatur ab illo, qui erat militum doctissimus et rotundo ore.*[70] I admit that if the custom of those people was to be observed here *stricte*,[71] then an ordinary man like myself would be greatly embarrassed to have such a task given to him by my superior, for whoever does not praise someone's merits as adequately as he should downgrades himself. But since *ferreus Mars aureos calcat contemnitque fastus*,[72] my Minerva,[73] covered by a cloud of niter and lately intimidated by the storms raging over the Baltic Sea, has nevertheless decided to praise, though inadequately, *dignissima gesta*[74] of the companions in arms, the late lords Jan Rubieszowski and Jan Wojnowski. These two knights even in their youth—I could almost say already *a cunabulis*,[75] so young were they—did not engage in the teachings cherished by Pallas Athena[76] but eagerly applied themselves to the harsh and bloody school of Bellona.[77] They did not devote the least amount of time to those pastimes which *naturaliter*[78] lie in Apollo's sphere, but in the manner of old Polish warriors, like *generosae aquilae pulli*,[79] they have chosen for themselves the harsh Gradivus[80] as their leader. To him they have *plenarie*[81] pledged their entire life, to him they have dedicated themselves as eter-

[70][The law also stated that] he was [to be] praised by the one who was the most learned and the most eloquent in the army.
[71]Strictly.
[72]Iron Mars scorns and condemns triumphal splendors.
[73]Here meaning eloquence.
[74]The memorable deeds.
[75]In their cradle.
[76]Here meaning the humanities.
[77]Meaning here, they willingly joined the army, became soldiers.
[78]By their nature.
[79]The brood of a noble eagle.
[80]A Roman epithet of Mars.
[81]Fully.

nal sacrifices. For they had already fought in the battles at Merla, Cecora, and Żółte Wody[82] as comrades and later had been involved in the innumerable predicaments and misfortunes that were befalling the fatherland. If one were to speak in detail about each one of such occasions, namely how these two knights swam through such difficult deluges for the fatherland and endured such unfortunate periods for their state of knighthood as were the battles of Korsuń, Zbaraż, and Batoh,[83] an entire day would not suffice for recounting everything. About soldiers such as the two it came to be said at that time that if one of them were called a falcon and should come out of those battles alive, he could safely be termed a Phoenix.[84] All these experiences were not enough, however, for these men so greedy for fame, because *magnae mentes in ardua quaeque obstinatius.*[85] In those battles they were not deterred from exposing themselves to the fury of rag fate. They went on to yet other clashes at Beresteczko, Biała Cerkiew, Mohylów, and Żwaniec,[86] and being good sons of the

[82]Merla, a river in the Ukraine. The Merla expedition against the Tatars was under the command of Field Hetman Mikołaj Potocki, who reached it at the turn of 1645/46. Because of severe frosts the field hetman decided not to pursue the Tatar forces and turned back without accompolishing anything. The Polish Grand Hetman Stanisław Żółkiewski suffered a calamity at Cecora from the Turks in 1620; on May 16, 1648 the Polish forces were defeated by the Cossacks at Żółte Wody. Czapliński, *Pam.*, p. 109, note 166.

[83]The battle at Korsuń in which the Poles suffered a defeat took place on May 26, 1648; the siege of Zbaraż lasted from July 10 to August 21, 1649; on June 2, 1652 the Poles suffered a calamity from the Cossacks at Batoh, a village in the Ukraine.

[84]Greek name for the beautiful ancient mythological Egyptian bird which, after living 500 or 600 years, would burn itself. Then from its ashes it rose new and young. In Egypt the Phoenix was the symbol of the rising sun, but in Christian symbolism it represents resurrection and immortality.

[85]The greater the hardships the more persistent do great minds become.

[86]At Beresteczko the Poles conquered the Cossack-Tatar forces in a battle which lasted from the 28th to the 30th of June, 1651; the battle at Biała Cerkiew with the Cossacks took place on August 21, 1651; the siege of Mohylów took place in 1659, but Pasek might have been

fatherland they did not begrudge either health or life. The
following must have been written about soldiers such as
these : *'Viri proprium est maxime fortitudo ; eius munera
duo potissimum sunt : mortis dolorisque contemptus.'*[87]
And now what can I say of the Swedish, Muscovite, and
Hungarian wars which followed all the foregoing, and of
those battles—Ruszenice, Gródek, Wojnicz, Gołąb, Warka, Gniezno, Magierów, Czarny Ostrów[88] and many other
battles ? With what resolution and with what bravery they
presented themselves there, how *hilari fronte*[89] they suffered all the adversities *fortunae et iniurias coeli*[90] in these
as well as in the ensuing battles, it is not difficult to find
many witnesses. The same should be said of these worthy
knights that was said of the soldiers of Alexander the
Great : *'Ubi miles contemptor opum et divitiarum bella
gerit disciplina et paupertate magistra, fatigato humus cu-
bile, cibus quem occupat, satiat, tempora somni arctiora,
quam totius noctis.'*[91] The world has beheld in these noble

thinking of the siege of Monasterzyska in the spring of 1653 ; the siege
of the Polish forces by the Cossacks at Żwaniec lasted from October
until the 16th of December, 1653. Czapliński, *Pam.*, pp. 110–111, note
177.

[87]The greatest quality of a man is valor. His two greatest rewards are :
contempt for suffering and for death.

[88]At Ruszenice, a village near Opoczno, Czarniecki defeated the Swedish rear guard ; the battle at Gródek between the Poles and the
Cossacks took place on the 29th of September 1655 ; at Wojnicze the
Polish forces were defeated by the Swedes on the third of October, 1655 ;
at Gołąb the Swedes defeated Czarniecki on the eighth of February
1656 ; at Warka Czarniecki and Lubomirski defeated the Swedes on the
7th of April 1656 ; at Gniezno the Swedes defeated the Polish forces on
the 7th of May 1656 ; at Magierów the Poles defeated the armies of
Rakoczy on the eleventh of July 1657 ; at Czarny Ostrów, immediately
afterwards, the armies of Rakoczy were forced to capitulate Czapliński,
Pam., p. 111, note 179.

[89]With a clear brow.

[90]The adversities of fate and bad weather of the skies.

[91]When a soldier scorns affluence and wealth and does battle in discipline and poverty, the earth serves him as a bed when he is weary ; for
nourishment he uses whatever he has, and his sleep lasts shorter than
the night. (*Curtius, De rebus Alexandri Magni* III, 2, 15).

knights the above mentioned attributes coupled with
bounteous squandering of their health and life. Especially
at Chojnice, when they were *circumventi multitudine*,[92]
they suffered *plus quam satis*[93] at the hands of the enemy.
Rubieszowski was wounded forty times by bullets, sword
thrusts, and rapier cuts. He was counted among the dead
on the battlefield and when we were removing him in a
blanket[94] from the area, this noble knight was almost halfway immersed in his own blood. He was almost floating
in it. All of us assumed that after such a grave mutilation
he would thereafter loathe war ; but it was not so, because
virescit vulnere virtus[95] and resembles the ball which the
more it is bounced the more impetus it acquires. The
brave Cynaegirus[96] did not shrink from his undertaken
task ; Codrus[97] lost his life for the sake of his fatherland,
and thereby both gained the eternal fame and respect of the
entire world ; and this knight offers his entire mutilated
body as the last sacrifice for his fatherland. Thetis used to
bathe Achilles[98] in some refined liquids so that no weapons could harm him. I can safely argue that the bath
which preserved the life of our native Achilles, our be-

[92]Surrounded by a mob.

[93]More than their share.

[94]At that time the custom was to carry a wounded soldier off the
battlefield in a blanket tied between two horses. Czapliński, *Pam.*,
p. 112, note 189.

[95]Valor grows stronger by wounds.

[96]Brother of Aeschylus and Athenian soldier who perished in the battle
of Marathon when he seized one of the Persian triremes with his only
hand in order to prevent its setting off. After losing this hand also, he
seized the ship with his teeth, 490 B.C.

[97]In Greek legend son of Melanthas, Messenian king, and the last king
of Athens ; during the Dorian invasion of the Peloponnesus (11th cent.
B.C.) it was prophesied by the Delphic oracle that the side whose king
would die would win. Codrus went to the enemy camp in disguise,
provoked a quarrel, and was killed. In fear of the prophecy, the
Dorians retreated when they discovered what they had done. Codrus
thus saved his country by his own death.

[98]In Greek legend a son of Peleus and Thetis. His mother dipped him
in the river Styx in order to make him immune to all wounds.

loved soldier, and kept him from perishing in spite of his
heavy injuries was composed of a more meaningful sub-
stance than those refined liquids, namely Christ's blood
itself. I will not here go into the genealogy of these two
knights because I have already taken up lots of time even
though I have only reviewed their lives briefly. I have
touched on the subject of their fame only as slightly as one
would touch the rim of a huge bell with a tiny blade. *Sufficit* that these two are descended from fine nobility of the
voivodeship of Mazowsze. I cannot discuss their origin of
birth however even if I wanted to, because time and my
poor *facundia*[99] are inadequate. But since *magnorum non
est laus, sed admiratio*,[100] I shall only apply to these most
worthy members of the nobility the phrase which Sallust
once used to the Carthaginians :[101] '*De vestra quidem lau-
de melius est tacere, quam pauca loqui.*'[102] I shall add only
this, that whoever lives his life in such a way has his nobility doubled. *Illi vere sunt nobiles, qui non solum genere,
sed etiam virtute sunt nobiles.*[103] And now the worthy deceased, having set out on the road to eternal life, through
me do bid farewell to the entire army, which was their
school of life. They bid farewell to their mother company
and to their dear comrades with whom it has been equally
pleasant to live through times *adversa* and *prospera*.[104]
They bid farewell to all their relatives and to their remaining descendants, wishing that these behave *non alia
methodo*[105] and spend the days of their lives serving the

[99]Eloquence.
[100]Great men should not be praised but admired.
[101]Caius Sallustius Crispus, Roman historian (86 B.C.—34 B.C.). He
wrote ("*Catilina*" or "*Bellum Catilinae*" about the conspiracy of Cati-
line, "*Jugurtha*" or "*Bellum Jugurthinum*," about the war with Jugurtha, and "*Historiae*" in five books.
[102]It is better to be silent about one's fame than to say little. (Not a
correct citation : Caius Sallustius Crispus, *Bellum Jugurthinum*, XIX.)
[103]Those are truly nobleman who not only through origin but also
through virtue are noble.
[104]Foul and fair.
[105]The same way, not in a different way.

fatherland. In bidding farewell to all of you honorable gentlemen assembled here, they thank you very much that you have condescended as Christians to accord them a last farewell and a *salve*[106] to new eternity. Once upon a time someone dared say about himself: '*Non totus moriar, multaque pars mei vitabit Libitinam.*'[107] This is what our *commilitones*[108] have also deserved in this world and therefore they make their *supplices preces*[109] that their *merita*[110] will not languish in the *dulci recordatione*[111] of you honorable gentlemen for *mens et gloria non queunt humari.*[112] And after all the efforts of you honorable gentlemen and your piously rendered kindness to the deceased, I humbly beg that you honorable gentlemen, in the name of his Lordship the Lieutenant and the entire company, will not refuse your presence *in domu luctus.*'[113]

When I finished, Gumowski, the cupbearer, began to speak very *facunde*[114] and *erudite*,[115] but his line of thought was confused. This became apparent immediately to the well-versed ones, *praecipue*[116] the clergy. Later he tried to justify himself cleverly by complaining that I had used several citations which he intended to use in his speech, but which he had to leave out because I had used them before. He also added that it is very difficult for an architect when someone takes away from him the already trimmed and planed wood which was intended for putting the building together. Everyone understood the analogy, and indeed it often happens that one speaker takes over the subject matter from another.

[106]Welcome.
[107]Not all of me shall die, and much of my entity will escape Libitina. (Libitina was the Ancient Italian goddess of gardens and vineyards; also known as goddess of death and burials.)
[108]Companions at arms.
[109]Humble requests.
[110]Merits.
[111]Sweet memory.
[112]The soul and the glory do not descend into the grave.
[113]In the house of mourning.
[114]Eloquently.
[115]Learnedly.
[116]Especially.

Wolborski, a lieutenant of the starost of Dobrzyń,[117] gave the eulogy on behalf of the army. Thus the burial of the two *Arcades*[118] took place. Wąsowicz, a relative, came in order to pick up the money which was due to Pan Rubieszowski. The money and other compensations belonging to Pan Wojnowski were sent to his wife.

Later official orders came to depart and to gather at Kozierady, because we had had news that the Muscovites were assembling. We made camp at Kozierady three Sundays before Pentecost.[119] It was a splendid and good army but, as the Lutherans say, *pusillus grex*,[120] because only six thousand men were in Pan Czarniecki's division.

It was wondrous that on the very day when a bower of birch brushwood was raised for me in front of my tent, a yellow bunting began to build a nest for herself in the bower hedge, right at the tent entrance. Fearlessly and in the presence of many people she carried materials for the nest, and after she had built it, she sat on her eggs and hatched them. In that bower there stood a pine table on crossed supports. At this table we ate, drank, played cards, engaged in gunplay, and shouted, but the bird remained sitting and was not afraid of anything, even though it was right above the corner of the table. When she wanted to eat, she picked oats right in front of the steed. She hatched her offspring, nurtured them, and flew away with them. Everyone thought that this was a sign of some extremely good luck. There was luck, but only for the bird, who had, quietly hatched her offspring, and not for me, because so many worries had befallen me that I barely managed to overcome them, and only with a large decrease in my fortune. These

[117]Jakub Rokitnicki.

[118]Here the word is an allusion to the *Eclogues* of the Roman poet Virgil, Publius Vergilius Maro (VII, 4), to the equality and the common fate of the two men.

[119]This was on April 25, since Pentecost fell on the 16th of May at that time. Czubek, *Pam.*, p. 117, note 1. Czarniecki was in Międzyrzecz in April and in the beginning of May in Kozierady. Czapliński, *Pam.*, p. 116, note 228.

[120]A very small flock. According to the teachings of Luther or Calvin only a small flock of men will get to Heaven.

troubles began at Kozierady and did not leave me *ad decur-sum anni.*[121]

Some officers from my banner,[122] namely the Nuczyński brothers, were drinking one day at their cousin's, Pan Mar-cyjan Jasiński, a companion of ours who had also invited me to this banquet. Oh, I wish it had not taken place! After we had drunk a lot, Nuczyński began to provoke me more and more. Even though I was as drunk as they were, I said to Jasiński: "Pan Marcyjan, you should not have invited me here, since they provoke me, and pour mead all over me." I left the hut to avoid trouble but I said the following: "Whoever has any grudge against me can tell me so tomorrow and not today while he is drunk." When I was already half way home, Nu-czyński overtook me and shouted: "Fight me!" I answered him: "You would not find me idle in this respect, Pan brother, but there are two *impedimenta*:[123] first of all, we are in camp, and secondly, because I went to a social gathering at a compan-ion's place and not to a fight, I do not have a sword on me. But if things cannot be otherwise let the duel be tomorrow out-side the camp, not inside it." I then went toward my hut while his retainer tried to stop and detain him. He hit the youth in the face with his fist, tore himself away, and followed me.

I had to come out with my sword. Every time he slashed at me he would say: "You will perish." And I would say: "God will decide that." At the second or third exchange of blows, I struck his fingers and said: "You see, you got what you were looking for." I thought that he would be satisfied with that. But he, being drunk, either did not feel the blow or just wanted to avenge himself. In any case he charged at me again, slashing at me with his sword once or twice while blood was splashing from his face. I cut him across the pulse and he fell over.

Meanwhile the other banqueters, who thought that he had

---

[121]Until the end of the year.
[122]Company under Czarniecki's command.
[123]Pan brother was the title used when addressing a fellow gentryman. According to the military regulations, duels in a camp were strictly for-bidden. Czapliński, *Pam.*, p. 117, note 240. Obstacles.

merely gone out for a walk, were notified about the incident.
A younger brother came running and began to strike at me
vigorously and briskly. God watched over the innocent one, however. We clashed with each other and soon after his hand and
sword fell to the ground. The companions came running after
it was all over. Then Jasiński, the host of the banquet, came
and said to me : "Oh, you scoundrel, you wounded my brothers ! Come now with me !" I answered : "They got what they
were looking for !" He began to call for his sword since he did
not have one on him, as he pulled me by the hand. His companions tried to plead with him : "You were the host. You
should have tried to reconcile them. Don't do that !" But he
did not let himself be persuaded in any way and kept pulling
me. Meanwhile a retainer brought him a sword. I was plain
scared of Jasiński because a few weeks ago he had mutilated
our companion Paweł Kossowski before the eyes of the entire
banner.

So I freed my hand from his, stepped away from his side
and said : "What have I done to you ? Let me alone !" His
companions halted him, but when he pushed Drozdowski aside
they let go of him. "Go on until you get killed !" There was a
small river over which we had to cross by a narrow plank
bridge. "We shall cross over yonder as far as the forest ; whoever kills the other cannot return to camp." He then pushed me
onto the plank bridge and said : "You go first !" I had hardly
stepped onto the planks when he struck me on the head from
behind. Fortunately I wore a cap of the best Venetian velvet.
God so favored me that the blow did not pierce through. Only
in one spot did the velvet give way a little. I had a wale from
the blow, as if from a whip. I lost my balance and I fell from
the bridge into the water. I got quickly away from that spot
because I was afraid that he would not stop at that, but give
me another blow. I crossed over to the other bank and said :
"Oh God, You see my innocence." I had hardly stepped out
of the water when he was already across the plank bridge. I
said to him : "So you strike stealthily, you pagan !" He came
up to me. "Soon I will bite you even more," he said. From the
camps people came to watch because all the banners were sta-

tioned along the river. He struck at me with such force that my sword shook in my hand but I sustained this first blow. We cut at each other about ten times and nobody was hurt. I said : "Enough of this, Pan Marcyjan." He said : "Oh, you scoundrel, you did not do anything to me yet and you say that's enough." God so willed that immediately after he said this I slashed him across the cheek with the very tip of my sword and jumped away from him. Now he attacked me even harder. I then gave him such a blow on the head that he fell heavily to the ground. I took my sword in both hands then and began to strike him with the flat side. Only now did men come running from our as well as from other banners. "Stop! Don't kill him!" they shouted. I struck him with the flat of my sword some fifty times before they could arrive because of his baseness of having hit me in the head from behind.

On that day such a tense atmosphere prevailed that about fifteen duels were fought in the various banners. God obviously protected me on that day, however, since He guarded me from mishap in the three duels. This was not the result of any kind of bravery on my part, but only because God took my innocence into consideration. I remember many such similar instances since: "Whoever gives cause for a duel is always the loser." I warn and caution the one who will inherit this manuscript from me to learn a lesson from this example of mine as well as from many other similar examples. Even if he were the most experienced fencer he should not esteem lightly even the most wretched man. He should not have so much confidence in his physical strength and bravery as to challenge another man and go to a duel with a haughty heart. He should know that almost anyone could do him in then. But, if he fights humbly to defend his honor and appeal to God for assistance, he will win every time. I have acquired this practical knowledge from my own experience and from that of many others: whenever I provoked someone to a duel I was always beaten, whenever I was challenged, I was always victorious.

As an act of reconciliation I paid them twelve hundred zlotys for their pains and wounds, especially in order to cover the cost of the physician. It is after all *practicatum axioma*:[124] "The defeated one cries." Jasiński got nothing for his wounded cheek, and received a severe sentence: "As punishment you must give six hundred zlotys to the Bernardine Monastery in Brześć and, dressed in full armor, you must stand holding your sword up high for the duration of three Holy Day masses, because as the host you allowed your guests to fight each other, you did not try to reconcile them, and you yourself challenged him to a duel."

Later, because we received news that the Muscovites had

[124]An established principle.

managed to fight their way nearer us, Skrzetuski[125] was sent on patrol with a group of men that included two officers out of every banner. On the way Skrzetuski's patrol encountered the large and well equipped Muscovite banner under Słoński and captured it. Afterwards, Skrzetuski and his men turned to go back to their own camp, and being afraid of enemy pursuit, rode the whole night through. Only at daybreak did they stop on the outskirts of a village. The horses were now allowed to graze in the surrounding meadows thereabouts while the weary officers went off eagerly to sleep. All the while, a strong vigil was kept over the captured Muscovites. There was situated near by, close to the river, a manorial house, to which a number of retainers rode in hope of finding nourishment. They used force in order to get whatever they wanted and shooting and shouting from their direction started. The patrol was alarmed by these news and assumed that the Muscovites were near the horses. Later they learned what had really happened.

Łukasz Wolski,[126] a native of Rawa[127] and an officer of the Royal Sewer,[128] was aroused from his sleep by this noise. He dashed to mount his horse and, astride it, jumped straight into the river, and swam across. Because he was drowsy and a coward at heart—for many a man who misjudges his character and guts enlists in the army when he should actually raise hens at home and chase kites[129] away from his chickens—he did not look around to see what had really happened but, once on the other side the river, galloped into the forest and arrived back in camp two days ahead of the rest of the whole patrol.

[125]Mikołaj Skrzetuski, a lieutenant in the service of Adam Uriel Czarnkowski, the starost of Osiek. In 1649 Skrzetuski succeeded in crossing the besieged Zbaraż with letters for the Polish King. He marched toward the Muscovite armies about the middle of May. Czapliński, *Pam.*, p. 120, note 261.

[126]Son of the Lord High Steward of Rawa. J. Czubek, *Pam.*, p. 123, note 2. Also an officer in the banner of Wacław Leszczyński. Czapliński, *Pam.*, p. 121, note 265.

[127]A city not far from Łódź in the central part of Poland.

[128]A household officer of rank, in charge of serving the dishes at the table.

[129]Birds of prey.

In the camp his arrival created a great state of alarm. We rapidly assembled at the Voivode's quarters when Wolski came to give a report. The Voivode asked him : 'What happened ?" Wolski related, to our great dismay, that Skrzetuski's patrol had captured about three hundred Muscovites, that it had seized a fully equipped banner, and had acquired much booty, but "later the patrol was pursued by other Muscovites, found asleep, surrounded, and wiped out to the very last man. Those who had been in charge of grazing the horses along the river banks all drowned." The Voivode asked : "What about Skrzetuski : was he taken alive ?" Wolski related that with his own eyes he saw a Muscovite shoot Skrzetuski and stab him. He added : "I can give account of all this for after I had swum across the river, I stood for a long time on the other side and watched. I saw that they did not let anyone escape alive."

I could not restrain myself and said : "How come they did not kill you ?" The Voivode remarked angrily to me : "Leave him alone." But he himself asked Wolski : "How did you manage to escape ?" He replied : "Because I did not sleep. I was holding my horse by the reins. When the Muscovites arrived I immediately plunged into the water. They shot at me several times but God spared me all the same." The Voivode asked : "How numerous could the enemy patrol have been ?" He said : "It was not a patrol, Your Honor, but Khovansky's[130] entire military might. I saw practically the whole army. It covered the field like a cloud, and still other regiments could be seen beyond the mountain. I also came upon an escaped nobleman who maintained as well that Khovansky was approaching with his entire army." The Voivode became alarmed. He did not show it however and said : "God is on our side ! There is nothing to worry about, sir. Let us sound the trumpets for the herds to be brought back right away." The trumpets were sounded and there was great commotion in the camp for the herds of almost every banner were being pastured in a different spot, several leagues away from camp. The spirits of everyone fell. We thought : "Our first misfortune !" They all

[130]Ivan Andreevich Khovansky, Russian commander-in-chief.

questioned Wolski about their companions. He told them how each had met his death. All around there was fear, grief, and bewilderment.

We went to our banners in order to make necessary arrangements. Meanwhile others were already rushing in full haste—on foot and on horseback—in the direction of the herds. When I arrived at my tent, my retainer was just saddling my steed. I asked: "Why are you doing that?" He answered: "I mean to fetch the horses." I struck him with a mace and said: "You pagan! My health is more important than all the horses! Aren't there already three retainers taking care of them? Other men will see to their own horses. They will bring my herd too: I keep this horse close by in case of some great emergency and you want to take it away from me. What would I do if something were to happen?"

I had things arranged at my place and went back to the Voivode's quarters. Walking past a bazaar I saw Wolski weighing captured silver spoons at an Armenian's stand. I said to him: "Pan Łukasz, didn't our Jaworski manage to escape, for he had a swift horse and was always a cautious man?" Wolski said: "Your Lordship will never see Jaworski again. That is as unlikely as being able to see your own ear!" I said: "For God's sake, Pan Łukasz! Perhaps you made a mistake or were separated from the patrol somehow. I know that you have always had a wild imagination!" He again began to reassert that what he had said was true. He angrily repeated the story. I let the matter be and went toward the Voivode's tent. Father Piekarski said to me: "Stop! Things are bad for us, Pan brother." I said: "Keep in mind, Pan brother, that not even half of Wolski's report is true. I know his character. He improvises gladly."

Suddenly the Voivode came out of his tent. He was twisting his beard, which was a sign of anger or worry. He went up to Father Piekarski and said: "What were you talking about?" The priest repeated my words. The Voivode said to me: "Does he really possess this *vitium*?"[181] I said that such was not only

[181]Vice.

his nature but that of his father, the tax-collector of Rawa, as well. Already in school we used to call him "General *nugator*."[132] The Voivode struck his velvet outfit with his fingers and said : "I am also of that opinion, for if a patrol really did overtake them, it is unlikely that they were completely surrounded and that all perished. It also does not seem probable that it was the entire Muscovite military might, for I have news that they were getting ready to assault Lachowice[133] tomorrow with their remaining force ! They had ladders and other appliances delivered to them, for they had lost all of them in the first assaults !" The Voivode then gave orders to summon Wolski and one companion said to Wolski : "Pan brother, haven't you made a mistake ? It's capital offense to alarm the army." But he replied : "I stake my life that it will not turn out otherwise."

Thus *inter spem et metum*[134] the entire army was in great disarray since early morning. The herds which were close by were brought back. Those whose herds were still to come were waiting impatiently for them. Towards evening the banners were ordered to go on patrol. The sun was just setting when we saw someone coming from the other side. I said : "Well, we shall have news !" We did not recognize him. He rode on a captured Tatar horse and wore a Muscovite calpac[135] mounted with pearls. He rode through the maidan,[136] past the flags, and shouted : "*Munsztułuk ! Munsztułuk !*"[137] We rushed toward him and asked whether it was good or bad. He said something and rode past Polanowski. We ran after him as fast as we could but he gave the report only to the Voivode himself : "Tomorrow, God willing, our commander together with a troop, larger than the one with which he set out, will pay respects to Your Honor. He will throw the enemy flag at Your Honor's feet. The only harm we suffered in this combat was the loss of an

[132]Liar.

[133]A little town between Słonim and Nieśwież, 18 km from Baranowicze.

[134]Between hope and anxiety.

[135]Pointed fur cap.

[136]An open area near a town often used as a market place.

[137]News, a word of Tatar origin, usually meaning good news.

officer under the command of the Royal Sewer, a great knight."
The Voivode said : "Let the name of God be praised. You
have not lost this officer yet. You shall lose him tomorrow.
Fetch that bastard." The Royal Sewer stood there. His Lieutenant Skoraszewski looked as if someone had slapped him
in the face. Pan Wolski was handcuffed. The occasion was a
merry and a pleasant one *ex ratione duplici*,[138] first of all since
God had let this first combat end so successfully and secondly
because we saw again, healthy before our eyes, those whose
death we had lamented ; but above all because a certain feeling
of hope already delighted us. People wanted to cut Pan Wolski's
neck by all means. Not even his fellowmen from Rawa went
to see him. We were ashamed for him. He sent for us begging
for intercession. No one wanted to intervene. Only Father Piekarski and Lieutenant Skoraszewski saved his life. He was not
tried, but ordered to leave the army at once. He was never to
reveal that he had served in Czarniecki's division at any
time.[139]

Our patrol returned safely a day after the companion's
arrival. It triumphantly entered the camp carrying the unfolded
enemy flag. It led almost as many shackled prisoners along as
it numbered itself. When the prisoners were presented, a crowd
of military men assembled at the commander's. I was also
there. After that ceremony I stood by the tent with Rafał Jarzyna, a native of Rawa. The Voivode addressed us : "I assumed that all men from Rawa were brave. Now I see that
there are also fools among them." I answered : "One finds the
like only in the Wolski family." Two companions by the name
of Wolski stood by, both brave men : Paweł, who later became
the starost of Lityń, and another one, who was nicknamed "the
molded one". The Wolski from the royal banner was reaching
for his weapons when the Voivode said : "He speaks of the
Wolskis from Mazovia and you are from Ruthenia !"[140] There

---

[138]For a twofold reason.
[139]Wolski is no longer listed in the banner register of 1661. Other
writers have also reported this incident. Czapliński, *Pam.*, p. 125, note
283.
[140]Part of Poland at the time.

are also those from Rome about whom Ovid has written: "*Saevit atrox Volscus.*"[141] The Wolskis from Ruthenia and from Italy are brave chaps because they are called "*atroces.*" But those from Rawa are fools. So do not intercede for them. Yet from now on I shall consider Pan Pasek a good judge of human nature, since he detected the entire fabrication of Wolski's report." The discussion ended with jesting. A number of prisoners were sent to the King.

As soon as we received news from the Lithuanian Hetman Sapieha[142] that also the Lithuanian army had prepared itself for combat as well as it could, we started out at once and marched on the road to Mścibów.[143] Also Khovansky, the Muscovite hetman, moved toward us with his entire military might, which numbered forty thousand men. He left only a small number of men behind in Lachowice[144] to guard the camp and to continue attacking the fortress which they had been assaulting for a long time, giving it no *respirium.*[145] He had promised himself to take the fortress immediately upon his return from the expedition after our debacle. He set out just like a wolf against a flock of sheep, for he had already trained himself in battle against the Lithuanians and always went toward them with a feeling of a sure victory. He sent Nashtchokin, the second hetman, with five thousand choice troops a few leagues ahead in order to greet us. On the eve of Peter and Paul they encountered our advance guard and since it was not so strong as the Muscovite patrol, it sent word to our main body that the enemy was in sight. Suddenly the Muscovites attacked them with impetus. Before the banners and the volunteers arrived, our advance guard found itself severely oppressed. Nevertheless it resisted the Muscovites vigorously. There were some casual-

[141]Wolscus the Fierce is raging ; not Ovid, but Virgil in the *Aeneid*, IX, 420.

[142]Jan Paweł Sapieha, Grand Hetman of Lithuania.

[143]A town on the road between Białystok and Wołkowysk, seventeen km west of Wołkowysk.

[144]A town in the voivodeship of Nowogródek between Słonim and Nieśwież. At that time it was the strongest fortress in Lithuania. It was the property of the Sapieha family. Czubek, *Pam.*, p. 126, note 3.

[145]Respite.

ties on both sides. When we arrived, half of the Muscovites turned toward us, the others were finishing the battle with our advance guard. They assaulted us with great might. They wanted to throw us into confusion with their first attack. We withstood them however, even though over a dozen men fell off their horses to the ground. When the Muscovites saw that we resisted them strongly everywhere, their second assault was no longer such a daring one. Suddenly out of the thicket came the banner of Tuczyński and Antonowicz's banner of two hundred Tatars.[146] They broke into a trot as soon as they reached free terrain. The Muscovites fell into confusion right away. We also pushed forward and attacked them. We broke through them immediately and took to swords. There was not much shooting now and we just kept slashing away. When the rest of the Muscovites began to run away, we pursued them. We kept catching up with them, and killing them. By sunset the main army arrived and made camp on the battlefield. We held our horses by the reins the whole night through, since two regiments were placed as camp guard. The Lithuanians also camped beside us. There were nine thousand of them under Paweł Sapieha, their Grand Hetman, while Gosiewski,[147] their treasurer and Field Hetman at the time, was in Moscow as a prisoner of Khovansky himself.[148] Khovansky expected to have the same luck with us. When he sent Nashtchokin ahead into combat, he gave him the following order: "Try to capture Czarniecki and Połubiński[149] alive so that Gosiewski will have company."

[146]Michał Antonowicz. Czapliński, *Pam.*, p. 127, note 293. Light cavalry armed with swords, bows, or guns, and made up of Tatars who had settled in Lithuanian Poland.
[147]Wincenty Gosiewski, who was taken into Muscovite captivity in 1658, from where he returned to Poland in 1662. He was executed for participating in a plot in November 1662. Czapliński, *Pam.*, p. 128, note 295.
[148]He was not taken prisoner by Khovansky but by Dolgoruky. Czapliński, *Pam.*, p. 128, note 296.
[149]Aleksander Hilary Połubiński was the marshal of the Grand Duchy of Lithuania. He distinguished himself in the war with Sweden; died in 1679. Czubek, *Pam.*, p. 128, note 298.

Against forty thousand Muscovites[150] there were only fifteen thousand of our men, including the Lithuanian army. This was a small number, but hope comforted us and also the fact that all the dead fell with their heads facing the Muscovites. Warriors always consider it a sign of victory when the dead fall with their heads toward the enemy. We had enough food during that night because we ordered our wagons and knapsacks filled with biscuits. We also had brandy in the ammunition boxes, which were in use at that time. After we had one sip of brandy and then another, it went to our heads a little and we began to feel drowsy. Many a man lay down on the grass and slept. We had with us a certain Kaczewski from Radom,[151] a great prankster. He said: "Pan Jan, why should we put our fists under our heads? Let us use this Muscovite for a pillow!" Near by lay a fat Muscovite, who had been shot. I replied: "All right! I'll keep you company! He put his head on one side, I on the other. We fell asleep like that with the horses' reins wound around our hands. We slept for about three hours, but toward daybreak the Muscovite groaned. Both of us jumped to our feet. Apparently he still had some life left in him. As soon as it had dawned muted orders to mount were sounded by trumpet mouthpieces. The army set out in order to begin the encounter early, with the help of God. On our way there everyone said prayers in his own way, singing and reciting the Little Office of our Lady.[152] Chaplains on horseback listened to confession. Everyone received the last sacraments in order to be thoroughly prepared for death.

When the army arrived at a point about half a league from Połonka,[153] it arrayed itself for battle.[154] Czarniecki de-

---

[150]According to Czapliński this number is an exaggeration. According to the relations of the Muscovite prisoners Khovansky had 24,000 men. The present day historians estimate the Russian forces at 11,000 and the Polish-Lithuanian ones at 8000. Czapliński, *Pam.*, p. 128, note 298.

[151]A city in central Poland.

[152]A popular way of praying among the Polish nobility at that time. Czapliński, *Pam.*, p. 129, note 302.

[153]A town halfway between Słonim and Baranowicze.

[154]The battle took place on June 28, 1960. Czapliński, *Pam.*, p. 129, note 304.

ployed his army, and Sapieha did likewise. The right flank was
entrusted to Woyniłowicz[155] with the royal regiment; the left
flank with artillery and infantry to Połubiński. We marched in
battle line and did not stop until *in prospectu*[156] of the enemy.
Oour leaders wanted the enemy to cross the river to our bank,
but since we could not entice them to do so we were ordered
to advance. Later about six thousand Muscovite infantrymen
did come across, but when three of our regiments attacked
them and poured fire on them from our side, they pushed the
Muscovites back across the river. The Muscovites fired on us
with cannon from their side and hit our men. An officer who
stood next to me had his horse shot in the head by a ball. The
ball pierced through the horse's tail. The companion flew from
his saddle more than three arm lengths into the air, but he
was unharmed.

At the points where the left flank and the *corpus*[157] were
advancing, the crossing over was difficult. By our right flank
there was a swamp of about seven furlongs or more, where in
places a horse would be immersed up to the saddle straps, in
other places it remained on the surface, though the intertwined
weeds yielded like eiderdown. Almost half of us went on foot
and pulled our horses behind. We were just getting out of the
mud when the left flank was already fighting a violent battle.
There was a farm, enclosed by a palisade, *directe*[158] opposite
our crossing. The Muscovites assumed that our men would try
their luck there. They had garrisoned it with four small cannon
and a few hundred infantrymen. But they did not come out into
the open until we were getting out of the swamp onto firm
ground. Only then did our infantry come out. They began to
shoot and fire on us with cannon. The balls fell like hail. Many
of our men fell dead; others were wounded. We attacked them
with full force, for we knew that almost all of us would perish
if we were to turn back. We went blindly into the fire. We

[155]Gabriel Woyniłowicz, a lieutenant of an armored banner. Other
sources give Wojniłowicz as the correct spelling of the name.
[156]In view.
[157]Here the center arrays.
[158]Directly.

became mixed with the enemy like grain with chaff, for there was no other way out.

A terrible massacre resulted among the commingling people. The most frightfully used weapons were the halberds. Still no more than a quarter of an hour had elapsed when we killed them to the last man. Not one managed to escape since it was in the open field. We were later told that they were one hundred in number. Our side also suffered casualties in both wounded and dead. I was astride a bay horse when it was hit by a shot in the chest and afterwards struck over the head and the knee with a halberd. I could still have ridden it had it not been for the knee injury. In the army I always had bad luck with horses. I don't remember ever having sold one after having bought it at a high price, for every single one ended up wounded, dead of natural causes, or killed. I would have been a soldier to this day had it not been for this lack of good fortune which forced me to leave the army because my father could no longer afford to buy horses for me and because I began to loathe my ill luck which made me cry many a time. I then changed over to my gray horse and told my retainer who had been riding it before to go back across the ford on foot. Soon after he overtook me on a much better horse which he had just captured.

We were finishing off the Muscovite infantry when Trubetzkoy, sent to their rescue, came galloping with ten banners of *duma boyars*[159] and three thousand regular cavalrymen. Now we stood in battle array with our backs to the infantry and faced the new enemy. They attacked us as if they wanted to devour us. We withstood them because we had to. When we noticed that they were pushing us toward the swamp, we closed ranks with them violently. Their mercenary cavalry fired at us heavily. Our men shot infrequently for we had used up all our ammunition on the infantry by now, and there was no time to reload. I say therefore that even though, at the outset of a battle, the most important weapon with which one goes against the enemy seems to be the gun, since there is no time to reload

[159]Members of the Muscovite Parliament, i.e., senators.

once the armies have already attacked each other, the sword is really the most essential. Now both sides were slashing at each other with swords at this opportune time. We attacked them so violently that they had no time to reload their guns. Once more we found that things were not going so badly for us even though they had fired at us. We exerted ourselves mightily, fighting each other like wrestlers, who would each force the other to bend.

Trubetzkoy bustled about like a top on a gray speckled Kalmuck horse. A multitude of dead bodies kept falling. Some six of the Muscovite flags already lay on the ground. An officer of the starost of Dobrzyń struck Trubetzkoy on the head so hard that his calpac fell off. Two Muscovites grabbed him under the arms right away and led him away. The Muscovite gentlemen began to run back to their initial positions and we followed them and kept slashing at them with our swords. We pushed them right up to the main body of their army; about half of them fell on the battlefield.

Everything was in a state of great commotion. The main body of the army was now fighting. Nor were the Lithuanians on the left flank idle; but the enemy did not turn his best forces as much at them as at us, for he esteemed them lightly. Some newly arrived regiments turned around and went back. Suddenly, when the Voivode saw our banners in back of the enemy lines, he sent word to Sapieha: 'For God's sake! Attack the Muscovites with all force and break them up. Otherwise we shall lose our royal regiment."

The Muscovites began to fall into confusion. They wriggled just like someone who feels too uncomfortable to remain sitting at the table. Their fear was already apparent. Those Muscovites who were turned at us no longer fought with eagerness. They would jump towards us, and then turn away. Suddenly the main body of our army dashed mightily at them. Our hussar banners rushed ahead. We fought from behind. Now we found some time to reload our guns. Suddenly the Muscovites began to run away.[160] Their entire army was head-

---

[160]The description of this battle agrees with that described by Łoś. Czapliński, *Pam.*, p. 132, note 322.

ing in our direction. Now we could strike whomever we chose for all of them looked nice.

A yellow bearded patriarch, a big man, who carried a gilded sword on a sling, attacked me. I jumped in front of him. He aimed his pistol at me. Assuming that it was unloaded and used as a mere threat, I boldly slashed at him. He fired. I struck him in the shoulder at the same time. Realizing that his shot had missed me, I dashed after him. I caught up with him and jumped in front of him, for even though he was on a good horse he somehow rode sluggishly. Either he was wounded or somewhat languid. I cut him across the forehead. He exclaimed: "Pozhaluy !"[161] He handed me his sword and fell off his horse. I had just taken his sword when a young lad in a multi-colored satin *żupan* who carried an ammunition pouch on a silver chainlet tried to escape on a pale Tatar horse. I rushed toward this lad and blocked his way. He was very young and comely and held a gem-studded cross in his hand. He cried: "*Pozhaluy ! dlya Christa Spassa, dlya Peretchistoy Bogaroditze, dlya Mikuly Tschudotvortze !*"[162] I felt sorry for him, but seeing that big crowds of Muscovites were rushing toward me, I feared that they would capture me. I did not want to waste time around him but I was sorry to kill him on account of his ardent prayer. I only took the cross from his hand and struck him across the back with the flat of my sword shouting: "*Utykay do matyery, dytchy synu !*"[163] The lad raised his arms and dashed away. He was out of my sight in an instant. It was difficult to take anyone alive *in illo fervore*[164] when their entire army was rushing directly at us in their attempt to escape. Should one hold onto the prisoner, defend himself with his sword, or load his pistol ? The cross which I had taken from the lad was beautiful. Its setting was worth about twenty ducats and I had tarried with that squirt of a youth for less than the

[161]Have mercy ! (Russ.)
[162]Have mercy for the sake of Christ the Savior, for the sake of the Immaculate Mother of Good, for the sake of Nicholas the Miracle-Worker !" (Russ.)
[163]Run away to your mother, you son of the devil !
[164]During this critical moment.

duration of the Lord's Prayer. Now I turned my attention to the bearded Muscovite again. He had already been stripped naked by another companion who was in the process of also taking his horse. I said to him : "I knocked the enemy off the horse and you are taking it ? Give it back or I shall use on you the cartridge which I had prepared for the enemy." The Walachian[165] did not argue much with me because he had seen that Muscovite shooting at me and had seen me knock him off his horse. He handed the beautiful horse over to me. It was not a Muscovite horse but one of those tall, chestnut-bay Ruthenian horses. I did not want to abandon it, but since my retainer was nearby I had no one to hand it over to. However, as soon as I came across another retainer whom I knew, I said : "Take this horse from me. If you manage to take it away from here safely, I shall give you ten thalers, or if you come across one of my retainers give it to him !" He took it and I dashed in the direction where the Muscovites were fiercely clashing with our men.

Now we were slaughtering the Muscovites like sheep. If I had had at least one retainer with me at the time, I could have picked out the most beautiful steeds for myself because we were fighting choice, well-dressed cavalry officers. But unfortunately retainers always busy themselves the most around their master when he drinks, not when he fights, and it is not befitting an officer to lead a captured horse by the reins. When there is no one to turn such a horse over to, it is better to give it up if one loves prestige. Seeing however that other companions were leading off the horses that they had captured as soon as the massacre was over, I took a beautiful black striped Walachian horse. This horse was slightly wounded around the ear, but this did not harm it in any way. Hardly had we come out of the mob when a retainer of mine came running. I gave the horse to him and ordered him to stand by. That fool had only swiped saddle-blankets for his nag and whatever else he could get hold of. Had he been with me he could have swiped satins, velvets, harnesses, and good horses.

[165]A companion from the Walachian banner. Czapliński, *Pam.*, p. 134, note 334.

I noticed my squadron flag in a distance. I rode toward it. When I reached it not even six men were there. Other flags were also very poorly attended. All our men had dispersed as fast as they could : they were slashing, killing, and pursuing the enemy. I said to our standard-bearer : "God took my bay horse away from me but He gave me another one, a very beautiful one in its place. I gave it to a stranger however. I don't know whether I shall get it back." The standard-bearer asked : "And who does that fair one you are holding belong to ?" I replied that this one was also mine.

The left and central Muscovite flanks had already been depleted considerably when their right flank, the one which was fighting with our left one, began to run away. There was great commotion once again. You pursued one and another stood with a sword right over your neck. You finished off one and another came running at you like a frightened hare. You had to move your head as if it were mounted on screws in order to see in front and back of yourself at the same time. If you carelessly concentrated on one enemy soldier, then the other escaping Muscovites could attack you from behind as they dashed by. A husky Muscovite standard-bearer was escaping with his flag. I stepped in front of him and aimed the pistol. He pleaded : "*Pozhaluy*!" He offered me his flag. I proceeded to lead him away. He prayed fervently. He folded his hands. I thought : "I shall manage to take this one alive." But suddenly a large crowd of about four hundred Muscovites dashed straight for me. He began to hold back even though I had disarmed him. Realizing that I would not manage to take him alive and that I myself might perish, I struck him with the point of my sword. He fell and I jumped out of the way with his flag. Meanwhile the Lithuanians were galloping to encounter this group while other companions were waiting in front of them.

I flung that beautiful flag aside and dashed toward them, for I would regret if I did not fight when the opportunity was there. While we were finishing off one banner, a second one, of the same size or even bigger, would appear. We fought them and yet another would follow. *Sufficit*[166] that our hands were feeling numb, for all the Muscovites who tried to escape could do so only by passing by our banner which was directly in back of their lines.

The massacre stretched out over three leagues. Some of us began to retreat while others still pursued the enemy. I regretted not being able to take anyone alive, but I did rejoice on account of my horses, especially the bay one which was very beautiful, although of questionable use to me. Suddenly over a dozen Muscovites who had been concealed in a small forest grove came out into the open. We took after them as if they were a flock of deer. One of them was escaping in the hussar fashion on a beautiful horse, the harness of which was gilded and costly. He himself, dressed in silk garments and an embroidered calpac, had a rich appearance. We tried to overtake him from both sides. I came closest to him.

Assuming that he was Khovansky himself I shouted: "Stop, do not be afraid. You will be spared!" He restrained his horse a bit. He looked at me askance. I did not appear reliable enough to him since I was dressed in a gray *kontusz*. He must have assumed that I was some retainer or scamp of the kind whom the Muscovites fear the most because such people show no mercy. Later he himself admitted this to us. He saw one of our companions, dressed in a red frock, a worn-out crimson *kontusz*, in the distance. This companion was riding such a worn-out nag that he could not have overtaken the Muscovite before the Day of Judgment. But the Muscovite *supponebat*[167] him to be someone important and rode directly toward him. Another one of our companions among those who were trying to catch up with the Muscovite shot at him and missed. The Muscovite still kept riding blindly towards our first companion. He became confused. He squirmed on his nag and realizing that he could not escape me, he handed me his sword and his pistols, which were mounted with ebony and silver. He shouted: "*Pozhaluy!*" I captured him alive. Khovansky, who

---

[166]Suffice it to say. (Rendered in Polish in the original text.)
[167]Assumed.

had received two head wounds during his flight, escaped. The whole infantry, except the several hundred who were killed at the beginning of the battle, remained almost unharmed. There were eighteen thousand of them still alive. They went to a nearby birch wood forest and set up a protected encampment there. But the forest was not dense, so we surrounded them with cannon and infantry. We opened such a cannonade at them that balls flew clear through the forest from one side to the other. Later, after we had weakened them with cannon shot, we attacked them from all sides and killed them to the very last man. It is hard to look at such quantities of human blood as were found there, for their men stood very densely and as they perished one dead body fell on top of another. The birchwood forest was situated on a hill and blood came pouring down in streams, like water following a downpour of rain.

By the time all of us were gathered around our banner, the bay horse which I had captured earlier had been brought up, but wounded. Immediately after my retainer had taken this horse from the lad to whom I had originally entrusted it, it received a wound in the shoulder blade. I had to sell it to a nobleman for only ten zlotys even though it was worth a minimum of eight hundred or one thousand zlotys. The prisoners recognized this horse and said that the voivode Zhmiyev, Hetman Nashtchokin's brother-in-law, had been riding it.

We had taken prisoners the way one rounds up cattle. Khovansky, their Grand Hetman, who had received two cuts, escaped. Shtcherba,[168] another hetman, perished. In their army they always have several hetmans. A great number of voivodes, princes, and duma boyars had been killed. Out of an army which, according to the scribe who had been captured by Kaczewski, numbered forty-six thousand men, not more than four thousand managed to escape with Khovansky. They left behind sixty cannon and so many flintlocks, halberds, and various firearms that there were even enough left so that the peasants could have some.

---

[168]Actually Osip Ivanovich Shtcherbaty, the hetman, had not perished but fallen into captivity. Czapliński, *Pam.*, p. 137, note 348.

Our envoys[169] were in Mińsk negotiating with the Muscovites at the time. Czarniecki was afraid that Khovansky, who
had escaped, might grab these envoys as he fled deeper into
Russia. To their rescue he therefore sent twelve good banners,
including ours, on an allnight march. Paweł Borzęcki[170] was
given the command of this march. So even though we had been
fighting strenuously and had not even had a chance to dismount, we began our allnight ride to the city. By the time we
arrived on the outskirts of the city we were numb from fatigue.
Our commander said : "Gentlemen, we need a captive in order
to find out what is going on in the city. I ask all those who are
willing to gallop near the city and to capture just any peasant
you happen to come upon." No one volunteered because, to
put it simply, no one wanted to go. When he saw that there
was no one willing, he said : "I would like to have at least
fifteen mounted men as a convoy, and the remainder to be
ready if the Muscovites tried any attack." From his banner two
men rode forward, but no one else. I remembered Lieutenant
Borzęcki's kindness toward me during my misfortunes in Kozierady[171] and I too rode forward. When they saw me do it,
twenty other men from my banner did the same.

When we approached the suburb, we entered a hut but
there was no one there. In a second hut we found a lighted fire.
Apparently someone had been cooking food, but there were no
people in sight. We took lights and searched around in the
corners. We found no one, but as we were leaving the hut we
heard a peasant woman cough out in the pigsty. There, we
found three women, "*Kash, su ster ?*"[172] One of my compan-

[169]They were Heronim Wierzbicki, the voivode of Sieradz ; Stanisław
Sarbiewski, the voivode of Mazowsze ; Jerzy Hlebowicz, the starost of
Samogitia ; Krzysztof Zawisza, Lithuanian grand marshal ; and Cy-
prian Brzostowski, grand referendary of Lithuania. Czapliński, *Pam.*,
p. 138, note 349.
[170]The son-in-law of the voivode Sarbiewski and a lieutenant of Margrave Myszkowski's armored banner. Czapliński, *Pam.*, p. 138, note
350.
[171]The incident refers to the duels with the Nuczyński brothers and
with Jasiński earlier in this chapter.
[172]What is this, sir ?

ions who could express himself in their Russian dialect asked :
"*Ne mash tu Lakhov* ?"[173] The peasant woman said : "*Ospane
nymash, ale trvokha welikaya. Prybezhalo tut tschetyry korakvi
nashych panov prevodnych* ; *tot tschas zabrali nashych komi-
sarov i pobezheli, znati shtcho khdes' tschuvayut Tscharnetz-
kokho.*"[174] The companion asked: "*Tschy poberemo ich* ?"[175]
The woman replied : "*Oy, poberyte, panunka* ; *pre Bokh zhy-
wy, postinayte dytschtschych synov.*"[176]

This spokesman of ours then sent word for our banners to
come and ordered the peasant woman to take us to the quarters
of our Polish envoys. The peasant woman, only in a shirt,
eagerly hopped ahead and showed us their quarters. Soon our
forces arrived in the market square. When our envoys were
notified by the guards that the city was full of soldiers, they
became frightened. Charlewski was ordered by our commander
to inquire in Russian about people stationed there and about
the Muscovite delegates. The anxiety of our envoys grew the
more. The infantrymen, who had stood by the wagons in the
market square, retreated, each to his own billeting house. Then
our commander and over a dozen of our men dismounted.
Charlewski said to a man servant in Russian : "Tell the envoys
that they have to get up and all of them get together." When
the servant returned from the house, lights were already burning within. The place he entered housed the quarters of the
Samogitian starost Hlebowicz ;[177] who was first envoy and a
foremost senator. In the second house, right next to this one,
Wierzbowski, the voivode of Sieradz, was quartered ; Sarbiewski, the voivode of Mazowsze, was in the third one. While the
envoys were assembling we went to our horses. Suddenly the
chief servant came and said : "Their Lordships are asking you
in !" He was followed by several other servants with large wax

[173]Are there any Poles here ?
[174]Sir, there are none, but there is great fear. Four of our Russian
banners escorting the envoys were here but they have taken our Russian
envoys and run away which means that they expected Czarniecki.
[175]Do you think we should capture them (Czarniecki's men ?)
[176]Oh, do capture them, Sir, for God's sake ; kill those sons of the
devil.
[177]Jerzy Hlebowicz. Czapliński, *Pam.*, p. 140, note 358.

candles. We went inside wearing Russian fur hats. The envoys
were making their way from the table towards the door in
a state of alarm. Now the voivode of Mazowsze recognized
Lieutenant Borzęcki, his son-in-law, and exclaimed : "God is
just ! God is gracious ! Our men ! Our men !" And then Borzęcki said in a few well-chosen words that we had come on
Czarniecki's behalf to report about our great victory. As first
envoy, the starost of Samogitia replied eloquently, but with
tears in his eyes. He could not finish his address for great joy.
Then they all rushed toward us, threw their arms around us,
hugged us, thanking God for such benefaction ! They asked
about the course of the war. Borzęcki was relating it to them
when one companion exclaimed : "Tell them no more, sir, until
they serve us some food." The servants and chefs of all the
envoys jumped to their feet in order to light the fires in the
stoves, to bake, and to cook. Meanwhile brandy, meads, and
wines were served. All of our men had dismounted. In the
midst of the immense joy we told them about the battle and
about our victory. They in turn told us that they had surmised
this when the Muscovite delegates had fled, they admitted how
afraid they had been that they would be taken along, and how
frightened they became at the sight of us, since they thought :
"Khovansky has sent for us." They also reported that they
were to sign the treaties next day, and told us how rude the
Muscovites had been toward them. Even though I felt very
sleepy at first, tiredness left me while I listened to these stories
and looked at such sincere joy. By then it was daybreak. We
said good-bye to the envoys and left the city. Just outside, we
stopped in the meadows in order to graze the horses and to rest
them. The envoys also prepared themselves for the journey and
left soon after us.

We went from there to Lachowice, where we found our
army in the abandoned Muscovite camp. To be sure, quarters
were reserved for our banners and a guard had been assigned
to protect them from plunder, but the guards had themselves
ransacked all that was of value. Lachowice is such a fine
fortress that one could write much about it. But since it is not
situated in foreign lands and thus is well known to many, it is

not necessary to do so. Briefly, there is no other one like it in Poland. It belongs to the estates of the Sapieha family. Thirty thousand Muscovites had perished there during the latest assaults.

Then came the Feast of the Visitation.[178] The military men quickly assembled there to hear Mass. Each one gave thanks to God for the blessing granted to him in this battle. Also many nobles were staying in this fortress. The women dressed themselves exquisitely : one beautifully, another still more richly, while the third one was so adorned with gems and gold that she could hardly walk. No wonder that the Muscovites had tried to capture this fortress at all costs ! And it could not withstand the siege for more than another month, because its provisions were running out. The haste with which our army had acted had brought us a twofold advantage : the rescue of the fortress and the breaking up of the negotiations. And all this had happened thanks to Czarniecki's valiance. For Sapieha had kept postponing things until the army would be better equipped with lances and other weapons. To which Czarniecki had said : "Soon even lances will not help us and in any case it is not difficult to find hop poles in Lithuania. If you do not set out with your army, I shall do so with only mine in the name of God." And this he did. We set out from Kozierady, whereupon Sapieha had to join us out of shame. So the poor souls set to work : they sharpened poles, painted them multicolored or white—just like beggars' canes—and tied linen pennants to them. As many metal lance tips as were necessary were brought from the towns. So we had to be satisfied with what we had, since there could be nothing better. A third advantage of our haste in starting combat was revealed when our leaders received news that Dolgoruky[179] was marching with a huge force to aid Khovansky. We on the other hand could not hope to receive reinforcements from anywhere, except from God himself. If those two armies had united, it would have been nearly impossible to break them ; and if we had managed to break them

[178]July 2. Czubek, *Pam.*, p. 145, note 1.
[179]Yury Ivan Dolgoruky, a prince of an ancient family dating back to the Ruriks ; died 1680. Czubek, *Pam.*, p. 146, note 3.

it would have been with great detriment and loss to our people, since we had a difficult enough time with each one separately, especially with that of Dolgoruky, about which I shall write below.

Thus thanks to the wise counsel of a good leader, those great military forces which together could have challenged even the Turkish Sultan did not manage to unite, the unfavorable peace negotiations were broken off, all the fortresses, with the exception of two in Lithuania which had been taken by the enemy, were liberated from Russian hands, and the troops which later, under the command of Sheremetev,[180] went against our hetmans had lost heart, a fact which contributed significantly to our victory at Cudnów.[181] Only Lachowice was not in Muscovite hands while all other cities and all of the Duchy of Lithuania were conquered by them.

When Czarniecki entered Lachowice on the Feast of the Blessed Mary, monks, noblemen and noblewomen, and all who had endured that heavy siege, came *processionaliter*[182] to greet him. "Welcome!" they shouted. "Come, unconquerable leader, enter, our Godsent defender!" There were also those, especially among the women, who shouted: "Our Savior!" Czarniecki muffled his ears with his cap, reluctant to hear such flattery. When Sapieha entered after him, however, the applause was not half as strong. He was only given a simple welcome, even though it was his own *domicilium*.[183] A multitude of knights, from our army as well from the Lithuanian one, dismounted in order to go to church. Then the *Te Deum laudamus*[184] was sung and we celebrated the triumph! Such a cannonade was set off that the earth trembled. Later a beautiful service was held with sermons of reverence and joy, and thanksgivings to

---

[180]Vasili Borisovich Sheremetev, ca. 1622–1682.
[181]On Nov. 1, 1660 at Cudnów, the Muscovite leader Vasili Borisovich Sheremetev was forced to capitulate by the Polish hetmans Rewera Potocki and Jerzy Lubomirski. Czubek, *Pam.*, p. 147, note 2. (In the *Memoirs* Czudnów.)
[182]In a procession.
[183]Abode (dominion).
[184]You God we praise.

God for His blessings. Great joy was mixed with tears all
around because all the magnates from the Lithuanian Duchy
had assembled in this fortress. This victory was especially
joyous because it had brought the first success to our fatherland after many misfortunes. Previously, the Moscovites had
had such an upper hand that whenever they learned about the
location of our army, they marched toward it, confident of
victory. They had logs and shackles all ready for the prisoners
which together with those found in their camp near Lachowice
came in handy, for we were ordered to shackle them in these.
Sapieha brought to Lachowice many beautiful captured brass
cannon, and not even one iron one was among them. Czarniecki sent over twenty of these to Tykocin,[185] adding also to
its artillery two long-range cannon.

When trumpets were sounded to give up the prisoners,
they were terrified of Czarniecki and wept. I delivered my
captive immediately before going to Mińsk after the envoys.
But others, who were not immediately delivered, wept and
begged not to be handed over. The Muscovite scribe,[186] whom
I mentioned before, the one who was fleeing from me, had
said to me : "Since your custom is to deliver the prisoners to
your commander, and since it is impossible for you to keep me,
here is what you should do : "Forsake your pay and property
and come to my capital with me. I shall give you fifty thousand
rubles, my daughter, and everything that I possess." And I, a
poor soldier, began to ponder about this et interim[187] we were
ordered to turn over the prisoners and I had to obey. The
Voivode found out that this scribe had promised me fifty
thousand. This estimate of the ransom was adopted and it had
to be paid. When the scribe negabat[188] to give so much and
argued : "I had promised this so that he would be tempted and
would let me go, but such a large sum I do not and cannot

---

[185]A city on the Narew in the voivodeship of Białystok. J. Czubek,
Pam., p. 148, note 2. The Tykocin starosty was given to Czarniecki for
his military merits. Czapliński, Pam., p. 143, note 373.
[186]Pasek referred to him earlier in this chapter.
[187]And in the meantime.
[188]Refused.

have," no one listened to that. The gentleman scribe, together with the other prisoners, was ordered to be assigned, in chains, to the wheelbarrows at the Tykocin embankments. He had to confirm the promise and pay it in full.

The Voivode received about two million for his prisoners. There was no one for whom they could be exchanged, since hardly any men from our division were prisoners in Moscow. But Sapieha had to exchange all of his prisoners because many of his noblemen, noblewomen, and soldiers were in captivity. A great number of Muscovite prisoners were released as the ransom for the Lithuanian field hetman Gosiewski alone, for, as is usually the case, the head of a hetman is expensive. And this head, which they had ransomed from the Muscovites so dearly, these Lithuanian scoundrels let perish so basely while they were drunk. They savagely and unjustly killed this successful warrior, good hetman, and worthy senator. About this I shall write below.

We stayed in the Muscovite camp near Lachowice for three days, where we had enjoyed affluence and an abundance of provisions of all sorts. Then we marched toward Borysów,[189] an important fortress on the Berezina river. We stopped there, hoping to take it from the Muscovites not by force but by alarm. We stayed encamped there for two months,[190] but when we saw that they would not surrender voluntarily and since we knew that a huge Muscovite military might was being prepared against us, the Voivode decided to abandon the siege of this fortress and did so. In order not to be idle, we went to the White-Ruthenian Mohylew,[191] which is a big and powerful fortress on the very Dnieper.

Działyński,[192] the starost of Bratyan, induced by the promises of the chamberlain and hetman Jerzy Lubomirski, sent

[189]Borisov. A city on the Berezina river about two hundred km northeast of Połonka.
[190]According to Łoś it only lasted two weeks. As cited by Czapliński, *Pam.*, p. 150, note 416.
[191]Mogilev. As opposed to the Polish Mohylew on the Dniester in the Podolia region.
[192]Adam Działyński. Czubek, *Pam.*, p. 150, note 3.

orders to his banner to leave our division, *sub praetextu*[198] of wanting to convert it to a hussar banner. This upset the Voivode considerably, not so much because of the loss of the banner, even though it was a very good one, as because of Polanowski, on whose advice he had depended a lot. He tried *omnibus modis*[194] to persuade him and begged him not to go, but was told that it was impossible. Since he failed to convince them he had to let them go, but did it with a curse which arose from his great sorrow. He uttered the following words at their departure: "May all of you, together with your commander, get killed during your first battle!" and such was the case. Upon their arrival in Cudnów, the next day, the cavalry captain,[195] twenty officers, and about forty retainers were killed. Change of place usually brings change of fortune. Polanowski himself escaped death by a hair's breath.

The Voivode did not want to await the enemy at such a huge and strongly garrisoned fortress. He realized that *melius est praevenire, quam praeveniri.*[196] We began to march toward Pan Dolgoruky on the road to Krzyczew[197] so that he would see that we did not intend to grovel before him. Our enemy was of the same opinion and began to march toward us more hesitantly. He marched *magnis itineribus*[198] at first but later not so rapidly. As soon as he had covered a distance of three leagues, he would rest for three days.

This was similar to the time when a prominent gentleman had threatened me with a duel once and informed me through some reliable persons that he would surely kill me. I did not wait for this fateful hour. Rather than to go fearing it, I preferred to pick it myself in order to be rid of its thought sooner. I rode to his courtyard and sent a lad in with the following message: "My master, whom your Lordship resolved to kill,

---

[193]Under the pretext.
[194]By all means.
[195]Działyński, who was indeed killed at Cudnów. W. Czapliński, *Pam.,* p. 145, note 389.
[196]It is better to surprise than to be surprised.
[197]A town, about 85 km east of Mohylew.
[198]At forced marches, great speed.

does not wish to cause your Lordship the inconvenience of having to look all over for him. In order to spare your Lordship any more inconvenience, he announces his presence." This gentleman thought things over. He did not kill me and sought reconciliation. Similarly Dolgoruky was in a great hurry to face us. He notified all the fortresses which were occupied by the Muscovites to block our way wherever we might try to escape. When we began to march toward him, however, his enthusiasm subsided right away.

Our army made camp in the open field, about one eighth of a league from the bank of the Basia river.[199] We still did not believe in such military might of the enemy. Whenever we managed to capture a prisoner, we forced them to talk by scorching their thighs. They said that Dolgoruky had an army of seventy thousand men fit for battle. Only then did we really believe it. We made thorough preparations to welcome him. We implored God for help.

I forgot to write that while I was stationed in Mohylew, some trouble, similar to that at Kozierady had befallen me as follows : Gorzkowski, an officer of the Chamberlain Branicki, brought charges of manslaughter against me for killing his brother, whom I had hit with a mace for the reasons which I had already described *anno* 1657.[200] I was stationed with Pan Bykowski in Radomsko at the time. It was right after the Hungarian War. Gorzkowski demanded that I account for it from prison. But the Voivode declared that during such a frightful war, soldiers, especially good ones, should not be imprisoned and imprisoned ones, if there are any, should be released and, if possible, for everyone taken to prison also to be released. I was therefore merely ordered to make a vow that I would go to prison if the law demanded it. When I had made the vow, I was allowed to go to the inquest *ad locum*

---

[199]Left tributary of the Pronia, falling into the Soża. the right tributary of the Dnieper.
[200]There is no mention of it under 1657 A.D. Either Pasek forgot that he had not written about it or that part of the *Memoirs* was lost.

facti[201] and the Voivode added: "God will punish you in the
ensuing battle if you are guilty. If you are innocent, you will
come through safely. This will be the test of your innocence."

My adversary returned to Poland in order to avoid the
battle. When he was leaving, I went to the Voivode and said
that I would not go to the inquest until after the battle but
I would let myself be tried according to the report of the
inquest, which he would bring back. These words pleased the
Voivode very much and he said in front of several companions: "Have faith that God will free you from this predicament
for your valiance in preferring to go to war with us. Your
adversary on the other hand may get killed by raiders in the
wilderness." I went along and participated in all the battles.
I was under that vow and I fought. Whenever the Voivode saw
me he always said: "What's new, sir, 'Under Vow'"? Apparently you are innocent, since after such a downpour of
bullets I still see you alive."

Soon after Pan Dolgoruky was only a distance of two
leagues away from us. A *consilium bellicum*[202] was held. Some
advised that we should let him pass to our side of the ford and
gave their *rationes*.[203] Hetman Sapieha sided with those. Others
advised that we should cross over to meet him, and Czarniecki
and Połubiński agreed with those. We remained encamped
there for a number of days. He did not move toward us and we
did not know why. We took captives and questioned them:
also they did not know why. It was incredible that he should
be afraid of us, since he had such a huge army at his disposal.
What secret was behind this? Finally Czarniecki heard from
some local nobleman that Zoltarenko was coming with forty
thousand Dnieper Cossacks. We resumed deliberations and
arrived at the conclusion that it was better to *praevenire, quam
praeveniri*.[204] We went across the ford which was very swampy

---

[201]According to the law a nobleman could remain in freedom after he
had committed a crime if he made an oath that he would appear before
the court when summoned. J. Czubek, *Pam.*, p. 153, note 1.
[202]Council of war.
[203]Reasons.
[204]To anticipate than to be anticipated.

at both ends *in accessu*,[205] and its bottom very boggy, even though the ford itself came up only to the side laps of the saddle. We wanted to erect a bridge but, since *res non patiebatur moram*[206] and since forests were far away from there, we crossed the ford. Everyone thought to himself: If God forbid we should not prevail, it would be better to thrust directly toward the enemy lines rather than to turn back across that ford. Our army was arrayed the same way as it had been against Khovansky, but the cavalry banners, of which there were nine, were divided up—one banner into three units—and behind each unit stood an armored banner. The army looked so splendid this way that it appeared as if we had about six thousand cavalrymen at our disposal. The army took up battle array. My banner was in the right flank again, under Woyniłowicz. All the detached retainers, ours as well from the Lithuanian army, were ordered to take battle formation under their banners and an officer was assigned to each such banner as captain. There were also several volunteer banners under the command of Muraszko. These retainers were attached to the volunteers and were drawn up behind a mountain, far away from the army, and were ordered not to show themselves until the battle arrays began to come together and close up. With the addition of these people our small army had gained in grandeur. When one looked at them, it appeared like a second such army; especially the Lithuanians kept a great number of these "provisioners."[207] Several thousand of these people were assembled.

We compensated with ingenuity where our strength could not suffice, for we did not have even one fourth of the enemy's military force at our disposal. Our hetmans sent word to Dolgoruky to give battle: "because we have come here to war and not to lie around." The envoys found him already marching in battle array toward us. After their return they reported on the

[205]At the access.
[206]The matter could not tolerate any delay.
[207]Here jocularly of the camp retainers who were always bustling about in their job of providing provisions for men and horses. It was one of their main duties. Czapliński, *Pam.*, p. 149, note 412.

size of the army and told of the *hulajgorods*[208] with which their entire army was engirded. These *hulajgorods* resembled the palisades which are usually used in ramparts, or bulwarks, or hollowed logs which are pierced through crosswise and at the ends one log is fastened to another log with iron clasps. The infantry carries them in front of the battle formations and when they come to combat they place them on the ground and put their muskets through them. There is no way to charge at them and no way to break up the enemy, because the horses would be impaled on them. The army stands behind these as if in a fortress. They are called towers.

As soon as Czarniecki had found out about this stratagem, he ordered [the army] to erect many small ramparts. Our infantry and retainers plunged into this work. They carried dirt in whatever they could—with caps, coattails—for we did not have many spades in our equipment. The ramparts were erected in the course of an hour or more. The infantry and the small cannon were brought behind them. This happened very rapidly. The battle lines were not to advance beyond these ramparts and were only to fight *defensive*[209] within them. They were to move ahead toward the enemy in regiments and to take refuge behind the ramparts if this proved to be unsafe. Things turned out differently, however, because we abandoned our ramparts and they broke their assault towers. I shall talk about this below.

The volunteers were ordered to run up to the enemy lines. There was a forest in the middle which was not wide but long and sparse ; because of this the armies still could not see each other. We galloped toward that forest, and when the Muscovites saw us, they sent their volunteers ahead. Their army followed immediately behind. Our army stood by the ramparts as if turned to stone. We began to come together then, and chased each other back and forth. And this was taking place still on the other side of the brushwood, about one eighth of a league from our battle lines : but now we could even dash

[208]A tall mobile military device used in the seventeenth century by the Muscovite armies.
[209]Defensively.

into the brushwood in the heat of pursuit. Among our volunteers there was a lad who could provoke and irritate them. When they shouted: *"Tsaru! Tsaru!"*[210] the lad would dash close to them and exclaim in a loud voice: "Your tsar is a such and such...!", or would stick out his buttocks: "Let your tsar kiss me there!" The Muscovites followed him and he lured out scores of them. The lad, who was riding a swift Tatar horse, fled as soon as he had led them out far away from their force. We galloped up from the sides, cut them off, attacked, killed or captured them. Suffice it to say that we sent about thirty captives to the Voivode from the skirmishes provoked by this lad. He would dash up to them again and say something else about their tsar to them. The Muscovites were raging with fury as they are more offended by an abuse of the name of their tsar than of that of the Almighty. They frantically rushed at the youth. This happened many times. They rode madly after him to the forest since they wanted to capture him by all means. They would surely have skinned him for such mockery of them. We in turn followed them. I pursued one and was almost captured myself. I directed my horse carelessly toward the brushwood which had been felled and was overgrown with new sprouts. My horse wanted to jump over these clumps—it was a small mouse-gray horse, swift and enterprising. I had ridden it many times during battle. I used to put two bridles on him *propter casum*[211] the bit would break, so that I held only one pair of the reins in my hands while the other was fastened to the saddlebow—the horse somehow entangled one of its legs in the suspended reins because my retainer, the scoundrel, had tied them somewhat too long. The horse seemed to start limping, and I assumed that it was wounded. Just then another bearded Muscovite dashed at me from the side. Also the one whom I had been pursuing turned back when he saw what was happening to me. The bearded one rushed upon me. I pulled the trigger. I aimed directly at his chest, and he fell off his horse. The other one, who was young, seized me by the

[210]Russ., tsar! tsar!
[211]In case.

neck. He apparently wanted to take me away alive, since they had not yet captured any of us but had only killed a number of our men, or perhaps he did not have anything to shoot at me with, for later I found both of his pistols unloaded. I seized him with my left hand by the arm in which he held his sword as he grabbed me by the neck. We kept pulling at each other, like two hawks clutching each other. Another Muscovite dashed by on a white speckled Tatar horse and the first one called to him : "*Khvyedore, Khvyedore, sudy* !"[212] But Fyodor was also concerned for his own skin because two of our companions were trying to overtake him. When my companions noticed what had happened, they rode toward me, abandoning the one whom they had been pursuing. The Muscovite shouted : "*Puskay, ta poydu do dydka* !"[213] Now I no longer wanted to let him go ; but if he had offered this to me a minute ago, I would surely have let go of him with pleasure without his having to beseech me for long. They cut the entangled reins and took both of us along. My companion stabbed the bearded Muscovite who was lying on the ground, since he was still alive. He wanted to dismount in order to search his pockets, but since the arrays were already penetrating into the brushwood and it was swarming with volunteers as with ants, he had no chance to do so. We struck the Muscovite's horse with the flat of the sword and rode toward our men ; but nevertheless it was difficult to take even this Muscovite away alive. Jakubowski struck him in the neck and then he fell. The Muscovites came out of the brushwood and we galloped to our battle arrays. They took position like blooming poppies before us. Now the two armies could see each other. The skirmishers were ordered to leave the battlefield. The Voivode went to the regiments and rode about, exhorting and admonishing : "Gentlemen, take care, for the sake of God, for whom we are sacrificing our health and our life in this battle."

Both frontlines remained quiet for about two hours. Neither attacked the other until the skirmishers were ordered

---

[212]Russ., Fyodor, Fyodor, his way !
[213]Let me go and I shall go away !

forward once again in order to entice the Muscovites into the battlefield. They went farther away from the forest into the field, so that both sides were already within cannon range. *Interim*[214] the enemy detached Prince Cerkasky[215] with twelve thousand men from the *hulajgorods*—as we were told later. I now mounted my own horse. We stood in battle array. When we noticed that Prince Cerkasky was heading directly toward our right flank, the Voivode dashed over to us and said to Woyniłowicz : "Well, old soldier, lead off in God's name, and luck be with you !" When he rode past our banner he said : "You must withstand the onslaught !" The enemy advanced toward us very slowly. When Prince Cerkasky was already near us, the Voivode said : "Beseech God for assistance and set to work !" Our banners began to move forward slowly. The commanders rode in front of us with their arms bare up to the elbows.[216] When the distance between the two armies was already less than four furlongs, the two armies dashed at each other. We came very close to one another. We could even grab each other by the chest. As soon as the Voivode had led us to the very battle line, he rode to the side and the two armies attacked each other. For a good quarter of an hour neither side yielded an inch. When Sapieha saw that we, who were in a small number, were having a hard time, he sent a thousand and a half good men from the left flank. These dashed at the Muscovites from the side and attacked them with such force that the banners became entangled instantly. Now a vigorous battle ensued and many dead bodies were falling. The Muscovites retreated ; we were getting through, and more bodies were falling. The Muscovites began to flee. Later the infantry loosed a terrible cannonade, but nevertheless, thanks to the grace of God, only at a small loss to our men, *ex ratione*[217] we had advanced very close to the cannons. The balls went above our

[214]In the meantime.
[215]Jacob Cerkasky (Tscherkasky), one of the most prominent hetmans of Tsar Alexey Nikolayevich. Died in 1667. Czubek, *Pam.*, p. 159, note 2.
[216]Such was the custom at the time.
[217]Because.

heads. Only over a dozen of our men perished. All those whose horses were shot from under them escaped alive. A horse was killed under Woyniłowicz. Many people were deafened, for at such close range the roar and violent impetus of the cannon were damaging to the hearing. I myself felt buzzing in my head for over three months, just as in a beehive.

After we had captured six Muscovite flags, had thinned their ranks considerably, and had given a hard beating to those who escaped, we retreated. A cavalry captain who was taken into captivity related later that Dolgoruky had scolded Cerkasky for letting himself be driven from the battlefield. To which the Prince answered *ex tempore*: "I shall see you in the same position soon if you try to withstand them in the same manner as you have instructed me to do. Those are wasps— wasps, not humans!" After this no fighting occurred for a long time. Only cannon fire was heard from the other side. Our commanders again sent word to Dolgoruky that we had come here in order to fight and not to be idle and that the evening was near. He answered: "Those whose death is delayed should not complain. You will not escape what is to befall you. Though the evening is not far away, I have such an army that it can bring you to reason and give everyone his due even in an hour. There is no need for a whole day."

After such an insolent answer, he ordered the regiments to be led out of the *hulajgorods* onto the battlefield. He left only some infantry and the cannon inside. Amidst the cavalry he mixed infantry and some light cannon. He hoped to conquer us with one blow relying on the greatness of his army. We sent orders to Muraszko to bring the volunteers and retainers from behind the mountain into the view of the enemy. They came with a great speed, looking like newly arrived reinforcements. Arriving at a good trot, they came to a stop at the left flank, at a small distance from the Lithuanian army. Muraszko bustled about under the *buńczuk*.[218] He galloped with his mace and arranged the troops, just as if a new hetman and army had

---

[218]A horse's tail mounted on a long staff; a sign or mark of a commander.

arrived. Such a splendid sight resulted that we also took heart when we looked at this throng.

The Muscovites assumed that new reinforcements had arrived and the noise which they heard coming from our camp they interpreted as joy over newly arriving help. By now they had brought their entire cavalry and half of their infantry out of these *hulajgorods*. Also our cavalry came out leaving the field-works behind. They fired cannon, and from time to time an arrow as big as a yoke fell among us, sometimes in the midst of our ranks and sometimes in front of them. The spear heads were like chopping knives. We marvelled at what the enemy's bows must have been like, if some giant were shooting from a huge bow, or what. We did not know that our assailants were the Astrakhan Tatars, who used bows so large that when one end rested on the ground, the other protruded above their heads.

A decision was made among our hetmans that Sapieha would be the first one to encounter the enemy since he had asked for it himself. But since the Muscovites were concerned more about themselves than about us, they thrust their first attack not in his direction but toward our right flank instead. Thus we were forced to fight again. The Voivode dashed up to us and said: "Gentlemen, I see that the enemy has taken a fancy to you, but don't be afraid, for the *corpus*[219] will back you up."

A bloody battle broke out now. The enemy stood very close to each other. Several of them could attack each one of us simultaneously. But we put up a mighty resistance and did not allow them to break our lines. Many were shot off their horses and the wounded ones were removed to our rear lines. Their infantry mixed up among their cavalrymen had caused us much damage. When we pushed the enemy backwards a little and met that frightful infantry, it felt like a slap in the face. The Lithuanians in our left flank fought much better than they had fought against Khovansky. They now recovered the heart which they had lost completely. Our volunteers and retainers attacked

[219]Main body, or center arrays.

the Muscovites with more daring than even the Tatars could show. Briefly, everyone fought with great zeal, for with such a display of military might before our eyes we could not have done otherwise. In the course of my entire military service, both before or after this battle, I have never seen our army fight better. People said of them : "If they fought us gallantly at all times they would conquer the entire world." The Muscovites trusted in their numerical superiority, and we trusted in God and in our valiance. Rivalry also existed between the Lithuanian army and ours. When each side saw how well the other fought both endeavored to fight to their utmost. Indeed everyone must admit that the Muscovite armies, and especially their boyar banners, are more formidable when standing in battle array than any other nation. They look so majestic with their beards that if one raised his hand against one of them, he would feel as if he were opposing a patriarch.

The Voivode made his rounds among the cavalrymen. He gave orders as to who was to attack. He also sent word to Sapieha to charge vigorously since the sun was setting. He then rode up to us. May more such leaders be born ! Happy is the mother who gives birth to such sons ! He said : "Gentlemen, whoever cherishes God and virtue, follow me !" When we attacked, a great clamor and massacre ensued for we could not overcome them and they could not repel us. We resisted them mightily, *ex ratione*[220] it is more commendable to die in combat than in flight. It was evident that when we rushed into the face of such an armed might God's hand favored us and that He granted us victory with only a small loss of our men. I shall never forget the incident, which I shall tell over and over and which I consider a great wonder. When three thousand Muscovite soldiers simultaneously fired at four of our banners, who, while in pursuit of the enemy, had been sidetracked and driven into the thick of the battle, only one officer in these banners and only four retainers were killed. The horse which I was riding was wounded. The following saying is really true : "Man proposes, God disposes," for at least half of us should have

[220]Because.

been unhorsed under such fire. Later the hussars tilted at them
with their lances as if at a wall. Some lances were broken. The
Voivode's orders were that anyone whose lance should become
broken should fight with a saber. If one let fly his lance and
lost it without piercing an enemy God help him, unless one
regained it. So did one banner of Czarniecki's cavalrymen and
another banner in full armor right behind them—whose, I don't
remember. The weaker banners were ranked behind the cavalrymen. When our men encountered a weak spot in a crowd
(as there were some of them who were afraid for their bellies),
they would step aside for us, so we were able to pierce *directe*[221]
through the enemy ranks like a drill, without getting many of
the lances broken. In this manner we pushed their way directly
to the very gateway of the enemy's movable towers which
sheltered the ranks and files of their army prior to their being
led from between them and out into the battlefield. In breaking
through our forces lost only one companion and one horse.
Once they reached and were directly facing their fortified gateway, they turned with their flag to face those enemy soldiers
who were fighting in the lines through which they had just
broken and at whose back they now were. The Voivode was
informed that his banner could be seen in back of the enemy
ranks. He was afraid that his men, surrounded by the enemy,
might be crushed, The Muscovites were also sorely disturbed
by this maneuver. The Voivode ordered his remaining forces
to attack. He himself jumped headlong in front of us. He
slashed and fired. He exposed himself as if he were a common
soldier, not a hetman. The Muscovites became confused and
then took to their heels. Now to the kill ! Slash and butcher !
Whenever a Muscovite banner rushed for their tower gateway
in order to ride behind the towers, those cavalrymen of ours
who had broken through to the rear of the enemy ranks, would
form a wall with their lances and cut off their passage into their
fortifications. The Muscovites were thus forced to deflect to the
other side. A great multitude of Muscovites were pressing to
get back the protection of those palisades and wanting to be

[221]Directly.

taken under cover fire by their men in the towers. But the latter could not provide covering fire for them because they would have done them more harm than to us. Nor was there any more firing of cannon because that too would have been futile among the entangled armies. Now we attacked them with both firearms and swords. For them, it was difficult to dismantle in a hurry their palisades firmly fastened with iron clasps. The enemy kept dashing for their towers—which we call palisades—and our men kept slashing without a pause. Right in that place a great multitude of them perished. Dead bodies lay over dead bodies in heaps. Those heaps of dead bodies were so huge that they were like high enbankments rising up above those palisades. And so they themselves fell into the trap which they had built for us. *Qui facit foveam, incidit in eam.*[222] Among our men not even one perished as a result of this stratagem, in which they had placed their greatest hope. God usually ordains that whoever builds a trap for others must fall into it himself. Almost all of their cavalry perished. Very few escaped. A multitude of voivodes, princes, duma boyars, and officials of the Tsar were killed because we had no time to fool around with taking anyone alive while facing such a mighty enemy force. To take the enemy alive *significat*[223] nothing else can be done, while, with God's blessing, each of us could kill several in the time needed for capturing one alive. I managed to kill a very important one myself, judging by his dress, as rich as if he had been going to a wedding. I did not even get a chance to take his calpac which was trimmed with about two handfuls of pearls and a diamond clasp, because it was impossible during such feverish fighting : you attacked one and ten of them would attack you. Our infantrymen had the greatest gain because they followed immediately behind us and could gather in the spoils. They found lots of money, because this had been a levy and many important and wealthy boyars had taken part in it. All of the Muscovite infantry which came out to the battlefield had perished ; the rest of them would

---

[222]Whoever digs a hole falls into it himself.
[223]Means.

have perished if night had not fallen and had not hindered us. They went into the forest, the night saved them. We gathered a few wagons of flags, a great number of good cannon, and a number of prisoners as well. And finally a few hundred infantrymen were taken captive for Czarniecki and Sapieha. But there were no significant ones, only three colonels, several cavalry captains, boyars, as well as over a dozen Englishmen and Germans. The night saved Dolgoruky and others because if night had not approached all would have perished.[224]

Zoltarenko[225] was with the Cossacks only three miles away during the course of the battle. One suspected that his main army was there, watched the battle and saw Dolgoruky's defeat, upon which it retreated at great speed. After that Zoltarenko received ukases from Moscow to unite at once with Chmielnicki, which he did in great haste. I don't know whether or not he was of any help there because our hetmans, most commendably, had attacked Sheremetev *gloriosissime*[226] at almost the same time[227] so that *nec nuntius cladis*[228] of the battle remained. Some of them fell on the battlefield, others were captured by those Tatars who were *e partibus nostris*[229] and who held Sheremetev himself as reward for having helped us fight the Muscovites. It was a glorious and great victory but I shall not write about it because I was not there. I write only about those battles in which I myself participated because my purpose here is to describe *status vitae meae, non statum Reipublicae.*[230] My purpose was *reducere in memoriam*[231] all of my *actiones*[232] by seeing them *in scripto in quantum*[233] my memory were to fail

---

[224]Actually in spite of the serious losses of the enemy the victory of the Poles was not decisive at the time. Czapliński, *Pam.*, p. 160, note 456.
[225]Vasyl Zoltarenko, a Cossack hetman.
[226]Most commendably.
[227]On the first of November at Cudnów. Czubek, *Pam.*, p. 167, note 2.
[228]Not a single survivor ; not even the messenger of the defeat.
[229]On our side.
[230]The course of my life and not the affairs of the (Polish) Commonwealth.
[231]To recall.
[232]Actions.
[233]In writing if . . .

me. But also this battle was a rather lucky one, thanks to God, since not even one man escaped out of such a huge hostile army (which supposedly consisted of seventy thousand men not counting the Cossacks). The Almighty God showed great mercy on the Polish nation and almost had torn the desolate fatherland out of the jaws of this ferocious enemy who would have conquered almost all of it had He not let us win this victory, for which may the most holy Name of God be praised !

After the battle of Basia,[234] the Ruthenian Voivode[235] sent mighty patrols to those places where supposedly the Cossacks were to be found in order to greet them as soon as our patrols traced them. But they had already slipped away. After they saw the reception which we had prepared for Dolgoruky they did not wish to be received in the same way. The prudence of a good leader is thus *praevenire*[236] the enemy and not to let him reinforce himself. What would have happened to our small army if these Cossacks had united with the Muscovites ! Yet the Muscovites had a beating, the Cossacks ran away, and those Astrakhan Kalmucks whom we feared also perished. And those of our men who had fought them had said because other regiments had attacked them) that the Kalmucks lacked any ability and after bustling with their ropes took flight even sooner than the Muscovites had, and I did not hear anyone complain of a wound inflicted by their weapons. So the good God blesses whomever He wants to. He inspires leaders, and lends valor and courage to the knights—all of which we had *visibiliter*[237] experienced in these battles with the Muscovites with such a small army and thus with no likelihood of our winning. When our patrol was returning home from beyond the Dnieper it passed through Mohylew. (As I already mentioned) when the army had passed through, people had abused it, shouted at it, and threatened it with Prince Dolgoruky, with shackles, and the Muscovite capital, but on its way back no one shot at them and did not even open his mouth. How

[234] At the Basia river.
[235] Czarniecki.
[236] To anticipate.
[237] Ostensibly.

14*

frightened is [n]omen victoris,[238] how God alters human conceit and self-confidence !

We now assumed that after such strenuous fighting, during which we had soaked in our own blood and in that of the enemy to the point of satiation, we would have some rest, but we received repeated and reliable news that Khovansky had already forgotten his former flogging and that in accordance with ukases of the Tsar had again gathered twelve thousand well-equipped troops, made up of the remaining duma boyars and court officials, and that he had crossed the Dnieper[239] and was marching toward us from its Polish side. Furthermore, he resolved, and told the Tsar, that even if he were to perish himself he would either attack us with impetus or would prohibit us from crossing the Dnieper and thus allow Dolgoruky, who was regaining his forces, to encounter us. But his plan failed, because it is difficult to catch a cautious fox asleep. As soon as Czarniecki—a man possessing the qualities of Lisowski's[240] soldiers—received news of Khovansky's undertaking, he ordered our army to retreat in forced marches to the Dnieper. We crossed the river, as well as we could, at Szkłów.[241] We swam some horses across while others were dragged by boats and ferries. Very cold weather prevailed already then, about which the poor horses complained and many of them bared their teeth. We made camp near Szkłów. The Lithuanian army camped in the open field, about a quarter of a league away from us, and we at the very Dnieper, on its flooded inlet. Sapieha sent Colonel Kmicic,[242] a good soldier, with three

[238]The name of the victor.

[239]From the right or western side of the Dnieper.

[240]Aleksander Lisowski was a famous commander of the Polish divisions who distinguished himself in the wars with the Muscovites under the reign of the Polish King Zygmunt III. The possibility exists here also of a play on words since the root of this last name comes from the word *lis* meaning fox, therefore a man as cunning as a fox or with the qualities of a fox.

[241]A town on the Dnieper, north of Mohylew.

[242]Samuel Kmicic ; later the standard-bearer of Orsza, the starost of Krasnosielsk and guard of Lithuania. Czubek, *Pam.,* p. 174, note 4.

thousand brave soldiers on patrol in the direction of Czereja[243] where Khovansky had set up a camp, carefully built and entrenched, since he was going to spend the winter in the field.

On the day following the patrol's departure, Czarniecki— supposedly guided by inspiration—ordered the trumpets to sound for our army to be ready in two hours, to mount horses, and to take provisions along. Such was the case. Muted trumpets were sounded and we departed without telling Sapieha anything about it. We moved on through the forests, with the same speed, ignoring why and where to. And Khovansky did the same : he went without transport and supply columns wanting to surprise us during the crossing. He met Kmicic at Druck,[244] or rather attacked him from the back, having passed him on another route ! (A townsman from Druck, whom the Muscovites had captured some place on the way, had told us this story.) When they clashed with each other then, the poor Lithuanian souls fought valiantly, but they could not withstand the Muscovites and their banner was split. Things were bad for the Lithuanians then ; and some of them were attacked, broken, captured, and tied up. Meantime, Czarniecki sent several banners ahead which arrived soon after at the ford at Druck, or rather Odruck because this little town has a double name. There had been bridges across the river Druć, but the Muscovites demolished these. Our men stopped at the river then and sent word to the Voivode that shooting and sounds of a battle were heard. Afterwards, our army proceeded at a gallop. Only now we guessed why we were going there. We soon caught up with the rest of our men at the ford at Druck. Things looked bad however because even though the river was not wide it was deep and rapid and its banks precipitous. It flowed in two streams, so we twice would have to swim a distance of half furlong. The simple-minded Muscovites felt secure, having blown up the bridges. Since they knew that our army was far away at Szkłów and therefore the Lithuanians could not get

[243]A small town between Orsza and Borysów.
[244]A small town and castle on the inlet of a lake through which the river Druć flows. It is half way between Czereja and Szkłów.

any reinforcements, they left no guard at the ford which they could properly defend.

The Voivode then said : "Gentlemen, *res non patitur moram*,[245] we have no time to build bridges here. You hear shooting and Muscovite voices there. It is already apparent that not the enemy but our own men are getting a beating. We have already swum across the sea and we also have to swim across now. Call God for assistance and follow me ! Put your pistols and ammunition pouches behind your collars !"

He was the first one to jump from the bank and since the river was very deep his horse immediately emerged on the surface. He swam across and stopped at the other bank. The banners then began to swim one after another quietly because the place where the fighting was taking place was barely fifteen furlongs away from us and only the forest had prevented the Muscovites from seeing us. The Voivode stood at the other bank and kept calling : "Keep in ranks, gentlemen, keep in ranks !" This was impossible, however, because not every horse swam alike : one would swim faster than another. Our first officer Drozdowski had a horse over which he had no control and which swam somewhat strangely to the side. As soon as the horse began to do this Drozdowski was thrown off the horse. He let go the horse and began to drown. I grabbed him by one arm, another companion grabbed him by another and we let him float so between us. When we had pulled him out of the water the Voivode said : "You have luck, Pan brother, because there are big fish here and some pike would have swallowed you even with your armor." (He scoffed him thus because he was of small stature.)

When we swam across another such armlet the Voivode ordered the royal regiment to dash into battle immediately while he himself remained behind in order to see the other regiments get across. We went to the field of battle at a trot. The Muscovites were astounded : "Did they drop from Heaven ?" Their army was in disorder ; some loitered in a crowd while others were tying the Lithuanians up ; still others were

---

[245]We cannot tolerate any delay.

wading in the pond and dragging the scattered men from among the bulrushes. They had not killed many of our men because they wanted to take as many prisoners as was possible in order to exchange them for their own men. And there was a huge pond, overgrown with bulrushes, near the city toward which the poor Lithuanians were fleeing from the rout. The Muscovites, assuming that we were just another patrol, attacked us and closed ranks with us. They noticed that all of us were dripping wet yet our guns fired. We dashed at each other. When they saw that more and more of our men kept pouring in as if shaken out of a sleeve, their courage sank lower and lower, while we kept picking up courage because as soon as one of our banners had swum across Czarniecki would order it to join us hastily. The Lithuanians were like lambs, several tied together in one heap. Kmicic, their colonel, dashed out of a hut somewhere as soon as his Muscovite guards had left him. He kept running among our men with his hands tied in the back and shouted : "For Heaven's sake, help me !" Finally someone did untie his hands. The Muscovites captured one of our retainers and asked him : "What kind of a patrol is this ?" And he answered : "Not a patrol but Czarniecki with his army."

The massacre was raging and dead bodies kept falling to the ground. In the pond some moved around and kept dipping in it. Earlier the Muscovites had pulled the Lithuanians by the beards but now it was the other way around. A reversal and a change of fortune thus took place. All in one hour fortune favored the Muscovites and left them in the lurch. When they had learned from the prisoner that this was an army and not a patrol, they realized the situation was dangerous. At the battlefield they were mightily pressed as our other banners kept constantly pouring out of the forest just like in some dance. Their officers began to flee and their army scattered. Their flight did not last long however because their horses were worn out from fighting the Lithuanians and from riding toward them some three leagues from another direction (as they had already passed them and then had to turn back). They also had very fat horses which stopped, spreading their legs out wide. We chased the Muscovites and pursued them for four leagues.

Those who did not perish within the range of the first league perished within the second or third one, because when we caught up with them their horses would stand there like a cow, and those who had already dismounted would kneel down and fold their hands. We would strike them across the neck then and would pursue the others. All of those who perished were killed within the range of four leagues. There were no more dead bodies beyond that distance. But very few of them managed to get back to their camp, according to the report given us by the peasants and the other prisoners which we found in this Muscovite camp. These scoundrels were playing the part of great gentlemen, because as soon as they had realized what was happening they ransacked the tents. We reached this Muscovite camp at Tołłoczyn[246] which was situated some seven leagues from the spot where the battle had taken place. In it we found all necessary provisions, wagons, and even horses in abundance; because even those Muscovites who escaped did not manage to take their own belongings along when we were pursuing them. From among those of them who remained in the camp, the wagoneers, whoever got hold of a horse, ran away and no one took along with him the belongings of those who had perished. We found cattle there, which we considered a great dainty. Whoever got hold of an ox or a heifer did not have to invite guests because they came, even from different regiments, as soon as they learned that a fresh piece of meat was being cooked. Prior to that it was very difficult for us to get cattle because near the Muscovite border most of them had been confiscated, while those who still had some in their possession would keep them, summer and winter, well hidden in the wilderness. We were all starved for meat because we had lived only on vegetables for several months, especially on baked red beets, out of which all sorts of special dishes were concocted. Dumplings were also baked out of these. The beets were brewed, mixed, spread on dough, rolled up like ordinary dumplings, and then placed in the oven. They were

---

[246]A town on the Druć, about ten kilometers north of Druck, formerly in the voivodeship of Mińsk.

then spread with ground hemp seeds on top and were served as a great specialty.

We made ourselves at home in this Muscovite camp and quarters were distributed just as if we were staying in a city. We no longer allowed the Lithuanians, who had followed us on the fourth day, to join us, but we did grant them provisions. We found the stables ready and with floors—the mud was already considerable then—and other solidly constructed buildings, for the Muscovites built their camps well. Our transport and supply columns arrived after us together with the Lithuanian army. Sapieha made camp separately, about a league away from us. Rains came pouring down and then there was much snow. The Lithuanians took quarters in the villages then since their horses began to ail. We on the other hand stayed in our camp for as long as we and our horses had things to eat. We had lost many horses in the previous battles because of bad autumn weather and because of having to swim them across in cold water, but we made up for our losses in this battle. Now we had plenty of horses and good ones at that, Astrakhan Kalmuck horses, Tatar horses, and various Russian ones.

The soldiers of today, who lose their horses often, should take example from our way of fighting. I claim that they do not engage now in more serious fighting than we had *et conse-quenter*[247] they lose fewer horses than we did, yet our cavalry was never changed into infantry as a result of that. To lose a horse was for us like letting a crab out of a basket, because we all knew that during a serious encounter with the enemy God would grant us others. If the enemy takes one horse from you, do try to take away from him two because you are as much a man as he is, as much a soldier as he, and neither his nor your skin is made out of a coat of mail.

[247]And consequently.

ANNO DOMINI 1661

By the grace of God I began the year at home. In this year God tested his servant with strange fates and alternated the *vicissitudes* with good and bad fortune, but everything turned out well in the end. I shall write about it below.

After the Epiphany I went to Radomsko to collect testimony.[1] Meanwhile Gorzkowski had already obtained his, I don't know how, and left. He returned to the army a week after I had departed from the camp. The Voivode said to him: "Your Lordship has amused himself with a black inkstand in obtaining the testimony, while Pan Pasek shed his blood here with us. Now you demand a trial *contra absentem*[2] which cannot be for he, wanting to defend himself, has just left for Radomsko, the place from which you have just returned. Also you, sir, should not have left to collect this testimony until now, for you have missed so many fine battles by doing so. Apparently officework appeals to Your Lordship more than war. Why don't you give up this aggravation, because if Pan Pasek survived such battles in which I myself saw him in, it is evident that he is innocent of your brother's death. You certainly must remember that I put him to the following test: 'If you come out of this war unharmed, I shall consider you innocent.' I shall judge the case as soon as he returns with his evidence, but if your lordship understood what I was hinting at, you would not bother the

[1] Regarding the death of Gorzkowski's brother. It was briefly mentioned under 1660 A.D.
[2] Against the absent one.

people. Pan Pasek does not deny that he struck your brother. He wants to prove however that the cause of his death was different. Moreover, you can take this case to the court of justice as one nobleman against another, for this happened such a long time ago and not under my command." The Voivode shut him up so effectively that he let the case be and moreover left the army at the end of the quarter.

When I arrived in Radomsko I found those people who were most essential to my testimony, and especially the landlords of the house in which this quarrel had taken place, dead. Only the priest, who had administered the last rites to him,[3] was still there. He wanted to give me *testimonium*[4] right after Mass that at the time of taking the last sacraments Gorzkowski's brother did not consider me guilty. However, the priest could not testify without permission from the local bishop and he urged me to obtain it. I hoped for the testimonies of my companions who were still serving under Pan Piekarski's banner, as well as for the testimony of Pan Olszowski and Pan Jędrzej Zaręba who were currently serving with me under the flag of the castellan of Lublin.[5] I left Radomsko empty-handed but with the intention of obtaining the said permission from the local bishop. Having arrived home, I learned that my adversary had left the army, got married, and settled on his estate. *Supponebam*[6] that he would drop the case and I no longer tried to gather the evidence. I used to see him later at the house of Pan Starołęcki, the castellan of Żarnów, in Studzianna[7] when Pan Michał Łabiszowski, an officer of Prince Dymitr,[8] was courting Panna Przyłuska, his Excellency's niece.

Pan Gorzkowski made no mention of the incident there. He only refused me a handshake in our first encounter. Those who had come there with me, my relatives and others, wanted

[3]Gorzkowski's brother.
[4]Testimony.
[5]In the armored banner of Stanisław Widlica Domaszewski, the starost of Łuków and the castellan of Lublin. Czapliński, *Pam.*, p. 175, note 9.
[6]I assumed.
[7]A village in the voivodeship of Kielce.
[8]In Prince Dymitr Wiśniowiecki's banner, since 1663. Czapliński, *Pam.*, p. 176, note 14.

to intercede for me, and especially Pan Potrykowski and Ra-
dziątkowski. They already pulled their swords but the host
stepped in. I too told them to drop the matter. "Let him be
content with refusing me a handshake." They left him alone
but Jan Rylski, the judge of Rawa, said to him : "Pan brother,
you are intervening since your brother was hit with a mace
while you should be hit with a stick for being so uncouth." He
sat there with us during those days of courtship but shunned
our cõmpany for he was afraid. We numbered more than one
hundred horsemen and all of us looked angrily at him for
refusing that handshake. He did not dance even once. When
some asked him what he still intended to do, he said that he
preferred to seek justice in the civil courts because he saw
favoritism in the military ones. I was very glad to hear this and
gave up gathering testimony. Later he did not even start the
civil suit since he supposedly felt that he could not prove me
guilty. After that I went back to the army. When the Voivode
saw me he said : "Are you returning with the evidence ?"
I answered : "I am." He said : "You are not likely to settle
this case since when one of you leaves the other arrives." I told
him that Gorzkowski intended to take the case to the civil
courts.

Soon after, the army began to prepare itself for a confederacy.[9] From the Field Hetman's[10] division we kept receiving
messages and letters inviting us *ad societatem*[11] and proposing
communem iniuriam et commune bonum.[12] Our division opposed the confederacy on the grounds that it would be very
harmful to the fatherland. The Muscovites no longer had any
means of resistance and in despair intended to surrender and to
beg us for mercy. All the Wolskis[13] had already moved their

[9]In order to collect pay which the Commonwealth owed them.
[10]Potocki's.
[11]To cooperation.
[12]A common fortune and misfortune.
[13]This refers to the story of Łukasz Wolski which was described in the
year 1660. Pasek here designates all men of little courage in this
manner.

belongings beyond Białe Jeziora.[14] Simply speaking, there was hardly anyone in our army who sincerely aspired to the confederacy. *Tandem*[15] the Field Hetman's party convinced us to meet *ad conferendum*.[16] Because of that I told my colonel to look for another officer to take my place. When the Voivode had found out about this, he ordered Mężyński, his colonel, to negotiate, with me to enlist in his banner. *Conclusum*[17] that I gave in.

Our army left Kobryń[18] and joined the field hetman's, but not all the banners did so because the royal banners, Czarniecki's own, those of his son-in-law[19] and of the starost of Kaniów[20] did not want to join. At the council of war a great commotion was raised *pro et contra*[21] the confederacy because the Field Hetman's army was already very much in favor of it. Our men found themselves at a crossroad. On the one hand *dulcedo*[22] of the prospective gains enticed them, on the other they regretted in such a state of affairs to be disobedient when an opportunity presented itself to extend the borders. Some regretted having come to the council of war while others said that it was absolutely necessary because, *quot capita, tot sensus*,[23] people have various opinions. We finally had to comply with their wishes, but under the following conditions : first of all that the head of the confederacy be chosen from our army ; secondly, that we were to receive good provisions, a considerable increase in pay, and were to march no longer *sub regimine*[24] of the various Field Hetmans but under our head of the confederacy ; thirdly, that administrators be appointed and left

[14]Beloe Ozero in Russian ; a city on a lake by the same name, over four hundred kilometers east of the Leningrad of today.
[15]At last.
[16]For reaching an understanding.
[17]We reached an understanding.
[18]A town forty-eight kilometers east of the Lithuanian Brześć, (Brest).
[19]Wacław Leszczyński. Czubek, *Pam.*, p. 185, note 11.
[20]Stefan Czarniecki.
[21]For and against.
[22]The sweetness.
[23]So many heads so many minds.
[24]Under the command.

behind on the royal estates and in the starostys who would manage them and collect the revenue *in rem*[25] of the army ; and finally, that the confederacy would not be disbanded until the army had been granted satisfaction *in toto*.[26]

Ad primum,[27] it could not be so, *per rationem*[28] the other army was twice as large as ours. *Conclusum*[29] that the head of the confederacy be from the Field Hetman's army, the second in command from ours. The army then singled out Świderski,[30] a plain and an honest man, as the confederacy's head, and Borzęcki, a lieutenant in the banner of Franciszek Myszkowski, the margrave of Pińczów, as the second in command. Borzęcki was a learned man with great ambition. Half of the counselors were picked out from our army, half from the other one. *Ad 2-dam illationem*,[31] they saw in it our army's invariable resolution to consume our bread while working and not while loafing on the estates. They had heard us declare *plenis buccis*[32] that we would not depart from our position and would defend it with arms in the case of their noncompliance. *Rationes*[33] had also been raised there *e contra*,[34] that we would hardly be a threat when we set to work, that the Polish Commonwealth would not care about us and would not settle our back pay if the defense were still available. The second in command supported our stand *potentissime*.[35] The head of the confederacy *annuebat*[36] but did not dare to speak his mind, fearing to offend his side. Then Karkoszka, an officer, I don't know from whose banner, spoke up as follows : "These are unnecessary inven-

[25]On behalf.
[26]In full.
[27]As far as the first point is concerned.
[28]Because.
[29]A decision was reached.
[30]Samuel Świderski, a lieutenant of Prince Konstanty Wiśniowiecki. Czubek, *Pam.*, p. 186, note 18.
[31]As to the second motion.
[32]Explicitly.
[33]Arguments.
[34]From the opposite point of view.
[35]Very strongly.
[36]Was in agreement.

tions of a few people. If there is to be a confederacy let there be one. If there is no confederacy, our arrears will be lost and we shall be made into dragoons. As I say, this is an invention of a few gentlemen only, and since the others do not say anything, surely, they think the way we do." The second in command glanced at the colonels and the lieutenants and said : "Gentlemen, what is your opinion ?" And they said : "We shall talk this over with our banners." The meeting was adjourned *ad cras.*[37]

Early the following day, at the conferences of the various banners, all of our men *unanimi voce*[38] resolved to abide by our terms. When, at the council of war, the lieutenants were ordered to declare their stand *nomine*[39] their banners, those who wanted to spoke for themselves, but whoever found public speaking difficult delegated the task to another. Our Krzywicki was a good soldier and certainly a handsome and stately man, but not much of a speaker, especially *in facie publica.*[40] He asked me to deliver the declaration. Our entire banner was to be present at the council. He himself stayed in his quarters to eagerly answer his correspondence. Since the royal banners, both of the Voivode's, and that of the Royal Sewer Leszczyński, the Voivode's son-in-law, were not present, the first declaration was made by the banner whose lieutenant was the second in command of the confederacy. Kraszowski, an officer, delivered it. The second declaration fell to the banner in which I had to serve until the end of the quarter, even though I had already given the Voivode my word. Our banner and a large crowd from all the other banners gathered *numerosissime.*[41] I began to speak as follows :

I do not know by what right someone would call himself a son of the fatherland who would completely forsake its public interests for his own private ones. The world calls prodigal such sons who barter away all their

[37]Until the next day.
[38]Unanimously.
[39]In the name of.
[40]At public gatherings.
[41]In a very large crowd.

property merely for the sake of short-range comforts and lose in one sweep the patrimony which they could *per portiones*[42] enjoy together with their own descendants. We hold *praetensionem*[43] against the Polish Commonwealth for withholding our back pay. But when I consider that this is not against the Hungarian, or the German, but against the Polish Commonwealth, our own mother, we should conduct ourselves as toward a mother, because every mother who finds herself with scarce bread usually rewards her children for a missed breakfast with a good dinner. She will not allow them *labefactari*[44] from severe hunger. If however her wanton children had pillaged her larder, probably even a missed breakfast would not be compensated for and the means of further nourishment would be gone . . .[45] *Mora est nociva.*[46] The enemy will be reinforced if we give him time to rest. God will get angry and when His Grace and His Divine Hand which protected us turns against us, we shall not receive the enemy's share and shall lose our own as well. It is obvious, gentlemen, quite obvious, that until now God's protection has fostered us. But we shall not read in history that such powerful and huge myriads have ever fallen from so few Polish swords. Let us keep in mind how these base Muscovites had plundered with fire and sword[47] three fourths of our fatherland. Let us keep in mind how often they have abused God in His churches. Let us keep in mind how they threatened us during the Swedish war. Let us prove that we also know how to look for nourishment beyond our borders, in the country of those who have destroyed so much of our land. Let us finally cast aside the degrading saying of our neighbors about our nation : '*Minatur bel-*

[42]In portions.
[43]A grudge.
[44]To grow weak.
[45]Two blank pages of the manuscript are found in this spot. Czubek, *Pam.*, p. 189, note 7.
[46]A delay is harmful.
[47]"With fire and sword"—these words might have inspired Henryk Sienkiewicz to write his novel which bears this title.

lum, et non fert : *sic gens tota Polona facit.*[48] This will
bring us greater fame and a better advantage because God
will continue to bless our deeds and our brothers. Even if
their hearts were as hard as diamonds they will have to
respect our sincerity. When we enter a prosperous land,
God might grant us greater gains than He has on our
native soil. I make this declaration therefore on behalf of
my entire company, *denuntio*[49] that if *pia vota nostra*[50] do
not appeal to someone, most likely his would not appeal
to us and to our entire division either (and I don't know
how to call these 'good intentions'). I permit myself to
speak so since we know everything about each other.
I solemnly *protestor*[51] before Heaven and Earth that were
the fatherland to suffer some misfortune as a result of
someone's obstinacy, may it not be through the *filialem
amorem*[52] which we want to render it.

They listened *modestissime*[53] for as long as I spoke, but
when I had finished, a loud murmur arose. One said this,
another that, and a third one : "Let it be." Still another said :
"He speaks wrongly. Nothing will come out of that." Later
several firebrands jumped up. They began to scream all at
once : "One should not be surprised that Czarniecki's officers
have scruples, for in their division Jesuits are chaplains. They
feed such scruples to them." But others hushed them up and
they grew silent. The second in command enjoyed hearing me.
He showed this *visibiliter*[54] because he realized that whatever
fame accumulated would fall on his good name for he was *vir
activus*[55] and a good soldier. The head of the confederacy was
also of the same opinion, but he did not show this in order
that he might seem to agree with the others. When that murmur

[48]The entire Polish nation only threatens with war but does not wage it.
[49]Declare.
[50]Our good intentions.
[51]Declare.
[52]Filial love.
[53]Very quietly.
[54]Openly.
[55]An active man.

calmed down, the declarations of the other banners followed, one after another. When the royal banner[56] finished then the other regiments followed in the same manner. Even those banners which held the opposite view to that of ours—and there were six of them—had talked things over with each other and then *recesserunt ab anteriori intentione*,[57] declaring themselves in conformity with our intention to march after a short rest and after getting things ready. The Field Hetman's men seeing our firm stand and that they could not override us in this, avoided irritating us. They realized that it would not be good for their cause if they lost our support and Czarniecki's, who was *totissimus*[58] devoted to the King, maintained the military power. *Conclusum*[59] that it would be so. The war council was broken up with the promise to reach a decision in its future encampment if God willed it so.

Camp sites were assigned next day. The sojourn of the marshal[60] and his second in command was to be in the castle of Kielce. Senior officers swore allegiance to the army according to a strict and intricate oath formula and vice versa. Some postponed the oath-taking (and I was among them) until further deliberations.

The regiments went *sparsim*,[61] each to his own position. Three thousand soldiers were sent to compel those banners, nine of which were from our division, to join the confederacy. And they, the royal and the commanders' banners, *per regulum*[62] of politics, only waited to be "forced" to join so that they could offer compulsion as a pretext for joining, which they then did. The starostys, royal tenures,[63] estates[64] and

---

[56]Pasek said only a short while ago that the royal banners were not present.
[57]Departed from their former stand.
[58]Completely.
[59]Finally everyone agreed.
[60]The head of the confederacy.
[61]Separately.
[62]Conforming to the rules.
[63]The royal estates which were leased out to the nobles.
[64]The income from these was used exclusively for the maintenance of the royal court.

revenues were taken away and were divided among the army. Once we had made ourselves at home at our posts, we soon took a liking to affluence and to drinking bouts. That pious intention which we cherished fell into oblivion. If someone recalled it he was instantly shouted down. False accusations were brought up against the King and against the Polish Commonwealth : "They threaten and press us. They promise to route us. Why should we try to accommodate them so much ?"

The Commonwealth went sluggishly about its affairs and everything turned out just as I, an ordinary man, had predicted. The confederacy lasted until the third year. The Muscovites gathered strength. By the time they began to negotiate with us they saw their power, they took our discord into consideration, and were much more confident of themselves. We, who were to take things away from them and get our share back, now had to give them a good reparation for having defeated them. I shall write about this at a greater length below. This is how God usually detracts benefaction from those who do not know how to enjoy what has been granted to them, as the saying goes : *"Vincere et victoria uti non idem est."*[65]

We had achieved such great victories over the enemy when thanks to a special divine protection we had liberated the Ruthenian, the Lithuanian, and the White Ruthenian lands. We had covered the fields with Muscovite and Cossack corpses and had soaked with blood the land which they had conquered and had wished to appropriate for themselves. We had liberated the fortresses conquered by them, some by assault, others in terms of treaties. We had extinguished their immense fervor. But after all this our triumphant army, instead of rushing into the Muscovite capital and making the intimidated and almost crushed enemy concede to us a victorious hand and accept from us the yoke of captivity (because their entire nation had talked about this already and would do so out of fear, which God sent down on them so that even from the capital they began to escape beyond the Białe Jeziora, about which I had learned later when I was in Moscow and about which I shall

[65]To conquer and to benefit by the conquest are two different things.

write below), the army formed a confederacy, not so much in order to receive back pay but more so because of intrigue and conspiracy which someone wanted to promote *sub umbra*[66] of pay withheld from the army, which gave them reason for remaining in the confederacy. The Muscovite Tsar did not begrudge resinous torches[67] to set this fire because the Muscovite nobles were generous with them. But this confederacy was formed because someone wanted to fish in muddy water, seeing that the King was *sine successore*[68] and that the famous Jagiellonian dynasty was drawing to a close.

Even though the Commonwealth had really indebted itself to the army, the army could have still held out if it had taken some more *ad rationem*[69] from the Commonwealth, because it was not that poor, and especially Czarniecki's division which had returned from Denmark rich and on horseback and which had not suffered losses, but had accrued profits in the Muscovite battles as well. The army could have done without pay and without this confederacy, but since it had been formed the army should have been treated with kindness, not harshness at first. This happened later, but it was already too late, since by then the army had taken a liking to *licentia*[70] and

[66]Under the pretext.
[67]Muscovite money.
[68]Without a successor.
[69]On credit.
[70]Dissipation.

the stag had already grown horns on his head; already sixty
thousand swords were drawn, as the saying goes—as if they
had been taken out of a dove's throat.[71]

In the camp at Kielce at the first meeting of the council
the subject matter of oath-taking was brought up. Those who
had not taken the oath of loyalty, secrecy, and adherence to
their commanders and had not pledged to remain faithful to
the oath until the general amnesty had to do so. Some banners,
especially those which had no desire for the confederacy, objected to this, fearing God's wrath. Some had to agree slowly
however, for they were enticed by the charm of the estates and
other great gains. I was as if *inter incudem et malleum*.[72] I, who
had as much coming to me in arrears as the others, which
amounted to a lot, wanted to be in the confederacy, especially
since I had already been assigned the secretary's office. But.
I did not want to bind myself by an oath by any means. I kept
evading it for as long as I could for I always avoided taking
oaths *naturaliter*.[73] At the fourth meeting, however, when the
lieutenants were handing in the lists of those in their banners
who had taken the oath, I was very much pressed to take it
without delay. When I took the floor and began to speak,
Borzęcki, the second in command, interrupted me. He told the
assembled army that he had taken it upon himself to persuade
me to swear to the agreed oath and added that I would do so.
He told me that he feared that if I spoke *crude*[74] or if I refused
to take the oath, some firebrands might try to pick a quarrel
with me. This would have most likely been the case, since I too
had had a few drinks in good company. *Soluta sessione*,[75]
Borzęcki really tried to persuade me by pointing out, *omnibus
modis*,[76] the gain to the entire division if the office of the

---

[71]The meaning here might have been : valiant or choice swords because
a dove picks out the best grain. For an exact meaning there is still no
explanation however.
[72]Between the hammer and the anvil.
[73]By nature.
[74]Sharply.
[75]After the close of the meeting.
[76]In all possible ways.

secretary were in our hands and the benefit to the entire Commonwealth if we, who had joined the confederacy *magnis inviti, quam invitati,*[77] were leading the councils. He elaborated on the gains and the betterment of fortune which this office could provide and added that it could benefit more than one banner. He also said that if more of us who wished the fatherland well and who desired to go to war under such conditions would enter *dispositionem consiliorum*[78] and prove that the army would go *ad opus belli*[79] under our leadership, for then our names would then be known to the world, the sooner we would put our terms into effect. But these savory promises, even though impressive, were not at all to my liking. Whenever I thought of the oath I felt opposed to it. Borzęcki got angry then and exclaimed these words: "You do not want to do this at my friendly persuasion. When you see several hundred maces raised at the meeting tomorrow you will be more easily persuaded. And I shall not be present there since you value my friendship so little."

Borzęcki did not come to the meeting next day and I was also in no hurry to get there, but they sent for me and I had to go. The matter of oath-taking was discussed and it was concluded that whoever had not taken it should absolutely have to do so. Chochoł was the first one to take the oath. Several other companions followed him. Suddenly Borzęcki came in even though he had been ill in bed. He was concerned that I might get into any trouble. He was very fond of me. When I was told to take the oath I said the following: "It is not a commandment of God that every companion should *de necessitate*[80] take the oath at the council of war. One can do the same at the meetings of individual banners, in front of one's own superior." They answered me: "It cannot be any other place but here so that you may have the honor which the army *intendit*[81] to give you." I still wanted to ask them to give

[77]More by force than by invitation.
[78]Into leadership in the councils.
[79]Into battle.
[80]Necessarily.
[81]Intends.

me time *ad cras*[82] for reflection, but something prompted me to speak my mind honestly. Somehow this confederacy and all these promises did not go to my heart, I don't know why. I began to speak to them then in the following words :

Gentlemen ! From the very beginning of my military service I have borne all the enemy attacks without frowning ; all the military endeavors I have taken *hilari fronte*[83] the various changes of fortune and misfortune in battles, which diminished my meager possessions, with a brave heart. No one has ever seen me behind the front lines unless it was next to my company, my mother, when so required. And I can boldly say this : Whoever knows that it is not, so let him throw a stone at me. I therefore consider myself to be on an equal footing with the well-deserving sons of this country. And if it is so, and since whoever is an equal at war should also have an equal share in the compensation, the same claims apply to me as to each one of you, gentlemen. I feel that I can boldly claim my deserved pay and reach out for my piece of winter bread,[84] as I am not reaching out for it when it is being taken out of the oven, as I have already fought for it beforehand.[85] I shall not ask for compensation then because I have already earned it, shedding my blood, and have a right to it together with the others. I do ask to be allowed to eat it *non adiurando*[86] however because I toiled for it *non abiurando*.[87] It is commendable of you, honorable gentlemen, *et specialiter*[88] of our older brothers to have found the means and to have chosen the time to

[82]Until the next day.
[83]A cheerful front.
[84]Figuratively here about the money and food supplies which the army was entitled to from the royal and ecclesiastical estates during its winter encampment.
[85]With sharp steel, i.e., when Czarniecki's division was sent to war with the Muscovites, meaning when we were fighting.
[86]Without adjuring myself.
[87]Without abjuring myself.
[88]And especially.

recover the arrears, for which we shall always be grateful. It was also necessary for those of you gentlemen who determine the ultimate course of our affairs—especially *in casu saevientis fortunae*[89] and who prevent (not knowing what *subsequentur*)[90] such instances in the future—to devise such an oath, which method *non reprobo*.[91] But since I hold some kind of an innate abomination toward it, I declared right at the first meeting of the council that I did not intend to take it. For just as an Arabian snaffle cannot restrain a hard-mouthed horse, this type of oath will not restrain someone without an innate sense of honor. It is far more serious and a real offense to God to take a knightly oath before Him and break it. I do not know whether Catilina[92] did not regret placing confidence in the oath by which he bound the accomplices to his plot. I do not know what good it did Hannibal[93] to have solemnly vowed the doom of the Romans while Heaven contrived for him a different cast of fortune. It is debatable what consolation Xerxes[94] derived in binding the

[89]In the case of an unfavorable fortune.

[90]Will follow.

[91]I do not condemn.

[92]Lucius Sergius Catilina (c. 108 B.C.–62 B.C.) Roman politician betrayed by his accomplices from the Allobroges and defeated at the head of the revolutionary forces by the army of the Senate while attempting to escape into Gaul. He was slain in the battle of Feasulae (now Fiesole), Italy, 62 B.C.

[93]The great Carthaginian general (247 B.C.–183 B.C.), eldest son of Hamilcar Barca ; sworn to eternal enmity to Rome. In 221 B.C. he became commander-in-chief of the Carthaginian army in Spain. He captured the Roman-allied city of Saguntum in Spain, which resulted in a declaration of war by Rome in 218 B.C. He successfully maintained a campaign in Italy for fifteen years, but had to retreat to Carthage in 203 B.C. as a result of Roman successes under Scipio Africanus in North Africa. He fled from Carthage in 196 after he was accused by Romans of breaking the peace. He then fought with Antiochus the Great, King of Syria, against the Romans. When Antiochus was defeated in 190 he was forced to promise to surrender Hannibal to Rome. Hannibal then escaped to Libyssa, Bithynia, where he committed suicide.

[94]Xerxes I (the Great), son of Darius Hystaspis and Atossa (c. 519–465

Spartan Demaratus[95] by an oath of allegiance when this
exile was more favorably inclined toward his own ungrate-
ful fatherland and sent sealed under a layer of wax secrets
of the enemy advancing upon his fatherland ; and later he
even instigated the brutal murder of Xerxes by his own
uncle Artabanus.[96] Surely, I could enumerate many more
cases showing prevalence of virtue and sense of honor
over compulsory oath. I say therefore that I do not know
in what way this oath which you honorable gentlemen
demand of me will become useful because it would be
contra rationem[97] of me to leave the Confederacy now.
Why should I, who never have been a *desertor castro-
rum*[98] even in times of greatest need when there was heavy
fighting and not much to eat, escape now when there is no
fighting but plenty to eat and ample to drink ? And even
if I were to desert the confederacy, regiments and troops
would not follow me because I am not a colonel. The loss
of my person in an army of scores of thousands would be
insignificant. If the oath is demanded, however, because
your Honors want to grant me the secretarial post of the
confederacy, I am willing to obey the will of your Honors
and to serve according to my ability, but under the condi-

B.C.) ; King of Persia (485–465 B.C.). Ahasuerus, who appears in the
Book of Esther in the Old Testament as the king of Persia, is identified
with Xerxes I.

[95]King of Sparta (c. 510–491 B.C.) ; deposed in 491 by Cleomenes in
favor of Leotychides ; fled to the Persian court at Susa where he was
received at the Court of Darius ; he became a friend of Darius' son
and successor to Xerxes ; he accompanied Xerxes on his invasion of
Greece (481–480) ; warned Xerxes of the bravery of the Spartans ;
after the battle of Thermopylae he advised Xerxes how to conquer
those Spartans still in Lacedaemonia. Xerxes ignored his advice, which
proved to be a mistake. Some claim however that Demaratus had sent
a message warning the Spartans of the intentions of the Persians before
they even left Susa.

[96]He was murdered by Artabanus, a captain of the guards, and not by
his uncle Artabanus (521–485 B.C.), who was in turn killed in 464 by
Xerxes' son Artaxerxes I.

[97]Unreasonable.

[98]Camp deserter.

tion that I shall not have to take the oath because I shall
not be brought to this by either this or any other office
or by the greatest gains derived from it. So I beg your
Honors to relieve me from the oath *si potest fieri*.[99] I declare that all the conditions which the army swears to
I shall observe even more strictly than someone who is
under oath, pledging my flesh and blood, which will
always be in the hands of your Honors. If, however, my
request is rejected and if I am not worthy of such confidence, then I do not want to enter *ad consilia*[100] and I do
not wish to know the secrets. But I shall not give up my
slice of bread because everyone who has well deserved it
can have it *sine comprobatione iuratoria*.[101]

Quite an uproar was raised *pro et contra*,[102] depending on
the individual sentiment toward me. Especially hostile was
Pukarzowski, an officer of the starost of Krasnystaw[103] at the
time, who was on the list as one out of six for the office which
had been offered to me and who heartily desired it. He spoke
up *ore om(n)ium*[104] then : "It would be better if those who do
not wish to march in line with us leave us, for we shall share
the cake only with those who share the bread with us." I answered : "You have misunderstood my words, because even
though *non arripio*[105] the new venture as *nocivam et perni-
ciosam*,[106] I nevertheless desire compensation and do not scorn
it because I have deserved it more and earlier than your lordship."

I went to say goodbye to the Marshall the same day. He
asked me where I was going. I replied : "To my banner in
order to fetch my retainers, and since I was not worthy of the
well-earned bread of the confederacy, my native soil would

[99]It is feasible.
[100]Into the deliberations.
[101]Without the confirmation under an oath.
[102]For and against.
[103]He was Szczęsny Kazimierz Potocki. Czubek, *Pam.*, p. 202, note 13.
[104]On behalf of all them.
[105]I do not grasp.
[106]Detrimental and destructive.

still feed me, thanks to the kindness of my father." Out of anger and grief, Borzęcki did not want to say good-bye to me, even though we were great friends. I confided, however, to my intimate friends that I intended to go to Czereja, in White Ruthenia, where Czarniecki had already mightily defeated Khovansky, the Muscovite hetman, for the fourth time,[107] as soon as I had rested the horses at home a little. The confederates learned of this. As soon as they found out about my intentions they immediately sent orders to the banner forbidding my release from the unit. This would have happened in any case since the Marshal's Cossack arrived in the banner sooner than I did. In such a way they contrived to dissuade me from my plans but to no avail, for I spent only a few days with friends enjoying their good company until departure time. Then I went home, leaving the retainers behind. I took the volunteers along and said only that I was going home.

My father praised my intentions very much. He thanked me and blessed me for my decision ; and my mother did so also. She was so disposed that she never tried to dissuade me— even though I was her only son—from the greatest and the most dangerous ventures because she *firmiter*[108] believed that no evil could come to any man against God's will.

I took care of things, and left the house on the feast of St. Martin.[109] I fed my horses well before that and purchased more of them with the money I had received, thanks to the grace of God, in Denmark and to which my father also added some. On my way there I came across our cavalry banner in Łysobyki[110] under the command of Lieutenant Kossakowski which, *post multas deliberationes*,[111] was going to join the confederacy. Many of my relatives served in his banner and I spent several days with them without disclosing my plans to them. I said only that I was going to Targoniów near Tykocin

[107]Czarniecki attained a victory over Khovansky on November 4.
[108]Firmly.
[109]November 11.
[110]A city on the Wieprz river, about forty-five kilometers northwest of Lublin.
[111]After many deliberations.

to see Kazimierz Gorzewski, my uncle, who was the commander of Tykocin. They believed it easily because he was my uncle. They might have tried to dissuade me from this undertaking if I had admitted the truth, especially Stanisław Trzemeski, a cousin on my mother's side, who was the second in command there. I left and arrived at the time of the first dawn Mass,[112] near Zielona Puszcza[113] in a village where his lordship Pan Stanisławski, the King's Butler of Warsaw and a royal courtier, was staying. When he saw me in church he, being a kind man, sincerely invited me to rest at his quarters or at least to dine with him, even though he had not known me before that. When I declined his invitation and frankly told him where I was going and for what reason I had left the confederacy, he begged me to join him all the more, because, as a *pars regalis*,[114] he wanted to be of service to me and promised to write to the court so that I would be treated with all kindness there. Since it could not be otherwise, I dropped in and I was greeted with such great hospitality that I, my men, and my horses felt as though we were in Paradise. Even my hunting dog was seated at the table on a silk cushion and was served food on silver plates directly off the serving dishes. And suddenly Mazepa,[115] a royal valet, arrived. He was a Cossack raised to nobility. He was on his way from Warsaw to see the King, who was in Grodno[116] at the time. While we

[112]The earliest special Mass said on the first Sunday of Advent. It was on November 27 at the time. Czubek, *Pam.*, p. 204, note 6.

[113]A former name of the wilderness lying between Grodno and Białowieża, south of Grodno and northwest of Białystok.

[114]Royal courtier.

[115]Ivan Stepanovich Mazepa (1640–1709), a Cossack and courtier of the Polish King. He left Poland after an amorous episode with a Polish lady which incident is the subject of Byron's poem "Mazeppa." He became Cossack hetman in 1687 ; he was given by Peter the Great the title of Prince of the Ukraine. He conspired with Poles and Swedes to gain the independence of the Ukraine. He fled to Turkey with Charles XII of Sweden after his defeat at Poltava in 1709. See Pushkin's poem "Poltava", Byron's poem "Mazeppa," Voltaire's poem "Mazeppa," and Słowacki's drama "Mazepa".

[116]In Grodno on the Niemen, a conference between the senators and the King was taking place at the time.

were sitting there we discussed various political questions and somehow he assumed from them that I was an important person. He took it into his head that it was impossible for me to be going into the Lithuanian and the White Ruthenian lands *sine mysterio*.[117] I went on my way slowly while he galloped ahead *magnis itineribus*[118] to the King and, curring favor, reported that a confederate officer from a banner of the Ruthenian Voivode was coming there. And he added : "He pretends to be going over to his commander in White Ruthenia, but on the basis of the circumstances this is impossible . . .[119]

. . . to men of merit, because *in manibus bene meritorum*[120] I hardly see one tenth of it. I have already lost half of my paternal inheritance and many times—the entire army and my hetman know this—I have shed blood for my fatherland. I even would have agreed to see my name placed last on the list *bene meritorum*,[121] and yet neither I nor many others, still more deserving than I, have had a chance to taste this bread. Yet I see here many of those who shed their blood by opening their veins with a French lancet[122] or being cut by the razor of a careless barber. And it is just such people as these, the

[117]Without a secret mission.
[118]Hurriedly.
[119]Nine pages of the *Memoirs* are missing here. Their contents may be surmised as follows : Mazepa falsely informed the King that Pasek was sent as an envoy to Lithuania by the confederacy. The King then sent an armed unit which arrested Pasek in order to deliver him to Grodno. On the way some Lithuanian confederates encountered them and, having found out that a unit of the royal armies was leading a captured confederate officer, they attacked the royal men in order to rescue Pasek but were unsuccessful. This made Pasek's situation even more embarrassing. When he was brought to Grodno he delivered a speech in his defense before the senators, the end of which is preserved. The passage following the break is the end of that speech. Czubek, *Pam.*, p. 206, note 3.
[120]In the hands of the very meritorious ones.
[121]Meritorious men.
[122]An old superstition which held that evil spirits were let out by bleeding. This was practiced by noblemen at the time.

ones who did not work for this bread, that rush after the
bread *bene meritorum*.[123] They want to be the first to
enjoy this bread and to become lords, and later they
oppress the poorer and quite meritorious ones and at the
sessions of the Diet and at regional councils they want to
pick quarrels and to scorn the better men. What is the use
of such men to the Commonwealth and to His Majesty ?
They take up the time of the Diet and the regional
councils in order to promote their own private interests
and take up the time for public action with unnecessary
extravagances and banquets. The bread thus torn out of
the mouths of deserving people they spend on party in-
trigues, corruption, and pursuit of their own interests.
They go blindly after the treasury of the Commonwealth
like a new-born kitten after milk. But if fortune were to
favor them less, if the smallest *adversitas*[124] appeared, if
the pleasant Favoniuses[125] ceased and cold Aquilos[126]
began to blow, they would fly to southern resorts with the
geese and forget the cares of the fatherland. They would
run to other lands ; like Gypsies they would allow themselves to be robbed in foreign cities. *Domi leones, foris
vulpeculae*.[127] We have a recent proof of this, the Swedish
war. *Saevire Fortuna et cuncta miscere coepit*,[128] when the
military might of almost all our bordering nations, *simul
et semel*,[129] began to oppress us, when for the resistance to
such severe enemy assaults, not a small frightened army
was required as reinforcements, but just as many *centi-*

[123]Men of merit.
[124]Adversity.
[125]In Roman mythology a gentle western wind, considered auspicious
since with it came spring and the rebirth of nature.
[126]Aquilo, a northern wind. The meaning of this metaphor is that at
this time they would fall short of allies and their troubles would begin.
[127]They are lions at home and vixens away from home. (Petronius,
Satyrikon 44, 14).
[128]When fortune began to rage and bring everything into confusion.
(Sallustius, *Bellum Catilinae* 10).
[129]Together and at once (suddenly).

mani Cotti,[130] then how many such zealots were found who *in necessitate*[131] supported, with counsel and fortune, the fallen fatherland ? Did a great number of them flock to the side of the King ? When they saw him *omni spe et consilio destitutum,*[132] each one ran in his own direction and was off, except for some very good and honorable senators and lords who either kept to the side of the King or to that of the army which ran from one place to another *inter viscera*[133] of the fatherland, resisting the fierce enemy like wild boars in the thicket[134] surrounded by the blood-hounds. When God looked at us with favor and when the fatherland shook off its misfortune a little, only then did the zealots show any eagerness to defend the fatherland. *Sero molunt deorum molae.*[135] Only then the number of people came pouring out, as though out of a mouse-hole, to nibble this bread. But they had not come out before, *ex equo Troiano,*[136] to defend it ! Such parasites should expect someday, perhaps even now, to suffer peril from the hands of the army, because it is unpleasant for a brave steed to have a wretched donkey take food from its trough.

I know very well that *captivatio ex consilio*[137] hap-

[130]Cottus, one of the Hecatonchires in classical mythology, the children of Uranus and Gaea. His brothers were Briareus and Gyges ; they had fifty heads and one hundred arms each.
[131]In times of need.
[132]Destitute of all hope and counsel.
[133]Within the boundaries.
[134]Pasek has in mind here the five banners which in 1655 did not surrender to the Swedes with the rest of the army and who, because of that, were not only not given winter quarters but were persecuted by the Swedes as well as by the nobility. Pasek might have served in one of these banners himself. Czapliński, *Pam.,* p. 200, note 288.
[135]The mills of the gods grind slowly. A Greek proverb meaning "Gods do not punish crimes immediately ;" Pasek understood it differently however : "After a while every master is ready." Czubek, *Pam.,* p. 208, note 9.
[136]In the case of the Trojan horse, i.e., out of which the warriors poured out for the peril of Troy.
[137]Imprisonment as a result of a senatorial counsel.

pened to me, but the world would recognize whether such
consilium[138] was beneficial to His Majesty and to the
fatherland. If my fate befell me out of virtue and love for
my fatherland, then I am innocently stoned ; if as an
envoy, then it is also *contra iura gentium*[139] and *contra
regulam iustitiae*,[140] since *quidquid non discutitur, iustitia
non putatur.*[141] Whichever of these two reasons it may be,
from this it immediately becomes apparent to him who
sins that he is doing the right thing, *vel peccantibus virtutis
species prima iucunda est.*[142] But let us wait for the end.
I was the only one out of an army of sixty thousand men
who did not join the confederacy, not because of any
necessity or misdemeanor, but only out of love for my
fatherland. I abandoned the repose and comforts which
the most obscure officer can enjoy now and I am going
to war. I am going to combat, disregarding severe winter,
I am going where they fight and where they drink blood
instead of savory liquors. My father praised my behavior,
friends of the family praised it, and all those who wish the
fatherland well did the same, almost *cum assecuratione*[143]
that I would somehow be rewarded with the fatherland's
gratitude. But apparently my reward began there in the
middle of a forest when I was stopped on a public road,
robbed, taken prisoner and brought here in triumph just
as the African prisoner[144] had been taken into Rome. Oh,
what a tremendous victory it is for so many to conquer
one man, to wreak rage on him and to cry shame upon
him ! Bravery should be displayed there where sixty thou-

[138]Counsel.
[139]Against the law of nations.
[140]Against the principle of justice.
[141]If something is not well disputed, it cannot pass as just.
[142]The old-time form of virtue is pleasant to the sinning ones.
[143]With the assurance.
[144]Jugurtha, c. 156–104 B.C., king of Numidia ; son of Mastanabal and
grandson of Masinissa, captured by the Roman general Metelleus and
dictator Lucius Cornelius Sulla and exhibited by the Roman general
Caius Marius in a triumphal procession at Rome in 104 B.C. He was
then put to death by strangling.

sand swords flash before one's eyes, and not here before one man ! The army will know how to repay for the disgrace suffered by my person, because, even though I am not a confederate, I am a soldier entitled to the same merits ; even though I am not an envoy I was dishonored as an envoy-*intentio pro facto*.[145] One should not fool around with Jaskulski's Confederacy[146] at the time when the better part of the army is beyond the sea ; their collective might can help or harm. *In quorum manibus arma sunt, in eorum potestate est conservare et perdere Rempublicam*.[147] I shall return to the army and I shall know how to relate the kind of gratitude they are to expect for their blood-earned merits ; I shall know how to put my claim before everyone who gave me and the entire army such foul service. And now I appeal to Heaven and Earth for my injustice and I sincerely regret with all my heart everything I did for the fatherland. *Cum vitia prosunt, peccat, qui recte facit*.[148]

As soon as I stopped speaking some of the senators began to raise objections and I had to retort to each one of them. First, the Lithuanian Vice-Chancellor Naruszewicz,[149] spoke as follows :

When I consider the actual content of this speech I find that it *accusat*[150] more than *excusat*[151] because in it Your Lordship disavows the confederacy and claims not to be an envoy, but sides with the army in such a way that an official envoy could not do or say more. Now even I myself, though I was not aware of this until the end of your speech, would not sin by suspecting you of being an

---

[145]Intention for the deed.
[146]The confederacy formed in 1659 by Marian Jaskulski was appeased with an advance on their pay. Czubek, *Pam.*, p. 210, note 4.
[147]The power to save or to ruin the Commonwealth lies in the hands of those who have the weapons.
[148]If crimes bring gains, decency means sin. Publius Syrus, *Sententiae*, 98.
[149]Alexander Naruszewicz. Czubek, *Pam.*, p. 211, note 4.
[150]Accuses.
[151]Acquits.

envoy when I take into account that credentials are not necessary for this, because everything which was to be expressed on paper could be stored in the head. The second reason for making this very probable is that since the soldiers of his Majesty were attacked by some rogues from the Lithuanian army it is apparent that they knew about it. Thirdly, because your Lordship speaks so haughtily, mistrusts us senators, and insults His Majesty the King, you are, for doing that alone, *hostis patriae et reus criminis laesae maiestatis.*[152]

He said more at length but it is difficult *exprimere*[153] someone else's words and sentiments *de verbo ad verbum.*[154] To which I answered thus :

I can say that the remarks of the Honorable Senator are just and correct because if I were in his position myself I surely would not have judged his Honor differently under similar circumstances. To his remarks I give such justifications. To the first one : I am grateful to my father who had me educated when I was young, and as the saying goes, *necessitas acuit ingenium.*[155] To the second one : Not I but those who wanted to liberate me should give explanation, as they did not know me and did not see me before and did this under the false assumption that I was an envoy. I am surprised however that your Honor calls them rogues, for I was unaware until now that rogues could be found in such a respectable nation as the Lithuanian Duchy, as there are none in our army. To the third comment I respond thus : a clever man should apply everything to himself. May your Honor, whose decency is unquestionable, condescend to teach me, I pray, how he would feel if he were submitted to the indignity of being captured on a highway, imprisoned and accused of treason to the Commonwealth, although obviously innocent and

[152]An enemy of the fatherland and guilty of the crime of offending His Majesty.
[153]To express.
[154]Word for word.
[155]Necessity sharpens the mind.

not even convicted under the law ? If your Honor tells me
that it would have been a grave affront *generoso pectori*,[156]
then *consequentia*[157] it applies to me, who can match
everyone as far as noble origin and virtue are concerned.
Though this worries me, I still do not feel embarassed
because I feel innocent. *Maximum solatium est vacare
culpa*.[158] And even if I were guilty it would not do a good
man any good, even if he were to weep his eyes out when
he is wronged in honor and reputation by an evil one.
This should never disturb an innocent man, even if one
were to trespass beyond law and justice, because he does
this at his own risk and this cannot upset a good man.
Bonus animus in re mala dimidium est mali ![159]—so say
the wise men. *In crimine laesae Maiestatis*,[160] even Cato's[161]
censure will not harm me ; someone else will suffer from
it sooner than I, *privatus*.[162] Because I do not speak of His
Majesty here, no one can find in my heart a reprimand of
the kind reign of his Most Gracious Majesty. Is it fit to
say that special atrocity was attached to this offense of
mine ? All this is the result *ex abundatia malitiae*[163] and
the guilty one is the one who has accused me and not the
one who rebukes me. I am addressing those who have
brought this charge against me, those who were at the

[156]To a noble heart.
[157]Consequently.
[158]The greatest consolation is when one does not feel guilty. Cicero,
Ad Familiares 7, 5.
[159]A good thought in misfortune is half the evil. Publilius Syrus, *Sententiae*.
[160]As far as offending His Majesty is concerned.
[161]Cato the Elder or Cato the Censor (Marcus Porcius Cato) 234–149
B.C., Roman statesman, Censor in 184. As Censor he tried to reform
Roman morals and banned foreign habits and customs. Upon his
return from Carthage, he used to end all his speeches in the senate with
Ceterum censeo Carthaginem esse delendam. "Also, I am of the
opinion that Carthage should be destroyed." His *De Agri Cultura*
survives. Of his historical *Origines*, in seven books, his speeches, letters, essays, only fragments have remained however.
[162]An ordinary man.
[163]Of an excess of spite.

16*

council and who imprisoned me here. I said before and
I say again—*nescit vox missa reverti*[164]—I shall know
how to rebuke for this all those who are my equal by
birth. Regional councils, tribunals and war councils serve
for this purpose. *Utraque civis*,[165] a nobleman and a soldier—I never retract my words. *Hoc mihi pietas, hoc pia
lingua odit.*[166]

Pac,[167] the Voivode of Troki, spoke up next. If I remember
well, his speech was as follows :

It is painful indeed when some misfortune befalls us, and
if the unfortunate one speaks *licentiose*[168] under such circumstances, it is not his fault but the fault of the one who
makes him lose patience. For they say that sorrow knows
no consideration. If he is innocent, I do not hold it very
much against him ; but if the guilty man speaks so haughtily then his sin is a double one, as the crime of *lèse-
majesté* and the offence to our senatorial dignity are
reflected in it as in a mirror. Having before one's eyes the
same reasons as his Honor the Vice-Chancellor, a lord
and brother, I also consider this man rather guilty than
innocent.

And presently he addressed to me this apostrophe :

You, sir, threaten us with the army, you threaten us with
vengeance, and you promise to return to the confederacy.
Are you sure that you will leave this place in good
health ? Did you ask whether you would be allowed to
take your head out of here ? Don't such actions as yours
deserve capital punishment ? We ourselves shall see to
this *et instabimus*[169] that His Majesty not allow to go un-
punished the insults to which we were subjected by
a person who cannot be either so important or deserving
because his age alone indicates this.

[164]A spoken word does not come back. Horatius, *De arte poëtica*, 390.
[165]I am doubly a citizen.
[166]This I consider as a virtue and my lips would not do otherwise.
[167]Mikołaj Stefan Pac.
[168]Harshly.
[169]And we shall insist.

And he continued to speak rather at large in this manner. To which I answered him with the following words:

Your Honor has admitted that it is very painful to suffer such great calumny, being innocent. Your Honor has also admitted that whatever sorrow the heart may possess, the tongue, as its natural *interpres*,[170] must proclaim it to the world. And, after all that, your Honor added *afflicto afflictionem*.[171] I must answer with the Scripture therefore: *Si veritatem loquor, cur me caedis?*[172] Your Honor threatens me with death—which is the lot of all living beings. *Quisquis ad vitam editur, ad mortem destinatur.*[173] Your Honor frightens me with old threats of death which may reach sooner the study of your Honor than my tent. I am not sure that they will not be more frightful to your Honor behind a golden bed curtain than to me on a poor soldier's felt pallet. Whoever serves in the war scorns death because he seeks death, and vice versa. I sought death, even at my young age, beyond the Dnieper and beyond the Dniester, beyond the Oder and beyond the Elbe, by the ocean and by the Baltic Sea. Your Honor would endeavor to avoid it. I, on the other hand, do not care because I know that such is the *sequentia*[174] of this life: *exilium, luctus, dolor tributa sunt ista vivendi.*[175] If one is to die let him die, but die well: and, supposedly, there is no better death than the one which befalls him who is innocent and who dies for the virtue and love of the fatherland. If it is considered *actus meritorius*[176] to die for the fatherland, it should also be meritorious for the sons of the fatherland to perish at the hands of the fathers of the fatherland. What gain can be derived from this

[170]Interpreter.
[171]Affliction to the afflicted.
[172]If I speak the truth why do you punish me? Gospel of St. John 18, 23; a paraphrased citation.
[173]Whoever comes to this world is destined to die.
[174]Exile.
[175]Exile, crying, and pain are things inseparable from life.
[176]An act of merit.

however can be perceived from the results. It was written that Perseus, who wanted to render his fatherland a service, *occidit anguem, e cuius collo guttae cadentes innumeros genuere colubros.*[177] My innocent blood will not put out the flame which someone has kindled—most likely to the peril of the fatherland—*malevolis consiliis.*[178] God, the army, and my poor *parentela*[179] will intercede for my innocence because it is not difficult for me to find kinship, being a nobleman. Even if my head were to fall, my teeth and some *nominis recordatio*[180] will be left behind. This is no great news. Men *magnorum nominum*[181] have found themselves in similar circumstances before. *Ita semper illustribus viris animo vivere longe antiquius fuit quam corpore.*[182] In spite of all these threats, I feel that I should not fear and lose hope, because I am innocent. *Aegrotus quamdiu animam habet, spem habet.*[183] The mercy of God is greater than the fury of the entire world. *Dei proprium est protegere, quos dignos iudicat.*[184] Since in the eyes of your Honor I lack any prestige, what am I to do? My age and my present rank do not demand such dignity as to scowl and to sit in a chair like a spider.[185] It happens sometimes that even such heights are levelled with the plains. Careful people will not step even on an old tire; wise people will not slight even the shabbiest man. *Nemo*

---

[177]Killed a serpent, whose blood flowing from his neck produced a multitude of serpents. Perseus slew the Gorgon Medusa and not a serpent; he did this by no means to render a service to his fatherland.

[178]With malicious counsel.

[179]Family.

[180]Memory of my name.

[181]Of great fame.

[182]Thus for many centuries men have lived longer in spirit than in body.

[183]A sick person does not lose hope as long as his soul is still in his body.

[184]God's purpose is to protect those whom He considers worthy.

[185]Here a malicious allusion to the senatorial chair. Czapliński, *Pam.*, p. 209, note 384.

est contemnendus, in quo aliqua virtutis significatio apparet.[186]

He spoke up again thus :

Quot verba, tot minaciae[187] or should I rather say *tot scommata.*[188] Whoever is listening can easily admit that the accused one should not be allowed to justify himself in such a way, should not be allowed to aggravate His Majesty and the Senate with such insults, should not be allowed to dissimulate his deeds by vainly boasting of his *merita*[189] toward the fatherland, listing adventures, places, rivers, and oceans, none of which we know to be true. We also were on the sea and beyond the sea, but we do not refer to that. (He cited a maxim here which I do not remember but it was appropriate to the charges). A man who reproaches his services to his country should rather do nothing for it, even if he did the most, for one evil deed *annihilat*[190] all these merits. If someone exalts the fatherland on occasion and then degrades it, if at one time he proves himself its son and at another its stepson, and if having done wrong he still *gloriatur*[191] and insults statesmen of the Commonwealth, such haughtiness should be repaid by the dungeon and the sword.

To which I gave the following answer :

To be accused and to be guilty are two different things : I find myself accused, but I do not feel guilty and therefore I defend innocence. My innocence *pro me militat.*[192] I have faith in God that in this whirlpool nobody will catch any fish. I do not twit the fatherland with my merits, but I merely recall them and give them *in lancem considerationis*[193] for deserving a recompense different from

[186]One should not slight anyone in whom any trace of virtue can be perceived.
[187]As many words, as many threats.
[188]As many jeers.
[189]Merits.
[190]Annihilates.
[191]Boasts.
[192]Militates for me.
[193]As the basis of consideration.

the one offered to me *ad praesens*.[194] If anyone has any
doubts as to my merits and whether or not I have earned
them, *cicatrices*, borne *adverso pectore*[195] are proof of
this. There are many companions at arms of mine who
will testify to this, those who were there and who watched
it, but it would have been difficult for anyone eating
oysters, snails, and truffles, while resting at home, to see
this. I do not want to argue about whether anyone has or
has not been on or beyond the sea, and I *facile credo*[196]
because *indicat vestis, quales intrinsecus estis*.[197] But after
all the nature of travel is different when one learns : *Pierla
italiano* ? *Pierla franciezo* ? and a different one when one
learns : *Wer do* ? Give the password ! It is a different
matter to listen to gracious melodies, to learn ballet, cap-
rioles, dances, to get ready to step according to the music
than to follow the sound of Mars' band. It is one matter
to pour out sweet liquors and another to shed blood.
I have always done *quantum potui pro patria*,[198] that I am
sure of ; and since I have neither now nor before done
anything *contra patriam*,[199] I can safely call myself her son
and not her stepson. I could sooner find stepfathers *inter·
patres patriae quorum machinationes*[200] have impaired the
Polish Commonwealth and have brought it to extreme
poverty, whose unjust actions have drowned its fame *in
profundissimo Democriti puteo*.[201] Through the valor and
bravery of the army, however, it was brought back out
from such grave labyrinths and restored. Without looking

[194]Now.
[195]The scars on my chest, which faced the enemy.
[196]Believe it without any difficulty, i.e., readily believe.
[197]The frock indicates what you are like inside.
[198]As much as I could for the fatherland.
[199]Against the fatherland.
[200]Among the fathers of the fatherland whose plottings...
[201]In the deepest well of Democritus. Democritus, called the Abderite,
and the laughing philosopher, Greek philosopher, born at Abdera, in
Thrace c. 460 B.C. (died c. 370 B.C.), the most learned of the Greeks
before Aristotle.

far for evidence I can ask what kind of damage and confusion did the Swedish war bring to the fatherland ! What
brought about the Swedish war however ? *Mala consilia
ordinis intermedii*[202] and the unjust judgment of Radziejowski.[203] And I do not explain in what way it was unjust
because I am speaking to those who are familiar with the
case. And if one had to start a war it should have been
started on a good foundation so that the end would not
shame the beginning and so that we should not regret what
we had started, of which the Swedish war is an obvious
example. It can be recalled how difficult it was for us to
leave our domestic pleasures, harvests, and possessions
and to wander abroad ; and on the other hand to recall
how pleasant it was, even though with a diminished purse,
to return *ad propria*[204] and to greet our *Lares* ![205] Who was
the cause of this ? Certainly not the one who, sitting
abroad, was asking what was going on in Poland. But
who ? This was made possible *per instrumenta*[206] the com-
mands of God, through the toils and the courage of the
army, through the efforts and alertness of good leaders, *in
singulari*,[207] simply speaking, *unus homo nobis cunctando
restituit rem.*[208] Now how should one deal with this confederacy or speaking *politius*[209] with the present alliance ?
I shall see if the one who formed it will dissolve it just as

<hr>

[202]Bad counsel of the intermediary body. The intermediary body
between the king and the knighthood was the senate. Czubek, *Pam.*,
p. 220, note 11.
[203]Hieronim Radziejowski, Vice-Chancellor of Poland, who was sentenced to exile, took refuge in Sweden, and then plotted with the
Swedes against Poland.
[204]To one's possessions.
[205]*Lares* and *penates* ; Roman benevolent spirits and gods of the household, thus cherished possessions.
[206]Through.
[207]Or rather.
[208]Because of one man who saved our fatherland by lingering. Cicero,
De senectute IV. The words of Aenius about Fabius Cunctator ; here
Czarniecki. Czubek, *Pam.*, p. 221, note 9.
[209]More politely.

quickly. This is the *nodus Gordius*[210] and it was easy to tie it with two fingers, but a moment later it could not be untied, even with the teeth. Whoever formed it is guilty before God and before the fatherland. A pious monarch exclaimed once to a bad administrator : '*Vare, legiones redde.*'[211] Our Commonwealth needs to exercise special caution *contra tot Varos.*[212] *Reddite rationem*[213] of the Swedish war which you have enkindled in the promotion of private interests against God and the law ; repay God for the indignation He suffered in His temples at the hands of the Swedish dissenters, return the cities, palaces and castles burned down and levelled with the earth, repay *nobilitati*[214] the suffered oppression and return their lost possessions ; return the blood shed because of this war and return the fatherland its perished sons, erase the forever ineffaceable disgrace to His Majesty and to the entire nation.

Turning *ad modernum statum*,[215] *redde* :[216] Give back! Return to the poor people the piece of bread, earned by them by hard labor and taken out of their mouths, and almost the last drop of their blood sucked out ! Restore to God His Holy Glory. Give back to the fatherland Smolensk, Kiev, Novgorod-Seversk,[217] the territory lying beyond the Dnieper and the more distant frontiers ! For the

[210]The Gordian knot. An intricate knot of Gordius, the legendary king of Phrygia and the founder of Gordium. Whoever could untie this knot was to rule all of Asia. Alexander the Great severed it with his sword.

[211]Varus, give me back my legions ! Caesar Augustus, Caius Julius Caesar Octavianus, the first Roman emperor, said these words to Publius Quintilius Varus, the commander of the Roman legions in Germany, after he was defeated by the Germans in the battle of Teutoburger Wald (9 A.D.), Svetonius, *Life of Augustus* 23.

[212]Against so many Varuses.

[213]Give an account.

[214]Nobility.

[215]To those presently assembled.

[216]I say.

[217]The land of Seversk, together with the city of Czernichów and Novgorod-Seversk, on the Desna, was occupied by the Muscovites in 1654. Czubek, *Pam.*, p. 222, note 11.

one of whose brain this confederacy is the coinage, one
needs a new hell. One should invent new and unusual
tortures. For him, one should summon a sharp sword and
the horrible hand of an executioner. Because before the
confederacy dissolves the enemy will gather strength. The
turn of fortune may be different. Later the enemy will
bargain with us. It will extract from us all that we could
have obtained from him, such is the custom with us ; once
we conquer the enemy we always give him reparation.

I stipulate and *praecustodio*[218] that I speak not to the
fathers, not to the respectable senators, but to the stepfathers of the fatherland. Whoever feels guilty let him be
offended if he wants to. I have never been a stepson but
a son to my fatherland, my mother. I could not be a stepson even if I wanted to, for I am a nobleman *ex nativo
sanguine,*[219] not one who has acquired his nobility abroad.
My innate love would not allow me to act as such. The
threats of the dungeon and sword should be reserved for
these good counselors, for I am not afraid of them. '*Etsi
caelum ruet, impavidum ferient ruinae.*[220]

Some tried to interrupt even while I was speaking, but
since I had said at the conclusion : "Whoever feels guilty, let
him be offended,"[221] which is a *dicterium tritum*[222] and familiar
to everyone, they were dead silent. The King, who had been
listening behind a portiere, as I was later told, had a good
laugh and said. "What a man ! What a blunt speaker.[223] He is
telling them the truth. Even if he were really an envoy I would
not have him punished for this quality alone." But this was
only related to me later.

[218]In advance.
[219]A true-born Polish nobleman, of native blood.
[220]Even if the heavens were to fall, the fearless one will be covered by
the ruins. Not an accurate citation from Horatius, *Carmina* III, 3, 7.
[221]The Polish proverb used here translates literally into English as :
"Whoever feels like scissors may be offended."
[222]Standing proverb.
[223]In Polish this reads as "realista." Brückner believed that the copyist
had made a mistake and that it should read *regalista* meaning royalist
rather than realist.

Everyone fell silent ; they just looked at each other for awhile. Then Jewłaszowski,[224] the voivode of Brest Litovsk, began to speak. He used many words and gave ample reasons. His speech was of somewhat the following content :

I consider it a heavy blow to the senatorial body when it is being called stepfathers, parasites, useless mouths, and finally traitors of the fatherland. I do not know whether such accusations are *debitae*[225] in anyone's case, but even though I myself do not consider myself guilty of them it hurts me, nevertheless, because I am a senator. If such insults are thrown at us by one cavalry officer we may expect the same logic of behavior also from others. *Expedit*[226] that his Majesty intercede in this abuse of his and our name. Since the army is subservient to us and since we are the *capita*[227] of this Commonwealth such behavior must be absolutely reproved.

He spoke eloquently and at length in that vein, but it is impossible to remember the entire speech. I had anticipated such and similar charges against me and considering the course of the case I knew such speeches would be made. I had prepared myself so that I would have *rationes competentes*[228] to refute them. *Ex occasione*[229] of those which came by chance God supplied the refutation.

I answered him as follows :

If an accusation directed at others who are guilty, even though small, seems unpleasant to someone who claims to be innocent himself, may he consider how difficult it might be for him who never deserved ingratitude from the fatherland but *meruit*[230] every recompense of gratitude, being *in plano*[231] innocent, but who is being

[224]Kazimierz Jewłaszewski.
[225]Justified.
[226]It beseems.
[227]Heads.
[228]Appropriate reasons.
[229]In the case.
[230]Deserved.
[231]Completely.

defamed and insulted by a long memorable offense, as I am now. But since your Honor said 'by one cavalry officer' and almost added 'and not a very important one' let his Honor be reminded that he himself rose from a cavalry officer to senator and even now should not slight the less significant ones. As the saying goes : '*Sacerdos de unamissa.*'[232]

. He became very angry and began to speak violently :

So you will insult us one after another ? I shall hurt you if I so desire. Remember this will harm you very much.

I said again :

I know that everyone's friendship is useful to me but also mine is useful to everyone else. May no one threaten me with such statements, because I prefer to renounce such support forever and I do not think that the slander thrown at me unjustly, since I am innocent, and my truthful words will harm me. '*Ei sane non multum poterit obesse fortuna, qui sibi firmius in virtute, quam in casu, praesidium collocavit.*'[233]

And I finished my reply with that maxim.

This senator got angry at me mostly for two reasons. First of all because I criticized him as "*Sacerdos de une missa,*" since he did not have many possessions, only one village, where the soil was ploughed by three hundred horses ; second, for that "cavalry officer" remark. And I purposely criticized whatever I could think of because I trusted in my innocence as much as in an army of one hundred thousand men. And they twisted it all and said that I wanted to evade the accusation under the pretext of innocence. Father Ujejski,[234] the Bishop of Kiev, came back while the Voivode of Troki was speaking. He

[232]A priest only for saying Mass, i.e., simpleton who only knows how to say Mass and does not know theology and is not capable of fulfilling other duties as a priest. Czubek, *Pam.*, p. 225, note 8.

[233]Indeed fortune cannot harm very much someone who has chosen for himself a stronger defense in virtue than in blind fate. Cicero, *Ad Herennium* IV, 19, 13.

[234]Tomasz Ujejski.

had gone to the room where the King and Queen were listening to the course of events behind a screen. He took the floor and spoke as follows :

Whatever one does not experience himself he cannot understand so well as one who has had the taste of it himself. I also experienced a calumny once in my life, as far as I can remember, and since it was undeserved, the bitterness of it still *haeret*[235] in my heart and most likely will not leave my memory until death. Also in this case I *facile credo*[236] and would swear to it, that it is a false accusation. When I consider all the circumstances, I see that he had a proper upbringing and the education of a nobleman's son. When I *in parte*[237] observed his modest and good habits and appearance, apparently such since youth, I can safely conclude that this is a false accusation. And if it is false it must hurt ; and if it hurts is should consequently not be taken amiss very much, for in grief someone can say too much. Even though I have been put in the post of this senatorial chair by the providence of God and the grace of His Majesty, our merciful lord, I am always favorably inclined toward the entire army—'*omnis mercenarius sua diagnus mercede.*'[238] That the army demands to be paid should not surprise anyone, for it must be granted them ; but I feel that this question should have been brought up once more *ultimari*,[239] irrespective of the confederacy which *infallibiliter*[240] will bring to the fatherland—*utinam sim falsus vates* ![241]—great *detrimenta*[242] and the harm which have been mentioned by the soldier standing now *prae oculis*.[243] The declaration of the Commonwealth and of His Majesty should be conformed to and

[235]Sticks.
[236]Readily believe.
[237]Somewhat.
[238]Every hireling is worthy of pay. Gospel of St. Luke 10, 7.
[239]For the last time.
[240]No doubt.
[241]May I be a false prophet !
[242]Damage
[243]Before our eyes.

ad violenta media[244] should not be so immediately resorted
to. One should not deal with His Majesty, our gracious
lord, so *inhumaniter*,[245] one should not arrest the King's
couriers on the roads, inspect letters, and fully disrespect
the estates of His Majesty. I openly say that I can not
condone such behavior and *quo motivo*[246] His Majesty,
our gracious lord, has to be very cautious of such uncalled-
for behavior. Thus, when someone presumed you to be an
envoy, he reported to the King that you were not only an
envoy of the Lithuanian conspirators who not only keeps
in touch with them as to further action, but also as to the
proceedings of the army which is in the service of His
Majesty and of the Commonwealth and *sub regimine*[247]
of the Ruthenian Voivode in order to *avocare*[248] them and
to invite them to join the confederacy and *orbare*[249] His
Majesty *omni praesidio et custodio corporis*.[250] If this
really were the case the King would have something to be
resentful about; if it is not so however (which I myself
believe to be the case), it should be attributed *infelicitati
temporis*[251] that such suspicion had fallen on your lordship
because of someone's invention. You should not be disturbed about this, however. This incident will not bring
any harm or disgrace to your lordship. On the contrary,
when your lordship proves that he abandoned the confederacy and set out to join those who are favorable to His
Majesty and the fatherland, His Majesty will be grateful.
He will cherish your lordship's merits in his memory and
will reward them with all kinds of favor. No judgment
should be too meticulous, because, as they say: '*Nihil
adeo malum est, quin boni mixturam habeat.*'[252] And

[244]Violent means.
[245]In such an inhuman way.
[246]For this reason.
[247]Under the command.
[248]Divert.
[249]To deprive.
[250]Of all means of defense and of his bodyguard as well.
[251]To the misfortune of present times.
[252]Nothing is so bad that it does not have some mixture of good.

I assure your lordship that this incident will never damage your honor nor your good reputation but will even grant you easy access to all sorts of rewards of His Majesty and of the Commonwealth. Sometimes paths leading to good fame are tedious, but what of it when such fame earns more durability in the world than one brought by the favorable Favonius of prosperity. And I can find more of those whose virtue is remembered in the world thanks to hardships. '*Hectorem quis nosset, felix si Troia fuisset.*'[253] May this affliction not disturb your lordship because the consequence of it will be good fame and all sorts of good fortune. And now even time itself tells us to part. May your lordship return to your quarters and await the further announcement of His Majesty.

He spoke *fuse*,[254] with choice words, but I wrote down only the very *essentiam* of it.[255] When he[256] finished this consoling speech it was apparent that it was not to the liking of the other senators, for they realized that it was *ex mente*[257] of the King. I also surmised this because he came out from behind the portiere. I replied to his words in the following manner :

Thank Heaven that *inter tot moderni collegii sinistras opiniones*[258] I finally have lived to hear, at last, one *iudicium pro innocentia*[259] of a poor nobleman and soldier. But they say that *facilius est consolari afflictum, quam sustinere.*[260] So whoever suffers, keeps on suffering. I humbly thank the *magno praesuli*[261] and a distinguished Senator of our fatherland, but after all *vulnera dum sanas, dolor*

[253]Who would have known of Hector if Troy had been happy ? Ovidius, *Tristia* IV, 3, 75.
[254]At length.
[255]Essentials.
[256]Bishop Ujejski.
[257]In accordance with the opinion.
[258]Among so many bad opinions of the presently assembled.
[259]Speech in favor of the innocence.
[260]It is easier to console than to lift the afflicted man.
[261]Great Bishop.

est medicina doloris.[262] This little word '*si*'[263] is a sign of doubt, and I feel hurt that others doubt my innocence. But what am I to do? *Iugulatur virtus,*[264] but this only makes me feel glad, for *oppressa gloriosior.*[265] If this befalls me from someone's false accusation, a mongrel[266] can also bark at a roadside cross, but I side with Seneca: '*Ille enim magnus et nobilis est, qui more magnae ferae(scit)latratus canum securus exaudire.*'[267] If I am proven guilty, *succumbam.*[268] And now, since I do not feel a traitor to His Most Gracious Majesty and to the fatherland, and if I am worthy *videre faciem domini,*[269] I ask your Excellency for help.

The Bishop replied: "Most likely your lordship will have an audience with the King, but not today."

They rose abruptly and I left the chamber. Only the regular guard and my retainers were at the door; the others were gone. I asked: "And where are my *custodes*?"[270] I was told that they had left an hour ago. *Supponebam*[271] that they had gone to my quarters and asked: "So the envoy could not escape if he wanted to?" Karpiński, an officer of the royal guard, replied: "Surely he could have done so long ago if he wanted to." I left. When I arrived in the inn nobody was there, even the guns, of which the hallway had been full, were gone; only my usual meal, regularly sent to me from the royal kitchen, was on the table. The innkeeper came in and congratulated me on God's granting me peace. I asked him where

---

[262]When one heals the wounds, pain is the medicine of suffering. Cato, *Disticha*, IV, 40.
[263]If.
[264]Virtue is represented.
[265]The repressed one is more meritorious.
[266]In the original text *Kurta*, a common dog's name in Poland.
[267]That one is great and noble who according to the habit of a huge animal, calmly listens to the barking of dogs. Not an accurate citation from Seneca, *De ira* XI, 32, 2.
[268]I shall give in.
[269]To see his Majesty.
[270]Guards.
[271]I assumed.

everybody had disappeared to. He told me that they had come from the palace, taken their things and those which they had left behind, and run back head over heels, cursing Mazepa. I sat down to eat and invited the innkeeper to join me, for Father Gostkowski was forbidden to visit me, since he allegedly brought to me whatever news he obtained from the courtiers. After I drank several bottles of excellent wine, I went to sleep.

I woke up shortly before daybreak when I heard some rustle by the walls and I called my retainer: "Orłowski, go and see what the commotion is in front of the hallway!" He went there and the stableman, who slept by the horses, told him that the men who had been here before had returned. When he told me that I wondered what it was all about. Did they test me the way children test a sparrow, having tied it and holding it back with the thread if it tries to escape, or what else? Outside, the weather was bad, it was snowing, and they kept walking around and pacing up and down. When they heard me talking they began to shout: "Oh, sir, may your lordship give the order to have us admitted to the hallway because we shall freeze here." I pretended to be asleep and my retainers called out from the hallway: "Do not wake the master!" So they stayed there until next morning, pacing in the snow, for on the following day I gave orders not to open the inn until an hour after daybreak. As soon as they entered the hallway I asked them: "Why do you leave and then return?" They said: "We don't know ourselves what they are doing with us and with your lordship. When your lordship was in the royal chambers we were told to leave this post with everything instantly, 'so that the officer concerned would not find any of you when he arrives in the inn,' and after midnight they sent us back here to watch most attentively." I reflected on this and thought that perhaps the King had already pronounced me innocent and was to set me free tomorrow, but that the senators had tried to convince the King that I was important and that I had offended His Majesty; they vowed and were ready to sell their souls to the devil to prove that I must be an envoy and the King let himself be persuaded and again sent the guard. Also

Tyzenhaus,[272] the starost of Uświat, a great enemy of mine, must have helped this along by saying : "Your Majesty now sees that my words were true when I said that this man, although young, is very mature."

The Bishop of Kiev came to see me then and advised me to avoid risking my life and to rely on the King's grace. He said : "It came through the mail that the army had sent you as an envoy, and it will be more to your advantage if you confess to everything voluntarily. The King will be gracious, will promote you, admit you immediately to his side, and offer you a good starosty. What will you gain by the grace of the army ? The King has already gotten to know you from your speeches, he already knows you as a person, and he will treat you properly ; he has already learned that you are of a stable character, and he has appreciated the fact that *inter tot anfractus*[273] you kept the oath given to the army and did not want to give away their secret, which is a praiseworthy virtue in every man. Great gentlemen gladly enjoy the company of such people and put their confidence in them. Listen to my persuasion, and my priestly conscience will see to it that not even a hair shall fall off your head and that you shall have much good fame, rewards from the King, and all sorts of honors as well. If it is a matter of the oath by which you and the army are bound together not to reveal the secrets, I shall absolve you from this. The King only wants to repay them for what they did. The letters of His Majesty which were destined for Vienna and France, they tore open and read *quae(dam) secretiora*,[274] they censored our good King, and they spied on him as on a traitor. There was nothing in them either *contra Rempublicam*[275] or the army, but he feels disturbed that such a thing could happen to a King."

He proposed to me these and similar things, and I listened in silence. I was both angry and amused, thinking why God let such strange things happen to me, for they wanted to talk me

---

[272]Jędrzej Tyzenhaus.
[273]In the face of so many attacks.
[274]Whatever was most confidential.
[275]Against the (Polish) Commonwealth.

into admitting to what they needed and I did not feel like
giving in. I realized now why the guard had been removed and
sent back after midnight. I reflected that the mail, about which
the Bishop had talked, must have arrived at that time and in it
they must have written about this suspected envoyship, but my
person was not identified, since I myself knew what my mission
was and where I was going. Someone hostile to me must have
done it in order to submit me to a plight, as I did not want to
join the confederacy. But I gave myself up to God and answered the Bishop as follows :

If the starost of Uświat[276] came to me with this together with the son of the voivode of Smolensk,[277] who had
been coming to see me before, I would have known how
to answer them because one layman can sometimes express something to another layman *per parabolas.*[278] But
since it is your Excellency, a great and distinguished
senator and my great benefactor, whose grace and good
intentions I know about, I must act more gently, even
though this matter is painful to me.

May God himself, who created Heaven and Earth,
your Excellency and me, humble man, testify for me as
the protector *innocentiae,*[279] since virtue and honor cannot
testify for me. May He punish my accuser and thus the
cause of this unnecessary trouble to your Honors. These
assurances are not necessary because time—as *omnium
malorum medicus*[280]—will prove this and my innocence
will float to the top like oil. If I had been foolish enough
as to be unaware that a clear conscience is a great defense,
I would have succumbed, I would have looked for a way
out. I would have managed to escape from here, not once
but ten times. But I know that, being innocent, no lies can
harm me. I said at the first hearing that even a mongrel

[276]Jędrzej Tyzenhaus.
[277]The voivode of Smolensk was Adam Maciej Sakowicz. Czubek,
Pam., p. 235, note 2.
[278]In figurative speech.
[279]Of innocence.
[280]As the healer of all sufferings.

can bark at a cross. Neither threats nor entreaties can
disconcert my resolution. The sun will not turn into
a poppy, truth will not change into untruth for a request's
sake. God sees that threats will not make me give in an
inch and even if something were to befall me in my innocence, I shall neither beg nor be afraid, heeding the
opinion of a wise poet :

*'Nescia mens fraudum inculpataeque integra vitae,
scomnata nullius, nullius arma timet.*

Omnia contemnit ventis velut obvia rupes,
mendacesque sonos unius assis habet.'[281]

Let the unvirtuous one rejoice by talking his fill about
the good qualities of the virtuous ones. May the one who
expects to be contended with the true reality entertain
himself *ad praesens*[282] by vain hope that he will be spared
disgrace. *Meum est*[283] to imitate the wise sentiment and
the fearlessness *antecedanei saeculi* :[284]

*'Qui sapis, ad vitam sapias ; gere conscia recti
pectora nec strepitu commoveare levi.'*[285]

Just as there was no likelihood of my being guilty
before, there is none also now. All the circumstances make
me free and I speak thus : Just as when your Excellency,
who walks away *a sacrificio missae,*[286] has confidence that
he possesses a holy soul, so I myself testify in the name of
God now that I am innocent of this calumny. I shall not
even blush at those insinuations hinted at in the mail. All
those false rumors shall not mislead me. I shall not be
frightened by threats for I am innocent. I am very honest
before your Excellency. Even *sub sigillo confessionis*[287]

---

[281]A man void of treason, immaculate and pure/Is fearless of assaults
and jeers/Like a rock exposed to winds/He is unconcerned, and
fearless of voices of deceit.
[282]Momentarily.
[283]I desire.
[284]Or former ages.
[285]If you are wise show your wisdom during your lifetime, but have
a clear conscience and don't be afraid of just any rustle.
[286]Having made the sacrifice of the holy Mass.
[287]Under the seal of confession.

I could not have been more so. Also before His Majesty the King himself—if I am worthy of the honor—I cannot justify myself differently and more sincerely than I have justified myself before your Excellency, who *sine fuco adulationis*[288] is worthy of it. I also beg *humillime*[289] that Your Excellency not reveal that I have behaved so frankly *cum invocatione*[290] of God's name. Let them think whatever they want of me until the apparent truth exonerates me from this opinion.

Now I believe *absolutissime*[291] that you are *innocuus.*[292] Even though I was going to defend you with *omnibus persuasionibus*[293] before His Majesty I shall be quiet now. For you have faith in yourself and I see that when this matter is cleared with an irrefutable deduction, it will do more justice to your reputation and honor. *Et interim*[294] you can be *bonae mentis*[295] for I am not worried about you.

Hhe then went and reported to the King, I don't know what, and he kept sending me food from the kitchen. Things improved for me now as food was delivered to me from both the King and the Bishop.

When I was summoned to His Majesty, the Lithuanian Vice-Chancellor[296] addressed me thus : "What your lordship wished to obtain from the grace of His Majesty, our gracious lord, is being granted since His Majesty does not refuse to listen to your Lordship's justification." But when I saw that there was not a large group of people with the King, only the Bishop of Kiev, the Lithuanian Vice-Chancellor and Sielski,[297]

[288]Without any shade of flattery.
[289]Most humbly.
[290]I.e.; calling or in God's name.
[291]Absolutely.
[292]Innocent.
[293]All sorts of arguments.
[294]In the meantime.
[295]Of good cheer.
[296]Aleksander Naruszewicz. Czubek, *Pam.*, p. 238, note 1.
[297]Aleksander Sielski.

the Castellan of Gniezno, and a few courtiers as well. I said to
the King :

Your Majesty, my gracious lord ! The innate kindness of Your Majesty is known not only to me, *privato*,[298]
but also to all the estates, lands of the Commonwealth,
and courtiers under Your Majesty's domination. We experience it since Your Majesty does not refuse to listen at
all times of need, for which I humbly thank Your Majesty.
Suppono[299] that I would have been free of this accusation
long ago if I could have received earlier the grace which
is being granted to me *ad praesens*.[300] *Nil restat*[301] to me
but to fall to the feet of my gracious lord and to humbly
beg to be so fortunate as to *exuere*[302] this 'frock' of infamy
which was publicly cut out for me in the presence of
a larger assemblage of their Honors, the senators, than
I now see at the side of Your Majesty, because in this
cloak of infamy—I was under suspicion like a real culprit.
For this reason I humbly ask Your Majesty for this favor
and consideration for my honor.

They began to whisper among each other and concluded
that it was already nighttime and it would take too long to
bring together all the senators stationed in different parts of the
city. The King said : "We shall do so, but since the time is
running short we shall recess *ad cras de mane*.[303] I bowed and
left with Father Piekarski,[304] but since the King detained Tyszkiewicz, we waited for him in another chamber. When he came
back he said to me : "Now I consider you a worthy man for
behaving so and realizing that you need a bigger audience.
I thank you for this courage."

They drank wine from the King's cellar and I also drank

[298]An ordinary man.
[299]I understand.
[300]Now.
[301]Nothing else remains.
[302]Take off.
[303]Until tomorrow morning.
[304]Father Adrian Piekarski, mentioned already in 1659, Pasek's uncle
and the King's preacher at the time, was the author of a number of
historical opuscules.

some, but they did not force me into drinking *propter cras*.[305] Later we went to sleep. On the next morning, after we had heard Mass at the Jesuits', we went to the palace but we had to wait for about two hours before all the senators assembled. Only then was I asked in. I saw the senators and other dignitaries there, all the royal servants, many noblemen, and whoever desired to come, since no one was forbidden to enter. The Vice-Chancellor said: "I hope that enough is being done to satisfy your Lordship's wish since His Majesty our gracious lord, called together all the senators who could *comparere*[306] at his side. They now permit your lordship an audience in their presence," and I began thus :

Most Gracious Majesty, my Merciful Lord! Truly the rule of human life is oscillation of misfortune and happiness, like a shadow following the sun ; misfortune alternates with fortune, evil with good, troubles and sorrow with prosperity. And even though this is unpleasant to our nature, one has to tolerate this humble struggle with patience, considering that such fate has been destined for all mankind. But when someone is recompensed with evil for good, with ingratitude for gratitude, with deprivation of honor and reputation, the dearest deposit of good fame, for voluntarily submitting his life to the vicissitudes of fortune for this fatherland; when on top of being innocent, he has to drink a mixture of bile with wormwood, such calumny is then *afflicti supra afflictiones*,[307] an ailment above all ailments, *crimen atro carbone notandum*,[308] because it militates against God Himself and against the law. As soon as I could handle weapons, my temper did not prevent me *servire ob domini* [*panem*],[309] I did not plunge into the category of coddled Adonises[310] but I

---

[305]Because of the following day.

[306]Appear.

[307]A blow above blows.

[308]A crime which should be marked down in black charcoal.

[309]From serving for the Lord's bread.

[310]Here meaning favorites ; Adonis was a young Greek and favorite of Aphrodite.

competed in the ranks of the laborious Dentatis,[311] I did
not find the constantly used weapons of Bellona unpleasant, I did not find the deep currents of rivers difficult to
cross *sine ramis et remis*,[312] and I was not fearful of the
depths of the waters of the Baltic Sea, even though they
were alien to the Polish nation. I did not loathe the *odora-
tus*[313] even though they came not from the censer of Jupiter
but from the saltpeter of Mars. I accepted all the *adversita-
tes*[314] of fortune *hilari fronte*,[315] I met the enemy's bullets,
thanks to the grace of God, without blinking of an eye and
I also shed my blood. And why ? Certainly not because
of a grudge or some jangle with a personal enemy, also
certainly not for wealth—I have already lost a considerable
portion of my own—but first of all for the defense of Your
Majesty, for the integrity of my fatherland. The reminder
of these instances is not a sign of boastfulness, as has been
inferred here, but a *testimonia vitae*.[316] There is the evidence of my comanders concerning all this, there are
wounds on my chest acquired while confronting the enemy,
and my back is gored with lead and steel.

It is not most important of all to have served in the
war or to have been a soldier for a long time, but it is
important to have fought often. Even now there are such
companies in our army, though not in my division, which
are called immortal because their officers served in them
until they lost their eyesight like old *lannerets*, until their
hair turned gray.[317] Yet during the entire course of their

[311]*Dentatus*, Manius Curius Dentatus, Roman tribune, consul, praetor,
and censor, a model of the early Roman virtues of simplicity, frugality,
and patriotism ; one of the greatest generals of antiquity.
[312]Without rods and oars.
[313]Fragrance.
[314]Adversities.
[315]With cheerful brow.
[316]Testimony of life.
[317]In this period of continual wars many lived to see their hair turn
gray in their military service ; Pasek mentioned two such comrades :
Rubieszowski and Wojnowski.

service they did not fight in one battle, did not shed their blood, but consumed the bread of the Commonwealth in idleness. Who then is more useful to the country, a hawk consuming his bread in idleness, or a young officer who constantly toils and is willing to shed his blood ? Surely I was not induced by forty or sixty zlotys[318] to do this—*tam vile sanguinis pretium*[319]—but by the innate love of a son toward his mother, the obedience and service due to His Majesty. I was stimulated by virtue alone, for which I would have easily borne even the most difficult perils ; but now when such unkind injustice befalls me I must lament with the opressed *Athenian* :[320] '*O virtus, ego te dominam putabam, et tu es serva fortunae* !'[321] Am I guilty because *non obiuravi nomen coronati capitis*[322] and the eminence of Your Majesty, my master, during the Swedish war and which even now I did not want to do in the confederacy ? Is it bad that I voluntarily abandoned such gains, being ready to toil not where the melodies of Hymenaeus[323] sound but where the *classica Gradivi*[324] call me as befits my rank ? Must virtue perish ? If this question is not appropriate I shall ask with a quote from the Scriptures : '*Quid mali feci*?'[325] Because it is said about the Day of Judgment

[318]Since 1658 the pay in an armored company amounted to forty zlotys per quarter of a year ; in the quota of sixty zlotys the additional twenty zlotys were called winter bread. Czubek, *Pam.*, p. 242, note 7.

[319]Low price for blood.

[320]Demosthenes, 384–322 B.C., Athenian orator and statesman ; greatest of Greek orators. He attacked Philip of Macedon in *Philippics*, orations of 352 ; was also author of *Olynthiaes, On Peace, On the Embassy, On the Affairs of the Kersonese,* and *On the Crown.*

[321]Oh, virtue, I considered thee mistress of fate and thou art its servant.

[322]I had not abjured the name of the crowned head. This might be another indication that Pasek belonged to those five banners which did not surrender to the Swedes with the rest of the army during the Swedish invasion of Poland ; allusion to this was made in the first senatorial speech. Czapliński, *Pam.*, p. 234, note 662.

[323]Or Hymen, the god of marriage, and supposedly the son of Apollo and one of the Muses ; originally the marriage song among the gods.

[324]Trumpets of Gradiva.

[325]What have I done wrong ? A travesty of the words of Pilate from the Gospel of St. Matthew 27, 23.

'that wrong deeds will be praised and good ones reproved then.'[326] Evidently this is also being practiced; and consequently, *si virtus profligatur, omnia pereunt.*[327] I try to find out : What was the reason behind my name being brought to your Majesty's eyes? I am not convinced that it was hatred, for *invidia bonorum noverca.*[328] If it was someone's recklessness, however, it should do me no harm for whoever is void of virtue himself dislikes the virtue of others. But people in previous centuries called such persons *patres calumniarum.*[329] It was said that such a man is *serpens, occulte mordens.*[330] It was said that such a man is *duplici lingua praeditus mel et virus uno spirans ore et halitu.*[331] Potentates and monarchs always shunned such men as poison ; they never heeded the counsel of such and even avoided them socially. It was written that Titus,[332] whom *dulcis recordatio*[333] calls *deliciae generis humani*[334] since he never harmed a citizen,[335] *iussit delatores fustibus et flagellis caesos deportari per castra et plat[e]as,*[336] in order to punish others having such vices. Those however who could not escape this pestilence easily

---

[326]Pasek might have had in mind here "Woe to those of you who call evil good and good evil," Isaiah V, 20. Czubek, *Pam.*, p. 243, note 16.

[327]If virtue is being oppressed everything perishes.

[328]Spite (jealousy) is the stepmother of good people.

[329]Fathers of slander.

[330]A serpent, biting secretly.

[331]Endowed with a double tongue which belches honey and poison all with one mouth and in one breath.

[332]Titus Flavius Sabinus Vespasianus (38–81 A.D.), Roman Emperor (79–81 A.D.).

[333]Sweetly remembered.

[334]The delight of mankind.

[335]Actually he was called that because of his free distribution of gifts to his people. He captured Jerusalem in 70 A.D., for which he was given a triumph at Rome. He succeeded to the throne on Vespasian's death, June, 79 A.D. He tried to better the lot of the Romans. He was succeeded by his brother, the evil and tyrannical Domitian.

[336]Ordered the informers punished with sticks and whips and dragged through camps and streets. Not correct citation from Svetonius, *Life of Titus* VIII.

lent an ear to the advice of such while they fed others
with insults, and thus fell under the proverb : *'Qui facile
credit, facile decipitur.'*[337] There is a multitude of such
examples under the sun. *'Contumelia Harpagi sumpsit
coronam Astyagis. Contumelia Narsetis inundavit sanguine Italiam.*[338] I do not talk about Poland, but here similar disgraces have taken place. How does this come
about? I have already said that I was put in this undeserved cabal,[339] as the Muscovites say, *perversis delatorum
consiliis.*[340]

Even though wise men say that whoever has a free
conscience should ignore all sorts of slander and people's
false talk, *fretus integritate conscientiae suae*[341] because a
good conscience and innocence are *memoria actionum
nostrarum bene a nobis gestarum*[342] and some recognition
and confirmation of our thoughts which approve of good
deeds and which give a true evidence of them. Still the
more innocent the case is the more painful it is. This
should not undermine the authority of Your Majesty before his subjects, however, because *'Planetae eo tardius
moventur, quo sunt in sublimiori sphaera; ita quanto
maior est principum auctoritas, tanto magis suos affectus
moderare eosque tem(p)erare debent.'*[343] And if I may be
free to express myself in this, for which I humbly beseech
with submissive heart, I would beg that these *consilia,*[344]
'utinam falsus sim vates!',[345] not deceive Your Majesty
and the fatherland because I have also found out *quantum*

---

[337]A gullible man is easily cheated.
[338]The contumely suffered by Harpagus deprived Astyages of the
crown ; the indignity of Narses flooded Italy with blood.
[339]Here meaning predicament.
[340]By the perverse advise of informers.
[341]And should rely on his clear conscience.
[342]The memory of our virtuous actions.
[343]The higher the sphere in which the planets rotate, the more slowly
they move ; in similar fashion, the greater the authority of the rulers
the more they should moderate and restrain their tendencies.
[344]Counsels.
[345]May I be a false prophet.

privato licuit,[346] that French thalers, rubles and Muscovite coins were being thrown around here and the present confederacy I could call a reversal of the Muscovite expedition and not a confederacy. But the truth should be sumarized briefly, I see Your Majesty *sine successore*.[347] Some direct the water toward their own mill while others accommodate their service in order to enrich themselves, and they violently impress their ideas on the fatherland. The confederacy seems trying to many now and steps should have been taken to prevent its formation, knowing that for two years someone was igniting this fire, the flames of which would have been usually easier to extinguish in a closed room than when it reached the roof. '*Melius in semente, quam in segete bella exscindere.*'[348]

The confederacy is bad ; bad are also those who do not join it. Someone has sinned, another will do penance for him. May Heaven pass judgment on this. Being innocent, I have above all God as a *testimonium*.[349] I have a thousand witnesses : my conscience, for they say that *conscientia mille testes*.[350] In time there will be even more of them because my innocence will be revealed to Your Majesty. The test of my virtue will open the eyes like a *lapis Lydius*.[351] If it does not happen just as I claim, let me go to prison.

My way was barred on an open road. If I considered myself guilty I could have escaped safely. Let them admit in truth that they could not surround me. I was sitting on a horse which even a Kalmuck and Astrakhan horse could not overtake and which could not have escaped me, had the necessity arisen. This horse would have denied a German Frisian horse's taking a sniff at it. But as soon as I heard Your Majesty's name and will and order, I did not resist.

---

[346]As much as a common man could.
[347]Without an heir.
[348]It is easier to subdue war in its seed than at the harvest.
[349]Witness.
[350]A conscience is equal to a thousand witnesses.
[351]Touchstone.

Frustra Pygmaeus in Gigantem pugnat[352] and I did not try
to escape (*quis nescit longas regibus esse manus?*)[353] but
gave myself up voluntarily. I was taken to Grodno, like
simulacrum[354] carried to Rome after the Spanish war of
Pompeius.[355] Some liked this while others reproved it
'*viri namque prudentes statuunt victoriam de civibus re-
portatam silentio obrui, non triumpho decorari debere:
quae enim gloria parricidis coniuncta esse possit?*'[356] This
was the intention in my case; they triumphed over me as
if over the entire army, they imprisoned me like a male-
factor. They searched and examined me; they put me to
torture, yet threatened me with the sword and death.
'*Necessitas misera, cum vel civi ob patriam, vel patriae
a cive mors inferenda est.*'[357] My *actiones*[358] were known
only to God. '*Vitae innocentia certissimum est corporis
praesidium.*'[359] Innocence itself stood on my side and I on
the side of innocence. In the meantime I always begged to
see Your Majesty and to have an audience with your
gracious lordship who, from the beginning of Your reign,
has kindly condescended to show benevolence to his subjects because *nullum dominium nisi benevolentia tutum
est.*[360] I know that Your Majesty, a gracious lord, condescends to abide by the rule that kindness will sooner conquer the hearts of the subjects than harshness. *Qui vult*

[352]It is in vain for a dwarf to fight a giant. Pygmies, dwarfs in Greek
legend; Gigantes, giants in Greek mythology.
[353]For who is not aware that kings have long arms?
[354]An image.
[355]Cnaeus Pompeius Magnus, Roman general, born 106 B.C., who after
his victorious war in Spain made a triumphal entrance into Rome
during which pictures of the countries and cities conquered by him
were carried in front of him.
[356]Because heedful people consider that a victory gained over the
citizens should be covered with silence and not honored with triumph,
for how could glory go hand in hand with patricide?
[357]Necessity is sad when either the fatherland must do away with the
citizen, or the citizen with the fatherland.
[358]Actions.
[359]The innocence of life is the safest defense which the body has.
[360]No reign without benevolence toward the subjects is a safe one.

amari, languida reget manu.[361] I know that love is the
unbreakable link between Your Majesty and Your subjects. '*Adeo regum stipator inseparabilis amor est, cui
stipendium clementia penditur.*'[362] I have no other *asy-
lum*[363] except in God. There is no one else to whom I
could complain about the injustice suffered and to whom I
could relate the oppression of my obvious innocence. Once
they made a traitor out of me, they took away from me
my treasure of good fame which *pari passu ambulat.*[364]
While everyone knows that I have been wickedly accused,
not many will know how I shall be cleared of this calumny: '*Nihil interest, utrum ferro, an verbo occidas,*'[365]
I appeal to those to whom my innocence is apparent. *Tibi
vindictam [relinquo]*[366] for whoever trespasses against the
love of his fellowman rebels against God Himself. *Quid
Deum colat, qui hominem laedit?*[367]

At those words of mine when I said that I had been
threatened with the sword and death, the King turned to the
Vice-Chancellor[368] and said: "A dog must have said that."
I was pleased to hear this and expected a good outcome
of my case. Everyone went up to the King and spoke with
him; I don't know what they were saying, I saw only that
the King shuddered with indignation. He took out of his pocket
my speech, the one which I had delivered during the council
of war, and flung it at the Voivode of Troki. They were reading it and meanwhile, the Vice-Chancellor began to speak
as follows:

> It was said a long time ago that accidents do not
> occur on earth but wander among people: a man would

[361]Whoever wants to be loved should rule with a kind hand.
[362]Love is an inseparable companion of kings to such an extent that it
is recompensed by grace.
[363]Refuge.
[364]Goes hand in hand with life.
[365]It does not make any difference whether one kills with steel or with
the tongue.
[366]I am leaving vengeance to you.
[367]How can someone who wrongs a fellow man worship God?
[368]Teodor Denhof. Czubek, *Pam.*, p. 250, note 5.

not be a man if he always abounded in favorable bliss-
fulness and never experienced adversity. The Scriptures
also assert clearly that he who undergoes troubles has
great esteem and respect in Heaven. God himself confirms
it in his own words : *'Quem amo, castigo.'*[369] This coming
from God should be tolerated especially by a Christian
with a grateful heart for it was even esteemed among pagans. When Philip,[370] the great Macedonian King, received
news that his commanders had achieved a great victory
in his name and had laid waste the enemy's army, that
the Dardanian[371] kingdom had given itself up to him in
eternal obedience, that a son had been born to him—
Alexander, with signs of a great hope in the world—he
exclaimed in a loud voice : *'O dii, mediocre aliquod infor-
tunium tot tantisque meis felicitatibus apponatis, oro!*[372]
Apparently he realized that great fortune tends to draw
great misfortune and that after periods of unhappiness
and affliction God usually looks on man with a favorable
eye. Also in the present case, whatever occurred happened
with the will of God. One should not blame His Majesty,
our gracious lord, for what happened, because he would
have wished, at least *pro custodia corporis,*[373] to preserve
in oboedientia[374] the small army remaining with the Ruthenian voivode. He had to assume that your lordship
was really the man he had been told to be, since he was
still unaware of the honesty and worthy deeds of your
lordship which *ad praesens elucescunt.*[375] This accusation

[369]Whomever I love, I whip.

[370]Philip II, 382–336 B.C. son of Amyntas II and Eurydice, and the
father of Alexander the Great ; king of Macedon.

[371]Dardanians ; people in Mezia on the Balkan Peninsula.

[372]Oh Gods! I implore you to add some small misfortune to so many
and such great fortunes of mine. Plutarch, *Life of Alexander* III, 20.
Philip, conquering Portideja, received three pieces of good news : about
the defeat of the Dardanians, about the birth of his son Alexander and
about the victory of his horses at the Olympics.

[373]For the safety of his own person.

[374]In obedience.

[375]Are now being revealed.

can neither hurt nor harm innate honor and worthy deeds, because once it is proclaimed false, it will bring to Your Lordship even greater fame than if it were allowed *subsequi in silentio.*[376] People say that nothing is so bad that it could not turn out well. '*Hectorem quis nosset, felix si Troia fuisset?*'[377] A diamond covered by stones under ground would not be so precious of a skilful human hand did not cut it, gold would not be so delightful to the human eye if it were not refined in a fiery fire, virtue would not have been known to the world if it had not been tested by all sorts of adversities. Neither discredit nor harm were done to Your Lordship's honor by this incident, for it will be rewarded with good fame, gratitude of the Commonwealth, and respect and promotion of His Majesty as well.

When he finished I went to the King and bowed low. The King placed his hands upon my head and said:

Forgive us! These traitors cause us much trouble. Because of evil people we must judge amiss also the worthy ones, especially when such calumnies and circumstantial evidence are given. But your accuser has been paid for his rashness by losing our grace, which he will never be able to regain.

Suddenly he got up from his chair and went to his room. Some went with him, others turned toward me. They approached me with:

How you have scolded us! How you have scoffed at us! But we are no longer surprised, since we have proof of your virtue. You must have said these things because you were innocent. Let us forgive each other now.

This *verba pro verbis*[378] went on until a courtier of the King came in and said: "His Majesty wishes that you wait here awhile, Sir." I thought to myself: did they invent something new against me again? But in less than a quarter of an

---

[376]To follow in silence.
[377]Who would have known of Hector if Troy had been happy? Ovidius, *Tristia* IV, 3.
[378]Word for word.

hour the courtier returned again and asked me to go to the King's chamber. I went. There, a more lengthy discussion followed about the confederacy's procedure, and I was questioned about other events as well. The King said again: "Forgive us, forgive us, we shall always remember this." Every time I bowed he would place his hands on my head. He gave me five hundred gold zlotys with his own hands and asked: "Where will you go now?" I said: "There where I started out to go, to my commander in White Ruthenia."[379] He said: "No longer to the confederacy?" I answered him: "Gracious Sir! Whatever is expressed once in indignation cannot be taken back later when one reflects on it." The King said: "All right, all right, someone who renders the King and his fatherland a good service should not be thrown over the fence. There will be credentials and letters for the Voivode." He then turned to Father Piekarski and said: "Be proud of your blood and have a drink on this occasion." *Interim*[380] the table was being set for the King's meal and we left.

When we arrived at my quarters good food as well as exquisite wine, which the King himself was drinking, were brought from the royal kitchen. We were in good spirits and even the retainers in the inn were given a barrel of mead, fodder, and oats for the horses, etc.

Thanks to the grace of God, I ended the year under more favorable circumstances, and I learned that one should never despair even though fortune grows somewhat dim, for God disposes of man and his fortune; He saddens man whenever He desires to, and He comforts him when such is His Holy Will. Even those who had considered me *extremis laborantem*[381] admitted the truthfulness of such a conclusion and may this be also a warning to everyone who reads this manuscript after me.

[379]Czarniecki was stationed there.
[380]Meanwhile.
[381]Doomed for eternity.

ANNO DOMINI 1662

By the grace of God I began the year happily in Grodno. The
King left for Warsaw soon after; since my credentials were
non in toto[1] drawn up yet, he ordered me to accompany him.
Only there a letter addressed to towns and cities containing
orders to grant me provisions *quantum satis*[2] was given to me
as well as personal letters to the Voivode. At the same time
dragoons from the Voivode's regiment, who had been routed
in Mścibów, were placed under my command. Since they had
been romping with something they were attacked violently.
Several of them were wounded. Eighteen of them came to the
King with their sergeant-major, and begged for a letter of safe
conduct. The King said to that: "I am sending a cavalry officer
there. Go under his command and obey him in everything since
you are so dissolute that towns cry out against you." Each one
of them was given a silver thaler. The King summoned me and
placed the dragoons under my command and admonished me
to rule them as their own officer would and to punish the
offenders. They went under the authority granted to me in
a letter which I still possess to this day and which was of the
following content:

> To all and to each one separately, whoever should
> know about this, and namely to the noblemen and our
> loyal starosts, leaseholders and administrators of our royal
> estates, as well as to the heads of villages, to mayors, town
> and city councillors, we make known that in order to pro-
> mote certain interests of ours we are sending to the army

[1]Not in full.
[2]According to my needs.

18*

which is engaged *in opere belli*[3] in White Ruthenia a nobleman, who is faithful and devoted to us, Jan Pasek,
a cavalry officer in the banner of His Honor, the Voivode
of Ruthenia, with several men, so that he may conduct
them *in disciplina militari*[4] to the camp where they are to
stay for the time being. We command and desire under the
penalty for opposing our royal will that the above mentioned cavalry officer as well as the soldiers under his
command be given sufficient provisions everywhere. For
better trust in which we ordered to set our seal and placed
our signature.

Written in Nowydwór[5] on the XXVII day of the
month of December of the year of Our Lord MDCLXI,
during the reign of our Polish and Swedish kingdoms XII.

(L.S.) JAN KAZIMIERZ king.

The two original letters in which the King commends me to
the Voivode I have even now in my possession because after
they were read I took them from the Voivode's secretary. They
were not written at the same time, however, because their dates
do not coincide.

"JAN KAZIMIERZ, by the Grace of God, King of Poland, Grand Duke of Lithuania, Ruthenia, Prussia, Mazovia,
Livonia, Kiev, Volhynia, Samogitia, Smoleńsk, Czernichów,
and hereditary king of Sweden, Gotland and Vandalia.[6]

My Most Gracious Sir :

We had the bearer of this letter under suspicion because of false evidence which indicated that he was going
over from the Polish army to that of the Grand Duchy of
Lithuania which is in the confederacy. But since he *eviden-
ter*[7] that he was heading directly to Your Honor the more
eagerly we send him back to Your Honor and commend
him so that you might favor him with your kindness as

[3]In a military expedition.
[4]In military fashion.
[5]Royal estates in the vicinity of Grodno. Czubek, *Pam.*, p. 256, note 4.
[6]The Polish kings of the Vasa Dynasty also claimed the Swedish
throne, which led to much hostility between Poland and Sweden.
[7]Proved.

a man who was tested in warfare *toties*[8] and who during the present difficult situation adhered to our side. The Cossack sent by your Honor as well as Wolski, the nobleman who returned a few days ago from his Highness the Khan,[9] we shall retain until the conclusion *consilii generalis*,[10] which we shall begin *quinta die Januarii futuri*[11] with the Polish and the Lithuanian senators in Bielsk.[12] You will have sufficient news about everything that will be decided there from us and from the reverend Father, the Polish Chancellor,[13] and, about further events, reliable information will come from this Wolski, the nobleman, or from a loyal Cossack. We wish your Honor good health from God *et felices rerum successus*.[14]

Written in Nowydwór on the XXVII day of the month of December, of the year of the Lord MDCLXI, during the reign of our Polish and Swedish kingdoms XII.

JAN KAZIMIERZ, King.

I do not know why not one letter but two were written and this latter one was written a little more openly and under a different date, even though they were given to me together. *Suppono*[15] however that they did not trust me at first and later they made up their minds to place confidence in me and to send through me *secretiora*,[16] since they now trusted me completely, supposedly because Father Piekarski had vouched for me. The King wrote the second letter as follows :

JAN KAZIMIERZ, by the Grace of God etc., as above, My Most Gracious Sir :

When we considered that it would be unpleasant to

---

[8]So many times.
[9]Aadil Girej ; the envoy was Paweł Wolski, the King's valet. Czapliński, *Pam.*, p. 248, note 17.
[10]Of the general assembly.
[11]On the fifth of January of the coming (year).
[12]Bielsk Podlaski, a town forty kilometers south of Białystok.
[13]Mikołaj Prażmowski. Czubek, *Pam.*, p. 257, note 9.
[14]And a successful outcome of affairs.
[15]I assume.
[16]More confidential matters.

your Honor not to know *ad praesens*[17] what the nobleman Wolski achieved with his Highness the Khan, it occurred to us *per litteras brevibus denuntiare*,[18] that especially his Highness the Khan and both the Sultans displayed great interest *in desideriis nostris*[19] and in particular they promised to put sixty thousand Crimean Tatars at our disposal *primo vere*.[20] We are going to have *ad minimum*[21] twelve thousand Prussians. When we add to this another army—whatever we manage to obtain—we hope to be able, with God's help, to organize for ourselves an adequate armed force in order to be able to do without those rebels, if the confederacy *non resipiscet*.[22] We shall not fail *constituere de nervo belli in consilio generali*,[23] however, in order to arrive at the sessions of the Diet *cum re parata*[24] and so that it will not take up time from other matters. *Caetera fusius*[25] by his lordship Wolski. And now for the second time we commend Pan Pasek to your Honor so that he may enjoy the respect of you, his commander, and of his captain of horse as someone whose great courage and valor are known to your Honor from all previous occasions. We are also familiar with his *actiones*[26] since they have been related to us and, especially *in statu moderno*[27] of our fatherland, he could not have done more. And it is also already known to us how he stood up *pro aequitate*[28] at the councils of war. It cannot be that such worthy conduct should remain unrewarded by us, unless

[17]Now.
[18]To inform you in brief, by letter.
[19]Our requests.
[20]By the following spring.
[21]At least.
[22]Does not come to its senses.
[23]To decide about the funds (money) at the general assembly.
[24]With this matter settled.
[25]Other things will be more thoroughly reported.
[26]Deeds.
[27]In the present state.
[28]For the right.

God should take our health away ! *Expedit*[29] that others also should know with what kind of gratitude we reward those who are *bonarum partium.*[30] Now we wish you good health from God *et felices successus.*[31]

Written in Nowydwór on the II day of January the Year of the Lord 1662, during the reign of our Polish and Swedish kingdoms XIII.

JAN KAZIMIERZ, King.

This letter was addressed as follows :

To His Honor Stefan Czarniecki, the Voivode of the Ruthenian lands, of Piotrków, Kowel, etc., our most obliging starost.

I received the letters and took leave of the King. He again placed his hands on my head and said : "Do forgive us now. Do try to attend the sessions of the Diet with the Voivode and come to see us then. We shall remember you."

I immediately gave orders to the men to proceed straight ahead, in a beeline, on the road of Lida[32] in such a way that I could overtake them in one day even if I left a week after they did. I sent my retainers and horses which I did not need along with them and returned with two other men to Pan Tyszkiewicz for I had given him my word that I would do so. There I was received as a welcome guest with abundant hospitality and merrymaking. I stayed a week there after the lapse of which I wanted to leave but they did not let me go. In order to inform my men of my whereabouts my host sent his Cossack with the message to slow down right beyond Białystok[33] until I should overtake them and to leave me word about themselves in Lida and Oszmiana.[34] I stayed at Pan Tyszkiewicz's another week and indulged in pleasant conversation where mutual compliments were paid and during which I was promised various backings and promotions, as well as the hand of his

---

[29]It is proper.
[30]On the right side.
[31]And success in your endeavors.
[32]A city eighty kilometers south of Wilno.
[33]A city in eastern Poland.
[34]A city fifty kilometers southeast of Wilno.

niece Panna Rudoniówna, an heiress whose possessions were valued at more than a hundred thousand, only she had just recently turned nine. We parted with the assurance of constant friendship and with curses upon anyone who would fail to keep his word. All the speeches which I had delivered before the senators as well as those during his presence before the King, Tyszkiewicz asked me to repeat to him, to copy them and to leave them behind. Even the one which I had delivered at the council of war he copied from Father Piekarski with his own hand, cherished it and was very much delighted—though there was really no reason for this, and said: "Even if you had no other wealth than the one stored in your head it is big enough for me to give you my niece's hand in marriage." I parted *cum plenitudine*[35] signs of sincere and unchangeable friendship and left. But I turned back several times, as is usually the case with good friends.

When I arrived at Oszmiana I neither found my men there nor any news of them. I assumed that they were moving at a snail's pace, since they were disciplinary and overly obedient. On the third day after my arrival the sergeant-major finally arrived with two other men, *quidem*[36] to assign quarters. I noticed them at a distance and ordered the gates closed so that they would not learn of my presence. They stopped at the mayor's, were rude and claimed that the company had 100 horsemen. They showed the King's letter, given to me, which specified that "we are giving men under his command," but did not specify how many. The townsmen consented, as they had heard a week before that they were roaming around the villages. They gave them seventy zlotys, a barrel of beer, bread, meat, etc. I told my innkeeper to watch out for the moment when they counted the money and to notify me. They acted hastily. The provisions were already in the sleigh, because he[37] intended to bypass the city, since he was ashamed of his men. The townsmen were collecting the money. He was sitting at the other end of the table, writing a message to me which he was

[35]With many such.
[36]Supposedly.
[37]Presumably the sergeant-major.

to leave with the mayor as I entered through the door. They saw me and seized their caps. The townsmen looked and wondered in amazement—since they had seen me in the city for three days—what was this? I asked: "What money is being counted here?" He answered: "The townsmen offered this to us for horseshoes out of grace." The townsmen did not say anything. They did not think highly of grace obtained by a mace aimed at one's neck. I asked the mayor: "What did you agree to?" He said: "Seventy zlotys, a barrel of beer, meat and bread. The provisions are already in the sleighs." I said: "The provisions are ours, the money is yours. Put it away for it is yours. There is no glazed frost nor clods now. The horses will not stumble. The snow is up to the saddle laps, the road is soft, so horseshoes are not necessary." The townsmen seized their money. They put it in a sack. "Sir Sly Boots" looked down in dismay. The townsmen dispersed instantly. They who did not know me before and did not even bring me a bundle of hay for I had not asked for it, instantly began to chip in and bring various things for me. But I did not want all this. I fed my horses and left. They voluntarily put a six-gallon barrel of vodka in my sleigh. I went on my way then and fed my horses well. In towns and villages we obtained food and drinks but—God forbid!—I never permitted money to be accepted. Driving along as far as Lepel[38] we were well provided for. Even if each one of us had ten stomachs, he still would have plenty to eat and drink. But the sergeant-major complained that I forbade him to take money. He said that with the royal letter I could collect several thousand zlotys before reaching the camp. He tried to persuade me to take money and pointed out the gains. I did not allow it however because my reputation was at stake. But these scamps found their own devices to make money. They would take provisions in one place and sell these to people in another.

When we were riding through a large wilderness once, we saw in the midst of the forest a big village from which sounds of screams and a commotion could be heard. In a manor there

[38]A city about eighty kilometers south of Płock.

a widow was living— I no longer remember her name. When we drew nearer we saw the manor being robbed and the noble-woman walking and wringing her hands. Some were strapping skinned hogs and flitches to the horses, some took costly objects while others dragged cattle on ropes from the barn. I assumed at first that it was an execution of some sentence of the court. I did not interfere and was passing by the gate. I intended to stop in that village overnight since the night was already approaching. But when that noblewoman noticed me she dashed out through the gate: "Have mercy, sir, they are robbing me, a poor orphan. They are worse than the Musco-vites, worse than the enemy!" I asked: "Who are these people?" She told me that these were the volunteers of Pan Muraszko." I turned back to the courtyard and said: "Gentle-men, don't you fear God since you are doing such violence to a nobleman's manor!" "What business is this of yours?" I said: "This is my business since I am a nobleman!" Later I said to her: "Your Ladyship, give orders to take these things back." And the volunteers said: "You are not going to take these back." The lady ordered her peasants to take back these things. The volunteers grabbed their guns and swords. We did the same and we clashed! We drove them out of the courtyard, both sides suffering damages. A horse was killed under one man when a dragoon shot among them. One of our horses was wounded in the side, but not seriously. They abandoned all their booty. The peasants took several of their horses but I ordered these driven after them. The noblewoman began to thank me very much and exclaimed: "Czarniecki's men are holy, Sapieha's are accursed!"

We stopped in an inn in this village for the night for I knew that they were encamped only two leagues away. This was a fight with riffraff. I was afraid that they might want to revenge themselves. And also at that time we were as dear to the confederates as a hedgehog to a dog who would like to devour it and cannot even bite it. Several of them had duly received scars and *supponebam*[39] that they would think of vengeance. Indeed such was the case.

[39] Assumed.

The poor widow sent us vodka and beer, whatever her household could offer. The dragoons drank these and the sergeant-major and myself helped ourselves to the liquor which was in the sleigh. At the resounding of the second cock we set up watch. Soon after, three hundred horsemen were heading our way. The watchman saw them in the snow at a distance and knocked at the window saying: "Gentlemen, please get up; we are having guests." When they sneaked closer he exclaimed: *"Werdo?"*[40] They answered: "Soon you will have 'werdo' you such and such a son!" The dragoons had no gunpowder; I gave some to them and ordered them to load the muskets. There were also no bullets, only I had some. I loaded my gun and gave them whatever I could spare. As they approached, the watchman called out: "Don't come closer, or I am going to shoot!" The sergeant-major came out and asked: "What do you want?" "We want to complain about the unjust beating given our men yesterday. Who is the senior officer here?" The sergeant-major said: "I am the senior one, since I am forty-five years old and all the others are younger." "This is a joke," they answered, "but who is in command here?" He then said that the commander was in the house. They said: "Let us in to see him." He replied: "We shall let you in but not in such a large crowd because one goes differently to complain." "Let about ten of us in." He answered: "Even twenty." Fifteen riders approached then. Some had their pistols at their belts and others in their holsters. As soon as they had reached the premises I ordered them to halt at the gate. Others stood in readiness by the door. Their horses were already saddled. They entered the room: "Greetings!" "Greetings!" One of them asked me: "His Honor, our colonel, wants to inquire who you are, whence and where you are going, and why you robbed and attacked us yesterday." I asked: "First of all I would like to know who is your colonel?" He said: "His Honor Pan Muraszko." Meantime the others puffed, gnashed their teeth, pulled and bit on their moustaches. The inn was surrounded by three hundred horsemen who shouted:

[40]Who is coming?

"Just wait, you royalists, soon we shall tie you up like sheep."
I answered : "Since I am a soldier in *servitio*[41] of the regular
army[42] of the Polish Commonwealth, I do not find it necessary
to explain to his Honor the colonel, who has less to do with
all this, from where I came or where I am going. But since
I am not ashamed of my actions even before the entire world
and would not *denegare*[43] to answer even to a beggar, taking
alms in the name of God, where I am going, I am also ready
to give an account to you, gentlemen, as to worthy soldiers
whom I saw together with us in previous battles." Since I had
uttered one Latin word *denegare*, one of them spoke up : "Do
not use Latin with us, sir, because we are ordinary soldiers."[44]
I replied : "I realize that you are an ordinary soldier, sir. I shall
explain myself to an ordinary man in an ordinary way and to
an extraordinary one, according to his wish." Meanwhile I said
to the sergeant : "Show the documents which you carry with
you." He took them out of his pocket and I handed them to the
colonel. He read them and asked : "Why did you attack our
patrol and wound several of our companions ?" I answered :
"Because it is not customary to rob estates of one's native
nobles, especially while being encamped. When we saw the
robbery we assumed that you were Muscovites. And since
I gave you an account, I demand from you the same. Let me
know what business or rather what claim you have against the
Polish Commonwealth ? As volunteers you have no pay coming to you from the state and in addition to this you have
joined the confederacy and hold up manors and rob them !
Secondly, why do you raid me at night as if you wanted to rob
me ?" The senior one said : "Because you deserve this." I realized that since meekness would not get us anywhere we should
let our weapons speak for us. As I held a mace in my hand,

[41]In the service.
[42]Volunteers did not belong to the regular army and did not receive
pay.
[43]Refuse.
[44]Muraszko's men were usually peasants and therefore could not be
expected to understand Latin. They were very hostile to the nobility.
Czapliński, *Pam.*, pp. 256–57, note 75.

I struck the lieutenant hard with it in the chest. He fell under the bench. At the same moment two of them fired their pistols at me and the sergeant-major. They shot through the uniform of the sergeant-major; God saved me, however, probably since I bent to the floor in order to pick up the pistol which had fallen from my belt when I had struck the volunteer. Now we attacked them. Half of them remained in the room; half dashed out into the hallway. We were fighting those in the room and our men in the hall took care of the others who were there. One dragoon had a frightful Muscovite mace with which he hit those fleeing from the room. When the crowd outside heard the shooting in the room they blindly rushed toward the huts. Fire was exchanged. Our men withstood them at the gate. Only three dragoons fired ; two of their men fell off their horses while one of our men was wounded in the neck. We subdued those in the room and locked them there. Those who were in the hallway got quite a beating and escaped stealthily behind the fence away from the horses. The bulk of them retreated by about a furlong and began to shout : "Come out here into the field !" I said: "Just wait and this might take place !" I returned into the room in order to tie up our prisoners. I turned them and two sleighs over to the innkeeper and ordered : "Hands off, peasant. Your neck is at stake if these should disappear. These sleighs contain the royal treasure, for I am transporting money for the army." The prisoners prayed and complained : "God punished us ! We were sent out to tie up others and now we ourselves are shackled." I stepped out into the courtyard thinking what was I to do. Should we ride out to them or not ? Some advised me to do so while others tried to dissuade me and most of all Chlebowski, a relative of mine : "It is a big crowd and we shall not be able to withstand them." The sergeant-major also remarked : "We shall see whether the lady for whose protection we interceded sends us some help, or tells the peasants ; still nothing is in sight." We wanted to put up a fight *defensive*[45] in front of this but when we saw that they were bringing sheaves, igniting them and already wanted to fling them at the hut, I shouted : "Wait, brave knights, you shall soon have us outside. Do not inflict harm on others for our sake." It was dawning. Our dragoons gathered all their belongings, mounted the good horses which we had captured and left our poorer ones in the courtyard. They loaded their muskets with stones and hobnails, whatever was available, because we had no bullets. They took some bullets from those who were tied up, from their ammunition pouches. One man,

[45]Defensively.

wounded in the knee with hobnails by Jankowski, a dragoon, groaned and wriggled before the gate. The other wounded man was carried off by his own crowd.

I exclaimed again: "Gentlemen, go away and give us up!" "Oh, this cannot be, you such a son! You shall not manage to escape from us. We shall rout you out of here like a badger out of a burrow." The sergeant-major said: "If you attack us we shall first of all kill those who lie here tied up." They answered: "We have already counted them as lost, but also you will not be resurrected, you pagan son!" Immediately after, they began to advance on the hut with fire: "Come out, you pagan sons, otherwise innocent people will suffer on your account." I answered: "Right away, right away, dear gentlemen." We went out as a body of over twenty men, including the retainers, advancing in a row. I ordered the second row from the back to turn facing our adversary ahead of our front row, if they were to surround us. I forbade them to shoot all at once, only two or three at a time, when ordered by me or the sergeant-major, who was in command of the back row, while I took over the front row. The sergeant-major turned over his own horse to a dragoon and sat on a splendid brown and white Kalmuck horse which he had captured from them. It jumped under him like a top. We had enough weapons since we had taken some from the prisoners. We had hardly stepped a furlong away from our quarters when they turned to the side. Then what I had predicted happened. They moved in a semicircle in order to come in back of us. When they were close I called out to my men: "*Alt!*"[46] The back row took position with their backs to the front row. Suddenly our opponents raised a shout and jumped at us *hostiliter*.[47] They fired densely from rifles and pistols, closely charged, row by row. I instantly fired from both pistols, since I had a third one in my belt and a rifle strapped to me; also three or four of my dragoons simultaneously fired from their muskets at my command. The one who closed ranks with me, apparently wounded, grabbed

[46]Stop.
[47]Fiercely.

at his saddle-bow. A dragoon jumped at him and struck him
with his sword across the neck. He fell from the horse. We later
found out that he was a distinguished Lithuanian, a dandy, by
the name of Szemet and that his father was angry at him since
he served with the volunteers. Also one of my dragoons from
the front ranks fell to the ground. The horse was killed under
him, shot in the side. When I noticed that the dragoon got up,
I ordered my men to march in a row. They retreated from us
a little and turned toward us again! Our Jankowski had
a musket with a thick barrel. When he splashed with these
hobnails he wounded many of them. A number of them
groaned in agony. The shot also caught up with several of
them in the back row. When they realized that they could not
break us they began to shout : "Return our men to us and you
may go to the devil !" The sergeant-major said to this : "They
will be useless to you dead !" They attacked us for the third
time but they shot only from a distance now, avoiding us from
close by. We were glad of that. We advanced toward them ;
two of us shot at one time while others were loading. They
kept retreating little by little. We pushed them toward the
garden. The hedges were dense. They began to break through
them. We pushed toward them. They began to flee ! They
broke through one hedge and ran toward another. Right behind the gardens was a forest. They fled for this forest over the
fences and left the horses behind. Now we were sure of the
game. I did not order a pursuit and only a few were caught at
the fences. Some were wounded and two were killed. Three of
my dragoons and an orderly of mine were wounded. I was
slightly injured in the left thigh. I did not feel it, however, until
everything was over. Six of our horses were wounded and two
were killed, but there were enough left to choose from.

Later an administrator dragged along from the lady with
a small firearm for shooting deer. He gave me a bag of powder
and bullets for the road. We took the three fettered non-com-
missioned officers along. I ordered the others whipped with
a cowhide so that they would remember Czarniecki's men. The
dragoons stripped them naked and chased them into the forest
behind the others in heavy snow. We picked out about forty

better horses and we left taking along our three prisoners. We took so many saddles and weapons in booty that the sleighs bent under their weight. Other horses, as well as some of our own which we exchanged for better ones and left behind as a sign of friendship, I gave to the peasants and the administrator. I also told him to gather those which were roaming around the gardens, since only a few of the enemy had escaped on horseback, as I did not want anyone else to profit on our account.

I left and did not stop until I reached Żodziszki.[48] Since we had captured so many horses that some dragoons drove as many as three by the reins, I decided that they should be returned, for although these men were hostile they were not our enemies. The sergeant-major thought that we should keep the horses, but I said that since it concerned my reputation this could not be. *Conclusum*[49] that the dragoons should take the better ones and to hand over their own in their place to supplement them. My retainers took two and left theirs behind. But there was no starost's office there and since I did not want to turn back to Oszmiana, I delivered them up in Narocz.[50] We entered in the municipal register that some rebels had barred our way, wanted to capture us and we were delivering three of them. The prisoners begged and swore that they would see to it that nobody would pursue this matter. They testified in a voluntary declaration that they had really raided us and wanted to rob and tie us up. This *oris confessionem*[51] of their's I took with me along with the town's seal, the mayor's and the entire office's attestations and left them together with the herd of horses behind. At parting we got them drunk and gave them their own horses, for which they asked, back. Even so, there were still enough to choose from. The sergeant-major kept his roan. He later sold it to Captain Gorzkowski for 340 zlotys which was very little. We were told that it was a captured Muscovite horse.

[48]A town on the Wilia river, east of Wilno.
[49]It was decided.
[50]A town on a lake by the same name, east of Wilno.
[51]Oral confession, statement.

I went by way of Dokszyce,[52] Dolcze[53] and further on toward Lepel where the Voivode had set up camp. Since I was moving slowly and had stayed at Tyszkiewicz's manor for two weeks, the King sent Father Piekarski to the Voivode in place of Wolski, since he had sent the latter again to the Khan. The priest bypassed me on the way and arrived at the Voivode's before I did. When the Voivode read the King's letter in which it was written "as we have mentioned in the letter conveyed through Pan Pasek," he said : "I have not even set my eyes on Pan Pasek." The priest became alarmed. "For God's sake, he had left such a long time ago. The King had put such and such people under his command." Once again there was alarm on my behalf, another suspicion : "So the traitor went to the confederacy because of the offense which had befallen him there. They will have something to read in the confederacy, especially what the King wrote with his own hand. How can I show my face to the King again ?" The priest could not even sleep. Next day, just as everyone got up from dinner, he stood with Matczyński, Mężyński, and Niezabitowski[54] when the Voivode said : "He could not have done so for he had already started on the way to join me and thus had voluntarily spurned the confederacy. He and his men are probably enjoying themselves, pasturing the horses, and riding along leisurely, for they receive enough food with the King's letter everywhere." And I was already standing in the door at that. Then there was joy ! "Here he is !" The Voivode turned around and exclaimed : "O desiderabilis !"[55] He seized me by the shoulders. "Your uncle[56] would have died out of concern if you had not arrived today. I thank you for the good deed which you have rendered to the fatherland and to me who is favorably inclined toward

[52]A city at the springs of the Berezyna, 160 km. northeast of Wilno.
[53]A city on the route from Dokszyce to Lepel.
[54]Marek Matczyński, the Polish Master of the Horse, a friend of Jan Sobieski ; Piotr Mężyński, a colonel ; Ludwik Aleksander Niezabitowski, a cavalry captain and and later Castellan of Sącz. Czubek, Pam., p. 274, note 5.
[55]Oh, longed-for one !
[56]Father Piekarski.

you. We shall make it worth your while. Now one officer who sticks by me is dearer to me than an entire company. But where are your men?" I said: "They are here." He stepped outside and saw the horses: "And what is this? Where did you get such good horses?" At first I told him that I had encountered Khovansky's men, had given them battle, and had smashed them and that these were the spoils. Later, I truthfully told him exactly how things happened. Everything seemed improbable to him at first but when I showed him *confessata authentica*[57] in which they themselves had admitted that they had numbered three hundred horsemen, he marvelled at the great miracle that a dozen or so men had withstood such a big crowd. He thanked me, but to the sergeant-major he said: "I would have let you hang for the scandal which you had created in Mścibów, but now I pardon you because of that encounter in which you did not disgrace yourself. Yet this is probably thanks to your commander's courage rather than your own. But since you arrived on good horses you shall be the first to receive cloth for uniforms."

Since the Warsaw Diet was to meet, the King wrote through Father Piekarski ordering the Voivode to proceed with his troops toward the Polish border. The Voivode had already intended to do so and had already left Lepel. It was three nights later I think that a messenger arrived from the Tsar in order to impart to him the following intention: The Tsar wanted to send his envoys to the Diet to negotiate *inter gentes*[58] but was afraid to send them across the border, fearing that they would suffer some indignity from the army which was in disobedience *ad praesens.*[59] The Tsar asked the Voivode to send an escort beyond the border who would conduct the envoys to his Majesty, the King.

The Voivode sent for me and said: "Pan Brother, His Majesty the King wrote to me in his first and following letters that I should express to you his gratitude and I myself agree

[57]The authentic confession.
[58]Between the two nations.
[59]Now.

that your behavior is deserving of every recompense. But His Majesty should be the one to reflect on the reward for I am not able to bestow on you such a recompense as the King. I cannot give you any subprefecture nor tenure because this is not in my power, but I shall not neglect to do whatever I can. Yet now do not decline in haste an offer which can bring honor and profit. His Highness, the Tsar, asked me to send an officer over the border to escort his envoys, who are coming to the Diet. I would like you to undertake this but you will have to go to Vyazma."[60] I answered: "My benefactor! It is your Honor's privilege to command and mine to fulfill every command of your Honor as master of my life. I am ready to go at the command of your Honor, my benefactor, not only to Vyazma but even to Astrakhan.[61] The road beyond the Baltic Sea was farther and even from there I returned, thanks to the Grace of God, in good health under the lucky guidance of Your Honor." He said: "Fine! I shall give you several dozen elite Cossacks and I shall order your credentials written. Leave tomorrow as early as possible and God be with you!" He called Piwnicki and ordered him to write the credentials. I went to my retainers and said: "Feed the horses well, for tomorrow there will be a 'short trip' in store for them—to Moscow." One of my retainers remarked: "Soon we shall even go to Rome!" I said: "What are we to do if such is the will of our commanders? Be ready!" We set about preparing when the valet Wilkowski came running and said: "His Honor the Voivode summons you!" I went there. He said: "Pan brother, I have here great entreaties concerning your assignment. Pan Żerosławski and Pan Niegoszowski were here and begged me to send them instead. Niezabitowski interceded for them. I did not want to embitter the old soldiers but said that I had already promised it to Pan Pasek and that it would not be right for me to take back my word, since even the King had written to me twice in his behalf requesting me to honor him for his noble

[60]A city 150 km northeast of Smolensk.
[61]A city by the mouth of the Volga.

behavior. If he voluntarily foregoes this, however, I consent on my part." I answered: "I am ready to fulfill the wishes of your Honor, and I believe that if I adhere to them I do not grab other people's priority. I can represent the honor of Your Lordship, my benefactor, as well as the oldest soldiers." He said: "Fine !" He sent word to Piwnicki to bring the credentials as soon as possible to be signed. I went to the horses. There I came across those officers. They instantly began to negotiate with me to make a deal and forego this mission in their favor. Żerosławski offered one hundred silver thalers. I agreed. They went to fetch the money. I reflected that the trip was long and the task difficult. I did not know how much I would profit by it and now I could make one hundred thalers, without any difficulty, for doing nothing. Then I thought it over again and concluded that the mission could not be a bad one if they fought so hard for it and were willing to buy me out. I went to Piwnicki and said this to him. He exclaimed: "Are you joking? This assignment promises thousands and great fame. Don't agree, for it will also be unpleasant to the Voivode if you scorn his favor." I begged Piwnicki to complete the credentials as soon as possible and to take them to be signed. Then I concealed myself from Żerosławski and Niegoszowski. They came with the money and asked: "Where is the master?" "I don't know; he went away with some captain." They looked for me by the banners but could not find me. In the evening I came to see Piwnicki. He told me: "The Voivode has signed everything. He has it all with him. Your rivals came again to see the Voivode. Pan Tetwin and Niezabitowski interceded for them, but the Voivode said that he had already signed the letters and turned them over to you." I went to see the Voivode but to avoid being pestered by them again I sent a retainer on ahead in order to find out whether they were still there. I entered and found the Voivode in his jerkin only and he asked: "Who is here?" As soon as he saw me he said: "And where have you been? He repeated what Piwnicki had said and gave me the papers. One letter entitled me to transit across the border on my way to Muscovy. I was to hide that one. Another letter, dated as the first, I was to show as soon as

I brought the envoys *inter viscera Regni.*[62] I possess both of them to this day. The first one reads as follows :

> Stefan Czarniecki of Czarnca and Tykocin,[63] the Voivode of the Ruthenian lands, General of the Army of his Majesty, Starost of Piotrków, Kowel, and Ratyń.

> To all those concerned and namely to their Honors of the knightly order to whichever nation and whatever rank, merit, or office, I make known and commend to their Honors and Brothers my services as well as to the mayors, bailiffs of villages, councilors, and to all my people in the towns and cities, that I comply with the wishes of the Tsar and send to meet his envoys, who are delegated to his Majesty the King, a convoy and an escort, a Pan Pasek, an officer of my regiment, who is to conduct these envoys of his Highness the Tsar, wherever he will meet them, along the speediest way to my regiment, from where they will be conducted by either the above appointed officer or another one until they reach their point of destination. That maintenance be not denied to them and, as soon as the envoys cross the border, the customary horse and cart be furnished them is required by the necessity of the Commonwealth, and to this I add my entreaties. This document I confirm with my own signature and with the mark of my seal.

> *Datum*[64] in Kojdanów[65] *die 1 Februarii, anno 1662.*[66]
> Stefan Czarniecki, the Voivode of Ruthenia.

He ordered me to hide this letter immediately upon my return from across the border with the envoys and then to show the other one which *subiungam*[67] below, because it was a question of an affront to the hetmans and the Lithuanian nation whose privilege it was, according to the law, to receive Musco-

---

[62]Within the limits of our kingdom.
[63]In the Constitution of the Diet of 1661 Czarniecki received Tykocin and its surroundings for life. Czubek, *Pam.*, p. 278, note 2.
[64]Given.
[65]A town southwest of Mińsk ; formerly in the voivodeship of Mińsk.
[66]On the first of February 1662.
[67]I shall add, or enclose.

vite envoys and to conduct them up to Narew, at which point a Polish escorting officer would take over. He penned his second letter so that it appeared he had received them accidentally and not deliberately after he had come across them on the way. He thus wrote a second letter of the following content:

Stefan Czarniecki of Czarnca and Tykocin, the Voivode of the Ruthenian lands, General of the Army of His Majesty, Starost of Piotrków, Kowel, and Ratyń.

To all concerned and namely to their Honors of the knightly order of whatever rank, merit or office, I make known and I commend my services to their Honors and Brothers as well as to the mayors, bailiffs of villages, councilors, and to all my people, in the towns and cities, and declare, that since the envoys of the Tsar, Afanasii Ivanovich Nestorov and Ivan Polikarpovich, a secretary[68] are sent with a message to His Majesty the King concerning urgent needs and business, I have assigned to them a convoy with an officer of my regiment, Pan Pasek, to enable them to make their trip as fast as possible. That maintenance be not denied them and that the envoys be furnished with horse and cart is required by the necessity of the Commonwealth and to this I add my intercession. This script I confirm with my own signature and with the mark of my seal.

Datum[69] in Kojdanów die 12 Februarii, 1622 anno.[70]

Stefan Czarniecki, the Ruthenian Voivode.

In order to pay due respect to the Lithuanian Grand Hetman,[71] however, he gave me a letter addressed to him in which he wrote that he had met the envoys on the way, assigned to them an escort, and sent back the one who was put at their disposal at Szkłów. But actually neither the officer nor the envoys were in Szkłów and all this was done in order to

---

[68]Either Czarniecki's secretary made a mistake since the envoys were Afanasii Ivanovich Nestorov and Ivan Mikhaylov or Polikarpovich was the patronymic rather than last name.
[69]Given.
[70]On the twelfth day of February, 1662.
[71]Jan Paweł Sapieha.

preserve the protocol. He advised me not to hand over this
letter to the Grand Hetman, even if I learned of his presence at
one of his estates deep in Lithuania, in Lachowice, or elsewhere, but to deliver it only to his administrator or steward
upon arriving at one of his estates in the vicinity of Narew, so
that the letter would reach him someday. Which letter was
written in the following way:

Most Honorable Voivode of Wilno, My Most Respected Sir and Brother:

On the Minsk highway I came across Afanasii Ivanovich Nestorov, an envoy of the Tsar, who was on his way
to His Majesty the King and I dispatched back the escort
who was assigned to him in Szkłów. So that he would
hasten as fast as possible from Urzysko to His Majesty,
I assigned to him Pan Pasek, an officer of my regiment,
whom I present to Your Honor through this announcement. I report this as I do not want to neglect what is due
to a field hetman's office and to the authority of Your
Honor since Your Excellency should be notified of the
crossing and entrance of all envoys *inter confinia*[72] of our
Commonwealth. May it be left to the discretion of Your
Excellency to appoint a different officer to accompany
this envoy *ad praefixum locum*[73] where His Majesty is or
to permit the officer designated by me to continue as his
escort. Since the White Ruthenian lands and the borders,
which are being attacked by the enemy, are abandoned by
the armies of the Grand Duchy of Lithuania, *incumbit*[74]
that Your Honor condescend *consulere*[75] how to prevent
the bitter rage of the enemy who has already begun to
grow in strength. I cannot do anything without cavalry,
with only my infantry in the field. I had to abandon the
undertaking to go deep into enemy territory because I had
been *omni destitutus succursu*[76] in my eager intentions to

[72]Into the confines.
[73]To his destination.
[74]It is necessary.
[75]To consider.
[76]Deprived of all support.

serve *pro Republica*[77] even though I had desired *ostentare in hostico*[78] His Majesty's *arma*.[79] Having made this known, I surrender myself and my services to the Grace of Your Honor.

In Kojdanów, Fully Benevolent Brother and Humble Servant of Your Excellency.

Stefan Czarniecki, the Voivode of Ruthenia.

As things turned out I delivered this letter to the Grand Hetman, but not until I had arrived some six or seven leagues away from Narew. He received it kindly, answered it, and offered me his hospitality about which I shall write below. I begged him to let Czarniecki's letter be given back to me and I mentioned that I preserve such and similar documents so that *maneant posteritati pro testimoniis vitae meae*.[80] He right away ordered his secretary to return the letter to me, and asked : "Will you also preserve my reply ?" I answered : "Certainly, because such is my habit. My sons, if God grants me any, should see someday that I did not waste *florem aetatis*[81] in idling, but took part in various occasions as befits a nobleman." (About which, more later.) Now I return to the matter from which I deviated because of the contents of these letters.

When the Voivode returned the letter to me he said : "I have already assigned forty good men to you ; leave as early as possible and do not give way to any foolishness because you can make more by this mission than you would have from the confederacy. And how much is fame itself worth ? What will the King say when you will often be in his sight ? He will have to remember then what gratitude he owes you. Also I shall not fail to intercede as soon as I, if God grants it, go to Warsaw. Now go to sleep but have a drink before you go. What would you prefer, Spanish wine or mead ?" I told him that I would prefer mead because I knew that it was very good. He remarked :

[77](The) our Commonwealth.
[78]To show in the enemy's land.
[79](Military) might.
[80]They would remain to posterity as a testimony of my life.
[81]The best years of my life.

"Fine, I also shall drink mead since it turned out especially well." He drank to me and I emptied my cup ; I also emptied another beaker. He then said : "Drink also a third one to the Kolding doll[82] (he never lost an opportunity to remind me of her).

I bid him good-night. He asked then : "Have you eaten, Pan Brother ? Have you come after supper ?" I replied : "I shall eat in my quarters." I went and found Żerosławski sitting at my place with a bag of thalers before him. When I saw him I pretended to be drunk, having really gotten a little tipsy, as I had emptied three silver beakers containing more than a quart and the mead had tasted good.

He began to speak to me about this transaction and I said : "I am glad to see you." He said : "I have come with the money according to the agreement." And I said : "Pour some liquor !" He said : "Have the money recounted Sir." And I said : "To good health !" He tasted some mead. "Where did this mead come from ?" I said : "Out of a barrel !" He said : "Is this mead from the Voivode ?" I said : "It is mine and yours since we are drinking it." He asked : "Did you already get the credentials ? I said : "Please drink to it. Let us eat !" He saw that he would not get anywhere with me and said : "We shall talk about it in the morning then." We began to drink. He got so drunk on that pot of mead that when he was leaving he had to lean on his retainers' shoulders. I also indulged in drinking and he did not interfere, assuming that I was very drunk.

I got up very early on the next day, had the horses saddled, and went to the Voivode. Only now he elaborated on his instructions. When the elite Cossacks arrived, he ordered them to obey me, to behave sensibly, and to avoid trouble. I had just taken leave and had mounted my horse when Żerosławski came running. Gasping, he came up to me : "Yield this mission to me since you had promised me ! Take a hundred full thalers !" I said : "Do not make a fool out of me, Pan Brother ; I shall not dismount from my horse now !" He said :

---

[82]Here jokingly of the statue, mentioned under the year 1658.

"You can pull more out of me." "Even if you not only let yourself be pulled but torn in half, nothing will come out of this.

I rode in the direction of Smołowicze.[83] I did not find the envoys there.[84] I was given nice quarters, at the house of a well-to-do Muscovite. Only the master of the house himself cared and bustled about me, the lady of the house was not in sight. The food was cooked and we were amply provided with fish and meats. I spent four days there before the envoys arrived and I did not get to see the hostess. They hide their women so that they do not even get to see daylight; their wives endure great servitude and permanent confinement.

The envoys arrived then in good order and looking splendid; Afanasii Ivanovich Nestorov, the Great Master of the Pantry of the Tsar, of an old Muscovite family, and his son, the young Mikhailo, as if the secretary of the legation, Ivan Polikarpovich, over a dozen boyars and others, of lower rank, *circiter*[85] sixty in all. There were still wagon attendants and forty wagons with provisions and various other goods.

We greeted each other with great politeness. On the next day a tsar's banquet was to take place. In the evening Mikhailo Afanasovich, the son of the Master of the Pantry, and another boyar came to see me with this formal invitation.

"*Tsar', Gosudar' Veliki Beloyey i Chorney Rusi, Samoderzhtsa i Obladatel', tebe ster priyatel'a svoyevo prosit zavtra na beluzhye koleno i na lebedinoye khuzhno.*[86]

I was not familiar with their etiquette and I felt bad. I thought to myself what kind of custom it was to invite somebody for a rump and a knee and I still did not know what this

---

[83]Smołowicze, a town on the Polica, between Smolensk and Minsk, formerly in the voivodeship of Minsk. It belonged to the Radziwiłł family at the time. Czubek, *Pam.*, p. 286, note 1.
[84]In Vyazma.
[85]About.
[86]The Tsar and great monarch of White and Black Russia, autocrat and sovereign invites you as his friend for tomorrow to a beluga's (Russ. a white sturgeon of the Black and Caspian Seas) knee and a swan's rump.

beluga was. I wanted to say: "Let the Tsar himself eat this rump," but then I restrained myself. *Nemo sapiens, nisi patiens.*[87] I answered that I was grateful for the invitation from His Highness the Tsar to a banquet in his honor, but that, as a simple soldier, I did not enjoy delicacies. I shall show up but shall find something else to eat and shall leave the great delicacies to the gentlemen, the envoys. When the interpreter noticed that I frowned at that he said: "Do not be disturbed by this, sir. It is the custom of our nation that, just like with your country one is invited for a piece of boiled meat even though hazelhen and much other game will be served, so in similar fashion we invite for a *lebedinoye khuzhno*[88] even though many other dishes will be served. Yet whenever both of these dishes are listed—*lebedinoye khuzhno i beluzhye kole-no*,[89] it means a 'big banquet'." I then asked: "What kind of *beluga*[90] is this which has these special knees?" He said it was a big fresh water fish of which a part by its gills tastes as good as no other fish. Otherwise the *beluga* tastes like a sturgeon and this piece, which is removed from the fish, is round. It is served thus and therefore called the knee. I also asked why they invited one for the swan's rump and not the head, wing, or breast. He said because this part is the tastiest in the swan. I replied to this: "It would be better to invite one for an entire swan than for its rump. Also with us a rump of a fat capon is very savory and yet we do not invite one for a rump but *gene-raliter*[91] for a capon." He remarked that such was the custom.

I then attended the banquet to which I was again invited with the same kind of formal invitation as the day before. They immediately brought me a list of the titles of the Tsar so that I could learn them and would know what to say while drinking a toast to the health of such a great monarch, because God forbid that anyone should make a mistake or leave out one of the titles. It would be considered as a great insult to the

[87]Only the patient one is wise.
[88]Swan's rump.
[89]Swan's rump and the knee.
[90]Beluga.
[91]Generally.

name of the Tsar and all this eagerness would come to nothing. An abundance of food was served then, but it was bad and tasteless; only fowl was brought, mostly roasted. When we drank to the health of the Tsar I had to read the titles off the list; there was about half a sheet of them and they were very difficult and unusual. When we drank to the health of our King, only the Master of the Pantry knew the titles by heart and all the others read them off the list. At the slightest mistake we would have to start all over again even if we were already at the end. They also drank to the health of the hetmans, generals, and to Czarniecki because they were very obliging then. I wanted to repay politeness with politeness and drank to the health of Dolgoruky, Khovansky, and Sheremetev. They conceived this as an insult however. To be sure, they did not tell me anything right away but when they made friends with me they reproached me: "You did this as an affront to us." I replied: "After all they are field hetmans just like those of ours whose health you did not forget about." The Master of the Pantry said: "They are not even worthy of a dog drinking swill to their health because they lost our men."

They stayed in Vyazma for a week before they got ready. Then we went toward the border through Dorokhobuzh.[92] From there they sent their horses home and I had to requisition horses and carts because they allowed their horses to pull the wagons for only four leagues once we had crossed the border. And you, Sir Escort, worried that there would be something to harness, because such was the custom. It was difficult for me at first to hunt up teams of horses for so many wagons in such a devastated area but God did help me.

We moved in the direction of Minsk across Tołłoczyn, Jabłonica to Oczyża[93] and Mikołajów.[94] The farther we went the easier it was for me to get the teams; but at the start I regretted undertaking this mission.

The Muscovites were very happy that I was assigned to them as an escort and said: "*Kakzhe ster Gospod' Bog po-*

[92]A city on the Dnieper, 80 km east of Smolensk.
[93]A village east of Minsk.
[94]A city 30 km north of Nowogródek.

blagoslavil : *peredom vodil stary Pas, teper' budet nas vodit' molodoy Pasek.*"[95] For my uncle, a judge in Smolensk, had always escorted them and used to be a deputy to them. In the capital even the children knew him and everyone remembers him[96] well there. Even when I told them about my misfortune when a Muscovite had almost captured me during a battle with Dolgoruky, they said : "You would have been treated in the capital with all respect, and in consideration for your uncle's name and gratitude for his merits toward our nation you would have surely been released without ransom." But I said : "I thank you, I am better off at home !"

I moved at first *magnis itineribus*[97] in order to get out of the deserted area as soon as possible. When I reached populated land, things were easier for me ; I had no difficulty getting the teams, and I did not have to look for them because people there were acquainted with the custom. The towns notify each other when they hear that an envoy is passing through ; horses are to be provided then since as soon as the envoy stops in a town they are obliged to put food and drink at his disposal until the necessary number of horses is made available. So everyone took pains in order to be rid of the guests as soon as possible. They rode several leagues out of the city toward me, before I reached them, even on side roads which did not lead to the town and in which I had no intention of stopping. I did not even hear about the others and yet they would come, make an agreement, beg us to bypass them so that they would be free from the obligation to provide us with horses ; one brought two hundred zlotys, the next—three hundred, again another one hundred, according to the means available.

I still found the Voivode in Kojdanów even though he had taken leave of me in such a manner as if he did not expect me to return so soon from beyond the Dnieper. He gave me excellent information concerning everything *et sufficientem ex-*

[95]God meant well for us. Previously the old "Pas" had escorted us and now the young Pasek will convey us. (Play on words. *Pas* in Polish means belt and *pasek*, is the diminutive of *pas*.)
[96]Pasek's uncle.
[97]With forced marches.

peditionem.[98] But the letters he postdated for various reasons
as he did not intend to stay very long in this place. Since he
was encamped at a favorable spot, he did not want to leave at
once, but fed the army well and cleaned out the larder of the
Lithuanian confederacy, which was in concordance with the
intention of the Lithuanian Hetman Sapieha.

I sent someone ahead to inquire from the Voivode as to
whether he wanted me to present the envoys to him or not.
The envoys themselves begged to see Czarniecki. He ordered
us not to pass without seeing him. The envoys thus paid him
a visit : they drove in on their sleighs lying on bedclothes like
on a bed. It is not their custom to make up the sleighs for
sitting as we do ; they do not sit on them but lie stretched out
on a feather bed so that only their beards are in sight. The
poorer ones simply spread out any kind of a heavy blanket,
lie down on it and ride thus, complying with the custom.

After the audience the Voivode invited them to a camp
dinner. They came, drank heavily, and praised the good and
tasty food. And I remarked : "So you see that even though my
hetman did not invite you for the *khuzhno*, as you had invited
me, you ate well and you liked it." Then Polikarpovich answered : *"Kakzhe ster ? Vsyuda vorona govorit : ku, ku, ku !
U vas priglashayut na kura : u kura budet khuzhno ; u nas, priglashayut na khuzhno : pri khuzhno budet, sudar', golova."*[99]

With them the more the spirits stink the more they are
valued. Common brandy, so abominable that it is even sicken-
ing to smell, they not only drink, but enjoy as though it were
a great delicacy. They relish it and keep clicking their tongues :
"Slazheno zhe, sudar', vinko gosudarskoye !"[100] In the vicinity
of their capital they have a settlement[101] in which live only
Englishmen who, as cultured people, have many good wines

[98]And sufficient dispatch.
[99]How so, sir ? The crows cry everywhere : 'Ka, ka, ka !' With you,
one is invited for a chicken and the chicken will have a rump ; and
with us one is invited for the rump and along with the rump there will
also be a head.
[100]An excellent, royal wine !
[101]Sloboda near Moscow. Actually it was predominantly German.

and liquors. Whenever the Muscovites go on legation they procure from them various liquors, spiced wines which they call *Romania* and other wines, but they do not drink them themselves, but only treat others to them. This Master of the Pantry also did the same. He always poured vodka from a different bottle for himself than for me. I assumed at first that he drank a better one ; I did not say anything but I thought to myself : "Oh, what grossness !" As soon as we became familiar, however, and when he once poured a cup for himself and emptied it and then took another bottle from the table and poured liquor for me, I grabbed the one out of which he drank himself. He jumped at me and wanted to snatch it away from me but I had already put it to my lips. What an ill-smelling and awful thing it was ! I said then : "I assumed that you yourself drank a better one ! But now I consider you a polite man since you offer me a better one than you drink yourself." He was very much ashamed that he was suspected of it, but afterwards he was no longer embarrassed, even though he had been ashamed before for drinking such bad stuff. He called his retainer more often now : *"Mityushka, davai zhe, sudar', vinka gosudarskovo !"*[102] He would drain a cup and stroke himself across the chest saying : *"Kakzhe, ster, slazheno !"*[103] And that delicacy was such that even a goat would roar if one forced it down its throat.

Later, after we had parted with the army, I went through the Grand Hetman's estates. But since the Voivode had advised me not to make myself too burdensome, I merely notified the administrators that I was passing by. But still drinks, game and other things were sent to us.

I went to Horodyszcze[104] and then to Nowogródek. I felt bad as I was drawing near, since the townsmen did not send anyone to meet me even though they knew about the envoys. The towns which lay farther behind sent people in due time and invited those passing by to go with them. Those in Nowogródek said that no one can serve two masters : "We already have our own masters now for whom we fetch and carry." Indeed there was a Lithuanian regiment stationed there. I sent word to the townsmen ahead of time to have ready provisions and one hundred and fifty horses for the wagons of the envoys. They said : "Nothing will come of this ! We already have the Lithuanian regiment for whom we must supply provisions."

[102]Mityushka, bring me some of this royal wine !
[103]How delicious, sir.
[104]A town 35 km south of Nowogródek.

And they still did not send anyone to meet us. They did not suppose that I would dare to invade a town where a crowd of confederates was staying. Yet I said to the envoys, "Gentlemen! Please put your people at my disposal because this is a question of contempt for my King and your Tsar if they were to be impolite to us here." The envoys said to this : "Very well." They not only so directed their people but they also mounted their horses.

I grouped them as follows : the forty elite Cossacks and my retainers, in front, then the fifteen Muscovite riflemen who were guarding the wagons, and on both their flanks, infantrymen with muskets, and finally, the mounted Muscovites bringing up the rear. I myself rode ahead of all, close to the infantrymen. We numbered over one hundred horsemen. We entered the town with no resistance. I covered half of the length of the street when two officers and several dozen retainers armed with firearms came running toward us. They stopped there saying nothing, and we ignored them. (They were later followed by more armed men.) They took off their caps and we did the same. They stood there because they assumed that I only wanted to march through the town. When I saw some well-built houses I stopped. I pointed them out to the envoys : "Gentlemen, here are the quarters for your lordships." I myself stopped on the same side of the market place.

When they noticed that we were dismounting, they dashed toward us and said : "Do you, Sir, presume to invade our quarters ?" I replied : "And you, gentlemen, disregard the authority of two monarchs, the Polish and the Muscovite, since you forbid the townsmen to follow law and custom, *contra iura gentium.*"[105] One of them said: "An entire company is stationed in this street. Where you want to stop are the officers' quarters." I asked : "Does this company consist of people ?" He replied : "Certainly of people !" I said : "Even if they were devils, I would not be afraid of them. Leave me in peace. My business is not with you, but with his Majesty's town. If due service is not rendered to us, this contempt and disobedience

[105]Contrary to international law.

toward the King, our master, will cost the councillors their necks."

Some three hundred or more confederates already assembled. "You are not going to stop here !" I answered : "I am already here !" "You shall not stay here !" I said : "I certainly have no intention of remaining here forever, because I am in great haste. Be sure, however, that I will not leave until satisfaction is given me. In short, go away ! Otherwise, I shall give orders to shoot." The Cossacks and Muscovites held their muskets ready to fire. And I said : "Reflect upon it, and if you do not understand it yourself, let someone instruct you as to what importance is attached to every envoy. He is *publica persona*.[106] The eminence of two majesties and two monarchs is represented in his person, that of the one who sent him and the one who is to receive him".

We conversed thus to our heart's content. Then they left, and I gave the order : "Drive their horses away !" My men drove their horses into the street and let our horses in. Our wagons arrived, and we set up quarters. Some of their men came back later. They wanted to retrieve their saddles, harness, and guns off the pegs.

I sent word to the mayor that he would be subjected to punishment, that he and all the town would be summoned to court within a week at the latest if I were denied carts and horses. Not half an hour had elapsed before he and the councillors arrived and paid their respects. I asked who the presiding mayor was. "There he is !", one of them said. I dealt him a blow with a mace, and he fell to the ground. I had him tied up and guarded. "You shall go to Warsaw with me. The rest of you may leave, but take care that I be attended to, and that I have the horse teams, tomorrow. I will not leave this place until satisfied."

The Muscovites said : *"Oy, milenkie zhe, sudar', pristav, umeet koroleyskoye i tsarskoye sderzhat' velichestvo."*[107]

---

[106]Here meaning "public official."
[107]Oh, what a good man to command an escort ! He knows how to preserve the dignity of the King and the Tsar.

Later two lieutenants came. They exchanged some words with each other, and said : "Be at your ease, sir. The town will put provisions at your disposal. But carts and horses cannot be supplied." *Et interim,*[108] in their presence, I had those wagoners summoned who had just accompanied the wagons for the last two leagues, and I said to them : "Well, children. You observed law and custom. You did not try to break away from your obligation, but on the contrary went willingly. I am taking into consideration, therefore, that you come from a poor town. I am giving you a break, and shall not take you any further with me. I am in a big town now, and my demands shall be satisfied. I dismiss you. Go back home in the name of God !"

The wagoners fell on their kness before me. They thanked me. Then they rushed to their horses ! As soon as the townsmen found out about this, they came running and begged : "Have mercy on us, sir. We are willing to pay, but let these men drive further with you." They offered two hundred, they offered three hundred, but I did not budge. They finally offered four hundred. Meanwhile the wagoners, as fast as they could grab their horses, flew from the town. Some of them even left the harness behind. Then I said, as if I did not know that they had left already : "Go tell the wagoners to wait awhile !" I was told : "All of them are gone already, except for one whose horse fell ill." The townsmen became frightened, and begged me to send after them. I refused. The lieutenants begged me to free the mayor. I declared that until I was *in toto satisfactus*[109] as to provisions and horse teams, I would not set him free. If even my smallest wish were denied he certainly would go to Warsaw with me with his legs in shackles. They presented their arguments, I mine. They insisted that so many horse teams could not be provided. They suggested that I send to the neighboring towns so that they too would be made to contribute. I answered : "*Quod peto, da, Gai ; non peto consilium.*"[110]

They became angry : "You are obstinate, sir !" I answered

---

[108]And in the meantime.
[109]Completely satisfied.
[110]"Give me what I ask, Gaius, I do not ask for advice." (Martial, *Epigrammata* II, 30).

"And you are impertinent, sir!" And they left. A sexton brought me the news that they had ordered the townsmen to absolutely deny me both provisions and horse-teams. He reported also that they personally intended to drive me out of town. Either he told me this as a favor, or they put him up to it in order to test me. I did not let this news disturb me. I gave orders to barricade the street with wagons. All way across, wagon next to wagon, both ends giving on the market place and the other, so that not even a rider could get through. I did not have to ask for provisions. The street I was stationed in was the most prosperous in town and accordingly lacked nothing. *Interim* I summoned one of the blacksmiths who were located in the street, and ordered two manacles put on the mayor's legs. My elite Cossacks stood on alert. All the Muscovites were under arms. No one took a step without a matchlock. Let them try to drive me away now. There was plenty of beer in the taverns, and my men drank heartily. I asked my inn-keeper: "Is there mead anywhere nearby?" He thought of his own good, that he would lose less beer if he told me, and replied: "There is some at such and such a place. But please, Sir, do not say I told you." Six boyars were staying in that inn. I told them to ask politely for a pot of mead for cash. They did so. When they had emptied it, the alewife went to the cellar for more. Several of my men followed her. They reported that there were six barrels of mead there. I ordered them confiscated: "Drink, and after you have thus drunk your fill shoot about the streets." We revelled thus all night.

On the next day, we went to the barns, which stood behind the stables, and brought back as many sheaves of grain and hay as we needed. Now the confederates realized that they could not intimidate me and I did not ask for anything, because we had everything in abundance. We were slaughtering fattening pigs, hens, and geese. Then those lieutenants who had come the day before came again with several other officers of noble birth. Among them was Pan Tryzna,[111] an acquaintance of

[111]Stanisław Tryzna, a judge of Wołkowysk. Czubek, *Pam.*, p. 299, note 1.

mine. They began to negotiate : "The townsmen want to come to see you, but they are afraid. We intercede for them." I replied : "You yourselves have made them insolent, and now you intercede for them. Let whoever understands all this explain it to me. For I, a simple man, took yesterday's behavior as a threat of expulsion. Similarly, I understand today's behavior as such. But whatever I said yesterday, I still repeat today. My business is with the town and not with soldiers. Your slight is not going to injure me, but the two monarchs, and God knows, perhaps even yourselves, because I shall not allow you to expel me from here. Do understand that even if men were to fall on top of each other, I should not leave until satisfied. And if the situation proves trying for me, my army is less than one hundred leagues away, in Kojdanów, and most likely it has already drawn nearer by now. We shall see then for whom things will be difficult here !"

At that, the townsmen arrived. The wife of the mayor whom I had shackled was waiting since early in the morning. She came with her children, with liquor, and with tears as her third argument. The bargaining began. They promised forty horses. "That is out of the question ! Even sixty would not be enough !" They had to consent to one hundred and thirty horses. Some of these they had to hire from the soldiers, for they did not have enough, but were still not ready by evening. Since I did not want to ride at night, we began to drink. I did all this to spite those insolent people, for my innate nature responds *durum contra durum*,[112] even to excess. I would do anything for kindness, however, even to my own detriment.

Bonis modis[113] thus, at the intercession of those confederate soldiers who were meeker than yesterday, but especially for the sake of Pan Tryzna, a companion, who was an acquaintance, a wise man, and a relative as well. I had the mayor unshackled and said to Him : "Mark how to behave under similar circumstances next time. Remember that even the soldiers who might be stationed in your town will not be able to

[112]Tit for tat.
[113]In a good way.

protect you, and even if they did in case the escorting officer were a simple-hearted man, such protection would be only temporary for one could take revenge on you later. 'Cloisters last while abbots pass.'"

We began to drink. Many Lithuanians joined us. Pan Tryzna came with as many of his companions as he could invite. They came, made merry, and played the violin. The envoy was well disposed and ordered spiced wine brought from his wagons. We had been drinking mead before that, but I did not mix drinks. The Lithuanians did, and many of them lost their belts, caps, swords, and purses.

Horses were delivered early next day. Our own horses had rested and been well fed in the meanwhile as we obtained from the granges whatever fodder we needed. Even oats were brought later. I ordered preparations for departure.

The revelers of yesterday returned. Many invited me to their places. Even the colonel requested my presence but I had already promised Tryzna and said : "Pan brother, if I accepted your invitation, all the others would have reprimanded me for rudeness. I must decline the invitation therefore." He begged that I visit him before departure. I did not want to do so and I did not go. We again drank plenty at parting. "To your courage," they said. But they reproached me for executing my orders and for their confusion. They said that to give willingly or by force was all the same. They presented me with several greyhounds. Later we parted.

We headed in the direction of Mosty.[114] As soon as I left the town,[115] I sent an orderly back to the mayor with the message that they were to send enough food and supplies for their wagoners because I would not dismiss them before Warsaw or Narew at best. They were alarmed at that, especially those soldiers whose horses they had borrowed. Three leagues beyond the town limits two of the townsmen overtook me and began to plead. "No !", I said. "I shall deal with you the same way as you dealt with me concerning night quarters ! It cannot

[114]A city fifty km southeast of Grodno.
[115]Nowogródek.

be." They hastened then to the place of Pan Żeromski,[116] the Marshall of the confederacy, and the subprefect of Opesk and Czeczera. He was a wise and serious man. Very handsome, of middle height, young, not yet forty, he had a coal-black beard which reached his waist. He looked more like a dignified senator than a soldier. They wanted him to advise and to help them. But his answer to them was : "I cannot offer you help because of the seriousness of this matter. I know that those men have great pride. This would certainly lead to bloodshed, in which case it would be a capital offense. I shall give you the following advice however : if you have enough money, run after them. It will be the mediator between you." They said that they had one hundred zlotys. He answered that we would not even look at such a small sum.

The townsmen came galloping back. They begged and bargained with us. We finally settled on six hundred zlotys. They did not have the money with them however. They wanted to give me a promissory note with delivery in Warsaw. "This cannot be !" I said : "What are we to do then ?" "It is none of my business."

In the meantime the Marshal sent a comrade with an invitation for me and the envoys. He did not make the slightest mention of the townsmen in his letter. It was written as follows :

My Most Gracious Sir Pasek, Lord and Friend !

Had I learned earlier that Your Lordship is so kind as to escort an envoy of his Majesty the Tsar, I would have begged your Lordship already then for the privilege of seeing the legation with the envoy, for he himself had expressed the desire to see me in order to listen to him *in commissis*[117] of the Tsar. Since I have received news of the envoy and the liberated prisoners which he is conducting, I strongly beg your lordship not to hinder the envoy

[116]Kazimierz Chwalibóg Żeromski, a colonel in the hussar company of W. Gosiewski ; he was massacred by the Lithuanian confederates that same year. Pasek is mistaken here however by saying that he was also the subprefect of Czeczera. Czapliński, *Pam.*, p. 288, note 254.
[117]On behalf.

from doing so. For he does want to see me and himself desires it very much. It was no one else but I who had worked for the liberation of these prisoners, who are to be exchanged, and my intentions were guided by God. In the interest of myself and that of the entire army, I beseech your lordship *iteratis*[118] to allow this envoy *liberum aditum*[119] to my quarters in Wołkowysk.[120] I have assigned his lordship Pan Żydowicz, an officer of my army, to escort him to Wołkowysk. I remain your lordship's

    Benevolent brother and compliant servant
      Kazimierz Chwalibóg Żeromski
      Hetman of the armies of HRH of GDL.

The heading of the letter was as follows:

To my Most Gracious Sir and Friend, His Lordship Pan Jan Pasek, officer in charge of the Cossack company of his Serene Highness the Voivode of the Ruthenian lands.

Since he addressed me as "My Most Gracious Sir and Friend," and signed it "Your Lordship's benevolent brother and compliant servant," and again headed the letter "My Most Gracious Sir and Friend," he had, at one stroke, made himself both a brother and a friend.[121] From the beginning this was not to my liking. I answered this letter, which I possess to this day, in the following manner:

Most Gracious Marshal of the armies of the Grand Duchy of Lithuania, my most Gracious Sir and Brother:

When I looked at the heading of Your Lordship's letter, I was disturbed very much for I realized that I am worthy only of being Your Lordship's friend and not

[118]Once again.
[119]Free access.
[120]A city on the Rosia river, eighty kilometers east of Grodno.
[121]Only a merchant or townsman could be addressed as a "friend" in Poland at the time. A nobleman should have been addressed as "Pan brother". This is why Pasek feels slighted. Among the wealthier nobility the correspondence was usually taken care of by a secretary and only the conclusion of the letter was added by the nobleman himself. This probably accounts for the change in the form of address here. Czubek, *Pam.*, p. 304, note 2.

a brother. After reading your Lordship's letter *intus*,[122] and noting that your Lordship condescends to sign himself as a brother, I was somewhat consoled however. *Non peto vindictam*[123] on the heading of my reply therefore, *supponendo*[124] that this *error non regulatur*[125] to the attention of your Lordship but to the person of the secretary who, I believe must be a very old man, since he still remembers *hanc ideam*[126] of writing letters and has preserved it till this day. Such form of address was employed when one wrote to senators as 'Dear Sir'. If your Lordship's secretary is a young man, however, the possibility arises that he had previously served as a head raftsman who transported hemp, chipped oak parts, and oak boards to Riga. He must have been reminiscing about it while writing this letter and assumed to be writing to a merchant and corresponding with him *de anteactis*.[127] During the reign of King Olbracht such was the fashion. But during that of Kazimierz it fell long since into disuse.

I mentioned this *ex occasione*[128] your Honor's secretary and now I proceed *ad essentiam*[129] of your Lordship's letter. If I had been *requisitus*[130] by your Honor somewhat sooner, I would have surely changed my course upon leaving Kojdanów. I would not have the need to inconvenience your Lordship then because it would have been little out of my way or not at all . . .[131]

. . . .

The Ruthenian Voivode told me that I could appoint

[122]Inside.
[123]I do not respond in kind.
[124]Supposing.
[125]Error does not refer.
[126]Such a manner.
[127]About bygone matters.
[128]Concerning.
[129]To the contents.
[130]Summoned.
[131]One sheet is missing in the manuscript and then follows the conclusion of a word-of-mouth answer given to Pasek by Sapieha in answer to Czarniecki's letter. Czubek, *Pam.*, p. 305, note 8.

another escorting officer. I do not intend to change this but even confirm his choice. I consider your Lordship as one of us. We have a Pasek family here in Lithuania too. Also it was supposedly your uncle, the commander of Smolensk[132] who had escorted them before. There are also two men with your last name in my service. They are believed to be relatives of yours. Moreover Narew is not far away. What's the use of appointing a different escorting officer then? According to what I have heard you already escorted them through the world *cum conservatione* of your honor and that of your commander. Escort them then also to the side of his Majesty the King!

He was glad to see me and asked me to stay after dinner. He talked, drank to the Voivode's health, and recalled the victories attained in the previous year. He also asked: "Who was the officer who was held under suspicion by his Majesty, the King?" I told him that it was I. He said: "I asked because I have heard that his name was such. You have gained yourself a good name all over Lithuania for the courageous stand which you took." He drank to my health and ordered his soldiers to do so. He parted with me with great courtesy and gave me a reply to the Voivode's letter which was as follows:

Most Gracious Sir Voivode of the Ruthenian lands,
My Most Gracious Sir and Brother!

I humbly thank your Honor for respecting the prerogative of my office as a field hetman and the innate judiciousness and grace of Your Honor which is evident from all your Lordship's actions. *Renovo propositum*[133] to hold all the actions of your Honor in such esteem that whatever pleases your Honor cannot displease me. I do not have the intention to replace his Lordship, Pan Pasek, a high-ranking officer of your Honor, assigned as escort. I even adapt myself to the will of Your Honor and confirm the function assigned by Your Honor to his person

---

[132]*Horodniczy* in Poland. This office in cities the size of Wilno, Witebsk, and Smolensk was very important. Czubek, *Pam.*, p. 306, note 2.
[133]I renew my undertaken resolution.

and declare further that I could not have assigned a better
escorting officer myself, one who would know to preserve
so *dextre*[134] his and his commander's reputation. His *mo-
destia*[135] in escorting this legation is known to me, from
the contentment of towns and cities. His moderate behavior and his noble dignity are known and proper wherever they should be displayed.

Just *noviter*[136] in Wołpa[137] when people struck *contra
Maiestatem et matrem oboedientiam*,[138] of which your
Honor *suppono*[139] either already *innotuit*[140] or soon *inno-
tescet*,[141] he did not allow the *honoris palmam*[142] to be torn
away neither from himself nor from Your Honor. I cannot
reprove a good man therefore and if people say *Kyrie
elejson*,[143] I do not want to improve.

As concerns the abandoning of the White Ruthenian
lands, everyone must admit the *iustum dolorem*[144] of Your
Honor. This pierces my heart *non minus*.[145] What is one
to do however when such misfortune befalls the fatherland ? I, with my personal resources, even if I wanted to,
certainly *non subsistam*,[146] but I admit that Your Honor
had given protection to those lands with such a handful
of people too long *et cum summo periculo*.[147] What *subse-
quetur*[148] now is not our fault ; the one who is *auctor mali
reddet rationem*[149] to God. If the enemy would only leave

[134]Skillfully.
[135]Moderation, modesty.
[136]Recently.
[137]A town fifty kilometers southwest of Grodno.
[138]Against the Majesty to whom allegiance is owed.
[139]I suppose.
[140]Has come to the knowledge.
[141]Will do so.
[142]Palm (lit. "gem") of honor.
[143]Kyrie Eleison. (God have mercy ; an invariable phrase of the litany.)
[144]The just grievance.
[145]Nonetheless.
[146]Would not withstand.
[147]And with great peril.
[148]Will follow.
[149]The author of this evil will render an account.

us alone for the time, we could then assemble at the Diet and *consulere*[150] plans as to how to defend those lands as fast as possible. We could manage somehow then, but I doubt that this will be possible. In case Your Honor receives this entreaty of mine while crossing with his army, I beg Your Honor to be so kind as *divertere*[151] to my house for a short while, if my men fail to come across your Honor on the way. I very much desire to be able *conferre*[152] with your Honor about the further course of service to our failing fatherland. I do not doubt that such be the case. For the time being I commend myself to the grace of your Honor as a completely benevolent brother and a compliant servant.

Paweł Sapieha, the Voivode of Wilno,
Grand Marshal of the Grand Duchy of Lithuania.

Upon receiving this letter I went in the direction of Narew. Toward the end of the carnival[153] I stopped in Berezyny,[154] a village. We did not need a town however since we had plenty of everything in our wagons such as good drinks, meats, game, etc. We celebrated by the Russian *duhas*,[155] even though we had not known each other long. We went riding in search of the *kulig*[156] and we entertained other searchers. We had someone to dance with then.

On Ash Wednesday I left for Narew. The envoys had plenty of fish such as sterlets, and huge pieces of *beluga.* We also had enough fresh fish, as people brought it to us from everywhere. Wherever I sent for horses they also brought fish along with them.

Upon reaching Narew I no longer could take the Lithua-

[150]Discuss.
[151]Turn back.
[152]Confer.
[153]It fell after February 15 at the time.
[154]A village in the starosty of Knyszyn.
[155]*Duga* or *duha*, a wooden bow over the horsecollar joining two shafts, typical for Russian harness up to this day.
[156]Sledge parties during the carnival called *kulig* or *kulik* from the name of the bird *kulik* (curlew) in search of which supposedly a party of a dozen or so sleighs sets out and goes from manor to manor.

nian horses along with me because such was the regulation, even if I only used them for just a league. I had to acquire another set of horses right away.

From Narew we went through Bielsko, Siemiatycze, Drohiczyn,[157] across the Bug toward Liw[158] and from there to Warsaw. From our last stopover I rode ahead to the King. I reported about the envoys and asked for further instructions concerning them, how and where I should take them to.

The King received me cordially when he saw me. He recognized me right away and he had already learned from the Voivode that I was escorting the envoys. He was leaving for a Diet session when I entered. There were many senators and delegates in the chamber. Some of them I knew, others not. When he saw me he said: "Welcome Sir Quasi-Confederate!" I bowed and replied: "There can be no grounds for such suspicion now, Your Majesty, for I have come from Smolensk and not from Kielce."[159] The King remarked: "One could reproach you even more now, assuming that you were

[157]Bielsko; Bielsk Podlaski, a city thirty-six kilometers south of Białystok; Siemiatycze, a city not far from Bug, fifty kilometers northeast of Siedlce; Drohiczyn, a city thirty-six kilometers northeast of Siedlce.
[158]A city 36 km northwest of Siedlce.
[159]The headquarters of the confederacy were located there. Czapliński, Pam., p. 296, note 321.

won over by the Muscovites." I replied to that : "They may reproach me as much as they want to, Your Majesty, my gracious lord, will recompense me for it again, however." He laughed at that and hugged my head : "We shall never believe such a story again even if an angel were to say it !" Then he said to the senators : "I shall be detained for awhile. Meanwhile your Lordships may take their seats." He told me to follow him. We went to his bedchamber. He questioned me about everything then, asked about the envoys' business. I told him that they desired peace. He inquired whether I had opposition from the Lithuanian confederates during my escort. I reported the incident in Nowogródek. His Majesty said : "The Voivode has already written me about it. I thank you for the proper stand which you, as I see, know to apply under all conditions, *in adversis et prosperis*,[160] in order to preserve our dignity !" Later he summoned the Polish Chamberlain[161] and said to him : "Talk it over with Szeling as to where to quarter the Russian guests."[162] He talked with me for about an hour and then left for the Senate.

When I left his chamber, the deputies from Rawa and Łęczyca surrounded me : "Since when such familiarity with the King !" "How come !" "What is this." I told them and they exclaimed : "*Gratulor ! Gratulor !*"

I left the senatorial chamber and went to see Szeling. We dined together. *Interim* the envoys had arrived in Praga.[163] Since all the inns were occupied and we could not obtain quarters for them, I returned to the senatorial chamber and stopped in front of the King. He asked : "What is the problem ?" I told him of the envoy's arrival and that there were no quarters for them. He ordered Scypio[164] to go with me to commandeer some quarters and to stay in Praga until further orders.[165] We did so.

[160]Favorable and unfavorable.
[161]Teodor Denhof.
[162]H. Szeling was the King's courtier. Czubek, *Pam.*, p. 311, note 2.
[163]On the other side of the Vistula river, opposite Warsaw.
[164]Jędrzej Scypio, a courtier and a valet of the King.
[165]The Diet was in session at the time. It lasted from February until May 1662. The delegates were present at the royal castle therefore and all the inns were occupied. Czapliński, *Pam.*, p. 298, note 334.

On the next day a royal coach was sent for us. We were
assigned quarters in a Frenchman's manor. The King had me
consult with him concerning money for the provisions. I myself
had plenty of money, some of which was still from Denmark.
Just recently I had also received five hundred ducats from the
King and 17,000 for escorting the Muscovites. Since I had come
by it so easily, I did not respect it very much. I drank often
with the courtiers, since in Warsaw it is easy to make friends.

Mazepa had already apologized to His Majesty for that
slander in Grodno and again came to the Court. We saw each
other often, yet even though this incrimination of his did me no
harm, but, on the contrary, brought me gain and good reputation—even the confederates envied me this, while others congratulated me. I was, nevertheless, angry at him, especially
when under the influence of liquor, as usually all grudges come
out into the open then.

Once I came to the antechamber of the Royal chamber.
Mazepa along with several other courtiers was there and I said:
"Greetings Sir Cossack Officer!" He, the arrogant fellow,
retorted: "Greetings, Sir Corporal!", since Germans[166] had
guarded me in Grodno. Without hesitation I slapped his face
with my fist and instantly jumped back. He grabbed the hilt of
his sword, I grabbed mine. Everyone jumped to their feet:
"Stop! Stop! The King is next door!" But not even one
courtier sided with him. They did not like him very much since
he was somewhat of an impostor and, in addition to that,
a recently ennobled Cossack. They also knew about my justifiable grudge against him and respected me. I had already
made friends with them, and had not begrudged spending my
money on them during our meetings. A commotion arose then.
One of the courtiers entered the King's chamber and said:
"Your Majesty, Pan Pasek had slapped Mazepa in the face."
The King slapped his face at that and said: "Don't talk nonsense when you are not asked!" The Bishop became alarmed.
He knew that this was a capital offense and suspected that

[166]I.e., German infantry; such were the divisions called which were
under German command and in which also Germans served from
either Pomerania or Prussia. Czapliński, *Pam.*, p. 299, note 338.

insultus[167] would be raised against me. He came up to me and said : "I do not know you, sir, but for God's sake I advise you to leave because it is a great crime to slap a courtier in the face in the royal chamber." I answered : "Your Excellency does not know what this villain did to me !" The Bishop said again : "There is no provocation great enough to warrant such unbecoming behavior in this chamber. Leave, Sir, as long as there is still time and as long as the King does not know about it." I said : "I shall not go !"

Mazepa left the chamber almost in tears. It was not so much the slap that hurt him as that all the other courtiers did not side with him. I told the Bishop of the cause of my grievance. The Polish chamberlain came in later notifying the Bishop that he could see the King ; he threatened me with his finger as they were leaving. I surmised that they knew about it in the royal chamber already. They went out and I returned to my quarters.

It was Saturday next day and I did not go to the castle. I was afraid, the more so since one looked at things differently after sobering up. I cautiously inquired whether the King knew about it. I heard that he had but was not angry with me ; he even slapped the page boy who informed him about it in the face and said : "Here is one for you since you escaped harmless there. Don't repeat nonsense." On Sunday I went to see the Chamberlain of the Crown and asked if I could show myself before the King. He said that the King was not at all angry and had even said : "I don't blame him. A slander hurts more than a wound. Fortunately they did not run into each other on a road somewhere and Mazepa got off with only a slap. May he remember next time what making false accusations means."

When I came to the castle the royal couple was dining. The King noticed me and said : "By God, you have grown proud. It is already three days since I saw you last. Both you and the envoys should be given poorer sustenance, I believe. Then you would appear in my chamber more often." I answered : "Gracious King, they complain nevertheless, even though

[167]Charges.

Your Majesty has showered them with so much hospitality and kindness. If they were to be treated even more delicately I could not remain with them." Then his Majesty conversed with various people on different subjects. I was glad that he was not cross with me because of the Mazepa incident. A great number of delegates and officers were present. Dessert was being served.

A little bear was there, or rather a human form *circiter*[168] thirteen years of age whom Marcyjan Ogiński[169] had the beaters bait into a net in Lithuania and captured at a considerable loss of the marksmen since the bears defended him violently, most of all a big female bear, apparently his mother. As soon as the beaters had killed her they immediately captured the young bear. He looked just like a boy. His hands and feet had human nails rather than claws of a bear. He differed from man only in that he, including his face was completely overgrown with long hair, and only his eyes sparkled. Many controversial statements were made concerning him such as that he was *ex semine viri cum ursa*,[170] or that he had been carried off as an infant by a she-bear and brought up by her. *It ubera suxit*[171] and *assumpsit similitudinem animalis.*[172] The poor fellow possessed neither human speech nor manners. He only had animal characteristics.

The Queen handed him a sugared pear peel. He put it in his mouth with great pleasure but having tasted it he spit it out, all covered with saliva, and hurled it at the Queen between her eyes. The King began to roar with laughter. The Queen said something in French ; the King laughed even louder. Ludwika, being irritable, left the table. As a result of her fit of anger, the King ordered all of us to drink. Wine was served, music began to play and the ladies in waiting came. The party started.

[168]About.
[169]Marcyjan Ogiński, master of the pantry of Troki, later butler of Lithuania, then voivode of Troki, and finally (1684) Lithuanian Chancellor ; died in 1690. Czubek, *Pam.*, p. 314, note 4.
[170]A product of the sperm of a man and a female bear.
[171]Sucked the udders.
[172]Acquired animal characteristics.

The King had Mazepa brought before him, and told us to embrace and apologize to one another : "Forgive each other from the heart as now each of you is guilty before the other." We made peace. Later we sat next to each other and drank together. Nevertheless, a year later, Mazepa left Poland once again in disgrace. It was for the following reason :

He had a small village in Volhynia in the neighborhood of Falbowski, whose manor he very much desired for what reason I don't know. He often stayed there during Falbowski's absence. The house servants who transmitted the lovers' notes and were *conscii*[173] of the love trysts, informed the master about it. One day Falbowski pretended to be going on a long trip. He parted with his wife and left. He halted on the road which Mazepa used and soon after the servant who served as the messenger and who reported the matter to his master, came riding along. Falbowski took the note ; he read in it how they invited each other to pleasure and how she informed Mazepa that his Lordship had gone on a trip. He returned the note to the confidant : "Go on and ask him for a reply. Say that her Ladyship asks him to hurry." The servant left. Meanwhile Falbowski waited for his return with an answer ; the servant had to ride for two leagues.

As soon as Mazepa had sent him on his way, he rushed back. He handed his master the note in which Mazepa declared his readiness to be at her Ladyship's service, promising to come at once. After awhile Mazepa came riding by. At their encounter Falbowski exclaimed : "Greetings !" "Greetings !" "Where are you going ?" Mazepa stated another point of destination. "I beg your Lordship for a short visit !" Mazepa excused himself and said that he had an urgent trip. "Your Lordship is also going somewhere, I see !" "Oh, it cannot be," said Falbowski and grabbed him by the nape of the neck. "And what is this note ?" Mazepa collapsed ; he insisted that he was going there for the first time, that he had never been there before. The servant was summoned then : "How many times has this man been there during my absence ?" He answered :

[173] Aware.

"As many as I have hair on my head." They seized him and rode on. "Do you choose to die?" Mazepa begged not to be killed and confessed to everything. Falbowski vented his anger on him and tormented him. He stripped him to the skin and tied him to his own unsaddled horse; he turned his face toward the horse's tail, his back to the horse's head, his hands over the shoulders, and bound his legs together under the belly of the horse. The horse, which was rather wild from nature, was startled, whipped with knouts, and had his headgear pulled down. Then several shots were fired over his head and he frantically rushed homeward. The route took him all the way through thickets: hawthorn, hazel, clumps of dog rose and thorns. The road was not spacious, only narrow paths were there which the horse remembered since he had often taken that route, for just as on a raiding party one usually avoids taking main roads. Riders had to bend often there, even though holding the reins in their hands, and had to go round bad and thickly overgrown spots; still a branch would often hit them from time to time on their heads or tear their garments. It can be easily imagined therefore how bad a treatment was received by a nude man sitting backwards on such a swift and frightened horse who, from fear and pain, rushed blindly ahead wherever his legs carried him through the dense thickets. Falbowski also did not let Mazepa's two or three attendants go along, so that no one could rescue him. Frozen stiff, Mazepa arrived at the gate and shouted: "Watchman!" The watchman recognized the voice and opened up: When he saw the apparition he closed it again and ran away. He called out everyone in the manor. They peeked through the doors and crossed themselves; he assured them that he was really their master, but they did not believe him. Only when he could hardly speak, bruised and chilled to the bone, did they finally let him in.

Falbowski rode back to his wife. He knew all of Mazepa's ways. He knocked on the window through which Mazepa used to enter. It was opened and he was received as a welcome guest. She had to endure much, but it is not becoming to describe the details here, especially those concerning the spurs which were specially prepared for that encounter and intentionally tied somewhere around the knees. *Sufficit* that it was a considerable and renowned example for the punishment and the sobering down of licentious people. Mazepa barely escaped death; when he cured himself, he left Poland out of mere shame.

I spoke thus of two outstanding royal courtiers. The Cossack fled from Poland and as to the bear (the feral child), I do not know whether he turned into a man or not, but I know that he was sent to Frenchmen for schooling and that he already made good progress in speaking. I return to my undertaken subject matter however.

I held my office *in debita methodo, cum gratulatione*[174] from my fellow noblemen from Rawa, who were then present at the Diet. The army's arrears and the defense of the frontiers were on the agenda. I saw the King often; the only *obstaculum* was that the treasury was depleted and there were no vacancies of office, but as I was not ambitious *naturaliter*,[175] I was content with little. I later asked permission to go home, which was twelve miles from Warsaw, for Easter.[176] I mentioned my solemn vows which I had made beyond the sea to thank God for his blessings during these campaigns. The King granted me permission *cum regressu*[177] and he appointed Scypio, his standard-bearer and courtier, in my place as escorting officer to the Muscovites.

When I came to my parents' estate there was great joy, for they had heard things—although not right away—of the Grodno slander. Many relatives, neighbors, and good friends came together; we were all merry. After I had rested at home we decided to fulfill my vow with a pilgrimage to Częstochowa.[178]

[174]As was fit.
[175]By nature.
[176]At that time it was on April 9.
[177]Under the condition that I should return.
[178]City in southern Poland on the Warta river, famous for its monastery of *Jasna Góra* with the image of Our Lady; a major shrine of pilgrimage. Our Lady of Częstochowa, esteemed as the "Queen of Poland", has been a national symbol since 1655, when the monastery withstood the Swedish siege which lasted forty days.

We set out so as to arrive there on Ascension.[179] My mother rode, I walked on foot, and horses were led behind me on which I was to ride back. It was dreadfully hot, but on our way back snow fell which caused great harm, since the rye was already in bloom at that time. Snow, which fell up to the horses' knees, nipped the blossoms and ruined the orchards and other *fructifera*,[180] since it lay on the ground for a week. So there was little or no profit from rye fields this year. The other grain fields also suffered great damage. God and the people had taken away much bread from the fatherland this year which was a *poena peccati*.[181] Thereupon a great shortage of grain ensued and the people were in want.

During my stay in Częstochowa I went to confession and begged for absolution *ex voto promissi matrimonii*[182] to the young lady about whom I have written earlier, since it never took place. This promise was given in an injudicious spirit or, simply speaking, from falling in love. I was absolved, it is true, but I remember the penance and the admonition which I had to listen to and I shall remember it for a long time to come. I could instruct many how cautious one should be in using that little phrase : "I shall marry you."

From Częstochowa I returned to Warsaw where I found things in a great uproar since there was no agreement. Some wanted to break up the Diet, the army began to assemble near Warsaw and declared that it would not allow anybody to leave until the close of the Diet, and there were listening posts along the roads. The Diet was concluded as though in a state of siege. The unfinished business concerning the control of the army and the means of payment was turned over to a committee. At the closing of the Diet I sought a cash payment from the treasury for my escorting mission since I did not get the promised office and I had no luck in spotting one at that time, even though the King had said to me several times : "Pick one for yourself !" I was offered posts and I knew that I needed

---

[179]It was on May 18, that year. Czapliński, *Pam.*, p. 305, note 381.
[180]Fruit trees.
[181]Punishment for our sins.
[182]From a promise of marriage.

income. I treated the *titulum* slightingly and wished for myself a *vitulum*.[183] During the entire course of the Diet I failed to find a lucrative position ; it is easier to find one *occasionaliter*[184] than when one looks for it deliberately. There was talk about the King's promise to me and the King himself reminded me of it saying : "I am indebted to you and it feels as if you shouted into my ear whenever I see you, even though you do not say anything, for I know that I am indebted to you." Such good fortune went unrewarded however since there was no money in the treasury. King Kazimierz, though a good lord, had no luck with money ; it simply did not stick with him. *Conclusum*[185] to give me a promissory note for six thousand on the Lithuanian treasury *ex ratione*[186] I had carried out the duty for the Grand Duchy of Lithuania and because a Lithuanian should have been the escort and not a Pole. Possibly, however, the decision was more *eo fine*[187] to hoodwink me with an apparent hope of contentment and in order to be rid of me hastily, for in that treasury the same situation as in ours existed. Gosiewski, the Lithuanian Field Hetman and treasurer, who had been captured by Khovansky prior to our coming to Lithuania with Czarniecki, still walked around with a beard and shaggy hair ; he could not be rich, since he himself had just come out of prison. When I went with the promissory note to him, he looked at it and said : "For God's sake ! The King knows that I have not collected any money during these years and that the treasury is empty. This promissory note was given to your lordship in vain for at present nothing can be obtained. Perhaps later, after the dissolution of the confederacy, since even if I had some money now I could not hand it out, so do not cherish any hope, your lordship. Let the King find something for you from another source." I went back, repeated those words to the King, and returned the promissory note to him.

---

[183]*Titulum . . . vitulum . . . (title . . .* bull calf), play on words. In other words I slight titles and I desire funds.
[184]By chance.
[185]Finally the decision was made.
[186]Because.
[187]With the intention.

The King said : "Things will be different as soon as I see him."
The Treasurer did indeed promise me payment, but the King
ordered me to ride to the Committee in Wilno and said : "They
say one needs a swift horse for a promise, so we wish you to
arrive at the beginning of the meetings. The Treasurer is supposed to get hold of some money then and he promised to pay
you out of those funds immediately. Be sure to return soon in
order to escort this Muscovite legation back and we shall not
forget to provide you with something better *feliciori tempore*.[188]

When the Diet closed I parted with the King and went
home, where I rested a little and then set out for Wilno. I found
things *in turbido*[189] upon my arrival there since right from the
beginning of the commission, for which a great number of
military men had assembled, no session of conference had taken
place without some sort of uproar, commotion, or rushing to
swords. Since so many people had assembled, it was very difficult to find accommodations and I had to stay in an empty,
recently begun, unfinished house. Only the frame of the house,
without doors, stood there. I had to beware, day and night, of
thefts and robberies, which was very difficult among strangers.
But even in this isolated place I could not escape intruders,
about which I shall write more later.

I attended the meetings for as long as I was welcome, but
law and order were ineffective there. I then asked for what
I came for, as both the giver and the receiver were in imminent
danger.

As soon as the money came from some source of income
I was given a note on the treasury and I showed the note to
the clerk. We began to count the money, having locked ourselves in a very dark cellar, which had only one window and
which was located in a castle behind the church of St. Kazimierz. We counted almost stealthily. He gave me *partem* in
good money, *partem*[190] in Riga shillings, which at that time
were thin and only silver plated. I was accompanied by only
one retainer—the others had to keep guard in that empty

188At a more opportune time.
189In a turmoil.
190Partly . . . partly.

house—and he could not take all the money away by himself. The Treasurer then gave me two Haiduks from his own guard and they carried the money to my quarters in a wheelbarrow. As soon as I had arrived at the house my orderly told me that an officer had been there who claimed that these were his quarters and was furious that I had stopped there without his permission. He wanted to drive my horses out, but another man who was with him had dissuaded him from it. He declared that they would return. I ordered my orderly to let me know when they did so.

I had hardly dispatched the Haiduks when he came with six other men. Also the landlord, or rather the heir of the empty rooms in which I was staying came with them. They were all drunk. He asked me : "With whose permission and at whose command do you live here, Sir ?" I answered : "With the permission of the Almighty who permits me to live and to walk." He said : "But these are my quarters." I replied : "Then you are a poor gardener, since you allow those quarters to be overgrown with nettles and weeds." He insisted : "These are my quarters." I answered : "You are not a praiseworthy land-lord since there are no oven, windows, or doors in the house !" He said : "And why did you stop here ?" I answered : "Because I came to a Tatar state and not to a nation which should be polite and obliging enough to provide free quarters for a guest." The townsman, the landlord of these empty rooms said : "Oh, Sir, tell him to drive his horses out to the street. He is mocking you." And he ordered : "Drive them out !" "Don't drive them out !", I said.

This was taking place inside this structure among the horses. The townsman, the owner of the house, rushed to untie the horses ; my retainer gave him a hard knock on the chest and he fell. We rushed to swords and a commotion arose. I had a chestnut-brown Walachian horse, unusually swift, and a Lithuanian who meddled in the affair fell from a sabre blow under the horse. My chestnut-brown also worked another over with the hooves and that one too fell to the ground. Already two lay there thus. Then, *per appellationem*,[191] the case was

[191]On appeal. A legal term used jokingly here.

settled outside in the nettles. We rushed at each other there ; one retainer covered my back, two others covered my sides. Somehow the retainer in back was cut off and one of them struck me from the rear, but not hard and I immediately jumped to the side. The gentleman fell into the nettles at the same time and two retainers jumped with swords in front of him so that he did not get hurt and got up. He charged directly and slashed at me mightily but I withstood him. I retreated and cut him across the wrist ; he ignored it and we continued to fight. Meanwhile my retainer struck this lad over the head and he fell. "His Lordship," the townsman, charged again. He was again struck across the fingers, let the sword fall, and took to his heels. My retainer set out after him and "his Lordship" fell into the bushes. The retainer kept striking him until I exclaimed : "Stop!" Then the others took to their heels and I returned to the house, to my horses. The man who had been struck with the mace had already crawled out and escaped. The one who had been trampled by the horse still lay there, unconscious. Assuming that he was dead, I ordered him dragged out by his feet. He groaned. My men said : "He is alive ! He is alive ! We must revive him !" He recovered, got up, and left. We also picked up those of them outside in the nettles. They went away, scolding and threatening us.

I thought : "What am I to do ? Lock myself up ?" I did not know what with. About an hour after nightfall a crowd of about fifty or sixty men came along. My retainer called out : "Don't come near for I shall shoot ! What do you want ?" They halted and said : "Why have you, such and such, mutilated our men ?" I answered : "Whoever courts disaster will easily find it. We have not mutilated them. Our innocence has overcome them." He said again : "Not one of you rogues will escape !" I replied : "Consider, sir, who is to be called a rouge : the one who during night attacks another or the one who sits peacefully and does not provoke anyone." He answered : "That may be so, but you must shed your blood, since you spilled that of our brothers." I answered : "If you have come for my head, you have also brought your own ; if mine is to fall then also yours will certainly get hurt. Move further back, we shall pull our triggers otherwise." Then a considerate one among them said : "Stop it ! May I approach ?" I said : "You may." He came closer and asked : "Who are you ? Why have you come to Wilno ?" In order to avoid trouble, *in quantum*[192] any of them were to die, I could neither tell them who I was nor that I came because of the promissory note. But I did know that Dąbrowski, a colonel of the Lithuanian army, had several nephews in Podlasie who served in various companies of our army. I said : "My name is Żebrowski. I came to see my uncle Dąbrowski and since I could not find any other quarters I have stopped in this house. But I am assaulted even here." He said to me : "Your men told us that your name is Pasek." I answered : "That is correct. I have a double name, Pasek Żebrowski." He asked : "And is our[193] Chancellor[194] related to you ?" I replied : "His coat of arms is the same but he is not related. He is Pasek Gosławski and I am Pasek Żebrowski." Under such circumstances one had to deny one's own title and kin. He continued : "And was it you who was with the colonel in Warsaw ?" "Not I, but my brother. I was not present at the Warsaw Diet." He said : "In such a case we shall always be able to find you if we need you ?" I replied that I was ready to justify myself any place but that also those who rapaciously attack we would have to do the same because : "I am not at fault before anyone. I did not provoke anyone. I merely stayed in this empty house quietly and I did not do any damage here. Tomorrow will tell who will be punished." He replied : "I doubt if you will live until then." I said : "Even if all of them were to fall dead on the spot, I would not be afraid. The law is on my side. It was *licita defensio*[195] and *invasor a se ipso occiditur*.[196] He said : "Good night !" "Good night !" said I and they left.

I told them that I was not afraid, but I felt differently. God

[192]In case.
[193]I.e., of the confederacy.
[194]Reference to Jan Pasek, the son of Jan Pasek, the starost of the city of Smolensk and the commander of its fortified castle ; mention of this is made in the Constitution of 1662. Czapliński, *Pam.*, p. 312, note 413.
[195]Self-defence is lawful.
[196]The aggressor perishes from his own hand.

forbid if one of them were to die ! For even if I were acquitted,
I'd be faced with the problems of the lawsuit, its cost, the
inquest, etc. I began to think of how to run away from there.
Praeiudicata[197] had already taught me that it is easier to escape
from a forest than from a prison. I remembered my *praeiudi-
catum*[198] in Kozierady and recalled that I had regretted not
escaping when there was still time, relying on my innocence.
Even though the case had turned *honorifice*[199] for me, it made
my purse groan a lot. I prayed to God for assistance and began
packing stealthily. Having packed, we took the horses by the
reins. We went on foot and led them behind us through the
bushes of nettle.

As the area had been burned by the Muscovites the cellars
were overgrown with nettles and weeds. The night was pitch
dark and repeatedly either a horse, a retainer or myself would
fall into those overgrown pits. We helped each other quietly
until finally we reached a part of the field where we could
mount our horses. It was beginning to dawn when we entered
the area of those empty cellars. I don't remember, during all
my life, having been in so many cellars as during that night in
Wilno. There was no food or drink in any of them, even though
we took great pains to look for it.

I would have headed directly homeward if Gosiewski, the
Lithuanian Field Hetman and treasurer, had not asked me to
come to see him after I had received the money, for he was to
write about it to the King. I halted in a butcher's shed where
oxen were slaughtered ; several of them were hanging even
then. The horses did not want to eat anything at all and just
snorted at the stench of raw meat.

I changed into a *kontusz*, in which I had not been seen
before, and I went down town to my cousin's.[200] After I told
him what had happened, he also felt that I should leave and we
started out together to the Field Hetman's in order to settle this
more promptly. As we were coming down the steps we ran into

[197]Experience.
[198]Experience.
[199]Honorably.
[200]His first cousin, the Chancellor of the Lithuanian confederacy.

those men, who had noticed that I was no longer at the empty house and had learned who I was. They were going to my cousin's to report to him what had happened and to inquire about me. I recognized one of them right away and nudged my cousin : "Here they are." My cousin then acted *quidem*[201] he was only taking me to the door *per modum humanitatis*,[202] said good-bye to me on the steps, and turned back with them. I went to the Field Hetman and thanked him for his kindness. After I had told him what had happened I did not want to wait for the letter to the King. He *non urgebat*[203] and even said : "Go, in the name of God, since this is a serious affair." I went to an apothecary from where I sent for my cousin to come and see me, for I no longer dared to go to his home, as I was afraid of being recognized.

My cousin came there ; we sat down in a quiet place and talked. He told me that they had inquired whether I was really a relative. He told them that I was his first cousin on his father's side and they said : "Why did he give us another name ?" My cousin answered : "In order to be free of your unjust charge because he is *in functione*.[204] He does not have the time to enforce the law. He told me to report to you however that he is ready to account for his actions and those of his men *in omni foro*.[205] Concerning his rank, I can tell you that he is in the service of the Ruthenian voivode and whoever wants to look for him can find him there." They said : "We think that three of the wounded men will not survive, yet what hurts us the most is that before leaving those quarters he wrote on the wall verses which disgrace our nation."[206]

My cousin answered them : "Answer him verse for verse, and if you consider yourselves innocent demand justice when the armies come together again." After my cousin told me all this we took leave of each other and I returned to my inn, but

201As if.
202Out of politeness.
203Did not insist.
204On official business.
205In any court.
206The poem is left out here.

I did not leave until nightfall in order to avoid an attack. I no longer went on the road to Grodno toward Poland, as I should have, but I set out toward Uciana[207] and from there in the direction of *Polesie*. I got through safely. Later I heard that they had looked for me along those roads which lead to Poland since they wanted to take revenge on me. God did not favor them however. The wounded men, thanks to the grace of God, did recover and all this fell into oblivion.

I no longer headed for Warsaw as I learned on my way that the King had gone to Lwów to a commission and that my envoy had already been dispatched with another escort assigned to him. I returned home therefore. Many claimed the furs which I had promised to buy for them in Wilno and they were all disappointed. I did not even buy anything for myself. I barely escaped with my life ; I had no idea that such trouble would befall me from those drunkards.

After my departure from Wilno the drunkards got hold somehow of the treasurer's books in which I had signed the receipt of 6000 zlotys and assumed that it was their Chancellor,[209] my first cousin, whose name was also Jan z Gosławic Pasek. They *potentissime*[210] insisted that he, as a military official, had received some bribe *respectu machinationis*[211] and conspiracy. Loudly and with pretended eagerness, in the name of the good of the army, they brought it up at the council meeting that "There are those here among us in whom we confide our greatest secrets and who apparently want to sell us out for they take private bribes and that could not be in vain." A big *fremitus*[212] arose then. There was clanging of swords and they asked : "Who is he ? Hand him over to us and we shall soon make hash of him." *Ad tot instantias*[213] the man was forced to say what he *intulit*[214] at the council : "The Chancellor

[207]A town about one hundred km north of Wilno.
[209]Of the Lithuanian confederates.
[210]Strongly.
[211]For some plotting.
[212]Commotion.
[213]At so many demands.
[214]Had brought up.

took 6000 zlotys from the treasury which was not in vain. I saw
his signature in the books acknowledging the receipt." But the
boor did not know my cousin's handwriting, *simpliciter*[215] the
spelling of his name. They asked : "Will you prove this ?"
"I shall", he replied. Some blustered out at that : "Kill him !"
And others : "Let him give *rationem*[216] of himself." Relatives
and kinsmen on his mother's side became alarmed, fearing that
he would be proven guilty. He was not disturbed however as
he was not guilty. He said : "My Lords, I realize *in quo
gradu*[217] of confidence you hold me, that all, *minutissima quaeque arcana*[218] reach me. I realize that I could do much harm if
I were not governed by my honor and that *intaminata fides*,[219]
which you gentlemen have confided in me so *fraterne*.[220] I do
say therefore that if I felt guilty of the charges, the world would
see me voluntarily sentencing myself to the cruelest decree of
death ; and even if I had just taken these 6000 zlotys for the
sake of the money alone may I be considered a traitor nevertheless and punished as one, but let them prove this to me and
I then *succumbam*." The accuser kept raging : "I shall prove
it. I merely ask His Honor the treasurer to have those books,
which I have already marked, brought here." The treasurer sent
for the secretary to come with the books and to tell them[222]
what it was all about. The spirits of my cousin's relatives rose
at that, for they were thinking how to save him and not to get
themselves into any trouble at the same time. Among those
present were the Biernackis, the Sokolonickis, the Chreptowiczes
and other kin, who were worthy people. When they heard the
defense, they stepped instantly to the side of the accuser so that
he could not escape. Suddenly the books were brought in and
handed to him. They said : "Show where you saw it." The
accuser found the place right away and carried it with him to

[215]Only.
[216]An account.
[217]The level, i.e. to what a degree.
[218]Even the smallest secrets.
[219]Immaculate faith.
[220]In a brotherly way.
[221]Shall surrender.
[222]Apparently the relatives.

the marshal. My cousin remarked : "Please let me see this book," just as if he did not know what was inside. Having looked at it he said : "Gentlemen, I confirm now what I had voluntarily declared before, that I am ready to bear the penalty at the hands of you gentlemen, if the accusation proves to be correct. If the accusation proves false, however, I ask that penance be given to the one who accuses having no proof, for whoever takes my good name away from me takes away my life. I realize that only a few could be found in the army who are not familiar with my handwriting for I have served you, gentlemen, with it on all the documents. Here is the acknowledgment of receipt for the 6000 zlotys. Whether it was I who took them and whether I am guilty, I leave in sinum[223] of you gentlemen." Many looked at it : "It is not his, not his signature !" They asked whose it was for both the first and last names were the same, only the handwriting was different. He said : "A first cousin of mine received the money from the Polish army, for such and such a service, on a promissory note of his Majesty the King." All the insultus[224] which were raised against my cousin were turned toward the informer then. "Let us punish the pagan son who brings such gossip to the assembly of knighthood !" He tried to get away. Sokolnicki, a colonel, hit him on the neck with a mace and he fell to the ground. Others began to hit him too, beat him, and tread on him lying there on the floor. Marshal Żeromski barely managed to rescue him.

Ever since that day they[225] began to prepare the peril of Gosiewski, the poor soul, and this was the first occasion for suspicion against him. They exclaimed right away : "Indeed, Sir hetman, there is no money for the army, but for a promissory note of His Majesty the King it is found at once. Would it not have been better to hold these promissory notes until better times and to satisfy our interests first ? All right, all right, but this might prove harmful to someone !" The Field Hetman justified himself, said that he was compelled to do it at

[223]To the conscience.
[224]The accusations.
[225]The Lithuanian confederates.

His Majesty's strong intercession, and that he would have to put out the money himself otherwise. Those excuses bore no weight however ; they *diffidebant*[226] him from that time on more and more. Meanwhile greater commotions arose in the assemblies, military people took to drinking, and consequently only drunken brawls, not peace and order, could be expected. Evidence of which, soon after, was the massacre of Kazimierz Żeromski, their own Field Hetman and the starost of Czeczera, a very worthy man. Later they also murdered the Lithuanian Field Hetman and treasurer Gosiewski. They made him take the last rites and *deliberatissime*[227] shot him[228] on one small pretense and a false accusation ; many other military men were also killed during the commotion. For these killings several colonels, Niewiarowski, Jastrzębski, and others were sentenced and executed[229] at the following Diet in Warsaw. Those whom the law could not reach were sentenced to infamy. My cousin, who was forced to participate in the council of the horrible manslaughter as the Lithuanian Counselor and Chancellor, was also sentenced, but managed to escape death and disgrace in the following manner :

Since there was pursuit for those from the field hetman's division who were responsible for his death, my cousin was also trying to escape from the pursuers following his footsteps. He came thus to the Berezina river which was frozen over in the middle. My cousin dismounted and cut a thin layer of ice open with a mace making it look as if, not having noticed the fatal hole, he had gone down with the ice while trying to escape. He trod the snow around the edge of the ice as if trying to save himself, left his cap on the ice edge, and dropped the pistol's cover on the water to float on top. He then mounted his horse, turned to the same road from which he had come and from there he rode into the wilderness, accompanied by only one

[226]Distrusted.
[227]Deliberately.
[228]On November 29, 1662,, in Wołpa. Czubek, *Pam.*, p. 335, note 8.
[229]Krzysztof Niewiarowski, Konstanty Kotowicz, Jastrzębski, and Narkiewicz were sentenced in December, 1664 and executed January 3, 1665. Czapliński, *Pam.*, p. 320, note 482.

man. Since the wilderness along the banks of the Berezina river is very deep, he managed to escape to the estate of his brother, Pan Piotr, who had become a subject of the Muscovite Tsar and retained all the family possessions conquered by the Muscovites in the area of Smolensk. My cousin remained there until amnesty.

Meanwhile those tracing him came up to the Berezina and noticed the spot which was broken through in the river. They picked up the cap and the pistol cover which was floating on the water. Assuming that he had drowned, they returned to the nobleman from whose manor my cousin had started out on his escape. They showed the cap to those who knew him better and related that there was not a trace of him beyond the opening. *Conclusum*[230] that he had drowned. Those in the manor began to cry but the pursuers were glad and said : "*Poena peccati.*"[231]

At the Diet, the first and last names of those who had been directly responsible for the killing and those who were aware of the crime were submitted and made public in order to deprive them of honor. My cousin's name was among them. Several deputies—some believed him dead while his relatives and others knew that he was alive—spoke up at that : "Most Gracious King, he had been punished by God once by his death, why include him on the list then ?" His name was ordered to be blotted out.

After the Diet, he left Moscow and settled *secure*[232] at home while the other disgraced men prowled around until another Diet met at which a general amnesty was granted to all *ad instantiam*[233] of those present. Only a few were exempted from amnesty because the widow of the deceased[234] did not allow it. They were the more guilty ones and she hoped that they would be imprisoned.

When others came to thank the King for the amnesty granted them, my cousin also *comparuit*[235] among them. He

[230]They concluded.
[231]"A punishment for the crime."
[232]Safely.
[233]At the intercession.
[234]Apparently the treasurer's widow.
[235]Appeared.

was serving as deputy from Lithuania at the time. He tried to justify himself, arguing that even though he was present at the *consilium impiorum*,[236] he was required to be there as *munus*[237] of the entire army. The King laughed and said : "When advising others, you have advised badly but you counsel well for yourself to have your deeds properly recorded in history." Only at the third Diet was this matter finally cleared up.

I am returning *ad statum anni huius*[238] now. The conference in Wilno took place amid many drinking bouts and commotions. The one in Lwów[239] was conducted somewhat *modestius*[240] and in more orderly form than the one in Lithuania and brought better results because, thanks to the grace of God, a way was found to pacify the army. The *szeląg*[241] and the *tynf*[242] were ordered coined ; the *tynfs*, containing only eighteen pennies'[243] worth of silver, were assigned the value of a *złoty*[244] and were underwritten by the following statement : *"Dat pretium servata salus potiorque metallo est."*[245]

Walachian *szelągs* were introduced into Poland at the same time, for which so much silver and gold money was taken abroad that the culprits of this baseness are not worthy to be called Poles and owe a great account to God. These Walachian

[236]Gathering of the impious ones.
[237]A delegate.
[238]To the events of this year.
[239]The conference in Lwów took place in 1664, not in 1662. Czubek, *Pam.*, p. 338, note 7.
[240]More orderly.
[241]In former Poland, a small copper coin.
[242]Former silver-copper coin.
[243]Polish *grosz*.
[244]Eng. zloty, a Polish monetary unit then containing thirty pennies, *grosz*.
[245]The legal value represents a worth more valuable than the metal from which it is made. The monetary reform achieved brought one-zloty coins of little value into circulation, the rate of which was enforced by law. They were coined by a man called Tynf and were accordingly called *tynfs*. The old one-zloty coins contained 8.15 grams of silver, the new ones only 3.36 grams. The taxes were collected in the old money, *moneta bona*, against which the new coin was set off. The result of all this was an economic confusion and an outflow of good money abroad. Czapliński, *Pam.*, p. 323, note 508.

coins were the cause of impoverishment,[246] despair, and a great
number of suicides among people. Ever since the commission
in Lwów, people kept killing themselves because of these coins
at the fairs. Then they finally disappeared from Little Poland
and, just like a destructive locust, they established their domi-
cile in Great Poland as far as the Odra and the Baltic Sea.

The commission in Lwów came to an end, during which
Paweł Borzęcki, the substitute leader of the confederacy and
a great warrior, perished, *non sine suspicione veneni*.[247] Such
was the rumor. "It had to be so," people said, "in order to
extinguish the candle which shone for the entire confederacy so
that some greater flame would not be enkindled from its bright-
ness." For he was the most important figure in the confederacy.

[246]These Walachian *szelągs* were coined in Suczawa and poured into
Poland in the amount of twelve million. They indeed became to many
the cause of economic ruin. Czapliński, *Pam.*, p. 323, note 510.

[247]Not without a suspicion of poisoning. Borzęcki died in November,
1662. Czapliński, *Pam.*, p. 323, note 511.

ANNO DOMINI 1663

After the dissolution of the confederacy the army fell into disorder, the companies toward which greater ill feelings existed were disbanded, and who knows what has become of many a man? Some settled down at home and married seeing the ingratitude ; others, formerly good soldiers, became effeminate and took heavily to drink.

The King went beyond the Dnieper[1] *in persona sua,*[2] but the fortunes of war, the mood and the eagerness were different than before the confederacy. The enemy gained strength and we could not accomplish anything worthwhile.[3] We managed only to blacken several chicken coops[4] with cannon smoke, which before the confederacy we could have swallowed up completely, and we lost many good men in the siege and returned home with nothing. Thus experiencing a significant change of fortune, or *verius*[5] speaking, reversal of God's grace, which was evident in our actions, we ended the year.

---

[1]On a campaign against the Muscovites in an attempt to regain the Ukraine, which became divided by the Dnieper into two hostile camps. Jan Kazimierz with the support of Tetera, the Cossack hetman who favored Poland, and the Tatars wanted to reunite the Cossacks under Polish rule. Reddaway, p. 528.

[2]In his own person.

[3]The Russians refused to accept battle ; they either sought shelter in a fortified town or retreated. Because of the spring thaw the King was forced to retreat. Reddaway, p. 528.

[4]Contemptuous term for castles.

[5]More strictly, i.e. more truly.

ANNO DOMINI 1664

There was a battle at Stawiszcze,[1] but there is nothing to write about it and nothing worthy of praise. The war with the enemy had become tedious to us and we wanted to try war with each other, probably *eo fine*[2] of forming another confederacy by means of this occasion. We had already obliterated the *sagina*[3] from the first one ; we once again wished to fill our bellies with similar gains.

We made peace with the Muscovites[4] under poor conditions : we paid them enormous reparations for having defeated them and we not only left their possessions intact but failed to recover those which they had taken from us and yielded large provinces to them, thus increasing their own. We then happily began the civil war, which is *malum supra omne malum.*[5]

[1] A town near Kiev. Its siege lasted from July 14 to August 20. See Czubek, *Pam.*, p. 340, note 8. It was conquered by the armies under the command of Czarniecki, who died shortly after from a wound inflicted there. King Jan Kazimierz awarded him the office of Field Hetman, *buława polna*, shortly before his death. A royal envoy delivered the message when, mortally wounded in Cossack battles, he lay dying in a peasant hut in the vicinity of Brodów. Sobieski, p. 241.
[2] With the intention.
[3] Gain.
[4] After the Polish victory over the Muscovites in the battle of Cudnów, 1660 A.D. Pasek participated in that battle. The thirteen-year truce with Muscovy was not concluded until January 30, 1667 A.D. in Andruszów. Poland ceded to Russia the territories beyond the Dnieper and Kiev. Reddaway, pp. 528–529.
[5] An evil above all evils.

A Diet was called into session during which Jerzy Lubomirski, our hetman and grand marshal, was to be tried for aspiring to the Crown *post fata regnantis*.[6] The King himself had first reproached Pan Lubomirski about it : "Sir Marshal, the news has reached us that you wish for yourself the Crown." He replied : "Who would not wish well for himself ? I shall tell your Majesty a story, which I heard about the Castellan of Wojnicz.[7] When the Haiduks brought him from the royal castle and put him, in his armchair, in his room, he asked his favorite Haiduk : "Andrys, what do your people say about our Diet ?" The Haiduk replied : *"Ot, Milostivy Pane, koliyesmo Tvoyu Pan'sku Milost na zamok prin'esli, vsy kheydutzy, bratya na-shy, khovoryli tak: Ot, tomu by to panu korolem polskyem, shtcho khozhych pakholkov d'erzhyt pry sobij."*[8] For this piece of news the Castellan gave the Haiduk ten silver thalers for liquor. May your Majesty consider then that if such an invalid, who cannot even turn in his own bed of his own strength, is pleased to hear others talk of his reigning, I should not be displeased if someone ordered me to reign over him *ultro*[9] the more so since, thanks to the grace of God, I can still mount a horse without any help. If therefore *post fata*[10] of your Majesty, whom I do wish good health and a long reign, men like the Castellan of Wojnicz, the Castellan of Gniezno,[11] and similar candidates were to compete *ad regnandum*,[12] I would be among them. If men like the Russian Tsar, the Swedish or the

[6]After the death of the present ruler.
[7]Jan Wielopolski, the starost and voivode of Kraków, in 1661 the castellan of Wojnicz. J. Czubek, *Pam.*, p. 341, note 7.
[8]"Oh, gracious lord, when we took your Excellency to the castle, all the Haiduks, our brothers, spoke thus : 'Such a master, who keeps fine lads at his side, should be the Polish King.'" Andrys was probably from Slovakia or from Ruthenia, from the area beyond the Carpathian mountains, therefore his language is russified. Czubek, *Pam.*, p. 341, note 8.
[9]Himself, i.e., (out) of his own free will.
[10]After the death.
[11]Aleksander Sielski, marshal of the chamber of deputies in 1674. Czubek, *Pam.*, p. 342, note 4.
[12]For the Crown.

French King were to compete, however, I would give up my candidacy at once.

Even though the King laughed at this reply, he already cherished in his heart *praeconceptum odium*,[13] which was planted toward Pan Lubomirski by the *persuasiones*[14] of certain people, especially by Prażmowski, the blind Archbishop of Gniezno.[15] That villain was the main *fomes*[16] of this war, which was disliked by Heaven itself and which drew an obvious rage of the Almighty upon our fatherland, for as soon as its consultations were begun, a frightful and huge comet appeared in the sky, which remained several months and threatened the eyes of the people with its ominous look. The longer it remained, the more it frightened the dismayed hearts. It foreshadowed bad events which followed later as a result of the obstinacy and plottings of evil people, who in promoting their own interests were more instrumental in laying waste the fatherland than were its enemies. Pan Lubomirski saw the King, *ultimum in linea domus regiae, domus Iagellonicae, sine successione*;[17] he saw the bitterness and the intrigue of Queen Ludwika, who was French by birth, and who persisted in trying to impose *gallicismum*[18] on our freedom by bringing a French dandy[19] to the throne; he saw that the King was already being led by the nose and gave permission to proclaim manifestoes at the voivodeship's pre-Diet regional councils *proponendo novam electionem stante vita.*[20] There were more Frenchmen in War-

[13]Preconceived hatred.
[14]The persuasions.
[15]Mikołaj Prażmowski (1617–1673), Vice-Chancellor of Poland and Bishop of Łuck in 1658 ; Archbishop of Gniezno in 1666 ; a greedy schemer who participated in forgeries of mint leaseholders. Bribed by the French party, he supported the politics of the French-born Queen Ludwika. In 1672 the Confederacy of Gołąb finaly deprived him of his offices and sentenced him to imprisonment in a monastery. Pasek, together with the majority of the middle and lower Polish nobility, hated Prażmowski. Czapliński, *Pam.*, p. 327, note 20.
[16]Instigator.
[17]As the last of the Jagiellonian dynasty without an heir.
[18]To impose French customs.
[19]Son of Prince Condé, Henri Bourbon.
[20]Proposing a new election during the lifetime of the reigning king.

saw than were kindling the fire of Cerberus. They threw money around and they plotted, especially at night. They enjoyed freedom and esteem in Warsaw. They celebrated public triumphs in honor of their victories, even if they were not real but invented ones. A Frenchman could always enter the King's chamber, while a Pole had to wait sometimes half a day at the door. In short, they exerted great and excessive influence.

Among all their various privileges, I must mention this. They were allowed to celebrate a triumph on account of a victory obtained over the Emperor,[21] *in theatro publico.*[22] The performers, the music and fireworks were brought to the theater for this celebration and a large crowd of spectators gathered. Some, who were either leaving or arriving in Warsaw, came on horseback to watch this wonderful *spectaculum.* Whoever noticed it stopped, even if he was in a hurry, to see this prodigious show, and I was also there since I was leaving Warsaw. After leaving the inn, I stopped on horseback, together with my retainers, to watch those wonders. *Circa hoc spectaculum*[23] people of various estates and various temper stood about.

Different scenes were performed : how soldiers attacked each other, how the infantry and the cavalry closed ranks, how one side yielded the battlefield to another, how they took German prisoners and beheaded them, how they assaulted a fortress and captured it. These things were performed at great expense and magnificence. After the overthrow of the imperial army and the enemy's defeat on the battlefield, the chained Emperor was brought, in imperial dress, but without the imperial crown on his head. He carried it in his hand and handed it over to the French King. We knew that the man who played the part of the Emperor in chains was a distinguished Frenchman. He could imitate the Emperor's physique and protruded his lip just as the Emperor did. One of the mounted Poles called out to the Frenchmen : "Kill this son of a . . . , since you

---

[21]Probably over the so-called devolution war, which Louis XIV conducted.
[22]In the public theater.
[23]For the sake of this spectacle.

have already captured him. Do not keep him alive, for as soon as you let him free, he will take revenge, will resume the war, will shed human blood, and the world will never have peace. If you kill him, however, his Majesty the French King will attain the empire, will be Emperor, and God grant it, King of

Poland as well. If you will not kill him, I shall do so!" He seized his bow, nocked an arrow, and shot Pan Emperor in the side so hard that the point of the arrow pierced him right through. He killed him. Other Poles seized their bows. They began to shoot at that crowd and wounded many Frenchmen. They also wounded the one *in persona*[24] of their king but he fell on his head from the throne under the stage and fled with some other Frenchmen.

A great commotion started on account of this in Warsaw. Those who had been shooting dispersed. I also left Warsaw in order to spare myself unpleasantness, as I had also stood there among that crowd. I went half a league from Warsaw in the direction of Tarczyn[25] and left my bow with Pan Łęczyński, in order to avoid suspicion. Then I rode slowly ahead. I carried only a hunting gun with me, for I expected a pursuit.

Queen Ludwika, *imperiosus mulier*[26] to whom one could safely apply the saying coined for another monarch : *Rex erat Helisabeth, verum regina Jacobus, imperiosus mulier*[27] let go now of her pride and threw herself at his Majesty's feet. She begged him to pursue and to imprison the malefactors. The King ordered all those who were at hand to ride to the high-way, naturally *sine effectu,*[28] for as soon as they caught up with someone they would say : "Where are you coming from?" "Wasn't that you who killed the Emperor and shot at the French King?" "Not I!"—and they left him alone. Which question was also directed at me, but not until the following day. I stopped to visit Pan Okuń and he was glad to see me. I was relating that "tragedy" to him when over a dozen horse-men came to his village and asked : "Has anyone come through here from Warsaw?" They were told : "Someone came through, but we do not know his name. He was accompanied by five men and stopped in our Lord's manor." They went there and entered the room : "Your obedient servant!" "Your

[24]Who represented.
[25]A town thirty kilometers south of Warsaw.
[26]A power-greedy virago.
[27]Elizabeth was King, but James Queen, the power-greedy milk-sop.
[28]Without any result.

obedient servant !"[29] The master of the house invited them to sit down. They asked me : "Where are you coming from, Sir ?" I said : "From Warsaw." "When did you leave ?" I replied : "After the death of the Christian Emperor and the French King !" "Were you looking on when it happened ?" "I was." "Who was the one who first shot at the Emperor ?" I said : "Someone just like you and me." He said laughing : "Was it not you yourself ?" I answered : "People there were shooting with bows and I came here without such equipment !" He said : "Whoever might have done it has God's forgiveness for interceding in such a great outrage. His Majesty mourns only in front of the Queen and laughs over it in his heart." We laughed and rejoiced at this conversation. They drank a couple of the host's barrels of beer and left.

The Frenchmen enjoyed great esteem under Ludwika. They were allowed to do whatever they pleased. When one came to the royal chambers of the palace one seldom saw a tuft of hair, only heads like huge boxes[30] which almost obscured the light coming from the window. Heeding the situation, some complained of the court's taking such a liking to this nation. Some *ministri status*[31] were dancing already *ad Galli cantum*,[32] but Polish freedom disliked and scorned all this for *ad Galli cantum non timet iste leo.*[33]

[29] A form of greeting of the Polish nobility at the time.
[30] The Frenchmen brought big wigs into fashion.
[31] High dignitaries.
[32] To the singing of a cock, i.e. Frenchman.
[33] The lion is not afraid when a cock is singing.

When Pan Lubomirski saw what things had come to, he took *initia*[34] which were not to everyone's liking. He himself had great popularity among the army and the landed gentry without seeking it ; because of his humanity, he quite often encountered from officers words of compliments such as these : "Your Excellency should be our Polish King !" Considering his dignity and merits in the fatherland he used to answer : "This lies in your hands, my dear brothers." One should not be surprised at that, *quisque suae fortunae faber.*[35] I never read of someone turning down the opportunity to become King. Because of that some people suspected him of desiring the great honor of Kingship for himself. But even if he had openly shown it and had become a candidate, it would not have been sufficient reason for trying him, since usually everyone wishes well for himself, especially since we did not choose an angel for a king, but only a man ; we did not elect a son of a king but a Polish nobleman.[36] In support of my view I shall also recall that we had nominated Polanowski as a candidate, who was only a colonel at the time and who prior to that had been an officer, accompanied by only two retainers under Pan Lubomirski's command. If we could have summoned Wiśniowiecki[36] or Polanowski to this honor, we should not be aggravated at doing so with Lubomirski since the election was free and *spiritus, ubi vult, spirat.*[37] When God inspires a liking toward someone, it is a deed of His Will. But what would the *invidia, bonorum noverca*[38] do then ? The saying goes : When one shoes a horse also a frog lifts its foot." These *consiliarii Placentini,*[39] who always had advised the King wrongly, embittered his heart toward Lubomirski and when the Queen saw that her intention for the support of a French candidate would collapse if a Pole were elected, she tried the more so *per importunas instantias*[40]

[34]Initial steps.
[35]Because everyone is the maker of his own fate.
[36]Michał Wiśniowiecki, elected after the abdication of King Jan Kazimierz, was the son of the famous Prince Wiśniowiecki.
[37]The Spirit breathes, wherever it wants to.
[38]Jealousy, the stepmother of good people.
[39]Wheedling advisors.
[40]Through importunate petitions.

and through her advisors. Some of them wanted to render the King a service by this, for they guarded their sympathy and good will in order to milk the French goat even more, while others, *sub praetextu*[41] of court complaisance, had their own private affairs *prae oculis, supponendo* :[42] "Who knows if I myself will not be called to the Crown ?" The King, flexible as ever, did whatever he was told to. He especially believed in the advice of his blind advisor[43] and even if the Bishop gave him the worst advice, it seemed good advice to the King. He took it as if coming *ex ore Apollinis.*[44] Even if it were to bring about the doom of the fatherland, the King did not seem to care as long as it appealed to the other.

Conclusum to try Lubomirski. Witnesses were brought against him and people were bribed to testify. Some deputies from the provinces, decent men, who judged things *a fine*[45] and considered the possible consequences, defended him *potentissime,*[46] but it was difficult to overcome the opponents. There was great noise and commotion in Warsaw and all of the Ukraine was in rebellion again, yet we did not realize our plight. A decree was passed : *infamia, exilium* and *privatio.*[47] *Malevoli*[48] rejoiced, but the fatherland groaned, anticipating the effects. At councils and sessions some praised this, some disproved it. The army was already whispering about a confederacy, thick clouds of misfortune covered the sky, and no one could say that things would go well in our land in spring. We did not need any astrologers to clarify what awaited us in the coming year when the fatherland was devastated and so much innocent blood was shed.

[41]Under the pretext.
[42]Before their eyes, thinking.
[43]Prażmowski.
[44]From the lips of Apollo.
[45]With respect to the prospective end.
[46]As much as possible.
[47]Infamy, banishment, and deprivation of offices.
[48]Evil people.

ANNO DOMINI 1665

A civil war broke out *ex ratione civis oppressi.*[1] The army formed a confederacy which chose Ustrzycki[2] as Marshal with Borek[3] as his deputy; forty good companies joined the confederacy, especially those which had close relations with Pan Lubomirski—his own, those of his brothers, sons, sons-in-law, those of other relatives and those of some good friends. More than sixty companies joined the King. The Ruthenian voivode[4] retained all the regiments *in rem*[5] of the King and set out with them from Biała Cerkiew[6] toward Zasław; the confederates went toward Lwów, then toward Sambor,[8] which they chose as *sedem belli.*[9] Those of us who did not join the confederacy were ordered to break through toward Lwów and twelve thousand loyal Cossacks were enlisted. The entire Ukraine rose in a wild rebellion, however, seeing that the time was favorable for that. Such were the fruits of our shedding of blood in order to recover the Ukraine for those infamous people.

[1]Because a citizen was oppressed. The armed revolt actually broke out already in 1664. The Polish nobles in general looked upon Lubomirski as a martyr of the cause of liberty.
[2]Adam Ustrzycki or Ostrzycki. Czapliński, *Pam.*, p. 335, note 4.
[3]Józef Borek. Czubek, *Pam.*, p. 351, note 3.
[4]Stanisław Jabłoński, a friend of King Jan III Sobieski. Czubek, *Pam.*, p. 351, note 7.
[5]I.e. supporting the King.
[6]A locality southwest of Kiev.
[7]A town in Volhynia, eighty kilometers east of Krzemieniec.
[8]A city forty-three kilometers southeast of Przemyśl.
[9]The site of battle.

A call was sent to the Crimean Tatars to participate in this war and the Khan promised to come out with one hundred thousand men at first. Later he sent word that he would not do this ; he promised to make up for it on another occasion, but not in this war "when brother raised sword against brother."[10]

The King brought an orderly and good Lithuanian army into the field. These Lithuanians were so hungry and ate so much, however, that it was as if the door of ten pigsties had been flung open. They also plundered considerably. But they paid dearly for all this at Częstochowa for there, where people were granted grace and indulgence, they received a beating.

The voivodeships took different sides ; some sided with the King, others with Pan Lubomirski. The voivodeships of Kraków together with the castellan of Kraków Warszycki[11] *personaliter,*[12] as well as the voivodeships of Poznań, Sandomierz, Kalisz, Sieradz, and Łęczyca, took up arms on the side of Lubomirski.[13] The others wanted to do the same but did not dare to, since they were in closer vicinity of the King. Neither did the King summon *ad societatem belli,*[14] *ex ratione*[15] he did not rely on them, and secondly, because he trusted in the forces which he had at his disposal. He also hoped to win over all of Lubomirski's men, as well as Lubomirski himself, for his blind *consultor*[16] had promised him that.

[But evidently, you blind one, were not aware that blind fortune can do more than you and that it does not consider who is the stronger one but serves the one for whom God orders help in his innocence. You promised to support the King *manu, consilio, opere et oratione* ;[17] you have helped with

---

[10]The above statement is historically true according to Czapliński. *Pam.,* p. 336, note 17.

[11]Stanisław Warszycki. Czapliński, *Pam.,* p. 336, note 20.

[12]Himself.

[13]According to Czapliński only those of Poznań and Kalisz did so. *Pam.,* p. 336, note 22.

[14]Them to participate in this war.

[15]Because.

[16]Advisor, i.e. Archbishop Prażmowski.

[17]With your hand, advice, deeds and prayer.

your advice indeed. Look how your *consilium*[18] came in handy, to what it had brought the fatherland and his Majesty...][19]

This lampoon was handed to the Archbishop as he rode through the forest beyond Wyskitki.[20] It was *per modum*[21] of a letter and bore the inscription: "Her Ladyship the castellan's wife sends her best regards to your Excellency."[22] Thereupon the bearer of the message galloped away on a swift horse into a crossroad. Since the Archbishop rode unattended by many, without dragoons, there was no one who could overtake this messenger and summon him to take a reply. It was rumored that he carried the letter for several days in his pocket, kept rereading it, and then burned it. Nevertheless it was not difficult to obtain copies, since a great number of them were circulated among the army and around Warsaw. No one knew who had written it.

I now return to the historical matter from which my pen

18Advice.
19This lampoon, which according to Czapliński and others differs strongly from Pasek's narrative style, continues in this manner for several pages. Czapliński cites it in brackets and Brückner entirely excluded it from his edition, considering it to be of different authorship. It is excluded for the same reason in this translation.
20A town on the way from Warsaw to Łowicz.
21In the form.
22In the section omitted for the reasons stated above, note 19, insinuations were made as to the Archbishop's romantic escapades.

turned in order to make this reference to the Archbishop. The King led a rather good and orderly army onto the battlefield. I also appeared among them as a royalist, since my company was on that side, even though I did not feel like one. But even though we were on the King's side, we rather wished a victory to the other in view of the injustice to Pan Lubomirski and in his person to all nobility as well. For he was *potens manu et consilio*[23] and all that fury against him was solely in order to prevent him from hindering the election of the Condé, whom Queen Ludwika was trying to bring *omnibus modis*[24] to the throne. Even the French king himself sincerely helped in this in order to be rid of the Condé *ex ratione* of his scheming, for the Condé was very affluent and almost more popular[25] *in regno Galliae*[26] than the king himself. The French king feared that during some change of fortune the *affectus populi*[27] might turn toward Condé. Moreover, if a Frenchman were to reign in Poland they could squeeze the Emperor between the two of them and deprive him of the imperial crown. For that reason the French squandered much money in Poland.[28]

The army assembled in the voivodeship of Rawa and Mazowsze. There was news that Pan Lubomirski, having left the exile in Wrocław,[29] was already in the vicinity of Krzepice.[30] The King had a rather fine army, but what did this avail, when all his hopes fell because of Czarniecki's death,[31] to whom he had given the field hetman's mace and through whom he had

[23]Powerful in deed and counsel.

[24]By any means.

[25]The Condé really conspired against his king but became reconsiled with him in 1660.

[26]In the French kingdom.

[27]The sympathies of the people.

[28]The above cited French schemes of surrounding Austria with the help of Poland seem to correspond to the truth. Cardinal Mazarin (Giulio Mazarini) had chiefly this in mind when he agreed to the election of a French prince as King of Poland. Czapliński, *Pam.*, p. 351, note 185.

[29]Lubomirski was in banishment from December 1664 to April of 1665 in Silesia, mainly in Wrocław. Czapliński, *Pam.*, p. 351, note 191.

[30]A town near Częstochowa.

[31]He died on February 16, 1665. Czapliński, *Pam.*, p. 352, note 192.

expected to achieve everything ! Indeed Czarniecki could have brought Lubomirski *ad humilitatem et submissionem*[32] because he as a great warrior would have known how to go about it. They would have never achieved, the election of the Condée *per promotionem*[33] of Czarniecki for I knew what he *sentiebat*[34] of this election.[35]

His Majesty the King set out successfully with her Majesty the Queen, the ladies in waiting, and the entire court from Warsaw. It was appropriate that ladies be at hand for the "dance of pursuit," for it was not a war but just such a dance. We constantly kept pursuing Lubomirski from place to place while actually not pursuing at all and his forces were running away from us, while actually not running at all. Every now and then things were just as the Mazovians say :

> Look out ! I shall slash at you !
> Bang in the stomach with a fist.[36]

A certain noblewoman from Sieradz, who had suffered some great harm because of this pursuit, made an appropriate remark to the King concerning all this when she came to complain to him. The King contented her with some gift and said to her : "Forgive us, Your Ladyship, for war is capable of such things ; we pursue this traitor and he runs away from us." The noblewoman said : "Gracious King ! To be able to catch up and not to catch up is a strange pursuit indeed. Why I, an old woman, would still undertake to catch up with him today." The King became flustered and then ordered more money to be given to her.

Our army was encamped between Rawa and Głuchowsko,[37] a hereditary village of Pan Sułkowski.[38] The King wearied

---

[32]To humiliation and submission.
[33]With the help.
[34]Thought.
[35]According to Czapliński, Czarniecki sided with the French camp. *Pam.*, p. 352, note 195.
[36]This passage is damaged by the copyist.
[37]Now Głuchów, a village several kilometers west of Rawa.
[38]Wojciech Sułkowski, the vice-voivode of Rawa. Czapliński, *Pam.*, p. 353, note 200.

of this place, a Jesuit school,[39] and said to his people : "Isn't there some nobleman whom we could visit ? I have grown tired of staying several weeks in one place." They suggested several noblemen who lived two or three leagues away but His Majesty said : "We wish to go somewhere nearby in order to be back for supper." Someone spoke up then : "Your Majesty, a polite nobleman named Pan Sułkowski lives right here, very near the camp. He will be glad to have your Majesty." The King gave orders to get ready and left with the Queen.

Unaware of this, we drank beer and played cards. I was there since Pan Sułkowski was a good friend of my father's and mine. Over a dozen other officers were also present when a servant entered and announced : "Their Majesties are on their way to Your Lordship's. Is their presence welcome ?" The host jumped to his feet : "I shall be glad to see my gracious lord. I welcome him and await him with pleasure." Yet I heard his wife say : "Surely I shall be glad to see you ! The devil is within you. Just wait !", but we did not know why she said these words. Everyone rushed out of the house as the King approached. As he was entering through the gate with the Queen still behind him in the carriage, Pani Sułkowska asked me : "My precious, point the King out to me, for I don't know him yet. I know that he dresses in German fashion but there are several like that among them. I don't know which one he is." I, not knowing why she asked, said to her : "The one between those two, on such and such a horse." She approached him, went down on her knees before him, folded her hands and raised them to Heaven, and said : "Oh, Just God !" The King, who was just about to dismount, stopped and she continued : "If You ever punished with various plagues evil and unjust kings, extortioners, devils, shedders of innocent human blood, show today Your justice over King Jan Kazimierz so that lightning strikes at him from the bright sky, so that the earth devours him alive, so that no bullet misses him, so that all those plagues which You sent upon Pharaoh befall him for all

[39]In this college of Rawa, the building of which is preserved until this day, Pasek received his education. Czubek, *Pam.*, p. 370, note 5.

the wrongs which we, the poor people and the entire kingdom suffer !" Her husband tried to muffle her mouth but she kept scolding all the more. The King retreated to the gate. The host ran after him, entreated him, grasped at his stirrups. "By no means ! You have an evil wife, sir. I don't want to, I will not !" He rode away and met the Queen : "Turn back, we are not wanted here." When they returned to Rawa the King burst into laughter but the Queen was furious. "I will punish her !" The King said : "We must not do that. Let the wronged one at least be gratified by talking to her heart's content. But for God's sake let someone persuade Lubomirski to become reconciled because even women are beginning to blame us for this war."[40]

So bold was this woman that after she had abused the King she came to see him next day and asked for an audience. She let it be announced that she was that noblewoman at whose house the King did not want to dismount, and begged to be allowed to bow before His Majesty. The King was so kind-hearted that he had her admitted right away. She justified herself, saying : "I had to do that out of grief, for I have suffered great losses." She complained the most about a birch-wood grove which she had as a park right next to her manor and which had been cut down for the building of camp sheds. The King replied : "Then I shall give you, my lady, a donation thanks to which after six or seven years you shall have another birchwood grove just like the one you lost. I shall order that you be recompensed, but just don't be so evil-tempered." He ordered two thousand zlotys to be paid to the woman, though she would have hardly received fifty zlotys for it if she had sold it at the market in Rawa because it had only been a tiny grove.

But now I shall put aside the incidents which happened during the war and return to the subject at hand. When the armies drew close to each other, a few thousand royal Polish

---

[40]This incident is also related by Wespazjan Kochowski in his memoirs (III, 179) in very much the same way. Czapliński, *Pam.*, p. 354, note 206.

troops and the entire Lithuanian army, with the exception of the lancers, were sent out *per modum*[41] of a strong raiding party. They encountered Lubomirski's men at Częstochowa.[42]

When the poor Lithuanian souls began to pray for in-

[41]I.e., in a manner...
[42]September 4, 1665. Czubek, *Pam.*, p. 373, note 5.

dulgence and to offer themselves to God there, they prayed so ardently that they broke out in a bloody sweat and left such offerings behind that they were completely stripped of everything. They arrived elegantly dressed, on horseback, with beautiful saddles, but returned on foot and practically naked, with the exception of those who had such poor robes or boots that they were not accepted as offerings. How very pious this Lithuanian nation is indeed![43] But not speaking *figuraliter*,[44] when Lubomirski's men attacked the Lithuanians, whom they eagerly wished to destroy for having entered the civil war, they did not even give them a chance to get ready for attack; they slashed and struck a great number of them. The Lithuanians wanted to find refuge in the monastery but the monks closed the gates, angering the King. Still only a few of them were killed during the initial assault, before their lines were broken, but a great many were wounded, pushed off their horses, stripped of their robes and cuirasses; others were disgraced, being lashed with whips. Having thus been turned into infantry, they were let free to return to the King. Only the commanding officers, the captains of horse, and colonels were taken into captivity. When a certain jester, an officer by the name of Pustoszyński[45] congratulated Pan Lubomirski on this, he said: "Gracious Sir, God gave us more than we prayed for." Lubomirski asked: "How so?" He answered: "For we have always begged: *Da pacem, Domine! da pacem, Domine!*[46] We have prayed for one and God gave us five *Paces*." For among the prisoners there were several with the last name of Pac, all senior officers. There was the Chancellor Pac, the field hetman Pac, and several bishops Pac at the time; they promoted each other's

[43]Facetiously, of course.
[44]Metaphorically. This entire description of the clash at Częstochowa is a parody of the prayer for indulgence. Pasek speaks of the Lithuanians as of the pilgrims to the monastery of Jasna Góra at Częstochowa. Czapliński, *Pam.*, p. 356, note 216.
[45]According to Kochowski (l.c. 192) this is an invented name. The man in question was Sambor Młoszowski, known for his sharp wit. Czubek, *Pam.*, p. 374, note 3.
[46]Give us peace, oh God! Give us peace, oh God!

careers.[47] Flags and kettle-drums were captured. Some standard-bearers, however, handed over their flags to the monks and then bought them back the next day.

After this battle and the flogging which the confederates gave the Lithuanians, the rascals again began to run away from us and we to pursue them. The cattle mooed, sheaves and hay stacks went flying in the air! They slipped away from us to Great Poland and we thought with delight! "Stand still for awhile, you knave! Now you will no longer escape us for we shall corner you, unless you swim across the Baltic Sea to Sweden! We shall also enjoy by this opportunity Great Poland's lamb-shaped cakes and fat cheeses." But while we eagerly pursued them with good expectations of cornering them somewhere near the Oder or the Baltic Sea, they somehow slipped away from us on the side; we received news that Lubomirski and the confederates were already in back of us. Now we despaired of catching up with them and so we began to negotiate with them for peace. We kept pursuing and negotiating thus. It was just like that fisherman who was fishing by the sea and, failing to catch anything, sat down exhausted on the shore, took out a fife and began to play beautifully. He hoped that his melody would induce the fish to come out onto the sand and he could then catch as many of them as he wished. He rested and just before evening he once again cast his net. The fish had come evidently from other places as he pulled out a great number of them but they began to jump around in the net for such is their habit. He beat them with a stick, saying: "I played for you beautifully and you did not come out to dance, why do you skip boisterously now when I no longer play for you?" He hit them, he smashed them and put them in the sack.[48] Such was also the case with Pan Lubomirski and

---

[47]Krzysztof Pac, Chancellor of Lithuania (1662–1684); Michał Kazimierz Pac, Lithuanian Grand Marshal (1667–1682); Mikołaj Stefan Pac, Bishop of Wilno (1671–1684); Kazimierz Pac, Samogitian Bishop (1667–1692). According to Czubek Pasek exaggerates here; there were only three. Pam., pp. 374–375, note 5.

[48]The tale about a fisherman is the ninth fable of Babrius, the Greek fable writer, who possibly lived in Syria in the 1st century A.D. or somewhat later. Czubek, Pam., p. 376, note 1.

the confederates. They consented to these negotiations and called them the negotiations of Palczyn,[49] but they did not trust this fife and seeing that these were suspicious melodies they abandoned them, for they were afraid of falling into a trap.

We chased each other for some time. Then we went back to our camps in order to prepare better for the next campaign.

[49]The armistice of Palczyn was concluded on November 8. The Palczyn Treaty, contrary to what Pasek claims above, ended the military activities in the year 1665. Czapliński, *Pam.*, p. 358, note 223.

ANNO DOMINI 1666

This year was anticipated by the following prophecy: *Dum annus ter 6 numerabit, Marcus Alleluja cantabit, Joannes in Corpore stabit* (*...Joannes Casimirus regnabit*). *Polonia vae! vae! ingeminabit.*[1] St. Mark's day did indeed fall on Easter and St. John's day *inter octavas Corporis Christi.*[2] It also proved true that many among the military as well as among the poor landowners cried out *vae.*[3]

The Diet was called in session in order to appease the civil war, but it is difficult to extinguish a fire when the flames have reached the roof.[4] I attended that Diet at my own expense. I went deliberately to listen to the speeches and to see what took place. Oh Almighty God, the plotting which I saw on both sides was so devious and cunning that it would take an entire book to give an adequate description of what went on. In this place, therefore, I admonish any young man who reads this after me to make every effort possible, upon finishing school, to attend these sessions, to listen to and to observe the Diet procedures. If he cannot afford to be there at his own expense he should do it in the service of a deputy or some

[1]When the year will be three times six, when Marc will sing 'Alleluja', when John will appear on Corpus Christi (someone added later; when John Casimir will reign), Poland will groan: woe! woe!
[2]On the octave of Corpus Christi. The above statement corresponds to the truth. Czapliński, *Pam.*, p. 359, note 3.
[3]Woe!
[4]The Diet was in session from March 17 until May 4. Czapliński, *Pam.*, p. 359, note 3.

young lord just in order to be able to attend a few Diets. Or if he happens to be in the military service already, he should attend these sessions in the service of his field hetman or even his immediate commander during the winter encampment, as I had several times done myself. But everyone should be present there, should attend all the sessions, and should listen *diligentissime*.[5] And when the chamber of deputies moves upstairs[6] where conferences are sometimes held and when the marshals exclaim : "Whoever is not a deputy please leave !"— one should try to make the acquaintance of at least one of those marshals,[7] as I did. With the intercession of important people I begged to be allowed to remain : "I came *ea inten-*

[5]Most attentively.

[6]Usually at the end of sessions where the senatorial chamber was located. Conferences of both chambers took place there in the presence of the king. Czapliński, *Pam.*, p. 360, note 8.

[7]There were four such marshals in the senate : grand marshal of the Crown and court marshal of the Crown ; grand and court marshal of Lithuania. One of these presided. The noblemen who were listening to the sessions were asked to leave the halls of debates when an unsually important question was to be discussed. Czapliński, *Pam.*, p. 360, note 10.

tione[8] of learning something *in hac palaestra.*[9] I promise not to give away any secrets." Sometimes a marshal would say : "Very well, I admire such character in a nobleman." When other people were asked to leave the chamber, I merely bowed to a marshal while the others rushed headlong out the door. Occasionally, someone was even hit across the neck with a cane. My comrades were amazed at that : "What luck you have ! I hid behind the stove but was finally forced to leave and you stayed." They did not know I obtained permission to remain.

I listened so *diligentissime*[10] that I did not even want to eat. When they sat in conference throughout the night in order to end the sessions, I did the same. I maintain that all the public meetings in the world are mere shadows as compared to the meetings of the Diet ! There one learned etiquette, law, and many things which one never heard of in school. I wish everyone such chance.

The sessions of the Diet lasted the entire winter[11] at great expense and with much commotion, but nevertheless no meaningful conclusions resulted from them ; only more bitterness and exasperation.

On the Monday after Easter, the son of the Polish Treasurer, Pan Krasiński,[12] who married a Chodkiewicz,[13] moved to the palace of Lubomirski,[14] the Polish Master of the Horse. The King attended the festivities. The Queen, ailing since Lent, fell seriously ill. The King was notified that her Royal Highness was feeling ill, but he indulged in drinking and making merry. "She will be fine," he said. Messengers came again, since her Royal Highness the Queen was dying. The King slapped the valet's face : "Do not talk nonsense when I am merry." A large

[8]With the express intention.
[9]In this 'school.'
[10]Most attentively.
[11]The Diet actually lasted for the last six weeks of spring. See note 5, same A.D. Czapliński, *Pam.,* p. 361, note 157.
[12]Jan Bonawentura Krasiński, later the voivode of Płock. Czubek, *Pam.,* p. 379, note 2.
[13]Teresa Chodkiewicz, the daughter of Jan Kazimierz Chodkiewicz, the Castellan of Wilno. Czubek, *Pam.,* p. 379, note 3.
[14]Aleksander Lubomirski. Czapliński, *Pam.,* p. 361, note 17.

crowd of courtiers and officers, including myself, stood near
the King when this happened. We saw and heard him. Some
began to whisper : "The King would be glad to be rid of this
pest." And this wac actually the case. He was merry and danced
all night. He was hardly ever sad, in both fortune and
misfortune he always seemed the same. "Sir host," he called
out to the treasurer *in haec verba* :[15] "Urge the officers to eat
and drink. Show them how delighted you are to have them.
May they long remember your hospitality !" He encouraged
us : "Drink up at this miser's." We drank all the more, danced,
and were merry.

The headstrong Queen Ludwika who stubbornly persisted
in her design to establish a Frenchman on the Polish throne
finally realized that things were not going the way she had
hoped they would. She spent large sums for that, ruined her
treasury, and impaired her health in her efforts and worries.
She used to sit behind a partition in the senatorial chamber,
day and night, in order to see and hear the progress her partisan
hirelings were making. Finally she despaired of success and fell
ill just after White Sunday.[16] She barely lived through Easter
Sunday and then she died.[17] The French lost one of their
greatest supporters when she died ; their opposition gained
heart. The promotion of the Condé failed soon after. Those
who had supported it wholeheartedly, including the blind one,[18]
were disappointed in their undertaking. The Archbishop joined
the Queen in death and God turned everything according to
His Holy Will.[19]

Ad eventum belli civilis[20] I now turn my pen. God stood
on the side of the innocent from beginning till end. The armies
went into the battlefield. Lubomirski did not attack the armies
of his lord and king, but did defend himself when pressed

[15]In the following words.
[16]First Sunday of Lent.
[17]The Queen died on May 10, 1667. Czubek, *Pam.*, p. 380, note 4.
[18]Archbishop Prażmowski.
[19]This as well as the preceding paragraph belong under the year 1667.
They were placed here by the copyist by mistake.
[20]To the event[s] of the civil war.

hard ; we pursued his forces when they fled from us. The armies met at Mątwy.[21] The distance between them across the ford was more than a league away.[22] The King ordered our army to ford the river the next day[23] and the dragoons and part of our cavalry got across. The Lithuanians were just about to follow in their step when Lubomirski's cavalry came galloping, not in battle array or formation, but crowded in the Tatar fashion. They charged at our companies right away, thinking they were the Lithuanians. They clashed mightily. Many a man fell off his horse to the ground before they recognized each other : a brother, a son were on the king's side ; another brother, the father on Pan Lubomirski's. They stopped fighting. They dashed then, with all their might, at the right flank where, under the command of Colonel Czop, the dragoons and the Cossacks were standing. Having withstood the gunfire they took to swords. They slashed and slashed. They were shot at from cannon, from beyond the ford. That did not hinder them in the least. An hour and a half did not elapse before they wiped out our men. Many high officers perished there, but above all those fine men from Czarniecki's regiment, those valiant knights and old warriors who, in Denmark as well as in the Muscovite, Cossack and Hungarian battles, wrought *mirabilia*[24] and who were unconquerable at all times. They all perished in this civil war. The King and the entire army lamented their death and especially we, in my division, since we were witnesses to their bravery. God let this happen on account of our discords. He took the prime of our kinghthood which had always withstood the attacks of our enemies.

The battle was fought greatly *in confuso*.[25] In the midst of all the commotion, where it was difficult *discernere*[26] between friend and foe, and to know whom to attack, we mingled with each other

---

[21]A locality near Inowrocław.
[22]The flooded Noteć river separated the two armies. The ford led through wide swamps. Czapliński, *Pam.*, p. 363, note 32.
[23]July 13. Czapliński, *Pam.*, p. 363, note 33.
[24]Miracles.
[25]In great confusion.
[26]To distinguish.

without recognizing one another. Before one attacked he would first ask : "From which army are you ?" "From which one are you ?" If *contrarii* ;[27] "Let us fight !" "Go to the devil !"; "You may go to hell !" And they left each other alone. When acquaintances met, they just greeted one another and then dispersed for sometimes, one brother was with the King, another with Pan Lubomirski ; a father here, a son on the opposite side. We did not know how to fight this war. It is true that they had white scarves tied around their left arms but we did not notice this right away. I also wrapped a scarf around my arm, right below the elbow, and when the battle raged I did not shun them very much. They saw me from a distance and asked: "Are you one of us or not ?" I raised my arm with the scarf and replied : "Yours." They said : "You rascal, you are not one of us ! Ride away or join our side !"

After the battle an officer from the other army rode up from the side and Czop, the Cossack colonel, sat on his horse and did not pay any attention to him, assuming him to be one of our men. The officer rode up slowly, step by step, fired in his ear from a pistol and killed him instantly.[28] So treacherous is war when dress and manner of both sides are the same. May it never come to this in our Poland again !

I crossed over the ford to our ranks. The King, surrounded by our men, stood there wringing his hands. He was deeply worried and looked depressed. He sent word to Lubomirski and demanded that he face battle and not run so haphazardly like a wolf. Lubomirski replied to that : "It is not my design to fight my King in the open field, but being the wronged one, to defend myself to the best of my ability. Nor am I to blame for the spilling of this innocent blood, which I deplore, but His Royal Highness himself, along with his good advisors who have brought about this state of affairs in order to lay waste our fatherland. However, *propter bonum Reipublicae*,[29] I consent to the armistice of Palczyn with certain reservations. I am

---

[27]Opponents.

[28]Kochowski also mentions this incident. Czapliński, *Pam.*, p. 364, note 42.

[29]In the interest of the (Polish) Commonwealth.

willing to apologize to his Royal Highness even though I did not offend him, and I am even ready to accept penance as long as my reputation and that of my family is not hurt."

And so, just as I already described it, and just as the Mazovians would say : "Let's keep reaping with the sickle," he again began to run away from us and we pursued him all over Poland. The villages groaned, the poor people cried out against the devastation. The bishops and senators tried to persuade the King to take pity on the fatherland and to realize that this was obviously not to God's liking since we had no luck.

Delegates were sent to Lubomirski then and we entered into negotiations, but we continued the pursuit of him. At last, in order to put an end to it, the King made camp at Łęgonice,[30] in the voivodeship of Rawa. Lubomirski's delegates came to our camp at Łęgonice. The conditions for peace were set and signed, *ab utrinque*,[31] but not without great efforts by many worthy people such as senators and other worthy men who had assembled there *ad hunc actum*.[32]

Before I go into the terms of this treaty, I want to return for a moment to that unfortunate battle at Mątwy which I mentioned before. On the morning following that unfortunate battle I went to the royal tents. I stood around with the others and discussed various events until the King emerged from the tent reserved for meetings. All of us bowed to him, as before our lord, and he said to me : "If your commander[33] were still alive, everything would have been different." I replied : "Gracious Sir, if God had not taken him from us not only this misfortune but also the spilling of innocent blood would not have occurred, nor would the Poles have raised swords against each other." Tears rushed to the King's eyes and rolled like peas, one after another. He turned back to where he had come from and Father Wojnat, already dressed in his vestments, stood for about an hour and waited with the Mass before he

[30]A village on the Pilica river near Nowe Miasto.
[31]By both sides.
[32]Just for that purpose.
[33]Czarniecki.

came out again. The King did not even say a prayer during the entire Mass, he only knelt quietly on a velvet dais and sighed. He was remorseful over the loss of so many worthy men. He had pangs of conscience, as he realized that the confusion and hideousness of all designs had caused a great discredit[34] to his royal authority. He realized further that the advice of his corrupt and evil advisors had ruined his plans. This distressed him very much, even more than all his other wars and misfortunes. It brought him to despair and finally to abdication. He often used to say : "My head will not be free until I cover it with a monk's hood."

Whenever the King saw one of Czarniecki's men he would recall him *cum suspiriis.*[35] For Czarniecki was a man *in toga et sago,*[36] a dignified senator who spoke the truth, a soldier who did not spare himself in battle, and a lucky commander as well.[37] The King and the entire army lamented his death, *etiam*[38] those who had competed with him and had envied his fame. If he were alive, it would not have come to this civil war, *et potissimum,*[39] Lubomirski would not have taken up arms against the King but would have merely simulated allegiance. But as soon as God took Czarniecki away, everything in Poland and in the Ukraine became confused right away.

---

[34]"Designs caused a great discredit" are words missing in the manuscript which were supplied by Czubek.

[35]With sighs.

[36]In war and peace i.e., who excelled in times of war and peace.

[37]Pasek extolls Czarniecki as a truly national hero and as a military genius all through the *Memoirs.* It is interesting to note that most historical sources agree with his opinion. "Poland's greatest military leader of the time, Stefan Czarniecki." R. Dybowski, p. 45 "The foremost soldier of the time was Stefan Czarniecki, a man of austere principles of life, of unimpeacheble honesty and deep patriotism. An implacable foe of the magnates and political anarchy, he was one of the rare types that combine an exalted conception of civic duty with clear vision and force of action. He was a man of vision and force of action. He was a man of genius and of exceptional strength of character." Lewinski-Corwin, p. 251. Numerous other such examples could be cited.

[38]Even.

[39]And above all.

Everyone would openly show ungratefulness before God himself if among other gracious favors he would not accept with special thanks also the gift of such a knight sent by God in order to defend the country and on whose shoulders the badly afflicted fatherland could drowse and taste the freedom for which it had strived for many years. Italy gloried in her Aemilius [40] who was killed by the Phoenicians on the battlefield while boldly defending her safety. Greece compared the fame of her Protesilaus [41] with the sun, for he did not spare either his health or his life and was killed by the Phrygian army similarly to Aemilius. For what are we to than God the most for our Czarniecki? For having granted him in all the combats His graceful protection, for having pulled him out with His own Hand in times of crisis at all times, for having given him great and important victories over the enemy, with only a handful of the army, or for having preserved him in life and called him back from this earth in old age *placida morte.* [42] Let armorial swords shield the Polish Commonwealth; let lances defeat the enemy; let watchful lions guard the frontier; let axes preserve the bounds of justice, and let horseshoes [43] tread upon the insolence of rebels. Your [44] armorial boat [45] *meruit* [46] more in the world than the one which brought Jason the Golden Fleece of Colchis. Our fatherland will sorrow deeper over the loss of

[40] Lucius Aemilius Paulus, Roman consul in 219 and 216 B.C., killed in the Roman defeat by Hannibal at Cannae in 216 B.C. It was the greatest defeat the Romans had ever suffered.

[41] Greek hero from Thessaly killed by either Hector or Euphorbus, during landing at Troy. It is said that he knew of the prophecy that whoever would be the first one to set foot on Trojan ground would be killed. He did so nevertheless.

[42] By a gentle death.

[43] Heraldic signs: swords in various coats of arms; lances in those of the Zamoyski family; lions in the Lanckorońskis; axes in the Tęczyński and Ossoliński families; horseshoes in the Myszkowski and Żółkiewski family. These coats of arms here are used in place of the names of the nobles who bore them. Czubek, *Pam.*, p. 386, note 5.

[44] Czarniecki's.

[45] Czarniecki's coat of arms.

[46] Merits, i.e., deserved.

Czarniecki than did the countries which lost leaders such as Epaminondas[47] and the Scipios.[48] Our Czarniecki was a braver and more courageous warrior than Hector,[49] a victor equal to Alexander.[50] It would be impossible for someone who had looked at Czarniecki's military accomplishments not to cry out at the graceful recollection of him, even if someone's heart were as hard as the flint of a Caucasian stone and as a Rhodopian[51] rock. I admit that I almost consider leaving the military profession, although I intended to serve under this good leader *ad vitae tempora*,[52] for having learned how to conquer it would be difficult to be conquered; once accustomed since early youth to pursuing the enemy it would be unpleasant to be pursued in old age, and a loss of a good leader, or a change in commander is usually accompanied by a change in luck. We already had proof of this in the case of Czarniecki's invincible regiment which withstood many such violent attacks and won such great victories but which during the civil war was swept away completely. Many of us from Czarniecki's school would prefer now to give up Bellon[53] in favor of applying Ceres.[54]

War can be pleasant under a good leader, even in times of greatest troubles and hardships. A heart seeking fame does not

[47]Born c. 418 B.C., d. 362 B.C., Greek general and statesman of Thebes who defeated the Spartans at Leuctra, July, 371 B.C. This defeat marked the destruction of Spartan superiority in Greece which they had gained in the Peloponesian War, thirty years before.

[48]Scipio, the family name of Roman generals from the time of the Punic Wars ; Cnaeus Cornelius Scipio, and Publius Cornelius Scipio were brothers ; Publius Cornelius Scipio Africanus, called Scipio the Elder, the son of Publius Cornelius Scipio, was the greatest of them all. There was also Scipio the Younger, Publius Cornelius Scipio Aemilianus Nuncantius, the son of Aemilius Macedonicus and others.

[49]The chief Trojan hero during the Trojan War.

[50]Alexander the Great, Alexander III of Macedon, b. 356 B.C. and d. 323 B.C.

[51]Rhodope, a mountain range in Thrace.

[52]Until the end of my life.

[53]Meaning here to leave the military profession.

[54]Meaning here to take up the cultivation of land.

24*

fear the fire and swords of war nor the huge Syrtes,[55] Scyllas and Charybdises[56] when it is under the command of a great leader. Scaevola[57] was renowned throughout the world because he rendered justice on his own hand for having missed sinking his sword into his fatherland's enemy. Czarniecki knew how to use his hand so that it never deserved punishment. The enemy whom he touched with his sword was never safe. *Tot saecula*[58] elapsed since Cynaegirus[59] earned his fame for having seized an enemy ship in his teeth and for which he is even now often remembered. But the world sees Czarniecki's more recent *merita*,[60] when he fearlessly withstood the enemy's *tela ore*[61] even after he was wounded in the palate. Until his death, he wore a silver plate in his mouth to cover the wound ; he could not say a word whenever it had to be taken out to be washed.

Oh Almighty God ! Much paper would have to be written up to describe adequately Czarniecki's deeds of knightly courage since his youth ! I witnessed many of them myself. About his youth, I heard from the old warriors that this Polish Hector[62] faced death several times a day ! Ever since early youth he adorned his brow with the hard casque of Mars ;[63] just like a son of the valiant Gradivus,[64] and not with the delicate and golden one like Paris.[65] He preferred tempered

[55]Syrtes, a large bay of the Mediterranean in the coast of Northern Africa which is dangerous for navigation ; according to legend, when the Argonauts were on their way home from Colchis the Argo was driven there by a storm.

[56]Scylla, in classical mythology a sea nymph ; Charybdis, a monster or whirlpool in the Straits of Messina, i.e., treacherous rocks.

[57]Scaevola, Quintus Mucius, a mythical Roman hero who after being captured by the enemies and threatened to be burnt alive, thrust his hand into the flames in order to prove that he was not afraid.

[58]So many centuries.

[59]Athenian soldier, brother of the poet Aeschylus who distinguished himself by his bravery in the battle of Marathon, B.C. 490.

[60]Merits.

[61]Bullets.

[62]Here Czarniecki.

[63]Roman mythological god later identified with the Greek Ares.

[64]A Roman epithet of Mars as god of war.

[65]Or Alexander, in Greek legend son of King Priam of Troy.

armour to Chinese silk and Sydon purple.[66] Death did not seek
him but he always sought death, thus heeding Seneca's admonition that, *"Quia incertum est, quo loco te mors expectet, tu
eam omni loco expecta."*[67] He sought it in his youth in the
Czech and German provinces, where he carried a flag in his
brother's company; he sought it in the Tatar, Walachian,
Multan, Hungarian, Cossack, Muscovite, Swedish, Prussian,
Danish, and Holstein[68] lands; he sought it beyond the Dnieper
and beyond the Volga, beyond the Oder, the Elba and beyond
the sea, and everywhere he eagerly risked his life for the safety
of his fatherland. But death spares him whom God preserves
for further service to Him and the fatherland; the valor and
wisdom with which he withstood the Swedish invasion is proof
of this. During those trying battles he faced the enemy with
a small army on behalf of the King and Master and was like
a welcome bezoar[69] to the already failing fatherland; and he
happily restored it to the King. He drove the Swedish tyrant
out of the fatherland and he pursued him into his native land
beyond the sea. Then the Muscovite wars followed, but I shall
not write about them however for this is not a chronicle but
a record of my life, yet I can apply the following words to this
commander: *"Tuum tam spectatum exemplum, tenaci saecu-
lorum memoriae traditum, in ipsa astra sublime pennata Fama
fert."*[70]

Czarniecki never boasted of his deeds. The more he
attributed them to God and to his Sovereign, the more good
fortune was granted to him by the Almighty. Achilles is famous
for his strength, but it is written that Thetis bathed him in such
magic waters that no weapons could harm him. History has it

[66]Color of the robes of cardinals and monarchs and thus a sign of
dignity.
[67]Since you cannot be certain where you meet death, you should expect
it everywhere. Seneca, *Epist.* II, *Ad Lucilium* 7.
[68]Schleswig-Holstein.
[69]From Arabic: A calculus or a concretion found in the stomachs or
intestines of Persian goats or llamas; used as an antidote.
[70]Wings of fame lift among the stars this excellent example of yours,
conveying its lasting memory to ages.

that Hector valiantly fought and won the battles when the Republic of Troy, his fatherland, was in danger. Rome boasts of Scipio's valor when he conquered Africa on its behalf. But this took place when soldiers were hurling stones at each other. Those bygone leaders, were they revived, would probably find the present-day manner of war unpleasant, when thousands of flintlocks fill the air with smoke right beneath your nose, when huge cannon balls,[71] the size of buckets, are fired right before your eyes so that even the devil himself, *curiosus*[72] though he is, does not have the time to appear according to custom before the individual at the time of death, when those fireworks, bombs, cannister-shots and so many other devices which were invented for the destruction of mankind are flying in the air. Even those famous knights of that time probably would not equal those of the present age, yet our commander was already familiar with all these inventions. He always knew how to conquer, he knew how to benefit by a victory; he never lost an army, he knew how to preserve it and even if he exerted it too hard on occasion, he knew how to get it back into shape and how to reward it. The golden age was already transformed into an age of hard iron,[73] when our homeland with its hope and joy was transformed into a land of bitter tears by the loss of such a field hetman and senator. They say: *"Optimum est memorabilem mori aliquo opere virtutis."*[74] But the name of our late commander adorns the world with virtue and eternity, even though he paid the debt of mortality. *"Omnium animi sunt immortales, sed bonorum fortiumque divini."*[75] We lost a knight whose equal Poland will probably not see soon again. Poland laments its senator as Mars his Hector; only a graceful recollection and praise of his name remain in our hearts. *"De-*

[71]From cannon-royals.
[72]Anxious.
[73]In classical mythology the golden age represented the first and the best of the four ages, the iron age represented the last and the worst of the four ages of the world.
[74]It is best to die having performed some great deed. (Seneca)
[75]The souls of all are immortal but those of the virtuous and valiant are divine. (Cicero)

*cet eos laudare defunctos, qui res arduas praeclarasque fece-
runt.*[76]

Now I turn back the pen, pursuing Czarniecki's glory to
the treaty of Łęgonice.[77]

When the treaty was concluded and signed, we began to
march from Łęgonice toward Radom because Lubomirski's
army was encamped along the Vistula. We arrived at Jaroszyn.[78] Only there Pan Lubomirski was given an opportunity to
apologize and to swear his oath of allegiance. He came to our
camp in the company of several hundred of his comrades and
elders.[79] Only two royal armored companies stood guard[80] in
the field, the rest of the army remained in their sheds. But
a great number of officers assembled in front of the royal tents
in order to witness the ceremony. When Lubomirski finished
his speech and entered the royal tent where he was to take the
oath, all the tent flaps were raised so that everyone could watch
the event. At the conclusion of this ceremony, the King went
to Warsaw and Pan Lubomirski to Janowiec[81] in order to
prepare for his *exilium* abroad. It was an unfortunate departure
however since he died[82] in Wrocław[83] soon after. He died of
no apparent cause and complained only of a headache. He was
heard to say : "Whoever works with his head must die because
of it." Since he brought disaster to the Commonwealth, some

[76]One should glorify after death those who have accomplished difficult
and splendid things. (Plato)
[77]On the thirty-first of July, 1666. In the original manuscript the following material appears here : a declaration of His Majesty, a general
amnesty, a form of the oath to be taken by the deputies of His
Majesty, a form of the oath to be taken by the deputies, the citizens of
the voivodeships, and the military men ; a rescript for the election of
His Majesty. These texts were not written by Pasek and were omitted
in Czubek's edition. They are omitted in this translation for the same
reason.
[78]Nowa Góra Jaroszyn, a small town on the Vistula across from Puławy.
[79]On the eighth of August. Czubek, *Pam.*, p. 406, note 4.
[80]They guarded the King.
[81]A town on the Vistula, ten kilometers southwest of Puławy.
[82]On the thirty-first of January, 1667. Czubek, *Pam.*, p. 406, note 7.
[83]A city in the lower part of Silesia, in German Breslau.

lamented his passing, while others rejoiced at it. Soon after, the Field Hetman[84] also said farewell to this world. Apparently, Queen Ludwika, as the *primum caput*[85] of all the plotting in favor of Condé, needed a retinue for her ascent to the heavenly kingdom. At first she invited the Field Hetmans and shortly thereafter the blind advisor,[86] her most faithful conspirator, to come along with her. In due time many others followed the Queen in order to give account of themselves before that frightful Tribunal.

The year ended in great misery and the impoverishment *nobilitatis*[87] and of the peasants. However, the deceased were silently reconciled forever *in perpetuum silentium*,[88] and no one dared to open his mouth about the wrongs done nor turn to the law because the amnesty was to justify all. Would it not have been better to have made up without shedding of so much human blood, without the devastation of the poor fatherland? We could have accomplished something worthwhile with the enemies of the Crown without devastating our land, without wasting so many lives which could have been useful in face of another crisis of the Commonwealth, and above all we would not have angered God.

[84]Stanisław Rewera Potocki died on February 22, 1667. Czubek, *Pam.*, p. 406, note 8.
[85]The chief instigator.
[86]Reference to Prażmowski, who actually did not die until 1673. Czapliński, *Pam.*, p. 386, note 203.
[87]Of the nobility.
[88]In eternal silence, i.e. amnesty here.

ANNO DOMINI 1667

I spent the entire winter at my parents' home in Węgrzynowi-ce.[1] There I often conversed with Pan Lipski,[2] the voivode of Rawa, and Pan Śladkowski,[3] the castellan of Sochaczew. God inclined the hearts of those two gentlemen toward me so that each wished me to wed into their family. The voivode grew fond of me after hearing me speak at a regional council at which a chamberlain was elected, and he himself installed as a voivode, and after seeing me preside over regional councils several times. As a result, he found some *activitatem*[4] in me and loved me much. For even while I was still in the army, whenever I came to my father's house and a regional council took place, I never missed it. Thus I rendered many people services. Occasionally I was asked to preside. Sometimes my services met with general approval. For this reason these two gentlemen held me in esteem. I presided at a pre-Diet regional council during Pan Lubomirski's amnesty *in anno praeterito*.[5] At the pre-Diet regional council in Rawa, which took place on February 7 of the present year, I presided once again and was urged to be the council's deputy to the local diet. I refused on the grounds that my father, who was also present at the council, would not cover my expenses for this mission, during which

[1]A village near Rawa, leased by Pasek's father. Czapliński, *Pam.*, p. 388, note 1.
[2]Jan Albrecht Lipski. Czapliński, *Pam.*, p. 388, note 2.
[3]Piotr Śladkowski, the standard-bearer of Rawa. Czapliński, *Pam.*, p. 388, note 3.
[4]Ability.
[5]Last year.

one had to be generous with money. Adam Nowomiejski, the royal prosecutor, and Anzelm Piekarski,[6] the cupbearer of Rawa, were then delegated as deputies. I gave them rather precise instructions pertaining to the agenda of the Diet. These instructions read as follows :

> Given to their lordships, the deputies from the land of Rawa, to his Lordship Pan Adam Nowomiejski, the royal prosecutor and judge of the city of Rawa, and to his Lordship Pan Anzelm Piekarski, the cupbearer of Rawa, unanimously elected, at the assembly of knighthood, to the two-week sessions of the Diet.[7]

> It is apparent to the world how much the entire fatherland must grieve when confronted with serious complications and no hope for its defense during such a severe crisis and when faced with ingratitude instead of consolation as a result of malevolent and wilful people who break up Diets. Everyone who considers with what pains his Royal Highness, our gracious master, toiled as a kind lord in order to bring the fourth Diet to a good end, after three broken-up Diets, must admit how deeply concerned he was to extend a helping hand to the already failing fatherland and yet, because of envious fortune's adversities, his Majesty did not succeed in manifesting his goodwill to the fatherland. Everyone, seeing the immense sorrow, fatigue and discomfort of his Royal Highness, all at a considerable detriment to his health, must acknowledge his solicitude, as well as his deep concern for the public welfare. He now calls into session the fifth Diet for the states of our Commonwealth, after four were broken up, in order to set the Commonwealth on a solid foundation and to provide the threatened fatherland, through timely *consilia*,[8] with the earliest possible means of defense. And since this Diet

[6]Both Piekarski and Nowomiejski are listed as deputies in the records of the Diet of 1667. Czapliński, *Pam.*, p. 389, note 14, citing *Volumina legum*, IV.

[7]This Diet was summoned for two weeks but with the deputies' consent it lasted six. Czapliński, *Pam.*, p. 389, note 14.

[8]Council.

meets from the benevolent grace of his Royal Highness, we commission our deputies, to above all express our appreciation for the sorrow and fatigue which he had to endure. We also commission them to wish him a long and a successful reign and to give due thanks, *nomine*[9] of our entire assembly of knighthood, for his *bonum*[10] and fatherly care of our land.

1. And since the Diets are broken up *cum summo Reipublicae detrimento*[11] as a result of frequent vetoes not grounded on any legal basis, we instruct their lordships, our deputies, to discover *ante omnia*[12] a means to conclude the Diets by restricting such vetoes by some law so that we may, *tandem aliquando,*[13] see the sessions of the Diet successfully concluded.

2. Furthermore, immediately post *absoluta vota*[14] of the senators our deputies are to beg his Majesty the King to ratify the armistice made at Łęgonice, *in quantum*[15] all its conditions meet with the approval of the chamber of deputies, since this armistice is most essential for internal peace.

3. In view of the difficult plight which the Commonwealth is in, we find nothing more vital than the contentment of the army, which remains in the service of the Commonwealth with its pay in arrears, and which has so many claims on the Commonwealth that the Commonwealth and especially our voivodeship cannot *sufficere*[16] from the regular taxes *propter visibilem desolationem.*[17] Therefore, the deputies should suggest the following methods for a speedier payment of debts :

[9]On behalf.
[10]Good.
[11]At the greatest detriment of the Commonwealth.
[12]Above all.
[13]At least once.
[14]After the conclusion of the speeches (i.e., those which the senators delivered at the beginning of the Diet.
[15]Insofar as.
[16]Meet them.
[17]Because of the obvious desolation.

4. First of all, that their lordships, the commanders, captains of horse, colonels, lieutenant-colonels, captains, lieutenants, officers of noble birth and other officers who are in possession of the royal estates, upon accounting with the treasury how much pay is due to them from the Commonwealth, wait until a certain period of time when this sum be, *propter meliorem certitudinem*[18] of payment, secured for them on the same estates.

5. As another method for raising money for such an urgent need of the Commonwealth, the deputies *proponent*[19] that the *clenodia regni*[20] be registered and pawned, with the deputies' knowledge, for a certain period of time.

6. Our deputies should also beg our bishops, abbots, and parsons, to prove themselves sons of this fatherland *in cuius sinu*[21] they were born, raised, and adorned with considerable honors, and finally, since the entire Commonwealth is in a state of confusion, condescend to render *charitativum subsidium*[22] without grudging, since they obtained their incomes from no other source than from the Commonwealth itself.

7. The taxes paid by the merchants who bring to Poland various goods, liquors, and other things for their own profit, as well as the custom duties, merchants' taxes, Jewish poll-taxes, and all other taxes collected *in fructum Reipublicae*[23] should be doubled, since the prices of all goods rise daily.

8. Even though every son of the fatherland thinks of it with great sorrow, the following measure also seems necessary to us : officers should not collect pay for those soldiers who, on various previous occasions, presented to

[18]For greater certainty.
[19]Should propose.
[20]The crown jewels.
[21]In whose womb.
[22]A voluntary subsidy. (The offerings which were voluntarily paid by the clergy when the Diet passed regular taxes were so called.)
[23]For the benefit of the Commonwealth.

the fatherland their well-tested virtue, but during the Civil War, God be merciful, perished at the battle of Mątwy, but surrender to the state's use and especially the pay of the non-nobles.

9. The deputies are also seriously to demand that all the money which was left over after the closing of the mint be used to pay the army.

10. It has always been the custom to reward worthy behavior with worthy payments, and a poor one with poor payment. Since there are many companies which did not join the regiment of Pan Machowski, though ordered to do so by his honor the voivode of Kraków (Cracow), it is only fair that they be deprived of renumeration. Because calamity would not have befallen those companies which were there[24] if the army had not been so small.

11. And since in urgent needs one must look to various means, though they might appear futile to us, we urge that money be borrowed *in fidem Reipublicae*[25] from various people under security of one kind and another, and also that the deputies proponent[26] whatever other means would appear most feasible.

12. So that the debts of their Majesties, the Royal Couple, may not be forgotten, the deputies shall negotiate about them with the entire chamber of deputies.

13. As far as the artillery is concerned, the deputies shall strive to find some way of meeting its expenses.

14. Even though we know that new taxes have been devised in the debt[27] owing to his Highness the Prince of Brandenburg, the deputies shall nevertheless, having re-

---

[24]Sebastian Machowski, the commander of the Polish armies, was defeated on December 19, at Brahiłów, by the Cossack field hetman Doroszenko. Machowski's entire division, numbering about 6000 men, was annihilated.

[25]At the Commonwealth's service.

[26]Propose.

[27]In the treaty of Welawa (Wehlau) of September, 1657, Elbląg and Drahim were pledged to the Great Elector as security for a loan of 4,000,000 thalers, the starosty of Drahim for a sum of 120,000. However, the former city was never actually transferred to him, and he

ceived *iustam calculationem et relationem*,[28] exert themselves in this matter *in quantum*[29] something still has to be done.

15. Since Piltyn[30] was *ab antiquo*[31] annexed to the Duchy of Courland, and in order to prevent an unpleasant situation such as we had with the Prussians, there is nothing more just than to give due thanks to the Prince of Courland[32] for having waited so long, and may the gentlemen deputies endeavor to see that it be given to the Prince of Courland, to whom it rightfully belongs, observing, however, the rights of His Majesty as liege and direct lord and as the ultimate judicial authority.

16. There is not one among us who, seeing the faith, virtue and possessions of their lordships, the citizens of Livonia, our brothers, annihilated and seized, would not express the thanks due them. And we would not be *contrarii*,[33] that our deputies make strenuous efforts, together with other deputies, to see that their desires be satisfied.

17. Since the matter *anni*[34] 1662 was postponed until the next Diet, and until the credit of the Commonwealth be better established, *iniungimus*[35] our deputies that, either a *summa proveniens*,[36] the capital as well as the interest be

therefore demanded the return of his loan. See Czubek, *Pam.*, p. 414, note 4. By this treaty Poland recognized the sovereignty of Frederich Wilhelm over East Prussia, which was a fief of Poland at the time. In an additional compact, made at Bydgoszcz, the Elector pledged to ally himself with Poland against Sweden. For all this, he gained Elbląg and other small territorial acquisitions at the cost of Poland. After the death of Charles X, peace was signed on May 3, 1660, between Sweden and Poland. Reddaway, pp. 524–525.

[28]An accurate account and report.

[29]Insofar as.

[30]A town on the Winda river in Courland. This refers to the district of Piltyn, over which Poland had carried on a feud with Courland.

[31]Since early times.

[32]Jakub (d. 1683).

[33]Backward, contrary.

[34]Of the year.

[35]We enjoin.

[36]Adequate sum.

returned to the Orsettis,[37] or that such a sum as is described in the contract be assured to them.

18. May the deputies endeavor to see that the mint which was closed, and later reopened without the Commonwealth's consent, be closed *ex nunc*,[38] and that its dies be destroyed.

19. May the deputies see to it that the trials of Boratyni as well as those of Tynf, for which the entire Commonwealth has pleaded, be held.[39]

20. The administrators of the new tax as well as of the excise duties *reddant* [*rationem*][40] of their expenses, and should also be tried.

21. Since the states of the Commonwealth suffer great losses because of the unbearable costliness of materials, frocks and other things, may the deputies beg that *pretia rerum*[41] be established.

22. May the deputies also endeavor to see that the sum which was designated and assigned to us in the treasury by the Commission decree be paid to us.

23. May the deputies urge that the *auctores*[42] of false coins *reddant rationem*[43] of what they did with the great sums which they forged into *tynfs* out of good coinage, since as many as eight tynfs were coined out of a thaler.

[37]Wilhelm Orsetti made a loan in 1659 to the commissioners of the Commonwealth for the payment of tribute to the Tatars, in return for which he was to receive the starosty of Knyszyn until repayment of the loan. This agreement was not approved by the Diet of 1662, however. When Orsetti died his heirs demanded payment at the Diet, but the Diet of 1662 postponed the case. Czubek, *Pam.*, p. 415, note 11.

[38]At once.

[39]Tytus Liwiusz Boratyni and Andrzej Tynf were accused, as the leaseholders of the mints, of embezzling funds. Tynf fled abroad; Boratyni was cleared of the charges, and a new contract with him was drawn up. Charges against Boratyni continued to be raised, however, in 1666 and 1667. Of these he seems to have been acquitted. Czubek, *Pam.*, p. 416, note 5.

[40]Should give an account.

[41]Lit., "prices", "maximum prices" here.

[42]The coiners.

[43]Give an account.

And the tax-collectors should demand that their dues be handed over in sound currency into the treasury.

24. Since we have not received the salt assigned for our district for a long time, may the deputies beg His Majesty that it be given to us.

25. May the deputies insist that foreign envoys and residents who have settled down[44] here be expelled *ex nunc.*[45]

26. Let the deputies demand that private envoys not be sent to neighboring nations *et sine consensu ordinum.*[46]

27. And since our voivodeship, more than all the others, is devastated by the constant passage, presence, and encampments of the armies of His Majesty and of the confederacy, may the deputies beg that our taxes be deferred *ad feliciora tempora.*[47]

28. Since, in case of the field hetman's absence, disorder usually increases in the army, and since the consequent debauchery produces considerable calamities detrimental to the Commonwealth, the deputies *instabunt*[48] that the field hetmans or at least one of them always be present in the army at all times *propter meliorem ordinem et disciplinam solidam.*[49]

29. May the deputies firmly demand that colonels, captains of horse and other officers not abscond from their regiments and companies *sine legali impediment*[50] under penalty of loss of pay. If commanding officers make such hardships concerning our pay,[51] let them themselves observe their duty. The same should also apply to officers who miss a battle. In this way we would have companies

---

[44]Foreign envoys and temporary residents who made their homes in the Commonwealth even though their official business had terminated.
[45]Immediately.
[46]Without the permission of the estates.
[47]Until more favorable times.
[48]Will insist.
[49]For the sake of better order and solid discipline.
[50]Without a legitimate obstacle.
[51]Pasek must be thinking of himself and others as military men here.

which would be *pleno numero*[52] and up to strength at all times.

30. May the deputies also resolutely demand that our native noblemen and our officers be represented in foreign armies.

31. If time permits may the deputies demand that the *postulata et desideria*[53] of their lordships, our Brethren, which are listed in earlier instructions, be fulfilled. Thus we commission our deputies to request that, as soon as another abbacy becomes vacant, the provisions...[54] be satisfied with the consent of the entire Commonwealth *etiam non o[bstante] lege de incompatibilibus quoad personam*[55] his Excellency, the Bishop of Chełm, Vice-Chancellor of the Crown,[56] *ex officio suae eminentis dignitatis*[57] and the great favor which he deserves from the Commonwealth, and also because we wish it in just reward of his Excellency's deserts with respect to the Commonwealth.

32. Also that adequate compensation be made to his Lordship Pan Aleksander Załuski, the chamberlain of Rawa, for the villages and estates of Pawłowo, Szapoli, Borodyno, Putosze, Czerńcowo, Radzynowo, Piotrowo, Holemszczowo, situated in the voivodeship of Smoleńsk and subject to feudal law, which *post sterilem decessum*[58] of the late Pan Stanisław Kazanowski, starost of Krosin and Przedbor, were handed over to him by His Majesty, but which are now conquered and in the possession of the Muscovites.

33. Our deputies are to take care that the city of Rawa, which was ruined and devastated as a result of the army's many encampments, be exempt from taxes and other burdens.

[52]Fully represented.
[53]The demands and desires.
[54]One word is missing in the manuscript.
[55]The law against cumulative holding of posts or pluralities notwithstanding, concerning (i.e., to the benefit of).
[56]Andrzej Olszowski. Czubek, *Pam.*, p. 418, note 9.
[57]In consideration of his eminent rank.
[58]After the death without heirs.

May our deputies insist that the *desiderium*[59] of his
Honor the rector of Budziszowice, that the fief which was
bought for a hospital in Budziszowice and which is presently leased by Pan Piotr Śladkowski, the standard-bearer
of Rawa, could *iure ecclesiastico gaudere*,[60] a matter which
was raised so many times at our regional councils and
enclosed in previous instructions.

We thereby commission our deputies, and obligate
them *fide, honore et conscientia*,[61] to seek *bonum patriae*[62]
and negotiate in such a way as to turn things rather *in
[e-]lucidationem*[63] of her liberties and not to her oppression, and to counsel with the deputies of the other voivodeships about everything else as well.

Given in Rawa at an assembly of knighthood on
February 7, A.D. 1667.

Jan Chryzostom z Gosławic Pasek,
deputy chamberlain of Rawa and
marshall of the assembly of knighthood.

The office of deputy chamberlain was given to me several
weeks prior to the meeting of the regional council. The voivode
and the vice-chancellor forced me to accept it against my will,
saying that it was an *accessus*[64] to higher honors, which they
solemnly promised me in the voivodeships, and a way to keep
in touch with them. *Alterum*,[65] they insisted that by merely
possessing a voice at the regional council I could get promoted
faster than if I did not hold one.[66]

They really wanted my promotion, and expressed sincere
intentions toward me: "You will attain high office here in
three years at the most." They sent me as an envoy to the King,

[59]Demand.
[60]Benefit from the ecclesiastical law.
[61]With faith, honor, and conscience.
[62]The good of the fatherland.
[63]Elucidation.
[64]Access.
[65]Secondly.
[66]At the regional councils the floor was given first to those who held
office.

to the Archbishop, and to the Bishop of Kujawy.[67] On each of these occasions, I gained a good name for myself. They also wanted to employ me in more important affairs.

The voivode wanted to marry me to Radoszowska.[68] Pan Śladkowski, the standard-bearer of Rawa at the time and later the castellan of Sochaczew, pushed me at all costs toward Panna Śladkowska,[69] an heiress and only daughter who had a village called Boża Wola,[70] situated in the land of Sochaczew and free of even the smallest debt, for which her father had paid 70,000 at a time when ducats were worth six zlotys and thalers three zlotys each.[71] Each of these men upset my inclinations for the other's match. Śladkowski said that Radoszowska's mother was licentious and that the girl might turn out that way. The voivode said of Śladkowska *in haec verba* :[72] "So what if she has 70,000. She has certain *vitia.*[73] Above all, she is as evil as a serpent and drinks a lot. You should look for someone with good qualities. It would be a shame to see you marry her ! If you don't like Radoszowska, I can find you someone else, but I shall not allow you to marry Śladkowska." I listened to these things as if to two bands playing at the same time, and both playing well. I had a greater liking for Śladkowska, however, because I heard that in her village not only did wheat grow in every field in which it was planted but also onions grew. I had a greater preference *ad pinguem glaebam*[74] than for cash.

Neither of them let me out of his sight. When they got hold of me, I had to stay three or even four weeks with whichever one caught me. Whenever I came to my parents, a messenger appeared right away from the one whose house I had stayed

---

[67]Wacław Leszczyński, Archbishop of Gniezno ; Prince Florian Czartoryski, the Bishop of Kujawy. Czubek, *Pam.*, p. 421, note 8.
[68]Presumably a member of the voivode's family.
[69]Presumably a member of Śladkowski's family.
[70]In Polish, God's Will.
[71]Before the devaluation of coins in 1668, one could obtain nine zlotys for a ducat and five zlotys for a thaler. Czubek, *Pam.*, p. 421, note 10.
[72]The following words.
[73]Faults.
[74]For fertile soil.

25*

away from longer. Neither would celebrate any family festivity without my presence. The voivode gave his daughter away to the Bernardine Convent in Warsaw. He asked me to give her away *ad votum*.[75] This I did *in frequentia*[76] of many noteworthy people, as is the custom in Warsaw. Later he gave another daughter away in marriage to Grzybowski, the son of the starost of Warsaw,[77] and I also had to be there. After the weddings and receptions he treated me almost as a member of his family. In Glinnik,[78] during Shrovetide, Pan Jan Potrykowski gave away his stepdaughter in marriage to Pan Maciej Potrykowski. Since the bridegroom was a relative of mine, he asked me to be his best man. I went to that wedding, and did not know that people were preparing a wedding for me. It happened as follows :

Pan Śladkowski, the present castellan of the lands of Sochaczew, invited to his house for Shrovetide a young lady with her mother and Pan Wilkowski, her stepfather, without telling me anything about it. Śladkowski *simpliciter*[79] begged me to spend Shrovetide at his house. He did not tell me anything about the young lady's presence or of his intentions. Since I had promised to be at his disposal, I had to consent. I thought to myself that I would apologize later to Pan Śladkowski for not keeping my promise. I then went with them[80] to Osów,[81] and from there to the wedding. Pan Śladkowski, who did not know anything about it, expected me to come. He deliberately sent a letter to Glinnik begging me to come, but again did not mention anything about his plans. To speed things up, he and her mother had decided to marry me off to her right away without bans. A priest was waiting. My cousins, the Chociwskis,

[75]I.e., to stand in her father's place at the ceremony during which she took her vows.
[76]In the presence.
[77]According to Czapliński, Pasek is mistaken here, because at the time the starost Jan Grzybowski married Anna Lipska. *Pam.*, p. 402, note 142.
[78]A village in the district of Rawa.
[79]Merely.
[80]The Chociwskis.
[81]Now Osowice.

did not think of my leaving and said : "Even if you were to attack us with a sword, we would not let you go, for we are your relatives. You shall go tomorrow. Sacrifice this day for us." It could not be otherwise, as they hid the horses and my other belongings. And from Śladkowski messengers came running all day. In the evening a letter arrived from her Ladyship,[82] née Myszkowska, in which she candidly admitted the plot, and added : "My husband is angry with you because he wished that you be called the bridegroom on Ash Wednesday, and he is bitter now that you scorn his favor." My cousins intercepted the letter. Seeing that it was in a lady's hand, they were particularly inclined to open it in hopes of discovering secrets. Upon reading it, Floryjan Chociwski said : "We shall not be able to keep him now, and it is simply not right to hold him under the circumstances. I may even go with him myself, because this is a question of preserving a friendship." My luck was always outstanding so that people were amazed. Still, the outcome could be neither better nor worse than God willed. Next day—it was already afternoon—I thanked everyone and rode ahead at a fast trot, sometimes even at a gallop, seeing that it was already evening. I had not ridden half a league, when it began to snow. Later, dusk fell. By the time we arrived and dismounted, it was dawn. A fish supper was being served.[83] Some guests, including the young lady's stepfather Pan Wilkowski, were already asleep. Both[84] of them looked at me angrily. I said to them : "The reason is that you did not write to me honestly in the first letter, and the last letter was intercepted and not handed over to me until I was leaving the village." Only then did they calm down a little. They realized right away that I had not done it out of disdain. I had not lost my tongue and wit. I appeased them, and said : "My worthy Ladyship and Lord, the kindness which you were to render me today will also prove useful to me tomorrow. Why, a wedding even on Ash Wednesday is not a novelty, especially since we

[82]Pani Wilkowska, i.e., the young lady's mother.
[83]I.e., Pasek must have set out for Śladkowski's manor on Ash Wednesday eve, arriving the morning of that feast day.
[84]Pan Śladkowski and his wife.

have a priest who is not a stickler, and is not afraid of the
bishop. !" The castellan's wife—her husband was actually still
a standard-bearer at the time—liked the idea ; but he declared
that it could not be. Now the wedding had to wait until May.
"Postponed till May, blown away."[85] Apparently God had not
willed it so. This even the young lady herself admitted later at
someone's wedding : "Even though the village 'God's Will'[86]
was there, nevertheless the Will of God was not there." When
May came, Pan Śladkowski served as a delegate in Warsaw.
The young lady's mother died. Thus this prospective marriage
was deferred. *"Homo proponit, Deus disponit."*[87]

Later Lubomirski and the Field Marshal Potocki died. The
Lwów Comission followed. Meantime, since these matrimonial
plans were postponed, Pan Jędrzej Remiszowski, who was
married to a Pasek, a first cousin of mine, began to recommend
to me—as among relatives—his sister, born a Remiszowska,
the daughter of Stanisław Remiszowski. He tried to persuade
me to go to the district of Kraków, just to get acquainted with
her and, only if circumstances proved favorable, to consult
further about terms. I kept this in mind. After the Lwów
Commission came to an end,[88] he convinced me, and we went
there. Pan Remiszowski went to Olszówka[89] near Wodzisław[90]
to his sister's. I went to visit Pan Wojciech Chociwski, my
uncle. I thought to myself : "It will not cost me anything to
take a look at this widow. If nothing comes of it, I have another
prospect waiting for me. For surely no one will take Panna
Śladkowska before me. My uncle, his son, and I set out. We
arrived in Olszówka *ipso die festi Beatissimae Mariae Vir-
ginis,*[91] after attending Mass at the miraculous altar of the Holy

---

[85] A Polish proverb meaning here that things which are postponed
usually do not materialize.
[86] Boża Wola.
[87] Man proposes, God disposes.
[88] August 10.
[89] A village near Wodzisław in the voivodeship of Kraków.
[90] A town 35 km southwest from Jędrzejów.
[91] On the very day of the feast of the Virgin Mary, August 8. Czubek,
Pam., 426, note 6.

Mother.[92] We arrived without musicians so as not to imply that
we came courting. But having felt a sincere inclination—also
the hostess began to allude to musicians—I sent to Wodzisław
and before long they were brought. And then we began to
dance. My uncle asked: "Well, do you like the widow?"
I answered: "My heart feels strongly inclined toward her. If
I could only speak to her today and find out whether she feels
friendly toward me." My uncle replied: "It is not proper to
speak to her the first day. But as to her inclinations, I have
already surmised that she is friendly toward you. I can instantly
tell when a woman takes a liking to someone, even if she does
not say a word. You need not have any doubts. I see that if you
like her you will surely be accepted. It is a good match, indeed.
She is a worthy woman and a good housekeeper. There is order
and every possible affluence in her house. These villages[93] of
hers are on a leasehold, it is true. But she has money and
a dower in Smogorzów,[94] and even though it is in the hands of
her children's uncle Pan Jan Łącki, a rowdyish man, I am not
worried, because you shall know how to deal with him. Since
God has inclined your heart toward her, it is His Holy Will.
Tomorrow, God willing, I shall negotiate." After this conversation, I went to dance with her. After the dance, I sat down next
to her. I was already attracted to her. She must have been
pretty when young. She appeared young to me even then.
I would never have said that she was as old as I later found her
to be. She was forty-six when she married me; I *supponebam*[95]
that she was not more than thirty. I was heartened when I saw
her youngest daughter, Marysia, who was two years old at the
time. For I hoped that God would give me a son, which would
have happened if it had not been for the malice of the people
who caused her—such was the rumor—not to have any more

[92]In the nearby church of the Reformed Franciscans in Pińczów, there
was a miraculous picture of the Holy Virgin. Czubek, *Pam.*, p. 426,
note 7.
[93]Olszówka and Brzezie. Czapliński, *Pam.*, p. 406, note 166.
[94]A village in the district of Stopnice, five kilometers east of Stopnice.
[95]Thought.

children.[96] We used to find various objects in bed. I myself
found several rotten bones from a coffin. Because of my own
experience, I admonish everyone who reads this *praeiudica-
tum*[97] that whoever marries a widow should strive *ante omnia*[98]
not to keep any female relative about him, but should give her
a dowry and marry her off right away. We had plenty of them
about, and that was our peril.

But I leave all that, which I already yielded to the Will of
God, and return to my courting conversation with the widow.
I said : "My gracious Lady, I pay my compliments to you,
gracious Lady of this house. I am calling on you at the request
of his Lordship, your brother, for a while to pay my respects.
But the food here has appealed to me so much that I would be
willing to accept service in your household with that as my
only recompense until Christmas, and if I were well content,
I would not refuse to stay longer. If my service would be in any
way useful to Your Ladyship, I would propose this eagerly.
For I have grown tired of the bloody games of Mars, and
would prefer to change profession in my aging years to something more useful, that is, to learn husbandry at the side of
a good housekeeper, entering her service as a farmhand—or, as
they say, a herdsman. My very Gracious Lady, if you do not
have a complete staff of servants, which you need, and if
I could be counted among those who find favor with you,
please condescend either to scorn or to accept my eagerness to
serve you. I shall not enter into any discussion about wages,
however, until I first hear from Your Ladyship with what
courtesy this declared eagerness of mine to be of service to
Your Ladyship is to be accepted."

She answered me thus : "My Lord ! It is a fact that in this
part of the country we hire servants only from Christmas time
on. If anyone enters such service after St. John's day,[99] he is
not entitled to full pay, but only to whatever may be offered

---

[96]Pasek evidently attributed his wife's subsequent barrenness to a spell
placed upon her by his stepdaughters.
[97]Experience.
[98]Above all means.
[99]After June 24. In other words, in the second half of the year.

to him by grace. That custom concerns only less significant help, however. When a more important servant is hired, we do not contract with him only until Christmas, but for a whole year, which begins from the date he is hired. I do not wish to enter into such a contract with Your Lordship, however. For I am aware that as a knight Your Lordship has become used to high recompense, while I, a poor noblewoman, might not be able to afford to offer you such. But I would gladly hear Your Lordship's wishes as to what he might be content with. Then I, if I find I can afford it, shall consent to your proposal without even waiting for tomorrow."

I said : "My Ladyship, you have scoffed not only me but all knighthood as well by referring to our meager pay of forty or sixty zlotys at the most, for which we begrudged neither loss of blood nor health at all times, as high wages. May Your Ladyship know that, if all warriors were satisfied with such recompense, all of them, including myself, would surely not abandon it until decrepit age. Since, however, I am now willing to abandon the army for this present position, and do offer Your Ladyship my benevolent services, it is obvious that I am willing to accept the pay about which Your Ladyship does not wish to bargain. But I have confidence in your considered discretion, in which I do not doubt, and I await from Your Ladyship a declaration."

She answered : "My Lord, after all, everyone, including yourself, acts similarly when hiring an employee, and speaks frankly to him about his future duties and terms so that he will know in what capacity he is to serve his master and what recompense he is to expect for his services. I am allowed to act in a similar way. I myself shall explain to you the terms of the position, and I declare that if Your Lordship is disposed to accept them, he will be hired today. Or if that seems unseemly haste, tomorrow.

I replied thus : "In this matter, I must attribute to Your Ladyship not a woman's but a knightly consideration and discretion in speaking candidly. This is what I like, to speak one's mind right out. And an answer slips more pleasantly from Your

Ladyship's lips than from a Chancellor's,[100] and I look forward to it, whatever it may be, as to a piece of news desired from God. If the answer is comforting, I shall be grateful, if the contrary, I shall bear no rancor, assuming that Heaven does not will it so."

She replied : "It behooves nobody to meet sincere friendship with ingratitude. Also my conscience would bother me, if I did not respond to Your Lordship's sincere affection with similar feelings. And if you really desire to be a good servant, here you will find a place and a master. Since your services are offered at my discretion, they can expect a special consideration.

Only now I thanked her. To describe all sentiments from this conversation would take too much time. Afterwards, I had an orderly, Dzięgielowski, who played the violin and sang well, sing :

Let hope bring various luck
To other people's mind.
Mine is the triumph,
For I got a happy bargain.

From this song everyone guessed what went on between us. Her brother came up to us : "Indeed, sister, was it right not to consult with us ? But it is all right even so, and thank God !" She protested that there was nothing to it, that was just a song. But they kept on insisting that she had already made her mind. They drank a toast to her health. When they noticed her ring on my finger, they began to dance and drink even more, as was habitual. Then without any ceremony we began to speak *de tempore*.[101] She said : "Tomorrow, if it were not a Friday." I thanked her for her eagerness, but said : "My Ladyship, I have parents without whose blessing I cannot change my status. Such is their order. By Your Ladyship's grace, I received your agreement, for I trust that Your Ladyship intends to keep her word. You, too, can rely on my fidelity. In any case, let

[100]A Chancellor was the one who announced the King's reply to the Senate. Czapliński, *Pam.*, p. 409, note 181.
[101]About the (wedding) date.

this agreement be put in writing. I shall go and return in two weeks. Thus, I shall fulfill the will of my parents. I shall also bring some relatives back with me. I shall bow before Your Ladyship then and beg for the fulfillment of your pledge."

She said: "This simply cannot be. If the marriage is to take place, it must be right away." Then her brother Jędrzej joined in, supported her, begged me not to put it off. He promised all his help and many bequests. So both the brother and the sister molested me: "Certainly the wedding must take place Sunday, not a day later." "You may get later the blessings of your parents. It will be more important if they bless both of you together."

I felt sorry for this woman then, seeing her great love, and I said: "Does Your Ladyship really wish that it be so?" She answered: "I do wish it. God is my witness, for I don't even know why God inclines my heart toward you." Only then did I declare: "Let it be so, then, since such is God's and Your Ladyship's will."

On Sunday I wrote a letter to Śladkowski[102] asking him to come to the wedding and to bring musicians. Meanwhile we rode to the church in Mieronice.[103] When my retainer Orłowski arrived at Śladkowski's manor,[104] Śladkowski went to his wife, who was still in bed, and told her the news. She jumped out of bed, dashed out in her nightgown, and asked: "What are you doing in Olszówka, Orłowski? Are you telling me of some dream? I don't believe this." Orłowski answered her: "Not a dream, Your Ladyship, because it seems that by now they have left for the church." "If so, then write a letter as fast as possible! Run to his Lordship, beg him to wait until we arrive. Even if this costs me my neck, the wedding shall not take place!" Orłowski took the letter and rushed on his way. Meanwhile, Śladkowski's household was in a bustle: "Harness the carriage!" "Get dressed!"

Orłowski came galloping and found us already in the

[102]The Castellan of Sochaczew.
[103]Mieronice, a village in the district of Jędrzejów with a parish to which Olszówka belonged.
[104]Orłowski, the retainer, was evidently delivering the letter.

church. I read the letter, to which the Castellan's wife herself
had added a postscript : "I beg you for the love of God, I beseech you, to postpone the wedding until my arrival. It will be
more to your advantage." I surrendered to the Will of God, and
prayed : "My Almighty God in the Holy Trinity, I implore
You, oh, my Creator, to condescend to fill my heart with the
Grace of the Most Holy Spirit so that I may know whether or
not this marriage is in accordance with Your Most Holy Will,
whether I should wait or not." Meanwhile the Mass had ended.
I said to my future wife : "Your Ladyship, what am I to do ?
Should I or should I not wait ?" She said : "For Heaven's sake,
let's not wait. They will spoil things for us." We went up to the
altar. The *Veni Creator*[105] began to be played, and we were
married. We were already leaving the altar when Śladkowski's
band of musicians rushed in through the door. "We are at the
service of Your Lordship," they said. I replied : "You have
come too late to play at the altar, but you shall make up for it
at the dining table."

We went home with the guests, and only then the Ślad-
kowskis arrived. There were accusations, anger, fury. "Is this
the way it was to be ? You could at least have stayed the wedding for us." I made excuses, saying that their letter arrived after
the wedding, but all was in vain. They shouted angrily : "Why
didn't you stop off at our estate on your way there ?" Śladkowski was appeased soon after and after a few drinks was merry.
He said to his wife : "Let it be, now ! Evidently, such was
God's Will. May God bless him." But she was still angry. She
did not want to eat, made accusations, and did not dance until
the following day. In spite of all, we were gay. And it had to
be, for such was God's Will, though not men's. May eternal
reverence and glory be to His Name ! And I would have surely
been content with this marriage, if God had given me a son by
her. But I did not get any, and much trouble befell me because
of the interests of her children, about which I shall write
below.

I found in Olszówka an abundant and varied grain harvest,

[105]It is usually sung in Catholic ritual.

but what of it when excessive cheapness prevailed ! The lease-hold expired soon after. It was difficult to preserve the grain. A bushel was worthless, and the grains just wasted away.

A week after the wedding, Pan Komorowski, the vice-starost of Nowe Miasto, came to propose matrimony to my wife and almost arrived in time for the wedding. He and some friends stopped in Wodzisław. The inn-keeper said to him : "Will your Lordship order meat for dinner ?" "No, because I intend to dine in Olszówka." The Jew said : "I would sooner advise you to dine here, because there your Lordship will not be a welcome guest." "Why ?" "Because someone else is already the master there. It is already a week since her Lady-ship married." Komorowski was greatly perplexed then. He ate his fill, stayed the night, and left the following day. Later he and my wife sent back to each other *symbola amicitiae*,[106] such as rings, except for a pillow, which he did not want to give back. Later, when we had become acquainted, he congratulated me and said : "Since Your Lordship got what I liked, I shall not return the pillow, since you got the head which slept on it." He was always a good friend toward me. Soon after, he married a widow, a Pani Brzezińska, who was such an evil woman that he considered himself an unhappy man, and vowed to become a priest if God freed him from her. And it so happened, for she died, and he became a priest and died soon after, too.

The funeral of Queen Ludwika took place later in Kra-ków.[107] I attended it with my wife. As soon as we had arrived there, we made our testaments. She, *cum assistentia*[108] of her brothers, wanted to bequeath her dowry to me. I did not want this, however, and said : "I shall acquire wealth on my own, as long as I have something to work with." People were amazed at that, saying it was something new under the sun that some-one who married a widow would scorn her generosity. Others praised my behavior, however. I saw many of my relatives in Kraków at the funeral. They were all displeased with my mar-riage, as I lived so far away from them now.

[106]The objects indicating their affection.
[107]September 22. Czubek, *Pam.*, p. 436, note 1.
[108]In the presence.

The Field Hetmans Potocki and Lubomirski died this year.
Also a battle took place at Podhajce,[100] or, in plain words, our
army with the field hetman Sobieski was besieged by the
Cossacks and Tatars.[110] God liberated our people, however.
The army later made camp at Otynia,[111] where their resistance
prolonged the campaign. A commission met afterwards. The
delegates from Kraków began to slight me during my first
appearance there, calling me a newcomer. On that, I hit one in
the head, another in the nose, a third in the back—in this way,
I won peace for myself, and they no longer called me names.

[100]A city at Koropce, 48 kilometers southwest of Tarnopol.
[110]From the fourth to the nineteenth of October.
[111]A town 22 kilometers southeast from Stanisławów.

ANNO DOMINI 1668

By the grace of God I began the year happily in Olszówka. I contracted with Pan Stanisław Szembek, the burgrave of Kraków,[1] a lease on Miławczyce and Biegłów[2] at 4000[3] *per annum*,[4] for our lease in Olszówka had expired. We transported grain to the two estates after the feast of the Three Kings and by the grace of God we took over happily on the third Sunday of Lent.[5] But I came upon years during which prices were very low and the lease was demanding. Even parsley, cabbage and chicken eggs were counted as income. I kept the lease for only two years. I lost on it more than 2000.

There I married Jadwiga Łącka, my step-daughter, to Samuel Dembowski, a nephew of mine. They lived with me for a year. Later as part of their dowry, I had my father yield to them Kamień.[6] I established them in their first home there and took my parents to live with me.

The Diet came to session, during which the King *proposuit*

---

[1]In Kraków he was a high official appointed by the King. In some instances also an assistant to a starost or castellan.
[2]Villages 19 km southwest from Pińczów, and 15 km east of Wiślica. Czapliński, *Pam.*, p. 415, note 1.
[3]Most likely zlotys.
[4]In Polish in the original.
[5]March 4 at the time. Czapliński, *Pam.*, p. 415, note 3.
[6]A village by that name. Since there are many villages by that name in Poland, its exact location cannot be definitely established. Czapliński, *Pam.*, p. 415, note 8.

benevolam regni abdicationem.[7] The blind advisor,[8] *quidem*[9] for the assurance of a peaceful life in old age had constantly urged the King to do so. In his heart however the Archbishop had hoped to put a Frenchman on the Polish throne. Even the King himself had silently agreed to this and was abdicating for this very reason. The Commonwealth was on guard however and endeavored that this should bear no fruit. The blind Archbishop knew that *stante abdicatione*[10] the entire Polish government would depend on him. He insisted on the abdication, since he could attain his goal more easily, being *alter rex.*[11] God willed it otherwise however.

[7]Voluntarily proposed his abdication. The Diet took place from the twenty-seventh of August until the sixteenth of September, 1668. Czapliński, *Pam.*, p. 416, note 9.
[8]Archbishop Prażmowski.
[9]Who.
[10]In case of abdication.
[11]Inter-rex. The King abdicated on September 16, 1668, and ended his rather prophetic and pathetic speech of the day with the following words : "People of Poland, . . . It is now two hundred and eighty years that you have been governed by my family. The reign of my ancestors is past and mine is going to expire. Fatigued by the labors of war, the cares of the cabinet, and the weight of age ; oppressed with the burdens and solitudes of a reign of more than twenty-one years, I your king and father, return into your hands what the world esteems above all things, a crown ; and choose for my throne six feet of earth, where I shall sleep in peace with my fathers." Fletcher, Esq., p. 89. His reign was one of the most disastrous reigns in Polish history.

All the estates had tried to persuade the King to the contrary. They reminded him of the enormous indignation and the affront to the fatherland, which as yet it had not suffered from any other monarch. They reminded him of the disapproval by other nations. For until now they had nothing to reproach us for. We neither killed nor drove any of our kings out of the country. We bore patiently with each king whom God had given us for as long as He had left him with us, even though there have been some rulers arousing discontent. When none of the benevolent *persuasiones*[12] brought results, Ożga,[13] the chamberlain of Lwów, began to speak. I stood near him and I could hear everything well. The white-haired old man began to speak *zelose pro patria et maiestate* :[14] "Gracious King! Do not cast into perplexity yourself and us, your land and our land, since you were raised and placed on its throne by this fatherland! You were born here just as we were. You were raised with us and with us you have spent many years. You were called in free election to reign over us. Do not abandon us." Many cried, among them the King himself. When persuasions and petitions failed to yield results, the same Ożga said, deeply moved : "Gracious King! Since you no longer want to be our king, be our brother !" Later some joked and laughed at the King's indiscretion that he yielded to persuasions. Diverse opinions were voiced as to his title and form of address. Not Crown Prince, because he had already been a king, but rather Pan Snopkowski, *ex ratione*[15] "*Snopek*"[16] was his coat of arms.

Later the Diet adjourned. Kazimierz came to Kraków and lived in the tenement house at Krzysztofory.[17] He already began to regret his behavior but, not wanting to show it, began

---

[12]Persuasions.

[13]Piotr Ożga, who died three years later. Czapliński, *Pam.*, p. 417, note 21.

[14]Ardently in the cause of the fatherland and His Majesty.

[15]Because.

[16]I.e., of the Vasa dynasty. *Snopek* literally means little sheaf in Polish.

[17]In Kraków, the property of W. Wodzicki. Czapliński, *Pam.*, p. 417, note 25.

to drink, dance and be merry. He went to France later, where he was received with enthusiasm at first. But when the news arrived of King Michał's election, showing that things were not going the way France had hoped, the French began to esteem the ex-King less. He no longer enjoyed such comforts as he had done in the beginning. He felt anguished and said : "The Poles did this to spite me, when they elected the lad as King." He regretted his decision and he was bitter at those who had brought him to it. He recalled the speeches of his benevolent advisors. Later he fell into affliction and despair, was no longer in such gay spirits as before and died shortly after.[18]

So, Gracious King, such is the *effectum* of listening to dishonest advisors, who brought you to this with their advice guided not by your welfare, but only by their own interests. You established these people in the Senate. You granted them the highest eminence. You made lords out of them, but they have no conscience and no God in their hearts—and where there is no God, it is difficult to expect reason, *difficile est ex animo resipiscere.*[19] Until the bitter end each strived to attain his own interest. Even though they saw that they sinned against God and against the law, they did not care ; they tried to justify their behavior and said that they were doing the right thing. Each said that this was to the advantage of the Commonwealth. He said that the *status*[20] had ordained it so. But wait, oh statesmen ! *Caelestis status*[21] shall censure *terrenos status*[22] and shall judge it, you shall see !

According to the custom during *interregnum, iudicia*[23] ceased all over Poland. Justice was rendered by special courts,[24]

---

[18]December 16, 1672, in the modest Abbey of St. Germain near Paris. Czubek, *Pam.,* p. 440, note 4.

[19]It is difficult to make one see reason.

[20]Reason of state.

[21]The heavenly reason of state.

[22]The earthly reason.

[23]Trials.

[24]*Vehmgerichte.* During the *interregnum* a vigilance committee of the nobility was set up in order to preserve order and safety. This committee also elected judges, since all the courts ceased to function with the death of the King. Czubek, *Pam.,* p. 441, note 6.

as it was customary during the period of mourning of the Polish Commonwealth. *Promotores abdicationis*[25] rejoiced, for they hoped that now surely they would attain their goal. The *director monoculus*[26] triumphed *absolute*.[27] In the newspapers he already showed firm and invariable hope that the crown would go to a French candidate. He saw that the choice of a king rested in his hands. He boasted that from a poor rector he had turned into the *inter-rex*.[28] He saw that he had many followers, who were fed at the same public trough as he was. He rejoiced just as if he had attained everything. God willed it otherwise, however.

[25]The authors of King Jan Kazimierz' abdication.
[26]The one-eyed leader. Reference to Primate Prażmowski who took over the office during the interregnum.
[27]Completely.
[28]Prażmowski assumed his office on September 17, 1668. Reddaway, p. 532.

ANNO DOMINI 1669

I lived in Miławczyce and kept a leasehold on Smogorzów. My *collaterales*[1] began to slight me, since I was an *a(d)vena*[2] from a different voivodeship. I endured this patiently at first because I did not have an opportunity for retaliation and more so because I decided to put things off, realizing that such was usually the case when someone from another voivodeship settled *inter sympatriotas*.[3] When an occasion presented itself for retaliation however, I did not fail to retort.

Once Pan Stanisław Szembek, the Burgrave of Kraków, and Pan Franciszek Żelecki, both relatives of my wife on her mother's side, came to visit me. They brought a relative of theirs along, Kordowski,[4] a great drunkard. I was glad to see them, but I was very angry with Pan Kordowski, because he pinpricked the Mazovians constantly. He said they were born blind, that they were insignificant people, *et varia*.[5] The other two relatives enjoyed this very much and chimed in with him in order to confound me. They brought him deliberately for this purpose. When a calf's head was served he would say that this was the Mazovian Pope. When he saw the yellow piece of dough under the roast veal he would say that these were the

[1]Neighbors.
[2]Newcomer.
[3]Among our local people.
[4]Perhaps Kargowski Count Ostoja. Czubek, *Pam.*, p. 442, note 10. Kasper Niesiecki, the author of the Polish armorial, is not familiar with such a name.
[5]And other things.

Mazovian Hosts. Indeed he indulged in grave provocations. Realizing that these hints were directed toward me I said to him, "Pan brother, you should not refer to the Mazovians as night approaches because you might see them in your dreams and because there are none here. But since I am a neighbor[6] of the Mazovians I must answer your Lordship in their behalf." He still persisted, however. After supper Pan Szembek began to dance. Żelecki said to me: "Let's go and join him." I answered, "Fine." We began to dance the "Great Dance."[7] Shortly after, Kordowski stopped in the dance-line and began to sing:

The moustaches of our Mazovians are salty
From eating millet groats, so they soak them in beer ![8]

He repeated this song several times and I already felt angry. I took Żelecki in my arms, just as one would a child, for he was of short stature. Everyone assumed that I did this out of affection for him and I carried him so. When I came up to Kordowski, who was still singing this song, I hit him with Żelecki in the chest and he fell on his back—a man as huge as an oak tree—he somehow bumped the back of his head against a bench and was knocked unconscious. Also Żelecki could not get up since I hit Kordowski with him with all my strength. We grabbed our swords. Only several of their retainers were in the room. The others were drunk and asleep somewhere in the house. I chased them out of the room. Then I turned back to Szembek and put the point of my sword against his fat stomach. He cried out: "Stop, what have I done to you?"

[6]Pasek's native voivodeship of Rawa had been annexed to the Polish Crown in 1462, while the remaining part of the Duchy of Mazovia was not included until 1529. Czapliński, *Pam.*, p. 421, note 11. Pasek therefore considered himself a neighbor of the Mazovians only.

[7]The polonaise was called the "Great Dance," but also Oskar Kolberg's *Mazur* was later referred to as such. Czapliński, *Pam.*, p. 421, note 13. Kolberg (1814–1890) was a Polish ethnographer and composer of Polish national dances. He was also the author of ethnological works on Poland and of an edition of Polish folk songs (1857).

[8]Six stanzas of this popular song were published in "A Villager's Kermis", *Kiermasz wieśniacki*, (1613–1615). Pasek quotes with slight variation, the beginning of the third strophe. W. Czapliński, *Pam.*, p. 421, note 15.

And the other two still lay on the ground. Only then I said :
"I wish you would go to the devil ! What did you come here
for ? In order to confound me ? I saw that all day long you
were insulting me through this drunkard. I endured it patiently,
but I can bear it no longer." The women jumped to our side :
"Stop ! Stop !" We let each other go. They began to lift Żelecki from the floor and to revive Kordowski. They poured
liquor in his nose, forced his teeth open and later fetched the
barber-surgeon, since he had cut his head on the bench.

Pan Szembek and Pan Żelecki went to bed then ; I kept
drinking to keep my spirits up and I also ordered drinks to be
brought for my orderlies. Later my lads did funny things to
my guests' drunken orderlies ; they lighted papers and stuck
them in their noses, smeared their moustaches with various
things, and inflicted on them whatever discomforts they could
possibly think of, as those orderlies lay like blocks of wood
in the halls and other places.

We apologized to each other next day. They have treated
me with great reverence and respect ever since that day. They
were ashamed of this incident, as it became known among the
neighbors. They did not know what to do about it, however.
They began to think more highly of me.

When I lived in Miławczyce—prices were low and the
lease appraised too high—I lost more than two thousand zlotys
on the leasehold. I was glad however of being able to hunt
a large number of foxes with three greyhounds and no hunting
dogs. I used to bring three or four foxes home a day.

Later the election of the King was to take place. The
Archbishop sent manifestos to the voivodeships. He encouraged
the estates of the Polish Commonwealth to a speedy election, wishing that such be accomplished *per deputatos.*[9] The
voivodeships did not approve of this, however, and ordered
everybody to mount horses, just as if they were going to war.
They knew the Archbishop's disposition. They knew that he
would not depart from his French policy until his death. They
also knew that many new candidates were getting ready for

[9]Through the deputies.

this honor, as for example the Prince of Longueville,[10] the Prince of Neuburg,[11] and the Prince of Lorraine.[12]

The voivodeships assembled in an orderly fashion. Then they departed for Warsaw. Since my wife was from the voivodeship of Kraków, I went with those under the flag of that district over which Achacy Pisarski[13] presided. We went to Wysimierzyce[14] where we stopped for over a week. *Primis diebus Iulii,*[15] we arrived in Warsaw. Later representatives of the various voivodeships, great armies, lordly retinues, infantries, and quite a number of distinguished men arrived as if shaken out of a sleeve. Bogusław Radziwiłł[16] alone had about eight thousand very well equipped men with him. The so-called Prussian band, which played on the bassoons in front of the heavy German cavalry, was then heard for the first time in Poland.

The Archbishop's mouth dropped open at the sight of all this and he began to doubt the success of his schemes. Nevertheless he persisted in his endeavors and cherished hope.

When the sessions of the chamber of deputies began, however, different opinions were heard, that this one or that one would be king, but no one mentioned the one who was destined by God Himself to be king. All the candidates sent their delegates there to act in their behalf, and hoped that things would turn out according to their wishes. But he[17] did not

[10]Charles, Count St. Paul, Prince de Longueville, the nephew of de Condé.

[11]Philipp-Wilhelm, a nephew of Jan Kazimierz. He had the support of Austria, France, Sweden, and Brandenburg but France secretly promoted de Condé and the Hapsburgs, Duke Charles of Lorraine. Carsten, p. 560.

[12]Charles IV, who later married Queen Eleonora Marie, the widow of King Michał.

[13]He later became the starost of Wolbron. Czubek, *Pam.*, p. 446, note 1.

[14]A town on the Pilica river, some thirty-three kilometers northwest of Radom.

[15]In the first days of July, undoubtedly a mistake, should be June. Czapliński, *Pam.*, p. 421, note 29.

[16](1620–1669). Well known Swedish adherent during the Swedish invasion of Poland and the head of the Lithuanian Calvinists.

[17]Prince Michał Wiśniowiecki.

anticipate anything, for he knew that he had not the slightest chance to be king. The French representatives, as if intimidated, worked secretly. Those of the Prince of Neuburg and of the Duke of Lorraine worked openly. There was not even a mention made of a Polish competitor, however. In the foreign camp they offered posts and made presents. They squandered money and gave plenty to drink. They entertained and made promises. He, however, neither gave anything nor promised anything; he had not aspired to the crown but attained it.

After several sessions had taken place and after we had received the corps of the foreign delegates we heard each envoy's declaration of his candidate's intentions toward the Polish Commonwealth. The candidate from Lorraine appealed to us the most *ex ratione*[18] he was martial and a young lord. His delegate also used the following words at the end of his oration: *"Quotquot sunt inimici vestri, cum omnibus in hac arena certabit."*[19] The session was adjourned until the next day.[20]

On the following day[21] the senators assembled beneath the tent.[22] After the armies had covered the fields, different opinions were voiced. Various candidates were praised. A nobleman, standing in stirrups amidst the representatives of his voivodeship of Łęczyca, right next to the chamber of deputies, spoke up: "Followers of Condé! Bullets will fly over your heads if you utter a word!" A senator answered him *crude.*[23] They began to shoot. The senators ran between the carriages or crowded under the chairs. An uproar and a turmoil resulted. Some companies galloped from the side toward the infantry and forced it to disperse. The chamber of deputies was surrounded. People began to make threats: "Traitors! We shall destroy you all! We shall not let you out of here! In vain have you misled the Polish Commonwealth! We shall provide other senators. We shall choose a king *ex gremio*,[24] such a one whom God will make pleasing to our hearts." The session ended with a tragic spectacle. The officers brought their troops to order.

[18]Because.
[19]No matter how many enemies the Polish Commonwealth might have, he will fight them all. The envoy of the Duke of Lorraine, Count Chavagnac, had an audience on the twelfth of June. Czapliński, *Pam.*, p. 425, note 39.
[20]The events discussed above actually took place on June 17. Czapliński, *Pam.*, p. 425, note 40.
[21]Actually five days later.
[22]A special tent or shed erected in the electoral field.
[23]Sharply.
[24]From our midst.

The companies returned to their posts in the field. The bishops
and senators, half dead, crawled out from under the chairs and
ran between the carriages. They rode back to their quarters.
All those who were camping in the election field went back to
their tents.

No session was held on the next day, as all the gentlemen
were recovering from the shock. They drank medicated and
soothing potions out of fright.[25] Neither did the voivodeships
come out into the field but stayed in camp.

On the sixteenth of July the voivodeships sent word to
the Archbishop asking him to come to the election field and,
conforming to law, to promote *continuationem operis.*[26] He
answered : "I will not come as I am not *securus*[28] of my safety,
and the other senators will not come." Word was sent to him
again that the army was assembling around the tent.[29] And they
added : "Whoever is virtuous and a senator and whoever wants
to come with us, let him do so. We shall choose a king for
ourselves. All those who do not come we shall consider traitors
to the fatherland ; what the consequence of this will be, let him
guess !" Then the voivodeships took up a position about one-
eighth of a league from the tent. The senators no longer
assembled under the tent but with us. Warszycki, our Castellan
of Kraków, and other senators came to us. Only then a debate
started about the recent events. The Castellan of Kraków said :
"With His Holy Name, for such was his saying—I praise this
action. It demonstrates Polish dignity, since all *nobilitas*[30]
should elect the king *non certus numerus personarum* ![31] I am
not angry about it, even though bullets whistled over my head,

---

[25]The session of the eighteenth of June did not take place because of
a storm and not because of the reason given by Pasek. A special
meeting of the senate did take place however. Czapliński, *Pam.*, p. 426,
note 48.

[26]On the sixteenth of July. Wrong date. Should be June 19. Czapliński,
Pam., p. 426, note 49.

[27]Further course of activities.

[28]Certain.

[29]Senatorial.

[30]The gentry.

[31]And not only a certain number of people !

for I know that the *malevolentia*[32] of those people, already apparent to the entire world, *haeret in pectore*[33] of every nobleman. Moreover, if I happen to live longer, I shall insist that sessions of the Diets be conducted on horseback, otherwise our deputies will not be able to safeguard the freedom which our ancestors have earned with their blood." He cited examples from history demonstrating the golden freedom which *floruit*[34] as long as the Poles had conducted their elections in such a way. "Also now we must arouse ourselves from sleep. We must forsake leisure *pro tempore*."[35]

Suddenly the delegation from Great Poland sent word to us : "What are we to do, for the senators ignore us ?" We immediately answered them with the following message : "Don't worry. We have our own senators and we are moving to the tent where we shall confer among ourselves." The delegations set out *ad locum electionis*[36] and stopped there. Oh, how the coaches then came rolling from Warsaw, some at a trot and others at a gallop. They rushed to the election field in all haste (since they expected that their voivodeships would beg them to come and would not start anything without them) ! Later the Archbishop came also, after he had realized that we would not bow to him and had no intention of apologizing for the sharp words.

Then the council began, but it was no longer as well attended as before, for whoever happened to be a great coward pretended to be ill, being afraid of another such commotion or even a worse one ; others really fell ill out of fright or because their fat bellies had been shaken. One of them supposedly had tripped while trying to escape over a wagon pole ; he had almost broken his neck. His Haiduks scarcely managed to lift him off the ground and stand him on his legs again. When the senators took their places they sat there like convalescents but did not speak. Someone remarked from the crowd : "Gen-

[32]Wickedness.
[33]Sticks in the heart.
[34]Flourished.
[35]For awhile.
[36]For the place of election.

tlemen ! We did not come here to be idle. We shall not
accomplish anything by just looking at each other in silence.
Since his Excellency, the Pater of Prażmów, did not duly
exercise the function pertaining to his office, we ask his Excellency, the Castellan of Kraków, as the first senator *in
regno*,[37] to take over the leadership. We are not electing a pope
here. We can do without a priest."

The Archbishop[38] rose abruptly and began to speak : "Oh,
Gentlemen ! As long as I live I shall not cease to serve our
fatherland, and *specialiter*[39] each one of you gentlemen on all
the occasions *quae sunt mei muneris*.[40] Now let us begin happily and may God's blessing be upon us, for which I have
begged Him *cum toto clero*[41] on this day. May He condescend
to incline the hearts of all of us through the Grace of the Holy
Spirit to act in such a way as to contribute to His Holy Glory
and to the welfare of our fatherland," *et similia*.[42] "Gentlemen,"
he added, "nominate whomever among so many worthy candidates you like, and I, the older brother and servant of your
Lordships, shall approve." Voices were raised *pro et contra*.[43]
The candidates and we began to harp upon each other's arguments : "I am for this one." "I am also for this one." "I like
that one." "I also like that one." The arguments went back
and forth.

While this was taking place the people from Great Poland
were already shouting : "*Vivat rex* !"[44] A number of us rushed
to find out whose name they had called. We learned that it was
the name of the Duke of Lorraine. But in the voivodeships of
Łęczyca and Brześć Kujawski, this was proposed : "We do not
need a rich lord as whoever shall become our king will

[37]In the kingdom.
[38]According to Czapliński, Prażmowski was not present on that day.
The *Veni Creator* was sung by Wierzbowski, the Bishop of Poznań.
Czapliński, *Pam.*, p. 428, note 66.
[39]Especially.
[40]Pertaining to my office.
[41]With all the clergy.
[42]And so on.
[43]For and against.
[44]Long live the King !

immediately turn rich. We do not need anyone who is related to other monarchs[45] because this would be a *periculum libertatis*,[46] but we need *virum fortem, virum bellicosum.*[47] If Czarniecki were still alive he would have certainly ascended our throne, but since God has taken him away from us let us elect Polanowski,[48] his pupil." While this was being discussed I hurried *per curiositatem*[49] to the group from Sandomierz which stood closest to us. I discovered that they wished there *de sanguine gentis.*[50] They said : "It should not take long to find a king, since we already have him among us. When we consider the greatness and *merita*[51] of the late Prince Hieremi Wiśniowiecki's[52] character and his great merits to the fatherland, it would be right and fair to repay it to his descendant.[53] Here is His Highness Prince Michał.[54] Why should we not nominate him ? Does he not come from a long line of great princes ? Is he not worthy of the crown ?"

Meanwhile the Prince sat among the nobility, silent and hunched up.[55] I rushed back to my group and said : "Gentlemen, already among a number of voivodeships things look favorable for a Piast."[56] The Castellan of Kraków asked me : "For which one ?" I said : "For Polanowski in one group and

[45]Hitherto only members of ruling dynasties could be considered. Carsten, p. 560.
[46]Danger to our freedom.
[47]A brave and martial man.
[48]Aleksander Polanowski, Lieutenant of Adam Działyński's armored company in Denmark, under the command of Czarniecki, later colonel. He fought with Sobieski at Chocim ; died as Castellan of Lublin. Czubek, *Pam.*, p. 451, note 8.
[49]Out of curiosity.
[50]I.e., one of Polish blood.
[51]Virtues.
[52]Jeremi Wiśniowiecki (d. 1651), Voivode of Ruthenia ; was famous for his great military achievements in the wars with the Cossacks. Czapliński, *Pam.*, p. 429, note 80.
[53]Michał Wiśniowiecki. His mother was Gryzelda Zamoyska, member of one of the most prominent families in Poland.
[54]Prince Michał Korybut Wiśniowiecki (1638–1673) ; he was thirty-one years old at the time.
[55]Chrapowicki also describes the incident.
[56]Piast—the first dynasty of Polish kings ; here, a ruler of Polish origin.

for Wiśniowiecki in another." Meanwhile the group of Sandomierz shouted : *"Vivat Piast* !"[57] Dębicki, the chamberlain,
flung his cap in the air and shouted : *"Vivat Piast* !" *"Vivat
rex Michał* !"[58] Also our Cracovians joined in : *"Vivat Piast* !"
A few of us ran to the other voivodeships with the news and
shouted : *"Vivat Piast* !" The people from Łęczyca and Kujawy, thinking that this was meant for their Polanowski, immediately began to shout the same ; other voivodeships also
did. By the time I returned to my group, Wiśniowiecki had
already been taken by his arms and led to the chamber of
deputies.

Our elders from Kraków contradicted and objected, since
they had taken much money from other candidates and had
received great promises from them, especially Pisarski and Lipski.[59] They said : "For Heaven's sake ! What are we doing ?
Have we gone mad ? Let's stop this ! This cannot be !" The
Castellan of Kraków had already left us, for the newly nominated king was a relative of his. Many other senators joined
their opposition. Some raised objections, while others remained
silent. Pisarski said to me (because he respected me): "Dear Sir
brother ! What do you think of this situation ?" I answered :
"I believe in what God has inclined my heart to do :
"Vivat rex Michał !" I left the ranks at that and followed those
from Sandomierz. Everyone hastily followed me, even the
standard-bearer with their fans, all except Pisarski, who only
struck his head with his cap and rode to the side.

We escorted Wiśniowiecki to the senatorial seats. Once
there, *gratulationes* were conveyed, to the joy of the good men
and the sorrow of the evil ones.

The Archbishop performed all the ceremonies which per-
tained to his office *circa inaugurationem*[60] as well as the church

[57]Long live the Piast !
[58]Marcin Michał Dębicki, the chamberlain of Sandomierz. Czubek,
Pam., p. 452, note 7. "Long live the Piast ! Long live King Michał !"
[59]Jan Lipski, the starost of Czchów, who headed the delegation from
Czchów and Sadeck, later the son-in-law of Wacław Potocki. Czubek,
Pam., p. 453, note 2.
[60]Regarding the inauguration. The coronation took place on September
29, 1669.

ceremonies in which thanksgiving prayers were offered, but with what heart, with what reluctance ! It was just as if one had harnessed a wolf to a plough and had compelled it to plow. What happened later *in publicum*,[61] what was done to the new king I shall write below.

By the next day the King was richer by several millions ; so many presents he received, couches, harnesses, tapestries, silver, and various objects of value. Even the delegates of those princes who had competed for the crown gave him presents. Suffice it to say that God had inclined everyone's heart so much toward him that each brought his most valuable possession. They brought not only beautiful horses and steeds, but also armor—even if it was nothing more than a pair of pistols mounted with ebony or ivory.

The *nobilitas*[62] went home *sparsim*,[63] no longer under the flag of their voivodeships. I lingered with my countrymen from Rawa for awhile and then I also rode home.

The coronation took place on the twenty-ninth of September in Kraków and was attended by a great number of people. Immediately after, the sessions of the Coronation Diet[64] began, the outcome of which was bad, as they were broken up by Olizar,[65] the delegate from the voivodeship of Kiev. His veto was attributed to a plot.

The army was encamped at Bochryń[66] at the time but did not engage in any clash with the enemy.

After the sessions of the Diet were broken up, Father Andrzej Olszowski,[67] *nihilominus*,[68] the Bishop of Chełm, was

---

[61]Publicly.
[62]Gentry.
[63]Separately.
[64]The Diet was in session from the first of October until the twelfth of November, 1669. Czapliński, *Pam.*, p. 432, note 98.
[65]Jan Olizar, later chamberlain of Kiev. Czubek, *Pam.*, p. 454, note 7.
[66]A town on the Horyń, north of Ostróg.
[67]Bishop of Chełm ; author of a pamphlet and deputy chancellor of the Treasury of the Crown ; later archbishop of Gniezno. Czapliński, *Pam.*, p. 432, note 104.
[68]Nevertheless.

sent to the German Emperor to ask for the hand of his sister[69]
in marriage to King Michał.[70] The request was easily granted,
since this was in accord with the Emperor's wishes and had
been suggested by him.

[69]Eleonora Maria, the Archduchess of Austria.
[70]The Bishop left for Vienna on the twenty-seventh of November, 1669.
Czapliński, *Pam.*, p. 432, note 106.

ANNO DOMINI 1670

I began the year in Miławczyce, but in the middle of Lent I moved to Smogorzów, because I was not satisfied with that leasehold.

The royal wedding[1] took place in Częstochowa[2] with a large attendance of our Poles. The Germans made a rather foolish show, however, and the bride was not given away like an emperor's daughter.

When I lived in Smogorzów I involved myself for the first time in a river shipment of grain. Being a novice at this, I depended on the older skippers, who warned me that as a greenhorn I would be hit in the purse. With God's grace, however, I sold at a better price, at 40 zlotys higher than they did, and this in the following way : Piegłowski, the Starost of Ujście,[3] and Opacki,[4] the Cupbearer of Warsaw, angered the merchants, who plotted not to buy from them out of spite. At the same time they paid me, one of their group, at 150 zlotys for wheat to spite them. Pan Jarlach purchased it from me, while the others had to beg the merchants to buy. They were paid then at 110 zlotys. So those who had threatened me with being taken in were taken in themselves.

[1] The bride came accompanied by her Imperial mother. This marriage created much discontent among the Poles. The Hapsburg Empire had three Eleonoras, the Imperial mother, the Queen, i.e., Leopold's wife, and Eleonora his sister who after the death of King Michał became the wife of Duke Charles of Lorraine.

[2] On February 28. Czubek, *Pam.*, p. 455, note 4.

[3] Ujście Solne. Czubek, *Pam.*, p. 455, note 5.

[4] Wojciech Opacki. Czubek, *Pam.*, p. 456, note 1.

ANNO DOMINI 1671

I began the year in Smogorzów,[1] but in the middle of Lent I moved to Skrzypiów and paid Myszkowski,[2] the Castellan of Bełz, 10,000 fl. for these estates and for Zakrzów. I leased Smogorzów for a year to Pan Trembicki, who had held Skrzypiów before that, since he had no place to go. Also in the same year Myszkowski drew up a contract with me for the leasehold of Olszówka and Brześć, but since he could not reclaim these estates from the hands of the Chełmski brothers, I had to wait for them in Skrzypiów for almost six years, even though I spent 21,000 zlotys on them *in deportionem*[4] of various debts on the entailed estates. How much trouble and expense I incurred because of these estates I shall relate below.

In Skrzypiów things went well for me and I was satisfied with that leasehold. Also this year I sailed to Gdańsk.[5] I sold grain to Pan Wandern, a very honorable merchant.

This year the army was stationed at Trembowla.[6] At Kal-

[1]A village near Pińczów.
[2]Jan Aleksander Myszkowski, Chamberlain of Bełz at the time, Castellan, in 1674. A colonel and a brother of the deceased Franciszek. Czapliński, *Pam.*, p. 434, note 2.
[3]Marcjan, Lord High Steward of Sandomierz, Krzysztof, Lord High Steward of Kraków, and Andrzej; they were brothers. Czubek, *Pam.*, p. 456, note 4.
[4]In payment.
[5]On a river transport of grain.
[6]A town and castle in Podolia, Poland, on the Gniezna river.

nik[7] the Crimean Tatars were attacked vigorously and later it came to a battle at Trościaniec.[8]

At the request of his Lordship Myszkowski I paid off the entailment debts and gave the Captain of Horse Szandorowski[9] 4000 fl., her Ladyship Miklaszowska 3000 fl., his Highness the Prince Aleksander of Ostróg[10] 3000, and the chamberlain of Bełz himself 3000 for the dispatching of men into camp.

The pre-Diet regional council meetings were held *in Novembre.*[11] The Warsaw Diet met *in Januario.*[12]

---

[7]A city in the Ukraine, where on October 27, 1671 Sobieski defeated the Tatars. Czubek, *Pam.,* p. 457, note 2.

[8]Village in the district of Jaworów in Podolia, Poland. Korzon knows nothing of such a battle. Czapliński, *Pam.,* p. 435, note 9.

[9]Teodor Szandorowski, Minister of Finance of Brasławice, and Captain of Horse of an armored squadron. J. Czubek, *Pam.,* p. 457, note 5. He became famous at Rudnik, on the San, where he took the Swedes by surprise in 1656 ; a very brave soldier.

[10]Died 1673.

[11]In November.

[12]In January.

ANNO DOMINI 1672

I lived in Skrzypiów, since my wife never wanted to live in Smogorzów *ex ratione*[1] it was rumored to be a *locus fatalis*[2] where either the landlady or the landlord died. In spite of that I lived there often, and God preserved me even though I was for twenty years the master there.

Royal letters came out for a levy *en masse*. The Turks set out with a great military force. Our army, under the command of Pan Łużecki,[3] the Castellan of Podlasie, was at Batoh.[4] The little blind eye[5] did not cease to plot and wanted to throw another king off the throne, on which God Himself had placed him. Altogether, there existed great and terrible *inter viscera motus*.[6]

Rączki[7] fell this year to the Łącki family. I received, *per exdivisionem*,[8] the children's share. I bought a second share

[1]Because.
[2]An unlucky place.
[3]Karol Stanisław Łużecki, in 1682 the Voivode of Podolia. Czubek, *Pam.*, p. 458, note 6.
[4]In the Bracław territory in the Ukraine ; Łużecki suffered a defeat on July 18, 1672 not far from Batoh at Ładyżyn. Czubek, *Pam.*, p. 458, note 5.
[5]Prażmowski.
[6]Unrest within the country.
[7]A village on the Pilica in the voivodeship of Łódź.
[8]Through partition, i.e., inheritance. Jan Łącki, the brother of Pasek's wife's first husband, died childless. Only one share of the inheritance was due Pasek's stepchildren, but Pasek illegally set himself up in possession of the entire estate, which led to a five-year-long lawsuit, the records of which are still preserved.

from the co-heirs, both of which shares I relinquished to my wife's daughter Jadwiga, who had married Samuel Dembowski, my nephew. I relinquished those out of my own free will and demanded nothing for them, even though I had incurred many expenses in the course of several years in the upkeep of these shares. How much trouble, riding to and from the squabbles, brawls and duels, I had on this account, I do not count.

I leased Smogorzów for a year to Pani Wojciechowa Gołuchowska, a comely widow. She married Pan Tomasz Olszanowski there.

I rode from home into camp. I halted near Kosina,[9] where the voivodeship of Kraków was assembling, and from there we went to Gołąb.[10] The King came to our camp. All the voivodeships concentrated there.

The Turks had already captured Kamieniec.[11] *Verius dicam*[12] they did not really capture it, but bought it from the traitors to our fatherland. They also conquered all of Podolia and the Ukraine without pulling out a sword. The *Lipkis*, or rather *Czeremis*, the Lithuanian Tatar tribes trained by us,[13] betrayed us together with Kryczyński,[14] their leader. All went over to the Turks.

After the capture of Kamieniec the Tatars made incursions deep into our land. They had, thanks to the grace of God, no luck however, because our army, in the name of our pious King, was violently routing them everywhere. At Niemirów, Komarno, and Kałusza[15] the enemies perished like dogs. In

[9]A village on the road from Przeworsk to Łańcut.
[10]A city seven kilometers north of Puławy. The nobility of the voivodeship of Kraków assembled there on the third of November. Przyboś, *Konfederacja Gołąbska*, p. 78.
[11]Kamieniec Podolski on the Smotrycz surrendered on August 29. Czubek, *Pam.*, p. 459, note 5.
[12]It is more in line with the truth to say that.
[13]Cheremis in English. A part of the Lithuanian Mohammedan Tatars moved under the reign of King Michał to the present-day Bessarabia from where, together with the Crimean Tatars, they attacked Poland. Czubek, *Pam.*, pp. 459–460, note 7.
[14]Aleksander Kryczyński, a Tatar. Czubek, *Pam.*, p. 460, note 1.
[15]Niemirów, a town twenty kilometers southwest of Ruthenian Rawa ;

the forest and swamps great numbers were killed by the peasants.

We stood with the King at Gołąb. It was difficult to advance, however, and to unite with the regular royal army. We did not trust them, seeing what conspiracies had arisen *contra coronatum caput*.[16] They would have gladly delivered up the king to the enemy. At the time when the Crimean Tatars took captives in the vicinity of Komarno a raiding party was sent out. Selected, well-mounted men from the levy *en masse* were placed under its command. We were divided into two units. The command of one of these was given to Kalinowski,[17] that of the second one to me. We rode along two different roads out into the night. Since I well knew how to conduct raiding parties, I went toward Bełżyce exclusively along pathless tracts through forests. This did not please my militiamen. They began to complain and ask why we did not take a paved highway, for sometimes a horse stumbled over a tree-stump and sometimes some little branch cut across the face. Toward daybreak I halted before Bełżyce[18] at the edge of the forest, in order to rest the horses a little. We pastured them, holding the reins in our hands. When it began to dawn I said : "Gentlemen, we must explore what is going on in the town, so that we do not attack someone at our own peril. One can hear the barking of the dogs and no people are in sight. A few men must ride ahead to obtain information. If they are noticed, however, they are to entice the enemy into the field so that we can surround them and get a captive." No one volunteered. I became furious

---

not far from Niemirów Sobieski crushed on October 7–8, the Tatar companies and snatched away from them numerous captives. Komarno, a town 36 kilometers southwest from Lwów, where Sobieski attained a victory over a strong Tatar company. Kałusza, now Kałusz, a town 25 km northwest from Stanisławów ; not far from Kałusz, Sobieski crushed a company numbering several thousand of the Tatar horde. Czapliński, *Pam.*, p. 438, note 19.

[16]Against the crowned head.

[17]Jakub Kalinowski, master of the hunt of Podolia. Czubek, *Pam.*, p. 460, note 8.

[18]A town twenty-three kilometers southwest of Lublin.

and said : "Gentlemen, is this your *oboedientia* ?[19] How shall
we go on ? My authority is useless if your obedience is to be
such. I shall ride myself therefore. But you be in readiness at
least, in case I bring you guests." They became greatly alarmed
because it was rumored that the Tatars were already in the
vicinity of Bełz. There had been some there yesterday afternoon, but only a few. Chociwski said : "I shall go with Your
Lordship !" Sieklicki said : "I also !" For they were as if my
own men : one a first cousin, the second one a good friend.
Also the young Stroński said to me : "If Your Lordship goes
himself, I shall also go, but I won't go with anyone else." We
went then.

We rode ahead and came in front of the town—nothing
was heard. We entered the town and still nothing happened.
Only the dogs, which had already calmed down a little, became
irritated again. We searched for people in the houses—no one
was there. They were all in the forests. We rode out of the town
and halted quietly among the farm granges. It was already light
when a peasant peeked out of the barn, having raised a sheaf
from the thatched roof. We rushed to that barn. We called, we
searched, but we could not find him, since the barn was full of
grain. Finally I began to shout : "Peasant ! You desire your
own peril, no doubt ! You are hiding from Tatars and shall
perish from Christians. I don't want anything else here than to
question someone as to what goes on here. I come from the
King. I cannot find one man in the entire town and you do not
show yourself, even though we have already seen you. Since we
cannot take revenge on you in any other way, we shall smoke
you out." The peasant said : "My Lord, now I shall crawl out."
He did and we asked : "Have Tatars been here ?" "Yes, yesterday at noon. They pursued two peasants, but they escaped
into the forest. They then halted at the edge of the forest
and wounded a peasant who was dashing into the forest, with
a bow in the shoulder. Shortly before evening we saw about
thirty horsemen, but I do not know who they were since I only
saw them from a distance."

[19]I.e., is this how you obey me ?

I sent for my men. They came and we debated. Meanwhile a sheaf of grain was laid before every horse. Some men said : "Let's keep going !", others : "No, let us turn back ! You will destroy us. It is enough that we have reached this place. Do not lead us further." I persuaded them however and we went on. We rode for a league and another. There were already Tatar traces : on and off dropped or lost things, elsewhere also thrown away, upon finding something better. Cowardice overcame my men, but I argued that these things were dropped by people who were trying to escape, and not by a Tatar raid.[20] Suddenly some nobleman rode toward us from the forest and said : "Only a league away from here you can capture as many Tatars as you want, for they are roaming around the villages. It will not be difficult to find a captive for information. I rode among them yesterday. They did not dare to rush at me, since they are so overburdened and their horses are so worn out. I myself shall lead you through along footpaths and through brushwood." His story was very much to my liking and I said : "Well, gentlemen, now we have to show that God and *natura*[21] have created us humans and not mushrooms. We shall have more than the others when we show off to the King by getting him a captive. God Himself is giving this easy opportunity to us to attain a good reputation. Let us prove that we are men." Oh, my God ! How they shouted me down, "Are we the regular army ?"[22] Are we the Walachians,[23] or menial people ? We have a regular army which we pay to fight for us. We were not sent here to get a captive, but to get information which has already been obtained, we shall not go any further from here. I have a wife. I have children. I shall not be knocked so just to please someone else, because I should not." I sought to persuade them as much as I could : "We are also soldiers just like the regular army. Let us not be like the Jerusalem nobility but

---

[20]The bottom of the page is cut off here in the *Memoirs*.
[21]Nature.
[22]The so-called *kwarciani*.
[23]Inhabitants of Bessarabia and Valachia ; they enlisted in the hired armies of the Polish Commonwealth, in which they usually served in the light cavalry.

like the Polish one. Let us remember God and the fatherland. Let us be ashamed of this sun which shines on us if we are not ashamed of people." *Surdis fabula narratur.*[24] They argued on their own : "We should not and we will not go." I asked : "When you were leaving home *qua intentione*[25] did you leave, as for war or for a wedding ?" I could not persuade them by any means. I took *votum*[26] and expressed such a feeling : "I would prefer to pasture pigs rather than to command men from a levy on a raid." We turned back from this expedition. I had an orderly, Leśniewicz, who led my horse by the reins, a great shrewd fellow. I said to him : "Dear brother, let another take the horse from you and you find some means to alarm us." He promised to do so and left. *Interim*[27] I said to several confidants : "Soon we shall be frightened here, but do not say anything. We shall find out how brave the lads are." As we were approaching a village it was already evening and the orderly set those stacks of hemp on fire which in the fall are stacked in the yards, next to the huts. When they exploded, everyone assumed that this was done by the Tatars. A commotion and noise arose in the village. I said : "Gentlemen, let's rush toward them !" And the gentlemen ran away from them in all haste, each in his own direction. They called out to me : "Sir commander, it is better to flee, otherwise you will perish and will lead the army, and the King, into danger and will bring the enemy upon us." Nevertheless, I said : "Oh, I shall not hold out ; I shall jump under the fire and shall find out what is going on." Those who were *conscii*[28] of this incident said : "Let us go and rush : after all they won't swallow us up completely." We rushed ahead toward the village. The others went their way. When I returned no one was there. We found only the things which they had cast aside : bags with crackers and bacon, cheese, cloaks, whips and other odds and ends. Among other things a tin ammunition pouch on a leather belt

[24]It was like telling a fairy tale to the deaf.
[25]With what intentions.
[26]A vow.
[27]Meanwhile.
[28]Aware.

and a leather belt and a leather case, full of good liquor, about two gallons in it, lay around. They were so ashamed of it that no one wanted to admit to owning it, even though we showed it around, having tied it to a long pole.

I thought to myself once I returned and said to the others : "We have acted wrongly, for what if these cowards rush ahead and alarm the army !" Some said : "Indeed, it is true, it is true. What are we to do about it ?" "One should send someone to overtake all of them. If some coward should say something there he should testify so that they would not believe him." Pan Adam Sieklicki said : "Let my Wilczopolski go. He has a horse and I shall order him not to spare it." In a twinkling it so happened. We let him have a sip of that liquor and I said to him : "Do not spare the horse because this concerns an important matter. God forbid that the King and the army were to be frightened as a result of our jokes. Your neck would be at stake (because he and my orderly were familiar with the area, since he was from the gentry from Lublin). Even if your horse were to fall dead, do not spare it !" He was reluctant to go because, being a poor man, he was afraid for the horse. Then I said : "Mount mine, and give yours to my orderly." He did so. He caught up with them, overtook them, and by catching up with them he frightened them even more, saying : "I am no longer riding my own horse because I have lost it and I had to mount someone else's." When he overtook them he rode at a slower pace with those who were at the front. When they got out of the forest they had to go through the fields and he tried to persuade them to stop somewhere for pasturing : "Since our gentlemen are in the rearguard and if they were in trouble we could see them behind us." Those men also considered that it would have been a great disgrace to them if they returned without the commander and the rest of the company, and so they halted about a league or less away from the camp. Having gotten scratched in those forests, with lowered heads, some could not recover for a week. They drank oils and balmed their sides. We, on the other hand, stayed overnight at that campsite. We and our horses were comfortable. When it began to dawn we started out after them, riding

at an amble and collecting caps, whips *et varia*[29] along the way.
As we were leaving the forest, they saw us. They went to their
horses and began to mount them. I reached them and I said:
"Gentlemen, you should be ashamed of God and people. You
have missed a great occasion because of disobedience; we
could have taken many captives and obtained good fame.
There were over a dozen Tatars there. They ran away from us
because there was no one to surround the village. There were
too few of us. It was night. We could not *sufficere*[30] this by
ourselves. And if there had been several hundred men surely
not one of them would have escaped." They did not believe me
at first, saying: "You are just deceiving us." But when they
saw someone's nag which his orderly had taken in the bushes
they finally did believe; for it resembled a young Tatar horse.
The wooden bow of its saddle was bare and only covered with
leather in the shape of Tatar fashion. Then they rejoiced and
began to beg us to say that they did not see any Tatars, "because all that guilt and disgrace would fall on us." We stood
talking about this for about an hour in the field, having
relegated the retainers to the side, who were told later to say
that they had not seen any Tatars. I promised to their great
contentment that I would not tell, saying: "You will not insult
God by not telling the truth that you did see the Tatars. Just
consider what infamy and abuse to the nation it would be if we
did otherwise, for at regional councils and general assemblies
we talk a lot, we raise commotions, and when an opportunity
arises to do something we do nothing." I used to speak thus at
every meeting as if praising them *quidem*:[31] "These are my
companions at arms! We have undertaken raids together, we
had fought battles, we have done so and so." Whoever knew
the truth just laughed.

   We started out later for camp when Kalinowski came
along with his party. We joined together. He asked me how
things had gone for me. I told him that I would have preferred

[29]And various other things.
[30]Manage.
[31]As if.

to have pastured pigs during that time until the raiding party returned rather than to have the command over such people. He said *conformiter*.[32] We conferred about this, as we rode along to the side for the duration of the trip until we reached the camp square.

After we returned to camp we were ordered to report to the King. I did not want to go and pretended to be ill, but Kalinowski came to me. "Go, sir, for they will assume that this mission deprived you of strength." I said: "I don't want to. I am ashamed to go there. I have nothing to tell, as there is nothing to tell. I am unable to lie." Kalinowski said: "I shall give the report, as long as Your Lordship is with me as the commander of the second raiding division." I went with him to the royal tents. We found several senators and gentlemen there. Kalinowski gave the report, talked as if in tortures, exaggerated, and finally said that we had sincerely tried to get a captive but could by no means get one because the Tatar raiding parties had already withdrawn to the main camp. And he with this division had not even reached half way to where I had and did not even get to smell the Tatar trail, because his men did not obey him either.

When he finished the secretary of the confederacy, Stefan Czarniecki, said to me: "And Your Lordship was on a different track with his men?" I said: "That's right." "It is necessary therefore that you give a separate report of your services." Other senators said: "It is very necessary." Only then I said: "It is our duty as subjects to carry out the orders of Your Majesty, our present great leader and dispenser of our lives, which each one of the faithful subjects should carry out and lay down *in aleam fortunae*.[33] I put judgment on myself therefore, but with what heart and with what readiness *in praesenti termino*[34] necessary for the dignity of the Majesty of Your Highness, my gracious lord, who had offered a sacrifice,

---

[32]The same.
[33]For fortune to decide upon.
[34]Under the present circumstances.

non indago.[36] *Non expedit*[37] to praise my *actiones*[38] as well as those of my companions, even if they had been of the best ; if base, however, it would be *crudele*[39] to condemn them. Those things which can be weighed *in statera iudicii*[40] should be neither condemned nor praised ; it is not important because *eventus acta probat.*[41] I do not know whether we have poor eyes, since, having reached the enemy trails, having seen fires and clouds of smoke, we could not be of service to Your Majesty, my gracious lord. The meaning of the report of His Lordship, the Master of the Hunt of Podlasie, a lord and brother, is the following : "*Volui, sed non potui.*"[42] I on the other hand instead of insulting God doubly, with laziness and a lie, prefer *verius dicendo :*[43] *potui, sed nolui ;*[44] using the words of a great monarch, "*Veni, vidi, sed non vici.*"[45] *In posterum,*[46] if my services were to be of use to Your Majesty for a similar expedition, I would prefer *hanc suscipere provinciam*[47] with fifteen menial people who observe *oboedientiam*[48] rather than to do so with a couple of hundred gentlemen who guide military affairs, with their sentiments. For this I humbly beg the Majesty of Your Royal Highness, my gracious lord." They looked at each other and burst out into loud laughter. Potocki Szczęsny,[49] the Voivode of Sieradz, said to the King : "I have never seen such a truthful report before." Czarniecki, the Starost of Kaniów, the field secretary, answered :

[36]I do not investigate.
[37]It is not fit.
[38]Actions.
[39]Cruel.
[40]On the scale of reason.
[41]The result praises the actions.
[42]I wanted to but I could not.
[43]Telling the truth.
[44]I could have but did not want to.
[45]I came, I saw, but I did not conquer.
[46]In the future.
[47]To undertake this obligation.
[48]Obedience.
[49]Szczęsny Kazimierz Potocki, the Voivode of Sieradz, later of Kraków, and finally the Castellan and Field Hetman of the Crown ; died in 1702. Czubek, *Pam.*, p. 470, note 7.

"One should not be surprised, for he learned how to fight in good company."

This was made public then and they were angry with me. Old Misiowski[50] said before some : "Pan Pasek will not acquire fame in our voivodeship for such defamation of our brothers." I, on the other hand, claimed *e contra*,[51] "that they themselves earned such infamy and that I shall always blame them for this straight to their faces." Later Pan Sobieski, the Field Hetman and Marshal of the Crown, sent several Tatars ; but the masses of the nobility rebelled at the news that he was the second malcontent after the Archbishop. They began to negotiate through a confederacy, or rather to plot in order to concur *unanimi voto*[52] in the decision not to desert the King until the last breath, since he was very popular and was loved by all the estates. For this reason all the malcontents were vigorously attacked.

We moved on toward Lublin. After we halted there, the manner of consultation was discussed : "What to call it : either the Crown Diet[53] or Convocational Diet or council of war ?" *Conclusum*[54] that it cannot be called Convocational Diet, since such is conducted *per certum numerum personarum* ;[55] not a Diet of the Crown, since such is conducted *per nuntios terrestres*,[56] while here the *tota Respublica*[57] participated and everyone was a deputy for himself. We concluded that it should be called a council of war, since the Commonwealth *in armis exsistit*.[58] We chose as marshal Stefan Czarniecki, the field

---

[50]Michał Misiowski, subaltern judge and owner of Tczyca and Jedlcza. Czubek, *Pam.*, p. 470, note 8.

[51]Contrary to that.

[52]Unanimously.

[53]Or Diet on Horseback, which in the *Memoirs* was corrected from the Polish *konny*, meaning on horseback, to *koronny*, meaning of the Crown. According to Czubek, Diet on Horseback is the correct form. Czubek, *Pam.*, p. 471, note 10.

[54]It was concluded.

[55]By a designated number of people.

[56]By provincial deputies.

[57]The entire Commonwealth.

[58]Finds itself up in arms.

secretary, the Starost of Kaniów, a man of initiative who knew
how to bring things *ad eum finem*[59] which would not become
damnificatio Reipublicae.[60] God himself evidently had inclined
the hearts of the people to elect a wise man, for if another from
among the candidates had acceded to the above-mentioned
command he, *infallibiliter,*[61] would have brought the Commonwealth into still greater turmoil. Some *zelabant pro parte coronati capitis*[62] taking its offense,[63] *pro basi et angulari lapide,*[64]
and they advised the King to adopt this standing and to support
it in *gradu absoluto.*[65] Others, on the other hand, considered
praeiudicata antecedentia[66] where similar occasions have arisen
concerning one person and to what a pass things were brought
to in the fatherland, to what a shedding of blood ! They felt
that this would draw behind itself great bloodshedding, confusion, and God knows, perhaps the last peril of not only this
one kingdom which is *antemurale Christianitatis,*[67] but of all
our Christian monarchies as well. Evidently it was God's Will
itself which *militabat pro nobis,*[68] since everything went well for
us. The fiery ones, however, desired the sword and the shedding
of blood ; they cried out, giving as a pretext that things cannot
go well in Poland until *perversa capita*[69] (which even with
a good master will not let us enjoy our freedom) are punished.

Czarniecki was elected Marshal. *Conclusum*[70] at the same
time that the counselling would take place through the districts
propter meliorem ordinem[71] and so that only the deputies

[59]To an end.
[60]Detriment to the Commonwealth.
[61]Without fail.
[62]Stood firmly by the royal head.
[63]Offence.
[64]As the basis and cornerstone.
[65]Decidedly.
[66]Examples from the past, i.e., Zebrzydowski's and Lubomirski's rebellions. Czubek, *Pam.,* p. 472, note 9.
[67]The bulwark of Christianity.
[68]Had fought for us.
[69]Perverse heads.
[70]It was concluded. Czarniecki was elected marshal on October 11.
Czubek, *Pam.,* p. 473, note 5.
[71]To assure better order.

themselves and the marshals would sit at the sessions and thus
promote *celeriorem cursum consultationum publicarum*[72] and
not in order to take up the time with speeches, and so that
each deputy would declare his district's stand in each matter
instead, *non praeclusa via*,[73] however, for every nobleman to
speak up, even if he was not a deputy, once he obtained permission to do so from the Marshal and on the subject about
which he should have been well informed by his deputy. Two
deputies were elected then at the individual district councils.
I was told by the gentlemen from the Lelów district to serve as
a deputy together with Pan Wojciech Giebułtowski. We would
sit in the field in front of the royal tents, having formed a big
circle with several, sometimes even over a dozen thousand
arbitraries[74] on horseback, some of which were sober, and some
drunk, who were right in back of us. The Marshal opened the
meeting *facundissima oratione*.[75] *Gratulationes*[76] from the King
and the senate followed it *apprecando felicem eventum*.[77] The
Marshal answered each one *in forma amplissima*.[78]

  Materiae consultationis[79] were proposed, but *specialiter*[80]
the cardinal points, that is *defensionis patriae*[81] and of the
resistance against the Turkish might, and secondly the guarding
of the person of the King, the lord, *et securitatis ab impetitione
et insidiis malecontentorum*.[82] The Marshal *petit consilium*[83]
from the council with which to begin. They began to take the
floor, arguing that *utrumque necessarium*[84] but that *cura salu-*

[72]A speedier course in the debate of public matters.
[73]Not excluding the (possibility) way.
[74]Those who are present at the council but do not participate in the
debates. Czapliński, *Pam.*, p. 450, note 117.
[75]With an elegant speech.
[76]Congratulations.
[77]Wishing a successful outcome.
[78]In a very ornate style.
[79]Subjects for discussion.
[80]Especially.
[81]The defense of the fatherland.
[82]And securing him from assaults and attempts on his life by the malcontents.
[83]Demanded a resolution.
[84]Both were necessary.

tis[85] of His Majesty, our gracious lord, would be in such consideration that *ante omnia*[86] a means of defense should be figured out for His Majesty, and only then should we *consulere*[87] other matters. Our lord was so beloved that all agreed to this *unanimi voce* and *libere*[88] and declared that fifteen thousand military men, together with the levy *en masse*, should be selected right in the camp and left at his side and which, after the royal call to arms, would go into the field *omni necessitate*.[89] This matter did not take up more than three hours. *De methodo contribuendi*[90] for this expedition they could not come to an agreement in the regional councils for several days, as some proposed taxes on the fiefs, while others proposed taxes on chimneys, etc. And since one could not set out very soon on this expedition if one had to wait for the collection of those taxes, then in this respect also the love of the subjects for their master did not prove itself lesser, because whoever had money lying around, in deposits in his house, voluntarily spoke up in his eagerness: "I shall lend my voivodeship fifty thousand." "I sixty thousand," etc. Soon the total sum was above that which was needed. They themselves collected their sums, they themselves gave them to their captains, in return for promissory notes. The captains were chosen by the voivodeships themselves. Others also, who were closer, brought their money right away to camp and instantly a means of defense was figured out for the King. All this was brought about by the true love of the subjects toward their King, who was really in need of defense as he no longer trusted the other army which was under the hetmans. As to the resistance to the Turkish might, one considered that whatever we were doing now for the King *hoc bonum* was *publiciter bonum*,[91] for if we were to have a strong king these bitter attacks on him would

[85]The concern for the safety.
[86]Above all.
[87]Consult.
[88]Unanimously and freely.
[89]Whenever necessary.
[90]About the method of paying taxes.
[91]Good in the public sense of the word.

not be so worrisome. A means of defense was devised. We began to discuss those who *consurgunt*[92] without cause against the master, and concluded that they should be summoned to court. Others spoke, especially the Marshal, who argued that "during a frightful war one should not only [*non*]*irritare crabrones*[93] but also suffer in silence the injustice done to him. His Majesty the King, as a merciful lord, *non urget*[94] this *propter bonum pacis* ;[95] if such a person, were to be found however, there would be no time for claiming when, if God grants it, this frightful Turkish war comes to an end." Nevertheless, this was in vain ; and people demanded : "Try them !" Whomever they recalled *ex magnatibus*,[96] they would only say : "Traitor, worthy of the executioner's sword, etc. For how will these traitors disturb us with their treacherous deeds ? King Kazimierz, was bad according to them ; they did not stop testing him until they brought him to eternal disgrace. God has given us now a father, not a master ; neither does this one appeal to them any longer. We have to shake off these leaders who take such great care of us, for otherwise we shall never have peace."

This was negotiated at the council of war. A deputy would answer another deputy *rationaliter* ;[97] and from those standing around a commotion would be raised as a result of any word ; the crushing of swords, waggling with maces, pulling of pistols followed. The deputies would then rise from their seats to intercede each for his own man (because such were the orders : everyone who came riding or came on foot to the council of war *non capiat*[98] a position save behind his own deputies). And it boiled as in a pot ; anything on the agenda, even the least significant matter, took up an hour or two. Even the banner councils which were conducted *ante sessionem*[99] within the

[92]Rise.
[93]Not irritate the hornets.
[94]Does not demand.
[95]For the sake of a pleasant peace.
[96]From among the magnates.
[97]With reason.
[98]Would not take up.
[99]I.e., before the council of war.

different banners did not take place without great commotion. Suffice it to say it was not only useless to utter anything and even to murmur anything against the King; he had captivated the hearts of all men because they said that "this is our king, our blood, *os de ossibus* ;[100] we have rejoiced at having a King from our own nation for a long time."

The secretary of the lands of Bielsk did not say anything important at the council of war. When the Starost of Środa[101] spoke *zelose*[102] against the malcontents and finally tried to prove through writing that "this should be cut out," this secretary of Bielsk,[103] a man as white as a dove, *quidem*[104] a great soldier, a deputy at every Diet from Podlasie, said only the following : "Sir Starost, you will not stand it !" (because he too was a deputy as the starost). Oh, God ! when a commotion started : "How so, you pagan son' He will not stand it ? We will stand it. We will not abandon each other till the very end. Evidently you too are one of them. Seize him, kill him, hand him over to us outside the council. We shall send his head as a present to Pan Sobieski !" They began to slash at him. The old man jumped like a he-goat behind the Marshal. The Marshal exclaimed : "Infantry, infantry !" And about six hundred infantrymen stood directly behind the Marshal with the muskets quivering in their hands. The officers said : "How are we to raise arms here ?" The bishops jumped up, the senators jumped up, they hardly managed to shield him. We in the council squeezed together so that they could not get through to him, because they pushed forward in order to drag him out and to massacre him. Also those who were suspected to be *eiusdem spiritus*[105] (since some of the malcontents were *protunc*[106] at the council of war), when the commotion arose, fled to the tents,

---

[100]Bone of our bones.
[101]Jan Cerekwicki, deputy to the Diets of 1670 and 1683. Czubek, *Pam.*, p. 477, note 7.
[102]Ardently.
[103]Most likely Krzysztof Żelski. Czapliński, *Pam.*, p. 454, note 164.
[104]As if or apparently but here probably implying also.
[105]Of the same opinion.
[106]At the time.

distrusting justice, especially some of our captains from Kra-ków.

Several times it almost came to the shedding of blood, and a few days later[107] it did come to that during a tragic *spectaculum*[108] in which a certain Firlej Broniowski,[109] having arrived at the council of war drunk, first halted on his horse behind us, that is, behind the deputies from the voivodeship of Kraków, and began to call out, to shout and interfere with those who were speaking. I assumed that he came from the highlands until my colleagues told me : "He is not a man from our voivodeship." Later, when he began to shout even louder, I said to him : "Pan brother, we do not need a bailiff here. This place is reserved for the voivodeship of Kraków ; either you, sir, stand still or leave !" He became indignant with me and began to scold : "I can halt wherever I want to." My colleagues jumped up and said to him : "You may not ; don't you know the orders that each one is to stand behind the deputies of his voivodeship ? Step aside or you will get killed ! Are you ashamed of your voivodeship ?" Our men on horse-back who stood next to him said : "Leave, sir brother, to your voivodeship !" and they pushed him out. He crossed over to the other side and again continued to make noise. They already knew that he was a malcontent and someone said to him : "Oh, Pan brother, be careful or else !" But he continued in much the same way ; later he said something against the King. They took swords against him. He fled to the sheds of the voivodeship of Bełz, but was pushed out of there also. In the field they killed him. We in the council of war were unaware of this until they dragged him to the council of war and shouted : "Step aside !" Two orderlies dragged him in by the legs—the body, already turned blue, wore only one boot ; they threw him in the middle of the council saying : "Here is the first malcontent. The same will happen to others !"[110] It was painful and horrible to look at that massacred man. The other malcontents were almost half

[107]October 13. Czapliński, *Pam.*, p. 455, note 169.
[108]Spectacle.
[109]Jan Firlej Broniowski. Czubek, *Pam.*, p. 478, note 6.
[110]Jemiołowski in his memoirs also mentions about this fact.

dead with fright as he lay there bloodstained like a slaughtered animal. After we had sat so for about half an hour the marshal suspended the meeting and we dispersed.

Later bad weather came, snows, frosts, so bad that many could not recognize their own horses, having gotten up in the morning when they were covered with snow. We held our sessions then in the tents because of it. The nobility began to go home, only we, the deputies, had to toil together with the Marshal until the end. Zamoyski,[111] the Castellan, was almost

---

[111]Marcin Zamoyski, Castellan of Lwów, later voivode of Bracław, Lublin, finally treasurer of the Crown ; died in 1689. Czubek, *Pam.*, p. 480, note 2.

killed before the end of the council in the same manner as Broniowski. One nobleman accused him, saying, "You have said this about the King : He is more likely to carry soap in a basket in Zamość than to reign." He escaped being massacred by a hair's breadth. He knelt down, and swore that he had not said this, and he folded his hands. The Marshal interceded for him : "For God's sake, gentlemen, enough of this bloodshedding !" The King sent word : "Even if he said this or something worse, I forgive him and beg for his safety." They left him alone. We finished the council of war on *10 Novembris* and we deputies signed its articles and we said good-bye to the King. The Marshal made a speech *nomine omnium*,[112] a very splendid and eloquent one. Not many people knew of his eloquence ; he became known as a great *orator* only in the capacity of a marshal. We then dispersed happily.

When I arrived at home *16 Novembris I* found everyone in mourning over the death of my beloved mother, who had passed away on the eve of St. Simon-Judah.[113] *Utinam in sancta pace requiescat.*[114] We buried her in the Reformed Franciscan Fathers' church in Stopnica.

[112]In the name of all.
[113]October 27.
[114]May she rest in holy peace !

ANNO DOMINI 1673

By the grace of God I began the year in Skrzypiów. I took back Smogorzów after a one-year lease to Pani Olszanowska, who had married there.

The Warsaw Diet[1] followed, during which Archbishop Prażmowski closed his eye in eternal sleep. He had only one eye, but it saw plenty and did plenty of evil. He died in Ujazdów[2] from worry that he could not promote the French interests. After him Prince Czartoryski,[3] a very worthy lord and a senator of great piety, became Primate.

During this winter the Turks did not leave the battlefield, but entrenched themselves at Chocim[4] and were encamped there. Our Field Hetmans, who had a good regular Lithuanian and Polish army as well as additional reinforcements[5] at their disposal, wanted the Turks to challenge them to a battle. The Turks did not want to fight, however, because the Tatars had

[1]January 4 to April 13, 1673. Czapliński, *Pam.*, p. 458, note 1.
[2]Now a section in Warsaw. Prażmowski died on April 15, 1673.
[3]Prince Florian Czartoryski, Canon of Kraków, Bishop of Poznań, Archbishop of Gniezno, finally Primate ; died in 1674. Czubek, *Pam.*, p. 481, note 6.
[4]A city on the Dniestr, across from Kamieniec Podolski, and Moldavian fortress.
[5]According to a resolution of the Diet of 1673 one armed and fully equipped soldier had to be sent per every twenty huts ; from hereditary landed estates one mounted soldier per every thirty huts ; by the clergy one soldier per twenty huts. They were called *dymowa* infantry and cavalry from the Polish word *dymy*, smokes, rising over the roofs of inhabited huts. Czubek, *Pam.*, p. 482, note 1.

already deserted them. In an unprecedented action our men resolved to assault them.[6] They moved up to the earthworks and surrounded the camp. The infantry mined the earthworks and demolished them in several places *nemine reclamante.*[7] The Turks did not fire even once at our army with cannon, even though they had many of them. God had probably blinded the pagans and taken away their courage, for they received our men, who tried to get through to them, as *modeste*[8] as if some guest had arrived and not the enemy. They waited on horseback in large groups behind the earthworks when our companies came toward them through the fortification holes. They did not attack our men until they were within the trenches, but could not withstand them long. They began to escape toward the Dniester bridge over to Kamieniec. Our men gave them a beating there. Since they had massed in a great crowd on the bridge, it collapsed. Some were killed on it, others drowned, others were driven to the rocky bank and fell head down, together with their horses.[9]

Our men took great booty of harness, silver and rich tents. In the trunks there were exquisite valuables, so that some trunks could be estimated at one hundred thousand. They also took richly embellished swords and Janissary rifles. Such a great number of camels was brought to Poland that one could even buy one for a nag. One son gave his father a special treat with his booty. This son was an infantry captain[10] and he had several captured camels. When he approached his parents' house, he wanted to greet his father in a Turkish outfit. He dressed himself in the entire outfit and in a Turkish turban, mounted a camel, and rode ahead to the manorial house. His old father was just going with a cane through the courtyard to some homestead when this apparition rode through the gate.

[6]This assault was presumed to be on November 11. Czubek, *Pam.,* p. 482, note 4.
[7]Without anybody's opposition.
[8]Politely.
[9]Almost the entire Turkish army was annihilated then; 120 mortars, 400 standards and the entire supply stores fell into Polish hands.
[10]Of one of the special infantry companies.

The old gentleman ran away as fast as he could, crossing himself. When the son saw that his father was frightened, he ran after him and called : "Stop, Sir : it is I, your son !" The father kept running even faster. Later he fell ill because of this fright and died soon after.

All of Poland was thus flooded with Turkish things : beautiful pieces of embroidery, fine horses, rich quivers, and various other valuables. God gave our nation a wonderful victory and most wonderful of all because the enemy had even forgotten to defend himself. Even earlier, when we overran the Walachian and Multan camps, the Turks did not come to help them and later they did not even defend themselves—except when they were driven out of their camp. But our men had also suffered : Pisarski,[11] the Starost of Wolbrom, a cavalry captain, perished with his lieutenant ; also Żelecki,[12] the Starost of Bydgoszcz, and others. This Turkish army had been supposed to move *primo vere*[13] to Lwów and after its capture still deeper into Poland. We had already asked them to terms and were willing to accept subjugation, because we did not have anyone *qui manum opponat.*[14] We begged the Turks to treat us as they did the Walachians and Multans and not to attack our faith. "This cannot be, since the Walachians and the Multans have

[11]Achacy Pisarski, Czubek, Pam., p. 484, note 2.
[12]Jan Żelecki, the Starost of Bydgoszcz, and Master of the Royal Hunt of the Crown. Czubek, *Pam.*, p. 484, note 3.
[13]In early spring.
[14]Who could withstand them.

subjugated themselves voluntarily and you were conquered," said the Turks. It is true that we had not yet sent any envoys on this matter, but we had already begun to negotiate through the Crimean Khan. Briefly, great fear and trepidation existed until God suddenly changed everything when He gave us a victory at Chocim. The Turks lowered their noses, for they lost the army which they had considered their best. They immediately agreed to peace and were content with only Podolia,[15] while before they had had an appetite for the entire Polish kingdom and said to the nobility of Podolia: "You cannot beseech us for such freedom as the Walachians have, because you are undisciplined; but we shall disarm you and use you for manual labor." God wanted it differently, however, and did not allow His temples and us to fall.

This victory stood to the credit of the pious King Michał,[16] who died right after it. Various people had various opinions about his death. There was *suspicio veneni*[17] in the garganey[18] of which he was very fond. I do not suspect anyone. I only record what people talked about.

[15]Podolia, Podole was given to the Turks already in the treaty of Buczacz on October 18, 1672.

[16]He actually died one day before the battle, on November 10, in Lwów. Czubek, *Pam.*, p. 485, note 1. He was thirty-three years of age at the time.

[17]A suspicion of poison.

[18]A kind of wild duck.

ANNO DOMINI 1674

By the grace of God I began this year in Skrzypiów. There was an *interregnum* and justice was rendered by secret courts.[1] I often went to Radom[2] concerning the estate of Rączki. The election of the new king took place *in Maio*[3] near Warsaw, but no longer with such a great assemblage as had accompanied that of Michał. Much competition existed also there, but once again God gave us a Piast,[4] *os de ossibus nostris*,[5] the Field Hetman and Commander-in-Chief of the Polish forces, Jan Sobieski. He was elected on the nineteenth of May and inaugurated on the twenty-first of the same month. He now reigns over us successfully. *Utinam diutissime regnet pro gloria Dei et utilitate Reipublicae Christianae.*[6] May God make his lineage strong, as He did once that of Abraham and may the crown not. fall from the heads of his descendants, as was the case in the Austrian royal family ; we all desire this.

The coronation did not take place right away, however ; not until the third year,[7] because great wars began with the Turks, the Tatars and the Cossacks. The Cossacks, who sur-

---

[1]Similar to the *Vehmgerichte*.
[2]The landed courts and the courts of first assistance were located there. Czubek, *Pam.*, p. 485, note 4.
[3]In May. Actually the election began on April 20.
[4]The name of the first dynasty of Polish dukes and kings.
[5]One of our own blood.
[6]May he keep reigning as long as possible for the glory of God and the welfare of the Christian Polish Commonwealth.
[7]February 2, 1676.

rendered to the Turk, invited him to war against us and wanted to destroy us through his might. These villains made their reputation even worse, and lost the rest of their might, about which will be written below.

The Turks, who regretted the loss of men in the previous year, let themselves be very easily persuaded by the Cossacks to wage war with Poland and took the Cossacks under their protection. Great armies went to the battlefield ; young Chmielnicki remained as hostage in Istanbul. This was a united undertaking against us, but God confused them. They quarreled and fought with each other and left us alone. The Turks took some cities by assault : Ładyżyn, Humań and others.[8] In all the cities, but especially in Humań it came to such great bloodshed that more than two hundred thousand Cossacks perished there. But also very many Turks perished during the assault. Thus those who threatened to shed our blood drank plenty of their own.

[8]Ładyżyn and Humań, cities in the Ukraine ; formerly in the voivodeship of Bracław.

ANNO DOMINI 1675

As soon as I had settled down in Skrzypiów I did nothing else other than make the necessary arrangements so that my daughters[1] could take the veil and make prefessions, because during my lifetime three of them—and while their late father was still living, a fourth one—became Bernardine sisters : Maryjanna, Aleksandra, Barbara and a second Maryjanna, the youngest. These young ladies became nuns neither from any compulsion nor necessity, because they were pretty and had dowries, but only out of divine vocation. I went into great expense for this purpose, however, because it is considerably more expensive than giving away a young lady in marriage. If there is anyone who is not aware of this, I will tell him what kind of an expense it is : it is not enough to give her a dowry and to endow her financially, but one must time and again give something to the convent.

In this same year I again made a trip to Gdańsk. I sold grain to Pan Wilhelm Braun.

The Turks attacked us in great hordes, plundered and burned in the vicinity of Wiśniowiec, Podhajce, and Zbaraż[2] and caused much damage. Our King-Elect defended himself from these villains as well as he could.

[1]Stepdaughters. The oldest, Maryjanna, had entered the convent still during the lifetime of her father in 1660. The remaining ones were given away to the convent by Pasek : Aleksandra, 1669, Barbara 1675, Marianna vel Katarzyna in 1681. Czubek, *Jan Pasek w oświetleniu archiwalnym.*

[2]Wiśniowiec, a town and castle south of Krzemieniec ; Podhajce, a town near Tarnopol ; Zbaraż, a city in the voivodeship of Tarnopol.

ANNO DOMINI 1676

In this year I lived in Skrzypiów. The body of King Michał was brought to Kraków ; that of King Kazimierz was also brought back from France. Even though Kazimierz had not wanted to end his life with us, he nevertheless returned to us after death. Dear King, you do realize after all : this is your *dulcis locus patriae* ![1] Of your own free will you scorned the country which raised you and kept up the spirit of love and faith at all times. Your corpse yearned, however, to return hither and to moulder here ! Kraków thus lived to see a great novelty—to simultaneously receive three Polish kings *inter moenia*,[2] two *simul et semel*[3] on a catafalque and the third one reigning. Our King-Elect, *Joannes Tertius*,[4] had defended the walls of our fatherland as much as he could from our enemies until he realized that he already deserved the crown promised him by the Polish Commonwealth. He thus arrived in Kraków on the twenty-ninth of January and was received with great enthusiasm and joy. Even those who had spoken against his election underwent such a change of heart that all rejoiced over his reign because they saw that he was a wise, good, soldierly, diligent, and lucky ruler. There were no malcontents then as there had been during the election of Michał, for God himself had so ordained.

The funeral of both kings took place on the thirty-first of

[1]Sweet fatherland.
[2]Within its walls.
[3]Together and next to each other.
[4]Jan the Third.

January in the Castle of Kraków. Both caskets were carried in the same wagon beside each other, both were put on the same catafalque next to each other, and joint ceremonies were performed. King Jan the Third assisted in all ceremonies *devotissime*.[5] The two kings were not buried in the same grave, however. Kazimierz was buried in the same grave, however. Kazimierz was buried in the Zygmunt[6] chapel of his father ; Michał, on the other hand, was buried in the right-hand corner from the entrance of the church, in a chapel of one of the Kings, but I do not know which.

On the third day after the funeral ceremonies, that is, [*secun*]*da Februarii*,[7] at the occasion of the feast of the Purification of Our Lady, the coronation of His Majesty Jan the Third took place. *Quam felicissime, diutissime regnet*[8] for the glory of the Almighty God as well as for the defense of the Christian Polish Commonwealth ! *Quarta Februarii*[9] the Diet *coronationis*[10] began, during almost all of which I had to stay in Kraków. I had a lawsuit against the Germans[11] about deeds of violence committed in Smogorzów. I obtained for Captain Chrzanowski[12] and for Lieutenant Demek the death penalty. They were shackled.

The vacant offices were given out : the big baton[13] went to Prince Dymitr Wiśniowiecki,[14] the small one[15] to Jabłoński, the

[5]Most piously.
[6]I.e., in the chapel of the Waza dynasty.
[7]On the second of February.
[8]May he reign most happily and as long as possible.
[9]On the fourth of February.
[10]Coronation.
[11]I.e., soldiers of foreign recruitment. Czubek, *Pam.*, p. 489, note 7.
[12]Samuel Chrzanowski, the defender of Trembowla. In spite of the verdict he lived for twelve more years.
[13]The big baton represented the office of the commander-in-chief of the Polish armed forces.
[14]Dymitr Wiśniowiecki (1628–1682). Voivode of Bełz (Bełżec) ; Field Hetman 1668 ; voivode of Kraków 1678 ; Castellan of Kraków 1680. Czubek, *Pam.*, p. 489, note 8.
[15]Stanisław Jan Jabłoński (1634–1702), voivode of Ruthenia ; Castellan of Kraków 1693. Czubek, *Pam.*, p. 489, note 9. The small baton represented the office of the Field Hetman.

small seal to the Bishop of Warmia[16] and the smaller staff to
Sieniawski.[17]

At Wojniłów[18] a battle was fought with the Crimean
Tatars. Later the camp at Żurawno[19] was besieged by the Turks
and the Tatars, with the result that our leaders, willingly or
unwillingly, had to negotiate with the enemy. Treaties were
signed with the Turks which yielded to them Podole and the
Ukraine. But the treaties with an enemy who always has an
eager appetite to devour our poor fatherland are short-lived.

[16]Stefan Wydżga. Czubek, *Pam.*, p. 490, note 1.
[17]Mikołaj Hieronim Sieniawski, Guard of the Crown, voivode of Volhynia, major-domo of the Crown ; d. 1684. Czubek, *Pam.*, p. 490, note 2.
The smaller staff represented the office of court marshal.
[18]West of Halicz.
[19]Northwest of Halicz. At Żurawno Sobieski's army of 10,000 men was
besieged from the twenty-fourth of September until the seventeenth of
October by a Turkish army of one hundred thousand. This finally led
to peace terms which superseded the Treaty of Buczacz.

ANNO DOMINI 1677

I took over Olszówka and Brzeście—God willing happily—
after a period of seven years in the following way : I had made
a contract concerning these estates and had paid the money
already six years previously. Pan Chełmski,[1] the Polish camp
commander, did not want to give up the leasehold, however,
until the expiration of the years stipulated in the contract, even
though there was an agreement with his brother Krzysztof that
he would do so. Also, when the designated time was drawing
near he began to threaten me, hoping to frighten me away from
this contract. I therefore made arrangements with the castellan
of Bełz,[2] who was departing for the Diet in Warsaw, that he
should order these estates to be turned over to me immediately
on the day of expiration of the leasehold. He left orders before
his departure that as soon as the designated time came, his
wife would go there and would turn the estates to me. And this
was the way it happened : even though they had locked the
gates, we chose an opportune moment when peasants were
being let out to go threshing ; a few of our men on horseback
rushed ahead and held back the gates until all of us had entered.
The estates and the peasants were turned over to me then.

[1]Marcjan Ścibor Chełmski. Czapliński, *Pam.*, p. 468, note 2.
[2]Jan Aleksander Myszkowski. Czubek, *Pam.*, p. 491, note 1.
[3]Subjects of the estate were handed over to the authority of the new
lease-holder, who had over them all the rights of an owner. Czubek,
Pam., p. 491, note 3.

But I shall let this go for now and shall return *ad cursum anni.*[4]

At this Diet, Gniński,[5] the voivode of Chełm, was assigned as an envoy to the Turks. A financial committee[6] of the deputies met in Sandomierz. Our army was encamped at Trembowla which proved to be convenient and lucrative, because the soldiers farmed for themselves, sowed, plowed and mowed the meadows[7] and during winter they were as comfortable as at home. In their bazaar everything was cheaper than in the cities, because beer and mead were locally brewed and loaded wagons with goods went for sale in the public square, as they had years ago to Kazimierz.[8] Such an organization of the army is very good ; if it were always that way, it would be better than to have the army roam all around Poland from one encampment to another and to wear out the horses.

I took off for Gdańsk this year on *7 Iulii*[9] and arrived there on *16 Augusti.*[10]

[Secund]a Decembris eodem anno[11] my beloved father died[12] *devotissime*[13] and in a really Christian way ; it was on the eve of St. Barbara, whom he had worshipped very much.

[4]To the events of this year.

[5]Jan Gniński became the chamberlain of Pomorze, voivode of Chełm ; in 1681 he became the vice-chancellor for the Crown. He participated in the Vienna campaign of 1683 ; died in 1685. Czubek, *Pam.,* p. 491, note 5.

[6]Concerning the speedier settlement of the army's back pay. Czubek, *Pam.,* p. 491, note 5.

[7]The estates of Trembowla and Krzemieniec were assigned to the army in the Constitution of 1677. The soldiers farmed and watched the borders. Owners of these estates were given compensation. Czubek, *Pam.,* pp. 491–492, note 7.

[8]Kazimierz Dolny on the Vistula, in the voivodeship of Lublin, was an important center of the grain trade at the time.

[9]July 7. It should probably be August, however. The trip to Gdańsk could by no means have lasted over a month. Czubek, *Pam.,* p. 492, note 4.

[10]August 16.

[11]On the second of December of this year.

[12]Actually in 1679. Czubek, *Pam.,* p. 492, note 1.

[13]Very piously.

He died in complete control of his memory and fully prepared for death, because he had no fever and it seemed as if he just fell asleep. I buried him in Kraków at the Carmelite cemetery on the Piasek. May God grant him eternal rest in His Kingdom!

ANNO DOMINI 1678

I began this year—*utinam feliciter*![1] in Olszówka. I suffered a great loss this year because of the following incident: His Lordship the gentleman from Bełz[2] asked for my attendance in a settlement with his Lordship Czerny,[3] the starost of Parnawa, about the depreciation of a rent in Kozubów.[4] When I went there, I took clothing and furs with me, because directly from there I was to accompany Pan Floryjan Łącki, the royal steward of Malbork,[5] to Kiełczyna[6] on his courtship of Miss Borowska. I was accommodated in an inn; the inn caught fire when we were in the manor house and my clothes were either burned or stolen. The damage amounted to at least four thousand. That's what happens when you do people favors! How much such friendly turns cost me in my life only God himself knows. I say that the friends to whom one renders a service on any occasion promise to reciprocate that service, to be sure, but they forget about it very soon. One rarely finds someone who remembers a favor even for three years; if you need his services then he either does not want to help, or he wants to but is

---

[1]May it be a happy one!
[2]The castellan Jan A. Myszkowski. Czubek, *Pam.*, p. 493, note 2.
[3]Michał Czerny. Czubek, *Pam.*, p. 493, note 3.
[4]A village in the district of Pińczów belonging to the Myszkowski family. Czubek, *Pam.*, p. 493, note 4.
[5]Marienburg.
[6]A village in the district of Opatów.
[7]We are mere ciphers and are born to consume bread. Horace, *Epist.* I, 1, 27.

not able to. When people need a friend, they will find you, but
when you need one, then you have to look for one with a
candle. There are also others whom God did not give the knack
to apply their ability, even if they had any. And so it is sometimes difficult to find a human being in a multitude of people.
Nos numerus sumus et fruges consumere nati.[7] Many a lazy-
bone lies around the house and does not want to know about
anything in the world : he thinks about neither the public welfare nor his reputation, but only plunges into domestic comforts and thus is of no use to anyone, ignoring *regulam vitae,*[8]
just as if he were not at all alive, for we were not born only for
ourselves, as the saying goes :

> Whoever fights for my sake, lends me money,
> Advises me well, and does not shrink from a long
> journey on horse,
> Such a man is a true friend and such I respect :
> Let him serve me with these four services, the rest
> I shall condone.[9]

There are such noblemen, however, who cannot be of service
in any of these instances, and yet every nobleman should have
de necessitate[10] one of these four qualities. If *ex his qualitatibus*[11] he possesses none, then things are with him as the Mazovians sing :

> Four girls
> For a bushel of chaff.

Sometimes to give a bushel of chaff even for ten such men
would be too much, or even to sell them as "dearly" as is
written in history about the Jews, that in a Roman military
camp thirty of them were sold for a penny.

I have made this digression *ex occasione*[12] and now I return
to my subject matter. I have spent almost the entire year en-

---

[8]The laws of life.
[9]In a somewhat changed version we find this poem in the *"Wirydarz"*
of Trembecki (I, 110) under the title : "Requirements of a Good
Friend." Czapliński, *Pam.,* p. 472, note 14.
[10]Necessarily.
[11]Out of these qualities.
[12]Incidentally.

gaged in friendly turns, compromises, congressional courts, endowments, agreements, wedding and funeral ceremonies.

In this year the Turks devastated Międzyboż, Niemirów, Kalnik and many other towns and villages.[13]

[13]Międzyboż, a town in Podolia ; Niemirów, a town in the Ukraine ; Kalnik, a village in the district of Winnica (Vinnitsa). These localities were given to the Turks under the terms of the treaty of Żórawno. Czapliński, *Pam.*, p. 473, note 23.

ANNO DOMINI 1679

By the grace of God I began the year there in Olszówka. God willed it that the year was peaceful, but very infertile and the harvest was poor. Yet prices remained very low, a situation which was bad for the leaseholders, and in some areas an epidemic was raging.

This year for the very first time a Diet was held in Lithuania at Grodno.[1] The Lithuanian gentlemen forced the passage of a resolution decreeing that two Diets would take place one after another in Poland, the third one in Lithuania. It is very inconvenient for our people to ride there; if something like this falls *in usum*,[2] however, it will surely be *perpetuitas*.[3]

Our army this year, which was encamped at Trembowla summer and winter, was not made up of soldiers but of farmers. They occupied themselves with farming : sowed, plowed and had an abundance of everything, just as if they were at home. The only thing they lacked was wives.

[1] From December 14, 1678 until April 4, 1679. Czapliński, *Pam.*, p 474, note 3.
[2] I.e., becomes a custom.
[3] Permanent.

ANNO DOMINI 1680

By the grace of God also this year I began in Olszówka. Right in the beginning of the year we lived to see something different, because the winter frosts passed and the weather became so warm, so nice, that the cattle went into the field. Flowers sprouted and the earth yielded grass; people plowed and sowed. I hesitated for a long time with the sowing, but when I saw that others had already completed half of their spring sowing, I also began to sow. When, during the carnival season, I accompanied people on their courtings or when I went to weddings, it was so hot that one could not wear fur-lined outfits, only summer ones, as *in Augusto*. There was no more winter ; only rain showers came and went. The grain which was sowed *in Januario* grew so high before Easter that the cattle were pastured on it. The cattle thus ate little hay during this winter, since they had very good nourishment in the field.

His Majesty the King sent to me Pan Straszowski, his courtier, with letters in which he urgently sought me to donate to him the tame otter which I had—such a delightful animal that I would have preferred to give away *partem*[1] of my possessions rather than it[2] whom I loved so much. The King learned of this otter at first from someone who said that it was *cum his et his qualitatibus*[3] and that it was in the possession of

[1]Part.
[2]Pasek always refers to the otter as "she". It is not clear however whether this merely refers to the gender of the Polish word for otter, *wydra*, which is feminine.
[3]Had such and such qualities.

a certain nobleman from the voivodeship of Cracow. My name was not known to him, however, and so they did not know to whom to direct the request. At first the Polish Master of the Horse[4] wrote to Pan Bełchacki—who later became the Vice-Chancellor of Cracow—and asked him to find out in whose possession this otter was and its owner's name. Since the otter was well known in the entire voivodeship of Cracow, and later even in all of Poland, Pan Bełchacki found out about it and informed them that I had it. Only then the King rejoiced in hope and said: "I have known Pan Pasek for a long time. I know that he will not refuse it to me." He then sent Pan Straszewski to me with a letter. The King and the Polish Master of the Horse wrote to me. Also Pan Adryjan Piekarski, a royal courtier and a relative of mine, begged me in his letter not to refuse the King this gift, since I would be rewarded with all possible grace and favor of His Majesty.

After I had read the letters I was amazed: "Who had reported about it there?" and I asked: "For Heaven's sake, what does His Majesty need it for?" The envoy said that His Majesty demanded it and begged for it very much. I said that there was nothing in my possession which I would refuse His Majesty, but I felt as if one had scratched me with a sharp curry-comb over the naked skin. Then I sent to the leaseholder of the brewery, a Jew, to send me a sleeve of otter skin. After it was brought to me, I put it on the table and said: "Here, sir, you have a speedy settling of the matter!" He looked at me, and replied: "But there was to be a living one, a tame one here, which the King is asking for!"

After this joke, I had to present it. It was not at home, however, for it was roaming somewhere around the ponds. We drank some vodka and then we went to the meadows. I began to call it by its name. It was called *Robak*.[5] The otter came wet out of the thicket; it began to fawn on me and then it followed us into the house. Straszewski was amazed and said: "For

---

[4]Marek Matczyński, a friend of King Jan Sobieski, and since 1676 Master of the Horse for the Crown. Czubek, *Pam.*, p. 497, note 6.
[5]In Polish *Robak* means a worm or a maggot.

Heaven's sake, how could the King not grow fond of it when it is so tame!" I answered: "Now, sir, you see only its tameness and you praise it; but when you see its virtues you will praise it even more."

We went to the pond. I stood on the jetty and said: "Robak! I need fish for my quests: jump into the water!" The otter jumped in and at first brought back a roach. I ordered it to go a second time; it brought out a small pike. The third time it dragged out a pike the size of a dish, which it only hurt in the neck a little. Straszewski grabbed his head: "For Heaven's sake, what do I see here!" To this I said:

"Would your Lordship like for it to bring some more? For it will keep carrying them out until I have enough; even if I needed a tub full of fish, it would fill it up, because a fishing net does not cost it anything." Straszewski said: "Now that I see it, I believe it; if someone had told me about all this, I would not have believed him." Straszewski caught me in my vows *et consensit*[6] to my proposal nonetheless, seeing that this would facilitate the description of its *qualitates*[7] to the King. Before his departure I showed him all its skills, which were the following:

First of all, the otter slept with me in my bed and it was so tidy that not only did it never mess up my bed, but not even under the bed. It went to one place where a container was put for it. Only there it obeyed the call of nature. Secondly: it was such a good guard at night. God forbid if anyone approached my bed! After it allowed my orderly to take off my boots he could no longer show himself, for it would make such a noise that I would wake up no matter how sound asleep I was. When I was intoxicated and someone passed by my bed, it trod on my chest and squeaked until I woke up. And during the day it would stretch itself out somewhere and would sleep so soundly that even if I were to take it in my hands, it would not open its eyes. This animal trusted me so much! It refused to eat either fish or meat raw. Even when on a fast day or a Friday it was served a chicken or pigeon without seasoning and parsley, it refused to eat it. It grasped like a dog when I said: "Don't let it be touched!" If someone pulled me by my frock and I said: "Seize him"—it would jump with a terrible shriek, would pull him by the frock, by the legs, aided by the dog, the only one whom it loved—his name was Kapreol and he was a shaggy German dog. It learned all this from him and the other tricks as well. It was friendly with this dog only. This dog was kept in the house and during travel the otter was also with him. It did not like other dogs and when one entered the room it immediately pushed it out, even if it were the biggest greyhound. Once, Pan Stanisław Ożarowski came to see me;

[6]And agreed.
[7]Qualities.

actually he just dropped in, since we were travelling together.
I was glad to have him ; the otter was also glad, since it had
not seen me for three days. It came toward me and was over-
whelmed with joy and tenderness. The guest had with him
a nice female greyhound and he said to his son : "Samuel, hold
this greyhound, so that she does not hurt it !" I said to this :
"Do not worry, sir : this animal will not let anyone harm it,
even though it is small." He said surprised : "Are you joking,
sir ? This greyhound attacks a wolf, and disposes of a fox in
a trice !" After the otter had rejoiced at seeing me, it saw this
dog which did not belong to the household. It went up to that
greyhound and looked her in the eyes, and the greyhound did
the same ; it walked around the dog and smelled her back leg.
Then it stepped away from her and went away. I thought :
"Maybe now it will do nothing more." We had hardly begun to
talk about something, however, when the otter, which had
stretched itself out at my feet, got up again and went quietly
under the bench, came in back of the dog again, and it bit her
in the calf : the greyhound jumped toward the door and the
otter chased her : the greyhound ran behind the stove, the otter
still followed her. When the greyhound saw that she could not
escape anywhere she jumped on the table and wanted to dash
out the window. Ożarowski grabbed her by the legs ; she broke
two fine wine glasses however. Later, when she was let out, she
did not show herself to her master, even though he did not
leave until after dinner of the next day. Other dogs were just as
afraid of the otter everywhere. Even on the road, as soon as
a dog smelled it and it squeaked violently, the dog immediately
ran away. On the road it was very useful on a fast day. In our
country, especially in this region, when one arrived in a town
and asked : "Can one buy fish here ?" they were even amazed
at the question : "Where are we to get fish from ? We don't
even see them here." But whenever I rode by a pond or by
a river and the otter was with me, there was no need of a net.
I would get out of my carriage for awhile and shout : "Robak !
Hop, hop !" Then Robak would jump in and bring out whatever fish that water had, one after another, until I had enough.
I was not as particular there as when near my pond at home ;

whatever it brought, I would take except for frogs, which it brought often, since—as I have already mentioned—it was not choosy, but took whatever it came across. Then I and my orderlies had it nice and sometimes even a guest was fed. When—as it happens—several guests stayed at one inn, people wondered: "I gave orders to look for fish in this particular town, and I could not get any. Where did Your Lordship find such nice fish?" To this I would say: "In the water!" Even on a meat day my retainers sometimes said to me: "Oh, sir, it's swarming with fish in this pond; let the otter go!" I would go with it—because it did not want to go with anyone else except with me—and it fished them out. When it was a good fish, like a pike, or a big bass, then I also ate it, not only the orderlies, because I would forsake even the best meat dish for a good fish.

There was trouble with it on the road, as wherever I traveled people were amazed. They gathered in crowds, just as if something had been brought from India. There were plenty of onlookers, especially in Kraków. When I rode through the streets there, a crowd of all sorts of people escorted me out of the city. Once I was at the place of Pan Szczęsny Chociwski, my cousin; Father Trzebieński was also there. He sat down at the table next to me and the otter lay next to me on the bench; the otter gorged itself and slept stretched out on its back, because such was its favorite lying position. After the priest had sat down for awhile, he saw the otter and thought it to be a fur sleeve. He grabbed the otter and wanted to look at it. The otter awakened, gave out a terrible shriek, grabbed him by the hand and bit him. The priest fainted from fright and pain; we hardly managed to revive him.

After Straszewski had seen the *qualitates*[7] of this otter, he also saw my aviary, that is: my huge bird cage, which I had built and had covered with wire grating. In it there were as many kinds of birds as could be found in Poland. The birds made nests in the little trees planted there and were hatched there. I not only had birds which could be found in Poland,

[7]Qualities.

but also other, foreign ones. I had whichever kinds I could get
and from wherever I could get them. Straszewski was also
present at the time when the birds sat on their nests and
hatched their eggs. He saw everything : that the birds obeyed
me ; he saw that they let themselves be stroked in the nest ; he
saw partridges hatching there and taking their offspring for a
walk in flocks—he also saw that when I called them they
came running like chickens when grain is thrown to them.

Straszewski went back to the King and reported on everything he had seen. He had hardly arrived and given his report
when the King was seized by such a fancy : "It cannot be
otherwise, you must go there again, and you must bring back
the otter by all means : I simply must have it !" Letters were
again written to me asking what I desired to have in return for
it. The Polish Master of the Horse and Pan Piekarski begged in
their letters : "For Heaven's sake ! Make no more excuses.
Give it away and you will be rid of the trouble ; you shall have
no peace otherwise, because the King keeps thinking about this
otter walking, riding and sleeping. So that nothing would be of
hindrance to it, he gave his beloved lynx away to the voivode
of Malbork ;[8] his cassowary,[9] a bird, he sent to Jaworów,[10] so
that he could enjoy the otter all by itself."

Straszewski came back again, delivered the letters and
related how grateful the King was for the promise of the otter,
how lonely he felt without it and begged for it with these
words : "*Qui cito dat, bis dat.*"[11] In the letters they made big
promises. Straszewski told me that the King wanted to offer me
a monetary compensation, but that Pan Piekarski advised him
against doing so : "Gracious King, it is useless to send money
because it will not be accepted. This nobleman has great pride
and he surely would not take it. One should send something
which would be more graceful to accept." The King sent then
to Jaworów for two Turkish horses to be sent to me. These

[8]Franciszek Jan Bieliński.
[9]On the margin a postscript : a cassowary is a big bird without any
feathers but only with a coat like a pig.
[10]Near the city of Lwów ; a favorite place of Sobieski's sojourn.
[11]He who gives readily, gives doubly.

horses were very beautiful and he ordered to have them delivered with rich saddlery. I said that I would take neither money nor the horses, because I would be ashamed to receive such *honoraria*[12] for such a trivial gift.

I then sent the otter off on its new mission. It accepted this most ungratefully, squeaking and screaming in its cage when it was driven through the village. I went into the house, because I did not want to hear this. I felt so sorry for it. On the way, wherever there was water *in plano*[13]—so that it would not hide away—it was let out of the cage several times in order to cool off and to enjoy itself. But even this did not help : there was plenty of squeaking and screaming. The animal longed to go back and pined away ; it was brought to the King ruffled as an owl. The King was immensely glad when he saw it and said : "The otter got homesick but it will recover." Whoever was ordered to stroke it, the otter grabbed his hand. The King then said : "Marysieńka, I shall dare to stroke it." The Queen warned him not to do it, as the otter would bite him. He nevertheless sat down next to it, after it was put on the bed again, and he stretched out his hand to it, slowly saying : "I shall consider this a good omen if it does not bite me ; and even if it does bite me it does not matter, the newspapers will not write about this." He stroked it then ; it bent toward him. The King became even more delighted and continued to stroke it. Later he ordered food to be brought for it and he fed it bit by bit. Reluctantly it ate a little on that gold brocade.

Soon after it began to crawl from room to room, wherever it wanted to, more and more freely ; it was already there two days. Water was placed for it in big containers and small fish and crabs were put there. It rejoiced at that and kept fetching them out. The King said to the Queen : "Marysieńka, tomorrow I shall only eat the fish which this otter will fish out for me. Tomorrow we shall go, God willing, to Wilanów.[14] We shall test it, if it can handle the fish there."

[12]Compensation.
[13]In a plain.
[14]Palace outside of Warsaw, on the Vistula, formerly Milanów. Sobieski acquired it in 1677. Czubek, *Pam.*, p. 505, note 3.

I had written a whole list of information, how one should deal with it. I had also written down that it should never be tied by the collar, but right next to the collar, because an otter's neck is thicker than the head. No matter how tight the collar were, it would be immediately pulled off its head. Indeed this happened. It was tied by the collar; it pulled the collar off itself together with the bells and it ran away. During the night it crawled around on the steps and, homesick, it somehow managed to get outdoors. At my place it became accustomed to go wherever it pleased, to roam around ponds and rivers as long as it wanted to, according to its wish, and then to come back home again. After it had crawled out, it wandered along the paths there not knowing where to turn. Early in the morning a dragoon came across it; not knowing whether it was wild or tame, he struck it with a halberd and killed it.

They got up—the otter was not there; they called and looked for it (. . .)[15] a great commotion. In the city an announcement was made with both threats and entreaties that no one should dare to keep the animal after he had found it. Then a travelling Jew came from Pińczów, followed the dragoon, who wanted to get paid for the skin. "What do you have here, man?"—a porter asked him. The Jew kept his hand in his pocket; the porter looked under his frock and found the skin stuffed with straw. Both the Jew and the dragoon were seized and brought before the King. The King looked at the skin; with one hand he covered his eyes and with the other he grabbed his hair. He began to shout: "Kill them, whoever is a man of honor! Kill them, whoever believes in God!" Both were thrown into the tower. *Conclusum*[16] to shoot the dragoon. He was ordered to take the last rites. Priests and bishops came to see the King. They argued and begged to realize that the dragoon did not deserve the penalty of death, for he had merely sinned in ignorance. The only thing that they *effecerunt*[17] was that the dragoon was not to be shot, but to run the gauntlet

[15]The manuscript is damaged in this spot.
[16]It was resolved.
[17]Managed to gain.

through the Gałecki[18] regiment. The regiment took the customary position in two files. The decree was that he was to run
the gauntlet fifteen times ; he was allowed to rest at the flanks,
nihilominus.[19] He ran so twice. There were a thousand and
a half men in the regiment and each one struck him once. The
third time around the dragoon fell in the middle of the file ;
contrary to the law he was hit even when lying down. Later he
was wrapped in a sheet. It was rumored that he never recovered.

Thus great joy turned into great grief, because the King
did not eat anything and did not talk to anyone for a whole
day ; the entire court was in a state of despair. So they deprived
me of a beloved animal ; yet they did not rejoice over it long
and even brought trouble upon themselves.

I also kept hunting game, which aroused admiration. I shall
begin with the birds. I used to have very nice falcons, hawks,
merlins, hobbies, and ravens all the time : they were used to the
hunting rod under which the partridges let themselves be
caught. These birds hunted a hare like a lanneret ; all of them
did their share. I once had a huge hawk which was so swift
that it could catch any bird. It was not even reluctant to go
after the smallest bird ; it would snatch it in his huge clutches
and every time it would bring it to me unharmed. Even if it
were set upon very big birds, it did not mind that ; he pursued
geese, ducks, storks, kites, ravens, as well as quail. He managed
to catch several quail a day. It was so strong that whenever it
fought with an old hare, it strangled him ; it then straightened
out its plumage and flew with it to another field, lifting the
hare from the ground like a partridge. I had the hawk for eight
years, until it died.

As for the hunting with greyhounds, I bred for myself
a leash of them from the breed of Pan Stanisław Pasek, my
cousin, who lived in the region of Sochaczew. These greyhounds
were tall and beautiful and at the same time so swift that it was

[18]Franciszek Gałecki, master cook of the Crown. Czubek, *Pam.*, p. 507,
note 4.
[19]Nonetheless.

not necessary to let them off the leash to hunt a hare or a fox ; they took turns, every hare was pursued by a different dog and none of the hares ever escaped. Against a wolf all the greyhounds dashed ahead however. The hunters in the nieghborhood used to say : "Woe to the animal which comes across Pan Pasek, for it will not manage to escape."

I enjoyed very much training the wild animals to become tame, to be friendly with dogs and to hunt with them their own wild brothers. When someone came to visit me, he saw a fox playing with greyhounds in the courtyard ; when he entered the house he saw a wolfhound lying under the table and a hare sitting on top of him. If some stranger met me on my way to a hunt, he saw several greyhounds, several scenting dogs and a fox, a marten, a badger, and an otter running among them ; a hare with bells hopped behind a horse, a hawk sat on the hunter's arm, a raven flew right over the dogs and from time to time it would sit down on the back of one in order to ride for awhile. The stranger would just cross himself then and say : "For Heaven's sake ! this is a sorcerer ; animals of all kinds run among his dogs. What is he looking for ? Why does he not bait these animals which run behind him ?" If another hare jumped out, all these animals followed him, even the tame hare did so when he noticed the dogs rushing ahead. But when the pursued hare began to moan, however, the tame one ran blindly back to the horse. My hunting was made famous in all of Poland, even in an exaggerated way. But I shall drop this subject now and shall return to the events of the year.

It came to an unfortunate demarcation of the borders in Podolia[20] with the Turks this year. The army was encamped in Mikulenice.[21] I sailed to Gdańsk with two barges ; I arrived there on the ninth day, since the current was strong and calm. I sold wheat to Pan Tynf at 160 zlotys. I returned by land and my barges arrived in the harbor[22] six weeks (. . .)[23] later.

[20]As a result of the humiliating peace treaty of 1676.
[21]A town south of Tarnopol.
[22]Of Nowe-Miasto Korczyn, on the Vistula. Pasek had his own gangway and granary there. Czubek, *Pam.*, p. 509, note 3.
[23]The manuscript is damaged here. Czubek, *Pam.*, p. 509, note 4.

At night, on the seventh of October of this year, my stockyards and my barns burned down in Smogorzów. Prices were
very low everywhere and for that reason I was not selling
anything ; in Gdańsk the price of grain was low, only wheat
paid well. At a conservative estimate I suffered a loss of twenty
thousand zlotys because of that. The peasants blamed the fire
on the overseer *ex invidia*[24] for him. According to them he
started the fire when he looked for his boar with a light. I had
a lawsuit brought against him and I had him tortured. He did
not admit anything, because he was innocent. The scoundrels
had accused him falsely out of hatred ; by doing so they also
led me to sin and deprived me of a good administrator, since I
took aversion to him for being in the hands of the executioner,
and I dismissed him. Later, after I had learned that the cause
of the damage was different, I regretted doing so. I learned
that the fire had started at the blacksmiths's, since a strong
wind blew directly at the stockyards ; the barn began to burn
most likely *ab extra*[25] and *non ab intra*.[26] Later also other barns,
stacks, ricks, and haystacks caught fire. Thus was the will of
God : *Dominus dedit, Dominus abstulit.*[27]

[24]Out of hatred.
[25]From the outside.
[26]Not from the inside.
[27]God gave it and God took it away.

ANNO DOMINI 1681

By the grace of God I began this year in Olszówka. Toward the end of the carnival season, I gave a wedding reception for his Lordship Aleksander Tomicki and her Ladyship Makowiecka, a widow,[1] née Gołuchowska in Kraków. On the twenty-first of June I became ill *periculosissime* ;[2] I nearly found myself at Heaven's gate. Let the Merciful God be blessed for my recovery and may He spare me from such an illness a second time! *In Augusto* I went to Gdańsk ; by the grace of God I sold my grain profitably and returned happily. Afterwards I helped to bring agreement between his Lordship Trzemeski, my relative and his Lordship Kiełczowski concerning the matter of Klimontów.[3]

Immediately after, I attended the wedding of her Ladyship Tomicka,[4] the daughter of the Castellan of Wieluń, to his Lordship Walewski[5] in Pińczów. The wedding was splendid and was attended by many guests.

From this wedding all of us went to Kraków to attend the

---

[1] The widow of Mikołaj Makowiecki, the master of the pantry of Halicz. Czubek, *Pam.*, p. 511, note 1.
[2] Very seriously.
[3] A village in the district of Jędrzejów. Czubek, *Pam.*, p. 511, note 6.
[4] Marianna Tomicka, the daughter of Konstantyn and Agnieszka, née Myszkowska, first cousin of the heir in tail Franciszek Myszkowski. Czubek, *Pam.*, p. 511, note 7.
[5] Aleksander Walewski, the standard-bearer of Sieradz. Czubek, *Pam.*, p. 511, note 8.

consecration ceremony of Father Jan Małachowski[6] to the bishopric of Kraków ; his Lordship Father Konstanty Lipski[7] was consecrated at the same time to the Archbishopric of Lwów. If one were to call the consecration ceremony of the bishop beautiful, one would find the consecration ceremony of the archbishop even more beautiful and beyond any comparison— it was accompanied with a rich and splendid hospitality.

In Stobnica the funeral of Aleksander Komornicki, a cavalry captain, was held. He was a great enemy of mine during most of his lifetime, but two years before his death a most devoted friend. He died in my arms. I was formally charged with inviting the mourners to the commemorative reception ; the eulogy which I delivered pleased everyone.

This year a comet appeared *ad occidentem.*[8] Prince Dymitr,[9] the Polish commander-in-chief, died. The army was encamped at Trembowla ; it was not engaged *in opere belli*[10] this year. The soldiers lay around, ate and drank, and we had to pay for it.

[6]He was captain of horse under Rewera Potocki. He became a priest after his wife's death ; was first canon of Kraków, then Bishop of Chełm, and in 1666 Deputy Chancellor of the Crown's Treasury. Czubek, *Pam.*, p. 511, note 9.

[7]Abbot of Jędrzejów. Czubek, *Pam.*, p. 512, note 1.

[8]In the West.

[9]Dymitr Wiśniowiecki. This is a mistake ; he died the following year. Czubek, *Pam.*, p. 512, note 4.

[10]In any military activity.

ANNO DOMINI 1682

By the grace of God I began the year happily in Olszówka. The winter this year was truly Italian, entirely without snow and frost. One did not ride in sleighs, the rivers did not freeze, the grass was green, there were leaves on the trees and flowers all winter long. People plowed and sowed at a time when otherwise severe cold persisted. Even March was so warm, dry and cheerful, that it was truly contrary to its own nature. Only in April there was snow and frost. Snow fell again during the Easter Holidays, whereby the already sprouting vegetables, especially peas, froze in certain areas. During the second week after Easter there was such a great snow and frost that one could ride in sleighs, although the calendar makers[1] had not written about it. They surely know what goes on in the sky, or rather, what is written there. It would be better, however, if they knew that their wives were writing love letters to others. But they don't know this and perhaps find out about it only when they are warned about it and manage to catch the go-between, snatch the love letter from her hand and read it.

The accession to the office of margrave[2] in Książ[3] by his

---

[1]The calendars at that time included also weather forecasts.

[2]Rather to the estate in tail of Pińczów which was established by Zygmunt Myszkowski ; the title of Margrave was given to him by the Pope, Clemens VIII. He was received to the coat of arms and family of the Duke of Mantua. This was confirmed by the constitution of the Diet of 1601. Czubek, *Pam.*, p. 513, note 4.

[3]Książ Wielki, a town near Miechów, in the voivodeship of Kraków. Near it is the castle of the Myszkowskis. Czubek, *Pam.*, p. 513, note 5.

Highness the Margrave Stanisław, as well as his taking of the oath,[4] took place *(pri)ma Decembris*.[5] It did not come to a good end, however, for he did not exercise his authority long.[6] One should always pay attention to these things and be on one's guard.

This year our armies remained stationary and did not do anything. Pan Jabłoński became Grand Marshal and Pan Sieniawski the Field Marshal.

[4]The oath which Myszkowski was obligated to take required a strict observance of the statutes of the estate in tail. Czubek, *Pam.*, p. 513, note 7.

[5]On the first of December.

[6]Pasek was shocked by this ceremony because it took place during Advent ; the church authorities forbade loud ceremonies during that time. Czubek, *Pam.*, p. 513, note 9.

ANNO DOMINI 1683

By the grace of God I began the year also in Olszówka. The year started with the wedding of his Lordship the Margrave with her Ladyship Bronicka.[1] God grant that it be joyful until the very end !

The Warsaw Diet began, during which *magno motu et deliberatione*[2] Poland joined in an Alliance *cum Imperio et Republica Veneta contra potentiam Ottomanicam.*[3] May God bless the pious intentions of these Christian monarchs *et totius Christianitatis* ![4]

Vienna was severely oppressed by the Turks. The armies of the German Emperor retreated because they could not hold out.[5] The Germans were driven off the battlefield *primo con-*

[1]Salomea Bronicka, daughter of Andrzej Bronicki of Kraków. Czubek, *Pam.*, p. 514, note 1.

[2]After many efforts and deliberations.

[3]With the Empire and the Republic of Venice against the Ottoman might. Pasek is mistaken here. The defensive and offensive alliance of March 31, 1683 was between Poland and Austria only. Poland's alliance with the Emperor, the Republic of Venice, and Pope Innocent XI was the so-called Holy League.

[4]And of all Christianity.

[5]The Turks had declared war on Austria already on January 2, 1683. Leopold and his court abandoned the city and went to Prussia. Charles IV, Duke of Lorraine, the commander of the imperial forces, retreated and waited for Sobieski and the Poles. Marriott, *East. Quest.*, p. 122. The Turks reached the walls of the city on July 14. The exact number of Kara Mustafa's army is not exactly known ; some have estimated it at 500,000 others at 200,000 or 300,000 ; according to Silähdar Mehmed Aga, the Ottoman historian, the engineer and artillery units alone had 60,000 men. Carsten, p. 513.

gressu[6] and great numbers of them were captured or killed. The Turks continued to assault Vienna ;[7] they mined its walls, broke its bastions and placed mines under its gates. The city *vix, vix spirabat*.[8] It was as if a strong man had subdued a weak one and then held him down and tried to strangle him ; the weak one then no longer tried to tear himself loose, but only implored for mercy. Vienna, to be sure, had a huge *praesidium*[9] under the command of General Starhemberg,[10] a good soldier. It had cannon and gunpowder, in *quantum satis*,[11] as well as sufficient quantities of provisions. But all this was to no avail, since no fortress under the sun could hold out *contra modernas inventiones oppugnationum propria virtute*.[12] Things were different in the days when only stones and spears were flung at the enemy and battlements were pounded with battering rams. Now grenades and case-shots are fired and balls, as large as buckets, fly from cannon-royals[13] and showers of steel pierce the body like a drill right to the very bone regardless of cuirass, elkskin and all the other protective *vestimenta*.[14] Now fireballs are flung which contaminate people with their terrible stench, killing them and sometimes almost causing *pestilentiam*.[15] Other destructive *elementa*[16] poison the life-giving water. And when

[6]At the very first encounter.

[7]The attack began on July 15. According to custom the Turks shot by arrow a message written in Latin and Turkish. They demanded the surrender of the city and the conversion of its inhabitants to Islam. They were guaranteed safe conduct if they wanted to abandon the city. Count Starhemberg gave no reply and the Turks began their assault. Carsten, p. 515.

[8]Was on the verge of collapse.

[9]Garrisons. The reports about the number of soldiers within the walls of Vienna vary.

[10]Ernst Rüdiger Graf v. Starhemberg (1635–1701), Austrian field marshal.

[11]In abundance.

[12]Against the modern inventions of besiegement with just bravery alone.

[13]These used forty-eight pound balls and were thus considered huge cannon at the time.

[14]Garments.

[15]Pestilence.

[16]Substances.

one finally believes that he stands on safe ground, made firm by God and nature, and does not know what goes on beneath him, at that very moment the spot on which he stands together with the embankments and the powerful buildings can be blown up toward the clouds like a fly with the gunsmoke. Fortresses serve now only to restrain coachmen from leaving a city before dawn without paying for the hay in the inn, or to stop a wolf from carrying away a mayor in his sleep ; but not a single fortress now can withstand an assault by all the modern inventions.

Such was the case with the fortress of Vienna. Who would not think, while looking at its splendor and fortifications, that only God's hand, and not a human one, could hurt it.[17] And just look at what destruction it suffered during a short siege of two months. It was not conquered but hard pressed, already *extremis laborans*,[18] having been drained of its strength, and *omni destituta succursu*[19] from its Emperor and its nation. The Germans were so frightened that they gave up all hope of not only opposing the Turks but even the Tatars. The Germans, the poor devils, were felled like trees in the forest. As I say, the only thing which kept Vienna from collapse was the hope of succor from the Polish army, about which Starhemberg had news through secret spies sent by the Emperor. The poor Germans used their own bodies to plug the holes in their fortifications. The surrender, which had been decided upon long ago and the conditions which had been described, they put off from day to day. The Turks knew that the Poles were coming to help or rather to relieve the Germans, but they did not believe that the Polish King *in persona*[20] would come with his entire army ; they *supponebant*[21] that only a certain part of the Polish forces would come. They worked slowly therefore, *et non nimis urge-*

[17]The fortress, i.e., the *Burg* was, by the standards of the seventeenth century difficult to conquer. Carsten, p. 515.
[18]Breathing its last, i.e., its fall seemed imminent.
[19]Deprived of all possible help.
[20]Himself.
[21]Assumed.

bant[22] for the capture of the fortress, because they did not much fear these Polish reinforcements. They reasoned that "If such huge German armies could not, from the start, withstand our assault and even now do not dare oppose us, though the capital of their country is threatened and though they fight on their soil, surely this small Polish army cannot possibly defeat us."

Prince Lubomirski[23] was already at the side of the German Emperor, along with those Poles who were recruited for the Emperor's money. And these men fought well there, even though some riffraff had enlisted among them. Any valet could become a Pan Captain or a Pan Lieutenant; any orderly who came on foot for recruitment was given a horse and could become a cavalry officer. The Germans heaped praise on them but all the credit was due to their good commander.[24] When the Polish King was setting out for this campaign the eagerness of his army was such that if they could have flown like a bird to the battlefield they would have done so. And this was already a sign of the prospective fortune. Even the King himself was as enthusiastic as though he were going for a certain and doubtless victory. So sure of victory was he that he took along with him historians and panegyrists who could observe the events and record the Polish victory *condigne*.[25] And he invited Kochowski[26] to this war with no other intention than to have him watch and give an adequate description of the victory. Even on the day of departure,[27] as he was about to mount his horse in Cra-

[22]Did not press too hard.
[23]Hieronim August Lubomirski, Knight of Malta and Marshal of the Polish Court, arrived, with a division which numbered 4000 men, in June in order to aid the Emperor. Czapliński, *Pam.*, p. 493, note 34.
[24]Lubomirski.
[25]Duly.
[26]Wespazjan Kochowski (1633–1699), a poet and historian, described the Vienna expedition in an opuscule entitled: *"Commentarius belli adversus Turcas ad Viennam et in Hungaria anno Chr. 1683 gesti"* (*Cracoviae* 1684). In the Polish language he described it in an unfinished poem under the title: "God's Deed" or "The Song of Rescued Vienna." (1684) (Song I). Czubek, *Pam.*, p. 518, note 3.
[27]August 15. Czubek, *Pam.*, p. 518, note 5.

cow, I heard the following words from his lips : "I pray to God that I will find the enemy still there. May it not be difficult to obtain Turkish horses in Poland." I wondered when I heard of his victory won so soon after his forecast. Some *murmurabant*[28] against his words at the time : "For God's sake may God not punish him with defeat for such conceited speech, because *cum potenti et victrici populo res est.*"[29] But apparently he spoke out of great confidence in God's help, since it came about so.

The King waited for the Lithuanian army a long time. Meanwhile, envoy after envoy came running from the German Emperor begging for the sake of God to hurry because Vienna was perishing. Unable to wait any longer for the Lithuanians, the King left. Before doing so, however, he made solemn *vota*[30] to God, settled his queen in Cracow, and entrusted Potocki,[31] the Castellan of Cracow, with the care of the Ruthenian lands.

When the King crossed the border, ample supplies and conveniences were provided for the army. He moved on with his army, *magnis itineribus*,[32] fearing that he might come to Vienna's aid too late. As soon as the Turks found out about the approaching Polish army, they began a violent assault on the city. When the Turkish Emperor[33] learned about the Alliance, he feared a defeat (which he would not avoid), and sent letters to his Vizier at Vienna as well as a rope assuring him that "this rope would not miss his neck if he did not soon capture Vienna.[34] Since it was you who wanted this war, you shall account for it if it goes *malo eventu*."[35] The villain bribed

---

[28]Murmured.

[29]I.e., the enemy is a powerful and a victorious nation.

[30]Vows.

[31]Jędrzej Potocki. Voivode of Kiev ; field hetman of the Crown in 1684. Czubek, *Pam.*, p. 519, note 3. Potocki died in 1691.

[32]In forced marches.

[33]Mohammed IV (1648–1687), dethroned ; died in 1691.

[34]Kara Mustafa, the Grand Vizier (1676–1683), brother-in-law of Mohammed Ahmed Kiuprili. He was indeed forced by the Sultan to perish by this silken cord.

[35]Unsuccessfully, i.e. if it fails.

the Janissaries[36] and plied them with liquor so that they would
fight boldly. He drove the captives ahead of the Janissaries in
the assaults and he himself ran about like a madman with that
rope around his neck. He summoned his men to fight, he besought them by the great prophet Mohammed to keep in mind
the fame of their invincible nation and to keep in mind also
his inevitable peril by means of the rope, which he wore around
his neck, if he failed to capture Vienna. So the heathens blindly
pushed forward to the fire, falling like sheaves. As the Polish
King approached Vienna with his army from Tuln,[37] the Turks
were assaulting the most. When the Polish army came to a stop
in order to join the German regiments,[38] the Turkish commander did not order the Janissaries to stop the assault, but turned
on us the Turkish cavalry, the Tatars, and Thököly's[39] Hungarians. The Tatars clashed twice with our men and then took
up a position away from them. The Vizier sent for the Khan[40]
and asked him : "Do you think that the Polish King is with the
army ?" The Khan said : "I think that I see that he is because

[36]A valiant Turkish infantry which consisted of Christian slaves (little
boys captured in other countries and brought up and trained as soldiers
in Turkey) at first. Later it formed the main Turkish force until it was
abolished in 1826.

[37]A city on the Danube, about twenty-three kilometers from Vienna,
separated from that city by the Vienna Woods. Sobieski's army crossed
the Danube there.

[38]Sobieski joined the Duke of Lorraine on September 5 and assumed
the command. Starhemberg sent a message for immediate help. On the
eleventh the allied armies took up their positions on the Kahlenberg.
On the twelfth they launched the attack. Marriott, p. 123. The two
commanders, i.e., Jan Sobieski and Charles of Lorraine met at Holla-
brunn to the north of Vienna ; Sobieski took over the command of the
entire allied army. The Turks learned of the advance of the allied army
on September 4. Carsten, p. 516. That Sobieski was the commander-in-
chief of the allied forces is confirmed by Prince of Anhalt, the Brandenburg general, as well as by Charles of Lorraine himself. Reddaway,
p. 548.

[39]Imre Thököly (1657–1705) a Hungarian magnate and Protestant leader
of the Hungarian insurgents who was proclaimed King of Hungary by
the Sultan. After the Turkish retreat he took shelter in Turkey, where
he died in 1705.

[40]Murad Girey.

if these Hussars[41] are present then also the King has to be."
The Vizier said : "Advise me !" To which the Khan answered :
"You counsel for yourself and I shall counsel for myself. I advised you long ago to withdraw from Vienna before the Poles
arrived.[42] Then the Khan galloped away from the Vizier to his
own men and exclaimed : "Allah, Allah !" Soon Tatars moved
away like a pitched ball. The Turks also began to weaken and
later fled.[43] Now they were cut at, slashed and pursued. In the
city,[44] when the besieged ones saw them escaping, they rushed
at the assaulting units and began to put them to the sword.
A multitude of heathens was killed. Others were punished by
being driven alive, in flocks, into Vienna to repair the walls and
fortifications which they had damaged.

All their cannon were left behind and their camp[45] was
abandoned with all its riches.[46] There was an abundance of
gold, horses, camels, buffalo, cattle and herds of sheep around
the camp. They could not rescue their beautiful and rich tents,
their chests filled with costly and magnificent garments, even
their money, because plenty had been found in their tents. The
Vizier's tents were as huge as all of Warsaw.[47] All these tents
with all their treasures became the property of our King. Even
sacks of thalers lay on the ground in huge heaps. The gold and
silver carpets were stretched on the ground. The bed with its

[41]Polish cavalry clad in winged armor. The Polish King set out for
Vienna with about 3200 of them.
[42]Fletcher describes the conversation as follows : "And you ; cannot
you help me"... "I know the king of Poland !" was the answer. "I told
you that if we had to deal with him, all we could do would be to run
away. Look at the sky, see if God is not against us." Fletcher, p. 122.
[43]The entire battle was under the command of the Polish King ; the
right wing of the allied forces was made up of the Polish hussars and
other types of cavalry. The Turks were panic stricken at the assault of
the Poles and soon were routed. Marriott, p. 123.
[44]The camp was located to the west of Vienna, between Grinzing and
Schönbrunn. It had 25,000 tents, 50,000 carts, mules, camels and buffa-
loes and looked like a large town. Carsten, p. 575.
[45]The entire Turkish camp with its treasures and provisions was lost.
[46]They had 10,000 casualties, as opposed to 5000 of the Christians.
Carsten, p. 168.
[47]Obviously the Old City of Warsaw.

bedclothes was appraised at scores of thousands of thalers. The
little rooms in those tents were so concealed that only on the
third day was one of the Vizier's mistresses discovered. Still
another mistress lay stabbed in front of the tent, a very beauti-

ful girl. It was said that the Vizier himself had killed her so that she would not fall into the hands of the enemy.

Other tents stood there for a week or two because it was impossible to remove them. When our Poles, who had taken much of this, were ordered to Hungary they threw them out of their wagons. When rivers were to be crossed and the horses became stuck in the mud, people would spread out a captured tent, which was worth a thousand or more, in order to pull the wagon across.

Our men told of the kind of comforts that the Turks had in those tents of theirs : bathtubs and baths with all the trimmings,[48] just like in the cities, and directly next to these, beautiful wooden pails, perfumed soaps lying in heaps on the shelves, fragrant perfumes in bottles, medicine chests with various balms, cologne and other objects, silver vessels for water as well as silver water pitchers and washbasins for washing, knives, Turkish daggers set with rubies and diamonds, unusual clocks mounted in gold, rosaries,[49] either sapphire or coral, set either with rubies or with some other precious stones. Bags of money lay in heaps on the ground or were just scattered in heaps on the ground in the tents ; never in chests, unless among the less affluent, who stored the money in cases. The Turks are not in the habit of stealing from one another, and there are no thieves to be found among them, hence they do not lock up their valuables. There were also various exotic *victualia*[50] such as rice, meats, breads, flour, butter, sweets, olive oil, other things. What discomfort could be felt in such a well-equipped camp ? But, as the saying goes, a rich household is easy to manage. One should not wonder too much at this immense wealth because the Turks were, after all, *depopulatores totius mundi et possessores quadraginta regnorum.*[51]

[48]Sobieski wrote in a letter to his wife : "It is impossible to describe the refinement of luxury which the Vizier had collected in his tents. There were baths, little gardens with fountains, even a parrot, which our soldiers pursued but could not capture". Winter, pp. 71–72.
[49]The Mohammedan rosary consisted of 33, 66, or 99 beads which were shifted according to the attributes of God. Czubek, *Pam.*, p. 522, note 4.
[50]Food supplies.
[51]The plunderers of the entire world and the masters of forty kings.

The war against the Turks should be pleasant and desirable to everyone and no one regrets risking his skin knowing that, as victor, he could afford to buy plasters with which to cover his wounds.

The Turkish horses also enjoyed great comforts. They did not get soaked, for they were kept nice and dry under a tent, not in the open air. They were well taken care of and covered with warm blankets and gold and silk-embroidered saddle-cloths. Everything one touched was something special. Quite rightly everyone should be eager to fight a war with Turkey, as one also renders a service to God when fighting an enemy of His. And this is now a pampered nation and no longer so industrious as it used to be ; their riches and possessions drowned them in luxury and made them effeminate. They fight only with the help of Tatars and their captives, whom they take from other nations and train for war. They make out of them Janissaries and spahis.[52] They themselves are already effeminate, however, and this *mollities*[53] will most likely bring upon themselves a speedy peril. And we have historical *praeiudicata*[54]

[52]Turkish cavalry at one time.
[53]Softness.
[54]Evidence.

that what is bound to happen to the Turkish nation *per nimiam mollitiem et voluptatem*,[55] happened to other nations which earlier had held sway and had been feared by the entire world. It is a good start for the conquest of the Turks, since God gave such means for their annihilation and for the recovery of so many kingdoms and holy places now in their possession.

This victory was achieved on the twelfth of September.[56] It brought joy to all of Christendom and it delighted the desperate Emperor, who had commended himself to the protection of God. It cheered up the entire German nation and especially the inhabitants of the city of Vienna, to whose backs this scourge was the closest. It brought eternal fame for our nation, a fact which other nations acknowledge even now. I heard from the lips of a distinguished gentleman, a Frenchman, the following statement: "*Poloni sunt genitores Germaniae.*"[57] For it is certain that Vienna could not have held out for three more days and, if it had perished, all of the imperial territories and subsequently all Christian nations would just as surely have perished. Thus, we have something for which we should thank our King and master who did not shun this war. His enthusiasm did much good for Christendom and was especially profitable in encouraging all the young Polish noblemen and lords to go *personaliter*[58] to war. They rendered the King a service and, thanks to their armed retinues, the army had a far larger and a more splendid appearance. The second advantage was the greater fear that had overcome the enemy once he learned that the King had arrived *in persona*.[59] The King's reputation as a warlike and a lucky master and his conquest at Chocim[60] on the Dniester *in anno*[61] 1673 had not been forgotten by them even then.

[55]Because of excessive coddling and debauchery.
[56]By the evening of that day the Polish cavalry entered the Turkish camp. Carsten, p. 516.
[57]The Poles are the fathers (here saviors) of Germany.
[58]Personally.
[59]In person.
[60]Khotin or Hotin in English. The Turks suffered a great defeat there at the hands of this Polish King.
[61]In the year.

31*.

All the people of the Catholic religion were and are content
with this resolution of our master the King. The Lutherans and
the Calvinists, however, were displeased, since they considered
this war as their own and begged God for a Turkish victory.
They thought this would be to their advantage; hence they
sided with the oppressed Thököly and other dissenters. I was in
Gdańsk at the time, and they begged God at their church gatherings to give the Turks a victory over the Emperor. Whenever they read in the newspapers that things had gone favorably for Thököly, when on a raid he had killed several Germans, they celebrated the event and said thanksgiving prayers:
"*Oh, Her Got! Oh, liber Got!*"[62] Pictures of Thököly on horseback, dressed in full armor, were sold. Those who were selling
the printed leaflets would also sing them right away. I was
walking past once when one of them was singing. I hummed
a little and then asked what he was singing about, since
others listened to him so attentively? I was told that this was
the news of Pan Thököly who happily defeated the Emperor.
When the one who was singing heard my question he showed
to me the script in German, saying: "Yes, Sir, buy them, buy
them!" I asked: "How much do you want for them?" He
answered: "A penny." I gave it to him. Many lads followed
me to an inn asking for some money. There was one shrewd
fellow among them and I said to him: "Dear brother, you shall
have one zloty if you wipe your bottom with this sheet!" The
peasant lowered his pants with great eagerness, he thoroughly
wiped his stark naked backside with those leaflets and then
flung them into the Motława river.[63] The German men and
women began to grumble and murmur, and I left. The Catholics, and those who had watched the scene from the ships
roared with laughter. And when I related it to the Catholic townsmen, the Dominican friars and to the Jesuits, they said: "Fortunately no commotion was raised against your Lordship, because these Germans here worship this Thököly with almost
divine respect."

[62]Oh, God! Oh, Dear God. (German, should be: "*Oh, Herr Gott! Oh,
lieber Gott!*"
[63]The inflow of the Vistula which flows through Gdańsk.

People advised me to buy horses from a merchant in Nowe Ogrody, a suburb of Oliwa,[64] I went there on a Sunday, in the late afternoon, at the time when almost everyone walked or rode out of Gdańsk for strolling. As I was returning from visiting that merchant, it began to rain. Since the weather was fine when I left, they did not take a cloak for me. I stopped in an inn in order to wait for the rain to cease and the strollers also ran under the porches wherever they could. A number of them dashed into the room where I was, sat down at tables and began discussing the war. I did not understand them, only very little, that is, only certain words. But the one of whom I am writing told me about it later (and it was pouring and water was flowing in the gutters like a river). One of them, looking out the window at the downpour, said : "Oh, may God grant that the Catholic blood would flow in Vienna in such streams as this water." Another one said : "There is hope in God." And one German, who sat separately from these, shrugged his shoulders, rolled his eyes to heaven and looked at me. He did not say anything and only shook his head.[65] I noticed this but I did not know why he was doing it and I did not understand most of what the others said. Neither did I ask him anything, because I did not know him and I did not trust him. They again said such words against the King : "Why did that fattened pig go there ? Of what use was he there ? May both he and the Emperor end up jingling manacles there !" In the meantime the one who sat apart from them could no longer restrain himself because he was a Catholic. He was a German, not from Gdańsk, but from some Prussian city. He was a broker among the merchants there and addressed them not in German, but in Polish, so that I could understand, and said these words : "I assumed that I was among Christians, but I see that I am sitting among pagans ; I assumed that I was sitting with people, but I see that I am among beasts. And is it really becoming to

[64]A locality north of Gdańsk with a Cistercian monastery. This is evidently a mistake because the suburb Nowe Ogrody was located west of the city, on the road toward Oliwa.
[65]The rest of this sheet is damaged here in the manuscript. "Shook his head" is an insertion of Czubek.

utter such slander ? May all of you get killed !" They grabbed
their swords while he had only a cane. One of them wanted to
slash at him with the flat of his sword, or to cut at him, but he
shielded himself with his cane. He was hurt a little. He then
called out to me : "Sir, they are saying this against the King !"
I grabbed my sword. The Germans ran out of the room. It
would have been difficult to chase them in Gdańsk. Only then
did he tell me more extensively what they had said. And I said :
"Let us go to the mayor." "I will," he said. "Will you swear to
this ?' "I shall." We went there. The mayor at the time was,
a certain Szuman, a brave and a wise man. When we arrived
we did not find him there, however, for he had left for his
estate. The German returned with me to the inn. Just before
night fall I sent to the mayor's once again. He had come back
but had already gone to bed, tired, and even without having
had his supper. We had to wait *ad cras*.[66] Pan Beleński[67] was
to come in the morning in order to go to the mayor's. He did
not come on the second and on the third day. By now he had
been bribed and he shunned me. I inquired about him however
from the other agents, or brokers, as they were called there.
Felski, an agent, told me that the German was staying at Kęp-
ka's rooms, I went and found him there. And I said : "What
happened to your word ?" He began to be evasive and said :
"I don't know those men, I don't know their names ; how am
I to denounce them not knowing who they are !" I understood
the situation and I said : "You poor soul, you were swayed to
their side. But you should know that it's an offence to tolerate
such a crime. It is *crimen laesae Maiestatis*[68] and besides that
it is also a great *scandalum*[69] against God." He admitted that
they had begged him not to charge them and that he had been
paid to be silent. I implored him to at least tell me their names
because I could surely have them arrested at the town hall and
then sent the city a summons to the court. He did not even
want to do this, pleading that they were influential men. And

[66]Until the next day.
[67]May have been Baliński.
[68]A crime offending His Majesty.
[69]Blasphemy.

he added : "I work here, I make my living in Gdańsk and I would have to leave this area." And so nothing came of it. I only regretted that during the mayor's absence I did not go to see someone else *ex magistratu*[70] and did not make that declaration right away, because once he had testified it would have been difficult for him to deny his words, no matter how high a bribe the others would have offered him.

Thus among the Christians some wished for a good, others for a bad outcome of this war. But God granted a lucky victory those who were *bonarum partium*.[71] He gave courage and strength to the good Christians and humiliated the dissenters[72] and their protectors.

Soon after that lucky victory the two monarchs, the Christian Emperor Leopoldus and the Polish King Jan III, met together *ad mutuum amplexum*.[73] How much jubilation and congratulating took place when the *principes Imperii*,[74] that is the Prince of Lorraine,[75] the Prince of Bavaria,[76] and the Prince of Baden[77] and others, had assembled there, and how they were received, history will write at length.[78] Later the King went to

[70]From the municipal office.
[71]On the right side.
[72]Pasek calls the Protestants thus.
[73]In order to greet each other.
[74]The princes of the Empire.
[75]Karl Leopold, i.e., Charles of Lorraine.
[76]Maximilian Emanuel.
[77]Ludwig Wilhelm, Margrave of Baden.
[78]Pasek idealizes the situation, for immediately after the victory of the Polish King, Leopold was overcome with envy and did not want to receive him at first, even though Duke Charles of Lorraine himself urged him to do so. It was finally agreed that the Emperor and the King were to meet on horseback in an open plain. Sobieski describes the interview thus : "I had my interview with the emperor the day before yesterday, that is, on the 15th. He arrived at Vienna some hours after my departure. ... We saluted each other politely enough ; I paid my compliments to him in Latin, and in few words. He answered me in the same language in picked terms. ... I presented my son to him, who approached and saluted him. The emperor only put his hand to his hat. ... He treated the senators and hetmans, and even his relation, the Prince and Palatine of Bełz, in the same say. To avoid scandal and comments of the public, I again addressed a few words to the emperor,

look at Vienna and at its devastation. Starhemberg had invited
him there and he dined at his quarters. When the Polish King
rode through the city, the crowd which assembled to greet him
was greater than the one which had defended the city against
the assaults. The people, the poor souls, cried out of great joy,
raised their hands to Heaven, begged for blessing and for
recompense from God, and called the King their savior, so that
he had to muffle his ears. Usually the innkeepers did not
accept payment from the Polish soldiers for the wines and for
other things, but some churls did.

   Later the imperial and the Polish armies went to Hungary
in order to look for Turks and to attack certain fortresses. They
bypassed Komara,[79] an imperial fortress which had not been in
the Pagan hands, even though other fortresses beyond it were
captured by them, as well as Nowe Zamki[80] which the Turks
had built, and, as they moved toward Strygonia[81] the Poles
came across the Turkish army at Parkany.[82] Even though our
army knew about it they assumed that it was a small army and
the Polish vanguard[83] proceeded carelessly. The Turks surpised
our men, who did not even have time to return the fire and an
entire regiment of dragoons of the Polish Guard Bidzieński[84]

after which I turned my horse ; we saluted each other, and I rode back
to my camp. . . . our people are very much piqued, and complain highly
that the emperor did not deign to thank them, except by touching his
hat, for so many pains and privations. . . . everything is suddenly changed ; it is as if they did not know us any longer. . . . They give us no
more forage or provisions". Fletcher, *His. of Pol.*, pp. 126–129.

[79]Komárom, Komorno, a fortress at the Waga and Danube rivers.
[80]Neuhäusel. A locality and an old fortress on the Nitra which was
recovered two years later. Charles of Lorraine was stationed there and
wanted to besiege it, but left the area in order to march toward Vienna
before the battle. Carsten, p. 515.
[81]Esztergom, Esztergan in Hungarian, a city located on the right bank
of the Danube. According to Czubek the Poles marched along the left
bank.
[82]A city on the left bank of the Danube at the mouth of the river
Hron.
[83]October 7.
[84]Stefan Bidziński, the guard of the Crown, later the voivode of Sandomierz.

was put to the sword. Many other dragoons assigned to the vanguard were also killed. The guard himself barely managed to escape but he lost more than two thousand men, young officers, noblemen, including many of his own relatives. Everything happened so quietly and fast that the army which was beyond a hill did not know about it. When the King arrived with his army and looked at these dead bodies, our men instantly lost heart.[85] The Turks at that point charged frantically at our forces, who resisted them somewhat weakly at first. When the Turks came in back of the company of the Ruthenian Voivode, the Polish Field Hetman,[86] the Hussar company began to flee ; then another one followed behind it, then a third one and then the whole army including the King, the field hetmans and everyone with great dishonor and German derision. They shamefully kept running for about a league, until they reached the imperial army. The Pomeranian Voivode, Denhoff,[87] a very fat man, perished ; Siemianowski, a lieutenant, also perished, as well as many comrades who dropped their flags, their lances and their drums.[88] The horse under the King began to stagger, but was struck with the flat of the sword from both sides and finally did carry its master out. And thus if God had not favored our army with a victory on Saturday, which was even greater than that at Vienna, the ineffable fame

[85]This took place on October 7. The Turkish cavalry was concealed beyond the hills. The King tried in vain to collect his forces and to lead them against the enemy. The troops were panic-stricken and dashed blindly ahead. The King stayed behind with only seven companions till the last, pursued by hundreds of spahis. Prince Jakub was separated from his father. A dragoon finally saved the King's life. Otto Forst De Battaglia, p. 241. The imperial troops were rather slow in following the Polish ones. Fletcher, p. 130.

[86]Jabłoński.

[87]Władysław Denhoff, the Voivode of Pomerania, was also the treasurer of the Prussian lands. Czapliński, *Pam.*, p. 508, note 136. The imperial army under the command of Charles of Lorraine brought the Poles to a halt and at that point the Turkish cavalry immediately turned around. De Battaglia, pp. 241–242.

[88]These were copper, semicircular and covered with leather ; they were used by the cavalry and were hanging from both sides of the drummer's horse. Czubek, *Pam.*, p. 532, note 1.

of the victory at Vienna would have been everlastingly obliterated with the infamy of Thursday's flight.

Evidently we grew proud when we heard such vows *blandientis fortunae ab ore populi* :[89] "Oh, our Deliverer, our Savior !" Together with our excellent victor we must have thought : *"Quis est, qui de manibus meis eripere possit populum hunc ?"*[90] So God struck dead cavalrymen before our very eyes to impress upon us that our lives, like the lives of those who lay there in heaps, were at the mercy of His Holy Will, and also that we would know that not the size nor the might of an army defeats an enemy, but Heavenly forces, and neither wisdom nor our *experentia*[91] but God's Hand grants and brings victory over the enemy. If our men were defeated on Thursday, let us then repent for our sins and let us humble ourselves before God on Friday and He will exalt us again and will let us revenge ourselves on Saturday, and let us believe together with the Psalmist that whomever He grieves today, He will grow fond of tomorrow.[92]

The Pasha of Silistra,[93] *victo[r] triumphator*,[94] having conquered our men with the Will of God and driven them off the field, gathered up from the battlefield those abandoned lances, kettledrums, drums, many flags, and captives and sent them all to his commander-in-chief at Buda along with the report that he had routed the entire Polish army. Later he also sent the head of the Pomerianian Voivode, Denhoff, and assured them that it was the royal head, saying that it should be instantly sent to the Emperor : and he humbly declared that *in triduo*[95] the same would happen to the German army as well since it was practically in his net. The commander-in-chief rejoiced over this victory and summoned people who knew the King

[89]From the lips of people these flattering words.

[90]Who is the one who could tear this nation out of my hands.

[91]Experience.

[92]According to Czubek this is an inaccurate citation of Jan Kochanowski's (Psalm XXX) : "Him whom evening grieves, Morning will grow fond of." Czubek, *Pam.*, p. 533, note 1.

[93]He was Kara Mehmed. Silistra is a city in present-day Bulgaria.

[94]The triumphant conqueror.

[95]Within three days.

well *ad recognoscentiam*[96] this head, but their opinions differed. The commander-in-chief then sent the army which was with him at the time to aid the Pasha of Silistra. He also congratulated the latter on his victory, begged him to continue this victorious start and also informed him as to further action.

There was a bridge over the Danube, between Buda and Parkany and on Friday the Turkish army crossed over to the left bank of the Danube where the Pasha of Silistra was stationed. Now the Pasha had a larger armed force than before and was so full of hope that the Germans could not resist him since God had favored him so. Our King, even though downhearted by Thursday's misfortune, was, nevertheless, of good cheer when he said to the Imperial generals that things would go differently now, even though God sent upon us *beli vicissitudinem*.[97] And so both sides found comfort in hope.

On Saturday morning, that is, 9 [*octo*]*bris*,[98] our army marched out against the enemy with the imperial forces directly behind it. When it reached Parkany it took a position on the battlefield. The Turks came out of their camp to the battlefield like bees after honey and without much thought they rushed at those companies which on Thursday had fled the attack ; and the battle began. Then their other companies attacked our other Polish regiments as well. The Pashas were commanding, especially the Pasha of Silistra, who dashed at the ranks like fire. The battle was on. *Caesariani*[99] followed close behind. They got us mixed together with the Turks and cut them in half. The Turks began to run away, some towards the bridge, while others fled to the fortress at Parkany. The Imperial men rushed at them from the other side of the battlefield. Now the Turks were an easy prey. Not all from among those who ran towards the fortress could squeeze inside and the gates were bolted by those who got in first, so that the others had to dash into the Danube. Our men slashed at them so that dead body fell on dead body and soon after, in one sweep, the fortress was captured. At

[96]In order to identify.
[97]As a war adversity.
[98]On October 9.
[99]The Imperial men.

first the Turks fired from it but then ceased to, not knowing
at whom to shoot because our men had become so entangled
with their own. Those of them who did not want to await the
Polish sword on land threw themselves into the Danube. Some
drowned there while others, tired of swimming, turned back to
land and surrendered. One Turk swam on his horse as far as
Strygonia, so that even a fish could not swim better. That horse
which was such an excellent swimmer came into our hands
later when Strygonia was captured. And it was supposedly
valued very highly since, as they say : whatever a wolf sets his
eyes on will not escape. Those however, who were escaping
toward the bridge, perished by still a worse death, because
during that commotion on the bridge they killed each other in
order to get ahead, while those of them who stayed behind were
put to the sword and shot down. The great mob which pushed
onto the bridge and the weight of those who still clung to it after being pushed off so overburdened the span that it collapsed.
Now the Ottoman gentlemen began to swim and to drown.
At the same time, others were drowning further upstream at
Parkany and their bodies came floating down with the water so
that the Danube was dammed up with these bodies and horses,
causing the water to rise an ell or more over its bank. Parkany
was captured with cannon, even though it was fiercely defended
by cannon from the side of Strygonia and some balls reached
over and pierced with walls while other splashed into the water.

Whoever lost his flag or his kettledrum on Thursday in
Parkany found them there now and retrieved them *sine con-
tradictione*[100] from his Excellency the Pasha of Silistra. Even
the captives which the Turks had taken alive were found there,
because the Pasha had sent only a few of them together with
the head of the Pomeranian Voivode to his commander-in-chief.
And there were such fools among them who claimed it to be
the royal head, since the Pomeranian Voivode was heavy-set
and similar in constitution to the King. A great number of
people perished then. Those who considered themselves victors
on Thursday were beaten on Saturday ; those who on Thursday

[100]Without opposition.

were the pursuers, were on Saturday the pursued : those who
on Thursday reached out for someone else's head could not get
their own away from the Polish sword on Saturday ; those who
thirsted for Christian blood with great appetite on Thursday,
were on Saturday satiated with their own. Altogether, six pashas with all their belongings were captured ; two were killed,
while the Pasha of Aleppo[101] as well as the Pasha of Silistra,
their chief commander, were taken alive. The Imperial soldiers
looted the Turkish camp before our men got there. Our men,
who fought *prima fronte*,[102] went in pursuit and took revenge
for Thursday's defeat and for the blood of their brothers, so
they no longer looked around for booty. But even the Germans
did not get as many spoils as in Vienna, as these were the same
Turks who had fled from Vienna, leaving behind their *pignora*.[103] Those who managed to save something in Vienna had
to lose it in Parkany and their lives as well. What an immense
consolation it was to all of knighthood when the merciful
Father, having warned us, turned His merciful eye at us again,
restoring *in triduo*[104] the fame of the Polish nation, allowing the
blood of our brothers to be revenged to our heart's delight,
filling the rapid streams and the impenetrable depths of the
Danube with them. It is nothing new for God to take care of
a nation which is under His Holy protection. What a pleasant
spectaculum[105] it was for all Christendom. One could kill as
many of God's and one's own arch-enemies as one wished,
until one's hand dropped from fatigue. At the same time one
could delight in seeing the downfall of the oppressors brought
about *a vindici manu Dei*[106] caused one another to drown when
they grabbed at each other, when they swam long distances in
an attempt to save themselves, or sank like stones to the bottom
while their turbans floated like a flock of ducks in the Danube.
It was wonderful to witness how the proud Pasha of Silistra

[101]Alil Basha.
[102]In the front ranks.
[103]Wealth.
[104]Just three days.
[105]Spectacle.
[106]By God's revengeful hand.

was pulled by the nape of the neck by an inconspicuous Polish officer to stand before the Field Hetman, how another one, the white-haired Pasha of Aleppo, was brought before the same Polish Field Hetman, Jabłoński, lamenting his captivity. Many other distinguished Turks were brought before the Polish King and the Field Hetman. It was also delightful to see just any ordinary orderly astride a beautiful Arabian horse and clothed in a captured fur coat and turban. In short, God granted our forces a great victory right away *in recenti*[107] and His grace was evident as we made up for Thursday's ignominious defeat.

The Germans, on the other hand, took no prisoners, but killed them *crudelissime*.[108] Even after their death they did weird things to them : they dragged the Turkish corpses around, cut strips out of their skins and made straps out of them for their own use. On the third day after the battle hardly one Turk could be seen on the battlefield with his back unhurt. Even when one of our men carelessly escorted a captive through the German ranks, they killed him in his hands. My nephew, Stanisław Pasek, was escorting a Turk who looked important because of his dress and beautiful horse. He had already disarmed him and was leading the horse, with the captive on top, by the reins when a German came riding out, and when he caught up with the Turk he stabbed him with his sword. The Turk just groaned and as my nephew turned around he only gasped and fell off his horse. The German who stabbed him immediately rode to the side. My nephew began to scold him : "Oh, you scoundrel, such and such a son ! You killed my captive ; was that fair ?" The German just laughed and replied : "Yes, Pan brother, Pan Pole, why should one feed this devil ?" My nephew kept scolding him : "You are a knave, and not a knight, to kill a captive in my hands." And the German just kept retreating and laughing. What could one do ? The Germans harbor a great hatred against the Turks *ex ratione*[109] they had captured so many lands, provinces, and fortresses from them, and sec-

---

[107]I.e., again.
[108]In a most gruesome way.
[109]Because.

ondly, because the Germans are *a natura crudeles*[110] moreover, because they had absolutely no luck with the Turks, for they defeated them in all the battles. Wherever the Germans went into the battle, the Turks rushed at them with swords and slaughtered them like cattle. And even when the Great Vizier marched in order to lay siege to Vienna, the Germans never dared *opponere* him *offensive*[112] until the Poles had arrived ; they merely sought shelter in the fortresses. When the Vizier marched through their entire country without pulling his sword, meeting no resistance, for there was no opposition, he first sent to Vienna, as a vanguard, the Tatars who, without the help of the Turks, attacked the German defences so resolutely that they put to the sword almost half of the fiery German regiments even before the Turks arrived. The Germans shamefully retreated beyond the bridges across the Dunabe which had been constructed at great expense and which they subsequently burned, leaving for the enemy free access to the city of Vienna. The German gentlemen experienced on those and on other occasions what a Tatar was capable of and what war with him was like. They jeered at us before *et toties exprobrabant*[113] us for fighting with such a poor, unarmed nation, a hundred of which ran away from one gun-barrel. But now they tasted defeat themselves when they discovered that their firelocks could not withstand the Tatar sword. Even their huge cannon did not help them. I maintain that not only the one who withstands an attack *pugna stataria*[114] can be considered a knight, but also the one should not be esteemed lightly who surrenders some ground but turns back again and fights. The former is lucky if he wins, and if he loses it will usually cost him his life ; the second one flies like a bird to safety and then turns back to the battlefield. *Fugiendo pugnat, fugiendo vincit.*[115] I also fought the Tatars, yet I never saw so many Tatar corpses in a heap after a battle

[110]Cruel by nature.
[111]During victory.
[112]To oppose aggresively.
[113]And so often reproached.
[114]In a regular battle.
[115]In flight he fights and in flight he conquers.

as German, Muscovite, and those of other nations. To see three
or four hundred dead Tatars in a heap meant a great victory,
while of the dead of other nations one could see as many as
logs in a pile. It is preferable to fight with a German. When he
conquers me he does not pursue me ; when I conquer him he
does not escape from me ; on the other hand, it is difficult to
escape the Tatar, and to pursue him is a burdensome task.
Even if one does overtake him, one will not get much booty
from him. I shall, however, return to the abandoned subject.

After this fortunate victory at Parkany and after the capture of Strigonium, our army marched toward the border
through Hungary. When the army entered the mountain area,
the Hungarian insurgents[116] came pouring out of the mountains
and forests. They continually harassed our men *in tractu.*[117]
They captured and killed the retainers on patrols and attacked
and robbed the slow-moving train and supply columns and then
when things were rough they ran into the mountains, exploiting
the advantage of the terrain. Later the foul weather came and
a great number of houses perished and many wagons loaded
with the spoils of Vienna were abandoned. Some preferred to
burn these rather than enrich the Hungarian rebels. Suffice it
to say that some did as follows : when their wagons got stuck
in the mountain passes they then unloaded a beautiful Turkish
tent, spread it out in front of the horses to enable them to get
out of the mud, and when they got the wagons out they abandoned the tents, which were worth several thousand but were
now stamped in the mud. Tinware, copper utensils, chests,
leather bags[118] and other costly Turkish items, how many of
them were cast into the marshes or into the river, when someone's horses were fatigued ! In fact the German Emperor had
wanted the Polish army to go to Poland by way of Silesia after
a rest in Moravia ; the Poles themselves, however, insisted on
Hungary, hoping to achieve something there. But a whole sum-

---

[116]I.e., toward Poland. On Nov. 3 the imperial and Polish armies separated. The Poles went North in order to cross over to Poland through
the western regions of the Carpathian Mountains. DeBattaglia, p. 245.
[117]Along the road.
[118]Which were used for water or wine.

mer was necessary for this purpose, not just late fall. Besides, apparently the will of God did not agree with our intention and therefore things did not go for us the way we had wished them to. However, during their march across Hungary our men did capture Levice[119] and Seczyn[120] where there were Turkish *praesidia*.[121] As they proceeded toward Seczyn they felt it was absolutely necessary to get a captive from the city. The Cossacks were ordered to do so and were promised a reward. Several of them went into the orchards, but they could not capture anyone because the Turks were cautious and did not leave the town. They then agreed upon the following trick. Over a dozen of them concealed themselves in the orchards while two others went toward the city and, watching intently, approached it closer and closer. As soon as those in town thought that these two men were within bullet reach they either turned an arquebus[122] on them or fired a Janissary gun at them. One of the Cossacks, although unharmed, fell to the ground while the other began to lift him up and then to undress him so *quidem*[123] to revive him. When the Turks saw this they fired at this one from several guns, and he, having partly undressed the other, began to run without turning around. He ran purposely over open ground so that it could be seen from the city that he was escaping towards the camp. The other one lay still, supposedly dead. He had gaudily dressed himself in a red robe. Soon one of the Turks reached him, glanced around in all directions, and, seeing nothing, came close to the Cossack and looked into his eyes—the Cossack had closed his eyes and bared his teeth—and then began to get ready to render that poor Cossack wretch the last service (he did not dress him but wished to undress him). He knelt down and began to unbutton his frock; at that point the Cossack grabbed him by the neck. The Turk shouted, and they began to wrestle with each other. The town was far away

[119]Levice in Czech, a city in Slovakia, north of Esztergom.
[120]In Hungarian Szecsény, a town and castle not far from the Ipoly river.
[121]Garrisons.
[122]Or harquebus, an obsolete portable firearm, a gun with a hook.
[123]As if.

and it was difficult to rescue the Turk from beyond the moat, while the other Cossacks came running from the ambush. The Turk tried to tear himself loose ; he would have gladly let go of the Cossack but the Cossack did not want to do the same. The second Cossack rushed up, grabbed him, and brought him before the King. What a display of Cossack ingenuity and skill this was ! When the King found out from the captive that, with the help of God, the above mentioned Seczyn or Syczyn could be captured by us, he gave orders to prepare for the assault. The Turks were thoroughly prepared for the visitors and when the Polish regiments began to move to the attack they fired *potentissime*.[124] Many of our men were shot down and some prominent officers were wounded. But when the Turks saw that the Poles pushed forward like hungry flies at a fat ox and paid no attention to their heavy fire, they surrendered and begged for mercy, and they were granted pardon.

In this assault the Turks shot Franciszek Lanckoroński[125] from Brześć, the starost of Stobnice, and a brave and valiant knight, in the knee. This incident so upset the King and the hetmans that they would have preferred not to have conquered this fortress, not to have known it, and rather to have passed it at a distance than to be deprived of such a worthy and indispensable gentleman. But jealous Fortune was very much disappointed in its desire to despoil our fatherland of such an indispensable son ! God's grace and protection did not let it triumph in this. There was still the same heart and eagerness as before, the same *activitas*[126] and courage as before, the same, or even greater, *vigor* and willingness to be of service to the fatherland. In short, we shall do whatever is necessary, we shall go wherever there is need to, we shall be there where others are ; let us not shudder to appear *Tyriis in locis*.[127] Evil fortune thus

[124]With all their might.
[125]Franciszek Lanckoroński, Chamberlain of Kraków, starost of Stobnice ; married to Jadwiga Morsztyn, was a a great friend of Pasek. Czubek, *Pam.*, p. 543, note 4.
[126]Bravery.
[127]In Tyrian places. *Tyria maria*. Tyrian seas implying "dangerous seas," Pasek changed to "dangerous places." Czapliński, *Pam.*, p. 518, note 215.

cannot harm the good sons of the fatherland whom God's Hand preserves in Its gracious protection ; on the contrary, by wanting to spoil things ill-fortune sometimes helps one to procure good fame and an everlasting reputation. May Heaven bring much happiness to such sons of the fatherland. Let us wish and say with the poet :

Vivite fortes frotiaque adversis opponite pectora rebus.[128]

After the battle of Seczyn our men yearned to capture Preszów[129] and Koszyce,[130] but time was the greatest hindrance because winter was drawing near ; the army just made an appearance before these fortresses and marched on toward the border. We lost Modrzewski[131] there by accident, who was killed by cannon fire. He was an old-time soldier and a valiant knight. He was both a colonel and a captain of horse who led regiments and used to command on occasions ; and there he perished, having recklessly halted at a target spot when in the city orders had been given to fire. One should always guard against coming to a stop while approaching a fortress where there is some kind of a range-finding mark or bush, and should pass through such places as fast as possible because usually the gunners have their guns aimed at them.

When the King was close to the border the Lithuanian army came to join our men. It was a beautiful and an orderly army, but what of it, since it was *post bellum auxilium.*[132] They set out reluctantly on this expedition and things would have been very bad if the King had waited for them, as some advised him to do, because time would have elapsed and Vienna would have been captured, being unable to hold out any longer. Even the Germans themselves had admitted this, *et consequenter,*[133] such a fortunate victory could not have been attained at the

[128]"Live, oh Valiant ones. And expose your brave chests toward adversities !" Horace, *Satires* II, 2. A long poem follows next in the manuscript in Lanckoroński's honor. It is ommitted in this translation.
[129]A city in northeastern Slovakia.
[130]A city in Slovakia on the Hernad river.
[131]Krzysztof Modrzewski, seneschal of Halicz, killed at Przeszów. Czubek, *Pam.*, p. 558, note 4.
[132]Succor after the war.
[133]And consequently.

fortress once it had been conquered by the enemy. And in accordance with the clairvoyance of King Jan III and a special inspiration of the Holy Ghost one could say everything turned out well. It was because the King had such firm hope in the future victory that he set out for Vienna *tanta festinatione et alacritate*[134] and without any delay, even though he had had only one half of his army with him. But in Vienna, the people were on the lookout for the King's much-desired presence like souls in Purgatory. They were in the same situation as when a wolf is catching up with a sheep and reaches its neck with its muzzle while the sheep, the poor thing, exerts itself even more, hoping, in the meantime, that some hunter might drive up and rout the wolf. Such was exactly the case with the German Emperor, when he, already frightened and despairing of success, was unable to rescue his own capital. He did not dare to look the enemy in the eye and to *opponere*[135] the disheartened army. He only turned to God with prayers and expected the Poles. He continually sent messengers to our King, asking him to arrive as fast as possible in order to help to extinguish this frightful fire, which supposedly would have devoured all of Christianity. The King, as a wise lord, considered all the circumstances, and wished to rush ahead as fast as possible, knowing that reinforcements were more certain and effective a year before a battle than an hour after a battle.

The Lithuanians were highly disturbed for having missed such a splendid campaign. Both their hetmans, Sapieha[136] and Ogiński,[137] heard plenty of sarcastic remarks from the King. They were annoyed at them and also, to a no less extent, by not having displayed such a beautiful army, which was dispatched with the proper equipment at the expense of the Polish Commonwealth, *in hostico*.[138] The Lithuanians on the other hand, the

---

[134]With much haste and eagerness.
[135]Oppose.
[136]Kazimierz Sapieha, the voivode of Wilno ; died in 1720.
[137]Jan Ogiński, the voivode and starost of Mścisław (1674) ; then voivode of Potycz ; died February 25, 1684 in Kraków. Czubek, *Pam.*, p. 560, note 5.
[138]In the enemy's land.

poor souls, turned green with envy as they listened to the Polish soldiers, who related to them how God had blessed them with such a splendid victory, how they enjoyed prosperity and abundance of everything in the Turkish camps. When they saw the wealth, silver, gold, the richly embroidered garments, various artful things, rare objects and rich spoils, their hearts bled all the more and they accused their leaders of negligence.

The army left Hungary by way of the towns of Spisz[139] to Podgórze, while the Lithuanians marched towards Volhynia, where they made up for their losses at Vienna on the lands of Podlasie, Polesie, and Volhynia for what they had failed to do with the Turkish ones, because they pillaged them.

While leaving Hungary, Field Hetman Sieniawski died.[140] He had already been ailing when he set out for the Vienna expedition, but because of his inborn eagerness he did not want to miss such a pious war. He went there eagerly, even though he remained ill the whole time. He died in the service of his fatherland and to the credit of all Christendom. After his death the field hetman's mace was given to Potocki, the Castellan of Kraków; he was a son of Stanisław Potocki, who had also been a field hetman in the reign of King Jan Kazimierz.

During that Vienna expedition Kunicki,[141] whom the King had directly made a field hetman over the Cossacks, dashed into the Tatar lands in accordance with the royal orders. He was a nobleman from Lublin. This Kunicki had a good time there together with the Cossacks because the better Tatar units had gone to Vienna. He had plenty of time and he burned and devastated whenever some unit of their army opposed him. His army constantly grew in size because he recovered very many captives who settled there while the others, further away, came to him when they heard about the arrival of a Christian army.

[139]The starosty of Spisz, which encompassed thirteen towns, lies southeast of the Tatra mountains. Originally Polish, it was given as dowry by Bolesław Krzywousty to his daugther Judyta and thus to Hungary. In 1412 it was returned to Poland. It remained a property of Poland until 1772. Czubek, *Pam.*, p. 561, note 4.

[140]In Lubowla in Spisz.

[141]Stefan Kunicki (Konicki in the manuscript). He was a Cossack ata-

The Cossacks behaved cruelly, sparing none. They killed women, they tore children into pieces and did the worst possible things to them. Rumor spread that three hundred thousand of their kind were killed there. Kunicki moved around boldly there and was not afraid of anyone. When the Khan was returning from Hungary, he picked out thirty thousand of the best men, different from average Tatars, and sent them as relief; there were also some Turks among them. Kunicki battled them at Kilia.[142] He conquered them, demolished them, and whatever spoils they had he took and he luckily returned from beyond the border. But later the Cossacks themselves killed him under the pretext that he had wronged them in the spoils. It was nothing new among them to kill a hetman on the slightest provocation. He did not wrong them in anything, but he had taken much booty which they could not grab from him by any other means, so they rebelled against him. Thus those scoundrels basely lost a good warrior who knew how to chase the Tatars, being so well trained against them.

When the Tatars found such devastation in their land, the corpses of their wives and children, their cattle and herds taken away, they deplored their misfortune.

In short, God blessed Christendom at that time everywhere: in Germany, in Venice, as well as in Poland. Later, Dymidecki,[143] like Kunicki, accomplished much in Walachia; he defeated the Turks together with the Walachians, routed them and captured Hospodar Duca[144] and put him in prison. In Turkey, *in contrarium*,[145] there was trouble, many protestations and rebellions against the elders over the unfortunate leadership of the war and over the loss of so many lives. The Turkish Emperor blamed it on the Vizier and ordered him to be strangled *in publico foro*,[146] trying to cast on him the people's

man who was ennobled at the Diet of 1673 for his loyalty toward Poland. See DeBattaglia, p. 248.

[142]A city at the outlet of one of the arms of the Danube.

[143]A Polish colonel, later killed at Kamieniec by the Turks. Czubek, *Pam.*, p. 563, note 2.

[144]Gregory III Duca. Czubek, *Pam.*, p. 563, note 3.

[145]On the contrary.

[146]In a public place.

wrath ; but later he did not escape it and was removed *de throno.*[147]

This year closed with great good fortune and with great relieve to all the Christian nations, except for the Lutherans who had begged God to give the Turks the victory because Thököly, the rebel, who stood on the Turkish side so that the Lutheran provinces would supply him with money, spread the false rumor among them that the Turks waged war *eo fine*[148] to destroy the Roman religion and to establish the Lutheran faith all over Europe in its place. Because of that the Lutherans prayed to God, conducted big services, took up collections and gave them to Thököly for the promotion of the war. I was in Gdańsk at the time they conducted those services and pestered God so very much. He did not hear them out however, since it turned out differently. When they were still at Vienna and *in spe*[149] to recapture it they sang incidental songs[150] on the streets, recited them on the avenues along the shore, flung copies about, painted portraits of Thököly as a defender, *suae religionis,*[151] sold them at a high price and almost each one of them wanted a copy for home. In the churches they held *gratiarum actiones*[152] whenever they heard something of a lucky turn of events for the Turks, and my heart always ached at that. I don't know what kind of satisfaction they obtained when they found out *de contrario rerum successu,*[153] because I was already at home when the victory took place.

Thus the year ended with all sorts of good fortune from God, not only in public affairs, but also in my private ones because I was healthy during the entire year and things went well for me in everything. Oh, kind-hearted God, condescend to grant benignantly such years as long as I shall live. And for this year may Your Most Holy Name be praised !

[147]From the throne.
[148]In order.
[149]In hope, i.e. hoped.
[150]Pamphlets and verses printed on leaflets.
[151]Of their faith.
[152]Thanksgiving prayers.
[153]About the contrary outcome of affairs.

ANNO DOMINI 1684

By the grace of God I began this year also in Olszówka. In public affairs it was once again a lucky year, but as for me, "you can't do much business after the fair is over."[1]

This year our armies no longer united *cum Caesarianis*,[2] as they could already *subsistere*[3] on their own ; for they took heart after the victory of the previous year—as the saying goes : "anyone can mount a tamed and broken-in horse, but not everyone can mount a proud and a swift one"—and also because *colligati principes*[4] had launched *aversionem belli*.[5] The Venetians held out against a large portion of the enemy's army, which *de necessitate*[6] had to be on guard from the other side of the sea. Our King went *personaliter* with the Polish army beyond the Dniester and conquered far and wide the lands there. The main might of the Turkish Empire, by which *imperium potissimum floret*,[7] was directed at him ; that is, the Crimean, the Nogayan,[8] the Bielograd and the Budziak[9] Tatars as well

---

[1] An old Polish proverb. During this year Pasek had as many as eight lawsuits. Czapliński, *Pam.*, p. 542, note 1.
[2] With those of the Emperor.
[3] Hold out.
[4] The allied princes.
[5] A diversionary attack.
[6] Out of necessity.
[7] The most mighty empire.
[8] Name of the Tatar khans.
[9] Between the Volga and the Danube various Tatar hordes spread across the steppes. They were : the Nogay, from the Volga to the

as the Walachians and the Multans ; all of it would have surely gone against the Germans if it had not been for this diversionary offensive of the Polish King. During the entire campaign our men had very many clashes with them and withstood their *potentissimos impetus*[10] with a great loss of their men, but also of our own as well. Many of our own retainers were captured on patrols, while mowing grass or pasturing horses—such is an old habit of this nation. Meanwhile the Germans kept defeating the Turks ; they drove them off the battlefield during the first attack twice this year, they captured fortresses and cities : Nowe Zamki, Buda, and others in the upper and in the lower regions of Hungary ; that is, lands conquered and occupied by the Turks a long time ago. The Venetians also captured many Maklaks[11] who surrendered to them voluntarily in a rebellion against the Turks ; they conquered *regnum Moreae*[12] and captured many other cities in *collateralitate*.[13] Simply speaking, things go smoothly when two unite against one. But after all, thanks to the grace of God, our Poles and especially the King, who decided to rise against this enemy feared by the entire world, were the main cause of this good fortune. The King *personaliter* went with the army against the enemy ; he began the attack and pushed the enemy to the side. But our allies, like lazy hunting dogs, having snatched the worn-out animal did not leave off pursuing it until they bayed it ; they also shall sooner fill their pouch than those who set the animal running. For often indeed base and lazy people will sometimes sooner . . .[14] also an improbable thing in this alliance of ours ; we began the war for them and we helped them sincerely and they

Crimea on the coasts of the Black Sea ; the Crimean, in the vicinity of the Crimean peninsula ; the Białogrodzk, between the Crimean and the Dniester ; the Budziak, in the southern part of Bessarabia, between the Dniester and the Danube.

[10]Mightiest attacks.

[11]Perhaps this refers to the Slavic tribe of Morlaks in Dalmatia on the coast of the Adriatic. That name, however, is only known since the XIX century. Czubek, *Pam.*, p. 566, note 7.

[12]The kingdom of Morea, southern part of Greece.

[13]In the near vicinity.

[14]Here the manuscript is cut off. Czubek, *Pam.*, p. 567, note 86.

made great booty and will probably make still more, because they were fighting with that portion of the enemy's army which became effeminate, weak, and unaccustomed to war on account of the long-lasting peace, for the *status imperii Ottomanici*[15] purposely wanted to leave them *imbelles*,[16] turning them over to farming and to other labor after the victory over us, *ex ratione*[17] they would not rebel. We on the other hand were left to fight the army of those nations which were always warlike and unconquerable in the past but which above all were in constant maneuvers, *in continuo belli opere* ;[18] *verbo dicam*,[19] their life consisted of continually waging war, and they lived off war. Even if our allies[20] had conquered them, they would not have acquired much booty from them, because they were impoverished wretches. Our allies had thus chosen a good lot for themselves ; as it were, a portion well seasoned with cinnamon and condiments, leaving for us one with horseradish or hot pepper. May God grant us that our teeth will not become numb from it, because it is an *uva acerba*,[21] as I can see ; since He gave us a good beginning may He bring about a good end !

[15]The political wisdom of the Ottoman Empire.
[16]Unwarlike.
[17]So that.
[18]In constant warfare.
[19]In short.
[20]The Emperor, Venice and the Pope, i.e., of the Holy League.
[21]A sour berry.

ANNO DOMINI 1685

By the grace of God I began this year happily in Olszówka. The *Sejm* was in session in Warsaw. Because of bad spring crops the cost of living was high in Great Poland this year. Also in Warsaw prices were high for the same reason. As soon as I found out about this I had a scow[1] loaded with barley and peas, I sailed on it myself, and made plenty of money from the inhabitants of Great Poland *in Maio.*[2] I arrived too late, however, for if I had done so a week earlier, before so much had been brought in, I could have received *altero tanto*[3] for a bushel. *Eodem anno*[4] Stanisław, the Margrave of Pińczów, died in Lublin while serving as a deputy to the Polish tribunal, leaving me in a great predicament *ratione*[5] of my leasehold of the margravate estates, Many people rejoiced at his death, and I also did not mourn him very much because he was—God forgive him!—a cunning and insincere man who never kept his word and indulged in lies ; whenever he told a lie he felt as good as if he had fully satisfied his appetite. Therefore I did not feel sorry for him even though he had died. *Suppone-*

---

[1] A river boat used for rafting along the Vistula ; it usually had a crew of about fourteen men and could load up to twenty lasts of grain. A last is a unit of measure ; a Gdańsk last is approximately equal to 1800 kg. Czubek, *Pam.*, p. 568, note 8.
[2] In May.
[3] Twice as much.
[4] During the same year.
[5] Because.

bam[6] that his *succedaneus*,[7] his brother Józef,[8] would be different, since he seemed sedate and good-natured. I see, however, that I was as much deceived in my expectation as that woman who begged God for a better master and who was followed by a worse one instead.[9]

Upon my return from Warsaw I began to prepare for Gdańsk. I was impatiently waiting with transport of my grain, which was getting very overheated in the granaries and which constantly had to be worked. But since there was no high water I and everyone else had to wait *ad Septembrem*.[10] When our hoped-for time finally came, I fell very ill *30 Augusti*, which was a Thursday. This illness befell me from drunkenness because of bad companions, who always brought me to this, as I do not remember ever getting drunk of my own free will, like some whom I know. But when someone was glad to see me or I was glad to see him, especially if a dear friend was concerned, then it was impossible not to observe our Polish fashion. I fell ill *periculose*[11] and I could not recognize anyone, since I was seized by high fever. What the doctors did with me I do not know ; *sufficit*[12] that they lost all hope and announced that things were extremely bad and that *convalescentia*[13] was impossible.

In the meantime the tide began to rise. A granary watchman[14] came with word that workers should be sent to start loading, while I lay completely unconscious. My wife told the watchman to go away ; he left, for there was no likelihood that

---

[6]I assumed.
[7]Successor.
[8]Józef Władysław Myszkowski. Czapliński, *Pam.*, p. 547, note 10.
[9]Pasek altered here somewhat the tale of Valerius Maximus (Roman author, 1 B.C. to 1 A.D.) about a woman who had prayed for the health of the reigning tyrant in fear that he would be succeeded by a worse one. Frogs begged for a new king in the fairy-tale of Phedrus (Macedonian fable-writer, 1 A.D.).
[10]Until September.
[11]Gravely.
[12]Suffice it to say.
[13]Recovery.
[14]From Nowy Korczyn where Pasek had his warehouses.

God would help me so suddenly and strangely. It happened as follows :

I had been lying in this delirious fever since *30 Augusti,* when just before dawn of Friday, [*Septi*]*ma Septembris,*[15] the eve of the Holy Virgin's Nativity, I felt ; as if in a dream, that someone shook me by the arms and said the following words : "Anthony stands over you !" I turned my head toward the wall then and saw a monk standing there dressed *in habitu Minorum sancti Francisci.*[16] I looked at him and did not say a word. All those who had waited on me were worn out and had fallen asleep. It was almost daybreak when the monk shook me. It seemed as though it were a dream, but nevertheless I felt fully awake immediately after. I was in full control of my memory. I realized that I was bedridden ; and I was aware what was happening to me, even though I had been completely unconscious before. I assumed some monk had been sent to see me, as is usually the custom when someone is sick. But he said to me : "I have guarded you carefully since last Thursday. Have no fear and get up !" Some feeling of joy came over me and I reflected that he was no ordinary clergyman but that he must be a holy person. I started up, wanting to fall at his feet, and exclaimed in a loud voice : "Oh, Holy Father !" I fell off my bed. Everyone heard this exclamation and rushed toward me with candles. And I asked : "Where did he go ?" They assumed that I was talking in fever and said : "Who are you asking about ? No one was here with you !" I said : "There was. Don't you have any eyes ?" And at that I sat down, not on the bed but on a stool. My wife said : "Summon Kazimierz !"[17] The barber-surgeon came and felt my pulse ; the fever was gone as if I had never had it. And after I came back to myself and rested a little, I gave thanks to God and to St. Anthony. I knelt down, and when I rose I began to tell them what had happened. They all wondered *cum stupore ;*[18] some believed that it had happened so and others did not. Even the doctor *suppone-*

[15] The seventh of September.
[16] In the frock of a Franciscan monk.
[17] The barber-surgeon's first name.
[18] In astonishment.

bat[19]—though he saw that the fever was gone *totaliter*[20]—that it had left behind some *debilitatem mentis*.[21] And so everyone was preoccupied with me until I said : "I see that you congratulate me and rejoice over my recovery, but you do not ask whether I would like to have something to eat ; you have starved me enough during those days of my illness." My wife jumped up at that: "Right away ! Right away !," she said—and she asked me what I would like to have. I said : "Whatever you bring me I shall eat with great pleasure." They were deliberating what to cook: not this and not that ; at last the doctor said : "You may fix something with butter even though it is a day of fast." I asked : "Why so ?" They said because it was the eve of the Holy Virgin's Nativity.[22] I was amazed, since I did not realize that I had lain ill for so many days, and I said : "I shall not eat anything prepared with seasoning because of the fast." They cooked for me a small pot of caudle. It tasted like an appetizer. I told them to cook it in a larger pot and to add plenty of spices to it. They did and I got dressed properly in the meantime. I also ordered someone to go to the fish pond with a net, to fetch a pike and to prepare it sour and without butter. When they saw that I drank and ate heartily (. . .)[23] they finally believed that I was *sanus mente et corpore* ;[24] about the latter especially the doctor had grave doubts. While I was eating, my wife said : "You have waited with the shipment of grain so long and now your illness stands in the way." I asked : "But why ?" She said that word had come that the water had risen considerably ; Pan Rupniowski and Pan Jaroszowski had left,[25] having sent the peasants for loading in all haste. I answered : "Then I shall go also !" Everyone began to laugh ; they assumed that I was joking but I felt vigorous. After

[19]Supposed.
[20]Completely.
[21]Impairment of the mind.
[22]August 8.
[23]Here a few words are missing in the manuscript. Czubek, *Pam.*, p. 572, note 8.
[24]Well in body and mind.
[25]For the Vistula.

I had satisfied my appetite, I walked about the room ; I ordered my bailiff to be summoned and I told him to have the peasants leave for loading immediately ; I also ordered my horses to be made ready and harnessed in the meantime. I was told : "Do not do this for God's sake ! Poor soul, health is more important ! I said : "Leave me alone, I know better how I feel and I also believe that He who gave me back my health will also preserve me and will take me safely to my destination." I ordered *necessaria*[26] sent after me then ; I took leave of everyone and left. In the open field I got out of my carriage and mounted a horse ; I rode at a trot, for I feared that the high water would ebb away. I found out that some had already sailed while others, who did not have the crew's provisions stored in their granaries, were still waiting for them to arrive. As my peasants could not possibly arrive before nightfall, since they had to walk a distance of seven leagues,[27] my neighbors put their peasants at my disposal. Two of my scows were loaded soon after ; I gave orders to load the rafts at a more leisurely pace without me. On Virgin Mary's Nativity I rode to the Franciscan monastery[28] at dawn. I attended Mass, which I requested celebrated at the altar of St. Anthony. Meanwhile the final preparations were made for sailing. Upon my return I got on board and departed before noon, since everyone else had left already. My peasants arrived almost in vain, since the others had been sufficient to do all that was necessary. I departed then and I managed to overtake even those who had left a day and a half before me, even though on the first day we did not make much progress—almost none at all—because the senior raftsman[29] had a bad boat and tried to get another for himself. We did not arrive in Leniwka[30] until *23 [Septem]bris,* because strong winds had hindered us. The rafts arrived four-

[26]The necessary things.
[27]The distance from Olszówka to Nowy Korczyn, where Pasek had granaries on the Vistula. Czubek, *Pam.,* p. 573, note 9.
[28]In Korczyn. Czapliński, *Pam.,* p. 551, note 47.
[29]One who goes ahead of the rafts in a boat and explores the depth of the river.
[30]A branch of a delta of the Vistula which flows through Gdańsk.

teen days later. From Łęka[31] the rafts reached Gdańsk in fewer
days than the barges because the adverse winds pampering the
barges ceased on the day when the floats left the harbor, which
was on the *21* [*Septem*]*bris*, St. Mathew's Day : and we were
already near Toruń at the time. There was a severe frost on
that day and along the banks more ice than usual. I made the
trip safely, thanks to the Grace of God even though I departed
so soon after my illness ; I did not even suffer a headache,
thanks to His Holy Grace, for which may His most Holy Name
be praised eternally. I also humbly beseech Him not to let us
out of His Fatherly protection in all times of affliction, but
especially illness !

[31]A village near Nowe Miasto Korczyn on the Vistula. Czubek, *Pam.*,
p. 574, note 6.

ANNO DOMINI 1686

I lived in Olszówka—God willing happily!—and I spent the year in good health and prosperity.

Eodem anno,[1] in Kraków, I was present at a ceremony during which Panna Sieklicka, the daughter of Pan Adam Sieklicki, a great friend of mine, and Pani Zofia Sieklicka, née Rabsztyńska, took the vows of the Augustinian Convent[2] with the consent of her parents. I was asked there, *in frequentia*[3] of many noteworthy people, to make a speech commemorating the occasion. I was not very anxious to do so, for I knew that I would be easily subjected to criticism. I was not reproved however, but perhaps they just flattered me—I do not know. The content of my speech was the following:

> Whoever leads his life with merely the intention to fill it only with worldly and trivial delights is not only disillusioned in his own undertaking but almost certainly deprived of eternal happiness. Lucky is that one who has not been trapped by the flattering favors of worldly delights, who has not been deceived in his stability, who has not been led into eternal disgrace by their caresses. Such *bona licita*[4] are not forbidden, it is true, and granted temporarily, to be enjoyed according to the will of God. If someone were to go against the explicit law, however,

[1] This year.
[2] It is located in a part of Kraków called Kazimierz.
[3] In the presence.
[4] Wordly pleasures.

and center his attention only on trivialities, the following
judgement would be read out to him by the last Assizes :
'*Proiecisti sermonem Dei, proiecit te Dominus.*'[5] And
someone was even driven out from the earthly kingdom :
'*Ne sis rex super Israel.*'[6] And soon there will be a lack of
both heavenly and earthly happiness for the world. So I see
that one has to deal carefully with the world and with its
trivialities, but not everyone can to this. *Sapiens et circum-
spectus animus etiam minutissimos praevidet cuniculos, in-
cautus etiam in visibilem incidit Charybdim.*[7] And since
the world sets such treacherous traps for worldly men,
I would assume that those who do not come into any
contact with it are far happier. Even happier are those who
have abandoned its events and who sustain in solitude, in
convents, and in various pious congregations their free
conscience with devotional meditation only, for they become sons of immortality and—since *servire Deo regnare
est*[8]—unquestionable heirs of the heavenly kingdom. An
obvious proof of which is here represented in the person
of her Ladyship Panna Helena Sieklicka, a descendant of
an old and distinguished family, whom nature has endowed
with so many splendid qualities. Through the illustrous
guidance of her noble parents, she did not heed the fact
that, being without a brother, she was the *legitima haeredissa*[9] to all their accumulated wealth, and did not look
around for wealth which could befall her with the blessing
of God. She voluntarily rejects all the adornments of this
world, she renounces its freedom and its delights forever
and enters into a contract with Heaven today. Today she
takes her first vows with Heaven and in choosing convent
life she sacrifices her maidenhood to God. Heaven will

[5]You have rejected the word of God and God has rejected you.
[6]So that you would not be the king of Israel. Both citations were taken
from the Holy Testament, Book of Kings I:15, 26.
[7]A wise and a cautious man, notices even the smallest pits, a heedless
one falls into an apparent Charybdis.
[8]To serve God is to reign.
[9]Legitimate heir.

not find her lacking in anything, for as I see it this maiden's wisdom possesses everything with which Heaven's eminence can boast and adorn itself with. But there are many saintly figures there already from among such maidens. Congratulations should be extended to the noble parents who, having brought up such an exceptional daughter as a human, can turn her over to God as an angel. I also congratulate their Ladyships, the novices and nuns, as well as the entire congregation, on such a spiritual sister and companion of the Holy Rule. I am to entrust her to their Ladyship and especially to her Ladyship the Mother Superior by the authority given me by her loving parents, His Lordship Pan Sieklicki, a nobleman and brother, and Her Ladyship Pani Sieklicka, and all the noble relatives on both sides who give her up as a sacrifice of theirs intended for God at His command as eagerly and as obediently as Abraham did, and have no regrets in giving her to the service of God. They surrender their dearest treasure, their beloved blood and the right and the authority of their prerogative to her Ladyship the Abbess, whom they beseech not to deny her, as a novice of the teachings of the Church, her gracious protection.

This veil-taking ceremony took place *24 Ianuarii*.[10] This year there was no winter ; there were no frosts or snow and no rivers froze. *In Februario*[11] the fields were prepared for spring sowing, flowers bloomed and there was grass ; the spring rye was sowed and the cattle ate grass. Barley and oats were sowed right at the beginning of Lent, even though they could have been planted before then. The sowing was completed before Easter[12] and there was no more winter and the harvest was good enough. It was an unusual occurrence and *supra usum*[13] in Poland that wild geese roamed around in large flocks all summer long in the vicinity of Kraków and Sandomierz, that is in places where they usually do not hatch. Even the grain had

[10]On the twenty-fourth of January.
[11]In February.
[12]Easter fell on April 14.
[13]An extraordinary thing.

to be protected from them for they spoiled it. These geese were somewhat different, however, not the usual kind, as if somewhat piebald around the neck ; they also nested with the native geese and they were not timid, and one could approach and knock them over with a stick. People made various comments concerning them.

Augusti 7-ma[14] I loaded four vessels with wheat and sailed to Gdańsk. After I had sold it I returned by land 17 [*Septem*]*bris*,[15] happily, thanks to the will of God. *Eodem anno*[16] I took over Madziarów[17] *modo obligatorio*.[18]

Eodem anno[19] his Majesty the King went with our army into southern Bessarabia and into Walachia, where they had several clashes with the Tatars and with other enemies. The most significant event of all however was that the ashes of St. Ivan were moved from Walachia to Poland.[20] All his silver utensils and several Orthodox monks from the monastery were taken along. God still blessed the armies of the German Emperor during this year, for twice they defeated the Turks mightily, captured the wealth of their camps and conquered several powerful fortresses. All this happened thanks to us, however, because the entire Tatar might was directed ar our Polish army.

[14]On the seventh of August.
[15]On the seventeenth of September.
[16]During this year.
[17]Now Magierów, a village near Stopnice, in the voivodeship of Kielce. Czubek, *Pam.*, p. 579, note 4.
[18]In lien.
[19]This same year.
[20]The corpse of St. Ivan of Suczawa was moved from there to Żółkwia in 1673 from where it was returned back to Suczawa under the Austrian occupation of Poland. Czubek, *Pam.*, p. 579, note 8.

ANNO DOMINI 1687

I began this year in Olszówka, where my lease had already expired; it was already the eleventh year of my leasehold. I moved things little by little to Madziarów, since I had yielded Smogorzów already a year ago to my stepson. I turned it over to him *in eadem qualitate*[1] in which I had received it and in which I had kept it for seventeen years, that is, I left the grounds, which had been neglected by the previous leaseholders, in good condition; the buildings were good and renovated, the orchards were grafted; the forests were planted, and kept intact; such treatment is a *raritas*[2] among stepfathers. The debts were also settled, for which I devoted much work and expense. The late Pan Łącki bought this estate on mortgage; since he did not have enough money for the payment, he borrowed from convents, and some *evictiones in fundo*.[3] Moreover *successores*[4] of his first wife, *de domo*[5] Grodzicka, that is their lordships Gomoleński and Lubański, brought a law suit concerning her share. Since both sides claimed the right of ownership of this inheritance, I had demanded that it be given to whom it *de iure debebatur*,[7] in order not to pay the same sum twice. Over this

[1]In the same condition, i.e. debts paid on time.
[2]Rarity.
[3]Some sums he secured on the estate itself.
[4]The heirs.
[5]Née.
[6]Both sides.
[7]Was rightfully due.

there were between us litigations, disputes, writs of execution, surprise attacks, banishments, fights and *consequenter*[8] also reparation payments. I had suffered great losses because of all this ; it also led to other affairs which were to my detriment. Such is the lot of a man who marries a widow with children and problems ; the first husband made the debts and left the problems, the children and the *litigia*,[9] and I withered and lost my health for the interests of others. What I could have earned for myself, I spent on lawsuits and I had still incurred ingratitude instead of thanks. I say this as a reminder : whoever is to marry a widow with children as I did, should come to me *pro memento*.[10]

I had slaved for such reparations, lawsuits, weddings, and arrangements when my stepdaughters, of whom there were five, took the veil and made vows. I reckoned up these expenses, however, and arrived at a figure of forty thousand.[11] All this I had laid out because of the urgent entreaty of my stepson and the intercession of friends. I even gave up my life annuity without compensation and even the ring which my wife gave me on our engagement. I behaved in this way so that nothing belonging to someone else would be with me. Even my stepson's relatives had admitted that I could have disclaimed his inheritance from Smogorzów if I had wanted to do so.

[8]Consequently.
[9]Litigations.
[10]For advice.
[11]According to Czubek, Pasek exaggerated here. There was only one wedding and three veil-taking ceremonies. Barbara and Marianna (the younger) became Bernardine sisters in the convent of St. Joseph in Kraków ; Aleksandra in Stradom and Marianna, the oldest, entered the convent of St. Joseph's still during the lifetime of her father. All four daughters had secured dowries in Smogorzów ; the oldest one was sent to a convent by her father. Czubek, *Pam.*, p. 581, note 8.

ANNO DOMINI 1688

I lived in Madziarów, but I could sooner say in Lublin, as I carried on a lawsuit with the Margrave.[1] My wife stayed in Olszówka's manor, *quidem incarcerata.*[2] But they[3] would have been glad to remove the fence for her, had she only wanted to leave.[4]

The Diet began on *26 Ianuarii*[5] in Grodno. I had to attend it because of the articles which had been passed at several regional councils *pro parte mea militantes.*[6] After a trip along poor, frozen, and cloddy roads I arrived *prima Martii*[7] in Grodno. The deputies of Kraków, especially such confidants of mine as Pan Lanckoroński, the starost of Stopnice, said to me *quidem* :[8] "The margrave is serving as a deputy of the guard of Sandomierz,[9] thanks to connections. But he is a harmless de-

---

[1]Stanisław Myszkowski.
[2]As if imprisoned.
[3]The Myszkowskis.
[4]Pasek did not want to give up his leasehold of Olszówka, since the Margrave had not returned him his loan as yet. He left his wife behind in Olszówka, who acted as if Myszkowski were keeping her there by force. Czubek, *Pam.*, p. 582, note 1.
[5]January 26. The Diet did not convene until January 27, but lasted until March 3, 1688.
[6]In support of my case.
[7]March 1.
[8]As if.
[9]Stefan Bidziński, who was married to Teresa Myszkowska. Czapliński, *Pam.*, p. 561, note 9.

puty, who does not open his mouth in public, sits like a night-jar . . .,[10] looks intently at others and concentrates mostly on card-playing. The courtiers and the Queen hold him in good grace, since they drain him of his money. You have failed to obtain a judgment by default on the margrave, so you want to find some other way of ruining him." I replied : "Precisely so *eo ipso*[11] he is an *oppressor nobilitatis et raptor substantiarum.*"[12]

When the margrave saw me in the chamber of deputies he almost froze with horror at the sight of me. His companions noticed his confusion and said to me : "For God's sake, the margrave is in need of some vodka to be revived. You will deprive us of a good deputy. Without his active participation the activities of the chamber of deputies will be paralyzed."

Interim consilia[13] of the Diet were hampered by the private controversies of Pan Słuszka, the Lithuanian field hetman, and Pan Dąbrowski, the deputy from the voivodeship of Wilno.[14]

I had the *consilium*[15] of good friends not to bring up my wrong before the chamber of deputies—my adversaries had already prepared themselves to raise a commotion if such were the case—but first to complain to the King and try to incur his *respectum.*[16] I followed their advice. I attempted to receive an audience and on the designated date I addressed him thus :

As the subjects of Your Majesty we consider Your Majesty our father whom we wish prosperity. In case of affliction we preserve the grace and protection of Your

[10]This spot is damaged in the manuscript. Only the word "gaping" can be detected here. Czapliński, *Pam.*, p. 561, note 10. It might read as "throwing his beak wide open."

[11]Because.

[12]The oppressor of nobility and extortioner of property.

[13]In the meantime the debates.

[14]Józef Bogusław Słuszka denied Dąbrowski the right to participate in the Diet for he had summoned him to the court as a result of a foray which Dąbrowski had committed on his estate. Actually Słuszka acted in concert with the King who wanted to remove Dąbrowski, a dogged supporter of the Sapiehas, from the chamber of deputies. Czapliński, *Pam.*, p. 561, note 16. Dąbrowski left the Diet in protest with the intention of breaking it up.

[15]Advice.

[16]Favor.

Majesty, our gracious lord, as an ultimate recourse in order to speak before him as honestly as the Crucified Son had done before His Holy Father. With submission and humility do I want to resort to these means now. I do want to apologize to Your Majesty, my gracious lord, however, for coming here as a private man to disturb the careworn and preoccupied ears of Your Majesty with problems concerning the fatherland. But I am not at fault, but those who having plenty of their own are eagerly trying to confiscate the property of others. I was a soldier *non per intervalla*[17] but *continue.*[18] I served *florem aetatis cum dispendio*[19] of health and fortune. I have witnesses : *cicatrices*[20] and my companions at arms, many of whom I still see *in ordine equestri*[21] and in the senate at Your Majesty's side. I don't feel guilty of any action deserving confiscation of my property. I don't owe anybody anything. His Highness the Margrave of Pińczów confiscated my property *ex bene placito.*[22] I could almost say—the remains of this piece of

[17]Not with interruption.
[18]Continuously.
[19]The best years of my life at the loss.
[20]Scars.
[21]Among the knighthood.
[22]Out of wantonness.

bread for which I did not cease to serve our native Commonwealth. I did not go *extra orbitam ordinationis*[23] because I did not give it *lege vetitum*[24] but for a lease which is *antiquo usu practicatum.*[25] I did not give it for private expenses but *in deportationem*[26] of the Margrave's debts which were left immediately post *fundatam ordinationem,*[27] about which the contract *docet.*[28] I gave the loan to the uncle,[29] *legitimo tutori,*[30] who had accepted this money which his successor had taken. He received the receipt *de tutela cum approbatione*[31] of the contracts *et certitudine*[32] of our claim.

I don't understand all this. I was expelled from the leasehold. My money was not returned and that which was . . . *et supellectili, per subordinatos,*[33] taken away from me *in praedam.*[34] It hurts me, Your Majesty, my gracious lord, to lose my meager possessions but also to see myself with this mark of misfortune sine *sine socio doloris*[35] because all the other leaseholders, even the *contrahentes, etiam obligatorii*[36] had been either *satisfacti ex asse*[37] or allowed to remain on their possessions *hucusque*[38] with the exception of myself. I don't know why these gentlemen shower me with so much 'grace.' Why they do not cease to

[23]I.e., transcended rules.
[24]Against the law.
[25]An old accepted custom.
[26]For the paying off.
[27]After the establishment of the estate in tail.
[28]Informs.
[29]Jan Aleksander Myszkowski from Mirów. Czubek, *Pam.*, p. 585, note 12.
[30]Legitimate guardian.
[31]To custody with the acknowledgment.
[32]And assertion.
[33]And any personal property by assailants.
[34]Like booty.
[35]Without a companion in my suffering.
[36]Leaseholders, even the pledged ones.
[37]Compensated for in cash.
[38]Until now.

saevire[39] at my meager possessions. The only grounds for such behavior it seems are a personal bitterness toward me.

The King listened *diligenter*.[40] When I finished he said : "To this one should reply with the Scripture : '*Habetis legem et prophetas.*'[41] We have tribunals and *subsellia*[42] in order to preserve justice, even in the case of such a powerful lord. Since this came to our ears however we *apponemus curam*[43] with great eagerness to see that such injustice does not take place."

Some dozen deputies and senators were in the room when his Majesty addressed Pan Chełmski, the Camp Commander of the Crown :[44] "You, sir, are a close neighbor. What is this case all about ?" Chełmski answered : "My gracious lord, I know that this nobleman gave the money and acted like an honest treasurer and not a leaseholder at all times. In times of need one could depend on him more than on other leaseholders. Sometimes he did not even hold on to a hundred zlotys overnight. As soon as he returned from Gdańsk people notified each other. They did not let him rejoice over his money long. They called him 'Benefactor.'[45] They extolled him for his congeniality and kindness, *pro exemplo boni amici*.[46] But when the question of returning something or of extending the lease on his estate arose, these things were not pleasant to hear. In short : two *potentiores*[47] joined against this nobleman in order to deprive

[39]Pick.

[40]Attentively.

[41]"You have the law and the prophets." According to Czubek the King merged here two places from the Holy Scripture and created a new citation which he needed : *Habent Moysen et prophetas* (Luc. 16, 29) and *Nolite putare, quoniam veni solvere legem aut prophetas* (Matt. 5, 17). Czubek, *Pam.*, p. 586, note 10. According to Czapliński this is merely an inaccurate citation of : *Habent Moysen et prophetas, audiant illos* (Luc. 16, 29). Czapliński, *Pam.*, p. 564, note 56.

[42]Courts.

[43]Shall take pains.

[44]Marcjan Chełmski, a colonel and camp commander of the Crown. Czubek, *Pam.*, p. 587, note 1.

[45]*Dobrodziej.* (Pol.) Also a very polite form of address.

[46]They set him as an exemplary good friend.

[47]Potentates, i.e., Stanisław and after his death Władysław Myszkow-

him of his property, *protractione litigiorum*,[48] *verbo dicam*,[49] in order to ruin the one who did *satis superque*[50] for their house. Much could be said about this. They just mistreat everyone. Against me too they raised God knows what a commotion concerning the same estates, which I had held after my brother. Your Majesty, gracious lord, knows in what kind of *litigia*[51] and costs they had involved me in. God knows that I spent more on the lawsuit than I had collected from Olszówka during these six years of my leasehold. Recalling those *anteacta*,[52] I could easily say *ad personam* :[53] *Perditi tua ex te*,[54] but since I am a Christian I should not rejoice over someone else's misfortune. I only say that in this case the outcome will be as it was with me, or even worse. They will involve him in expenses, troubles, will ruin him so that . . .[55] he will bow, beg for his own money which he had given to them eagerly, and later, they will give him whatever they want to because such is their way. Shortly speaking, great *inconvenientia*[56] occurs in this estate ; *expedit*[57] either be removed or brought *ad debitam formam*.[58] Because of these regulations, as the saying goes, neither a candle will be obtained for God nor a broomstick from someone else ;[59] this *onus*[60] which the law put *in capita*[61] of the ancestors

ski. Czubek, *Pam.*, p. 587, note 4.
[48]Delaying the lawsuit.
[49]Simply speaking.
[50]Enough and more than enough.
[51]Lawsuits.
[52]Former affairs.
[53]To this person.
[54]Your peril is well deserved. (Ozeas XIII, 9). Chełmski wanted to say : "You, yourself are responsible by fighting for the leasehold and trying to drive me out of Olszówka. Czubek, *Pam.*, p. 588, note 3.
[55]In this spot the text is spoiled.
[56]Injustice.
[57]It should.
[58]Into proper prospective.
[59]I.e., the devil ; Chełmski does not say the proverb in full because it would not have been proper to do so in front of the King. Czapliński, *Pam.*, p. 566, note 73.
[60]Burden.
[61]On the heads.

of Your Majesty *redundat*[62] now *in personam*[63] of Your Majesty and of the Commonwealth. *Incumbit subvenire oppresso*[64] as the one who, in the eyes of Your Majesty, *meruit*[65] all kinds of consideration and as the one who himself and whose relatives are worthy of it. Now his nephew,[66] an officer in my banner, who had been taken into captivity a year and a half ago, returned from Crimea *ante triduum*.[67] He had put another officer in his place so that he could sooner get ransom. Already *in parte*[68] an uncle of an important man brought a Tatar for him from Pan Gołyński, a lieutenant. He was ordered to procure a second Tatar in order to be released in his place. It is *hunc et non alium*.[69] He is among the prisoners of Your Majesty now. This slave humbly begs to see Your Majesty and I intercede for him as for a good soldier and a remarkable officer. He is there *ante fores*."[70]

The King said: "Bring him here!" The Camp Commander jumped toward the door. I preceded him. I stepped out but he was no longer in the chamber. I went to the chamber in the middle because we were in the Royal bed chamber. A royal valet was embracing him hugging (...) him, kissing him[71] and crying for joy. A crowd of deputies and various other men surrounded him because also (...) he had been there (...) at the time when the Queen (...) had sent through him and through another servant (...) a grant of twenty thousand ducats for the camp. These ducats were lost out of rashness.

I shall leave this for now to return *ad rem*.[72] I said to my

[62]Falls.
[63]On the person.
[64]One should help the oppressed.
[65]Deserves.
[66]Czubek discovered information about this nephew, a Stanisław Pasek, in the Act of 1692. Krzysztof Zawisza also mentions him in his memoirs. Czubek, *Pam.*, p. 589, note 1.
[67]Three days ago.
[68]Partly.
[69]That one and not another.
[70]Before the door.
[71]Accepted greeting form among Slavs.
[72]To the subject matter.

nephew : "Go, sir, to the King !" He did so. The King received
him cordially, asked who had imprisoned him and under what
circumstances. He asked about the sultans, the Tatar princes
with whom he was acquainted and about some captives. My
nephew told the King everything.

The session was just about to begin. The senators were
assembling in the chamber. The King said to Matczyński,[73] the
Polish Master of the Horse at the time, these words : "We wish
that Your Excellency may write an order of payment to hand
over to that Pan Pasek who has just returned from captivity so
that the Tatar in Żółkiew may be handed over *ad(pri)mam
requisitionem*."[74] When he turned to me he said : "It will be
curae nostrae[75] to obtain satisfaction for the injustice done to
you, sir." The Camp Commander said again : "Gracious lord,
a great commotion will be raised *in ordine equestri*[76] as a result
of this case, for there are regulations from several voivodeships
as well as from the council to oppose this and to propose it *in
facie publica*."[77] His Majesty replied : "I am aware of this. We
shall find a way to subdue this *sine maiori motu*,[78] however.
He then said to me : "Be of good cheer, sir. You have earned
due respect from your fatherland. You shall be *satisfactus*.[79]

Suddenly, a Black Friar in vestments appeared in the door.
He had been waiting there. The King heard Mass and then
went to the senate and sat down to work.

It was *15 Martii* at the time. The Diet was on the verge of
breaking up. The King was afflicted by the discords and the
recent news that the Crimean Tatars inflicted damages on the
Ruthenian lands and especially on his estates. I did not dare
to incur his disfavor. Sometimes even a Senator, having crossed

[73]Marek Matczyński, the starost of Grabowiec, 1674, Master of the
Horse of the Crown, since 1686 the voivode of Bełz, the treasurer of
the Crown 1693 ; died as the voivode of Ruthenia 1697. Czubek, *Pam.*,
p. 591, note 1.
[74]At first request.
[75]We shall try, i.e., our concern will be.
[76]In the chamber of deputies.
[77]To the estates.
[78]Without a big commotion.
[79]Satisfied.

the threshold, was told to turn back. I merely listened incidentally and looked for an appropriate time, since one should always act so with a master. I sometimes stood so that he could see me. He beckoned to me once. We stepped aside by the window. The King then said: "I spoke quite openly with the Margrave about you and he *firmissime negat*[80] his guilt. He claims that since his uncle took the money he is the one who should pay." I said: "The uncle took the loan, but had contracted an agreement as the guardian with me *in rem*[81] of his nephew in order to pay their debts about which the contract *docebit*.[82] The Queen remarked: Be kind to the Margrave, my Lord." I replied to that: "Gracious Queen, Your Majesty, be so kind as to persuade the wrong-doer and not the wronged one to do so. She said: "He is a good man." And I replied: "He is a good man but his deeds are evil." The King turned up his nose and grinned at this: "In return for this Marysieńka will give a jack of hearts to Your Lordship." He pinpricked her so because the Margrave played cards with her. The Queen turned gloomy and walked away. When she left the King said: "Just leave him alone. Let him be abused in the chamber of deputies. He will be cheaper then."

The King told me to see him after dinner, but suddenly he got into a coach and rode to the Carmelites. He was accosted by a Carmelite preacher there, who pronounced from the pulpit that allegedly His Majesty cared little for God's honor, since he failed to intercede for the injustice to Him and *contra ordinem equestrem*.[83] He argued about the nobility; what does being *nobile*[84] signify, what a *nobilis*[85] is and what his *vocatio*[86] is and who is a *vere nobilis*.[87] He cited an example of the following content: "I heard one worthy foreigner discourse about his

[80]Absolutely denies.
[81]On behalf.
[82]Instructs.
[83]To the knighthood.
[84]Noble.
[85]Nobleman.
[86]Call.
[87]A real nobleman.

travels and give various proofs of who surpasses whom, considering the *eminentiam*[88] and he said the following : "*Fui in
Italia* : *vidi praesules*[89] because the largest number of bishops
was there : *fui in Germani(a)* : *vidi principes*[90] because the
largest number of princes was there ; *fui in Gallia* : *vidi milites*[91]
because the best armies were there ; *fui in Polonia* : *vidi nobiles*[92] because the largest number of noblemen was there. But
forgive me, dear *nobilitas*,[93] for what I shall say. Your authority
has decreased tremendously, that authority which our ancestors
had so divinely earned for themselves among the nations, and
which they displayed to the entire world under the sun *pro
exemplari speculo* (*non sine*) *invidia*.[94] For such were the
Poles !" He furthermore argued, gave *probationes*,[95] mostly
about the fact that they did not care about God's honor. For
at that time the lecherous sect of Leszczyński[96] was formed
noviter[97] about which I shall talk *inferius*.[98]

In the afternoon I went to see the King, since he had ordered me to do so. He said : "The chamber of deputies would
have supported your case, but Tokarzewski broke up the Diet.[99]
Your Mazovians would have shouted down the Margrave to
death for I know which of them had intended to do so and we
would have helped from the side ; but now we have to take

[88]Prominence.
[89]I went to Italy, I saw bishops.
[90]I went to Germany, I saw princes.
[91]I went to France, I saw soldiers.
[92]I went to Poland, I saw noblemen (gentry).
[93]Nobility.
[94]As an examplary mirror but not without envy.
[95]Proofs.
[96]Kazimierz Lyszczyński (Lyszczeński), who was maliciously accused by
his debtor Jan Brzoska, the defender of Braśniak, of impiousness, was
at the Diet of March 5, 1689 sentenced to be burned alive. Later the
sentence was changed to beheading in the Old Market Place of Warsaw,
March 30, 1689. Pasek repeats merely a rumor. Czubek, *Pam*., p. 594,
note 4.
[97]Merely.
[98]Below. This part of the *Memoirs* is lost.
[99]Tokarzewski, cup-bearer of Brześć Litewski (Brest-Litovsk) ; an addition of Czubek. This place is damaged in the *Memoirs*.

another course. I hear that the Voivode of Sieradz[100] who is the tribunal marshal is present here in the castle. I shall summon him to me, I shall tell him to try this case justly and without delay." He told me to wait while he sent for him. When he arrived the King said to him : "Sir Voivode, we have here *hominem iniuriatum*[101] with us"—and he pointed to me. "He is a nobleman and a soldier and we have known him for a long time. He is a *potentioribus oppressus and desiderat iustitiam.*[102] I have a similar case in the tribunal register.[103] I recommend to your Honor both this case and the man as a *bene mer/itum*[104] to our fatherland and I beg that he be gratified in his in justice."

The Voivode replied : "Gracious Majesty ! I know this gentleman well. For many years we served in the army and I am familiar with the case. I know that my conscience would not be deceived even if I were to adjudge him without reading the inquest. Especially so, since the authority of Your Majesty *interponitur*[105] for him . . ."

(The *Memoirs* break off at this point)

[100]Jan Pieniążek, the treasurer of Przemyśl, 1661 ; starost of Oświęcim, 1666. Czubek, *Pam.*, p. 594, note 7.
[101]A wronged man.
[102]Being oppressed by the mightier ones, awaits justice.
[103]It included the list of complaints which the tribunal was to settle.
[104]A man of merit.
[105]Intervenes.